Portuguese Relative Clauses in Synchrony and Diachrony

OXFORD STUDIES IN DIACHRONIC AND HISTORICAL LINGUISTICS

GENERAL EDITORS: Adam Ledgeway and Ian Roberts, University of Cambridge

ADVISORY EDITORS: Cynthia Allen, *Australian National University*; Ricardo Bermúdez-Otero, *University of Manchester*; Theresa Biberauer, *University of Cambridge*; Charlotte Galves, *University of Campinas*; Geoff Horrocks, *University of Cambridge*; Paul Kiparsky, *Stanford University*; Anthony Kroch, *University of Pennsylvania*; David Lightfoot, *Georgetown University*; Giuseppe Longobardi, *University of York*; George Walkden, *University of Konstanz*; David Willis, *University of Cambridge*

Portuguese Relative Clauses in Synchrony and Diachrony

ADRIANA CARDOSO

UNIVERSITY PRESS

Great Clarendon Street, Oxford, OX2 6DP,
United Kingdom

Oxford University Press is a department of the University of Oxford.
It furthers the University's objective of excellence in research, scholarship,
and education by publishing worldwide. Oxford is a registered trade mark of
Oxford University Press in the UK and in certain other countries

Published in the United States of America by Oxford University Press
198 Madison Avenue, New York, NY 10016, United States of America

British Library Cataloguing in Publication Data
Data available

Library of Congress Control Number: 2016955208

ISBN 978-0-19-872378-3

Printed in Great Britain by
CPI Group (UK) Ltd, Croydon, CR0 4YY

To Ana Maria Martins and Mark de Vries

Contents

Series preface

Modern diachronic linguistics has important contacts with other subdisciplines, notably first-language acquisition, learnability theory, computational linguistics, sociolinguistics, and the traditional philological study of texts. It is now recognized in the wider field that diachronic linguistics can make a novel contribution to linguistic theory, to historical linguistics, and arguably to cognitive science more widely.

This series provides a forum for work in both diachronic and historical linguistics, including work on change in grammar, sound, and meaning within and across languages; synchronic studies of languages in the past; and descriptive histories of one or more languages. It is intended to reflect and encourage the links between these subjects and fields such as those mentioned above.

The goal of the series is to publish high-quality monographs and collections of papers in diachronic linguistics generally, that is, studies focusing on change in linguistic structure and/or change in grammars, which are also intended to make a contribution to linguistic theory by developing and adopting a current theoretical model, by raising wider questions concerning the nature of language change, or by developing theoretical connections with other areas of linguistics and cognitive science as listed above. There is no bias towards a particular language or language family or a particular theoretical framework; work in all theoretical frameworks, and work based on the descriptive tradition of language typology, as well as quantitatively based work using theoretical ideas, also feature in the series.

Adam Ledgeway and Ian Roberts
University of Cambridge

Preface

Relative clauses pose many challenges to syntactic theory. Chomsky explicitly acknowledges this fact by noting that "we still have no good phrase structure theory for such simple matters as attributive adjectives, relative clauses, and adjuncts of many different types" (1995: 382 n. 22). Bianchi, in turn, regards relative clauses as an intriguing empirical domain "both because of the complexity of the data and of the theoretical relevance of the construction (especially with respect to the syntax-semantic interface)" (2002: 242).

To further obscure the matter, relative clauses display some syntactic structures that, despite all efforts, remain poorly understood (e.g. pied-piping and extraposition). Other limitations can be identified that are not exclusive to analyses of relative clauses but emerge from much research within the generative framework, namely: (1) an overemphasis on the study of English; (2) the predominance of theoretically oriented studies (as opposed to corpus-based and corpus-driven studies); and (3) the incomplete coverage of relevant properties. The last two limitations are perfectly expressed by Bianchi:

> Each analysis is designed to account for certain aspects of a domain, and leaves others unaccounted for. But the choice of the "core" data to be analysed is to some extent arbitrary, for we cannot know a priori which set of data is fully representative of the empirical domain under investigation; and . . . the way an analysis is designed is crucially affected by more general theoretical concerns.   (Bianchi 2002: 242)

From these considerations it follows that many gaps remain in our understanding of relativization. This is not to say that little has been written about this topic; on the contrary, relative clauses have become a subject of extensive debate in the generative field (e.g. the Chomsky/Bresnan debate on unbounded dependencies and the Bianchi/Borsley debate on the antisymmetric/symmetric analyses of relatives) (see Bianchi 2002). However, most studies focus primarily on a specific contemporary language, neglecting the cross-linguistic and diachronic variation.

In the present book I try to fill some of these gaps by providing a comparative analysis of relative clauses in the diachrony and synchrony of Portuguese. In particular, I investigate three distinct phenomena: remnant-internal relativization (Ch. 2); extraposition of restrictive relative clauses (Ch. 3); and appositive relativization (Ch. 4). The data considered are mainly drawn from earlier stages of Portuguese and contemporary European Portuguese, but other languages are considered, including Latin, French, Italian, Spanish, English, Dutch, German, and Russian.

The research reported is theoretically oriented, broadly falling within the premises of the generative Principles and Parameters approach to the study of human language (Chomsky 1981), under its Minimalist version (Chomsky 1993, 1995, and subsequent work). It also takes the comparative perspective as a central guiding line (Cinque and Kayne 2005, among others) while seeking to explain the contrasts found in different stages of the same language and different languages with respect to the syntax of relativization.

Potential readers of the book are academics, researchers, and advanced students interested in linguistics (particularly, in theoretical syntax, historical syntax, Romance syntax, and Portuguese syntax). Although the book stems from a particular theoretical framework, it is meant to be relevant and accessible to readers of different schools, not versed in formal syntax theories. For those readers, the book provides: (1) comprehensive descriptions of the linguistic phenomena under analysis; (2) background information regarding the framework used; and (3) overviews of the competing analyses proposed in the literature to account for the relevant syntactic structures (e.g. relative clauses, noun phrase discontinuity, extraposition, and apposition). Moreover, it is not a book that interests only Portuguese or Brazilian linguists (or other linguists working on Portuguese), but it is useful for a wider public. For those not familiar with Portuguese, all examples are followed by a word-for-word gloss with the relevant morphological information and by an English translation. Concerning examples from Portuguese, all glosses and translations are mine.

The book is a substantial revision of my doctoral dissertation submitted to the University of Lisbon. The research was funded by Fundação para a Ciência e a Tecnologia under the grant SFRH/BD/22475/2005. The present book was prepared within the research project *WOChWEL - Word Order and Word Order Change in Western European Languages* (FCT PTDC/CLE-LIN/121707/2010).

List of figures and tables

Figures

Tables

List of abbreviations

Abbreviations used in the main text:

A	adjective
A′-movement	non-argument movement
Adv	adverb
AdvP	Adverbial Phrase
Agr	agreement head
Agr-A	agreement adjectival head
Agr-A-P	Agreement Adjectival Phrase
AgrO	object agreement head
AgrOP	Object Agreement Phrase
AgrS	subject agreement head
AgrSP	Subject Agreement Phrase
AP	Adjectival Phrase
ARC	Appositive Relative Clause
Attract-all-F	Attract all features
C	complementizer/chain
c-command	constituent command
CEP	contemporary European Portuguese
CI	comparative inversion structure
C-NSR	Nuclear Stress Rule (sensitive to asymmetric c-command)
Co	coordination/coordinative head
CONJ	Conjunction
CoP	Coordination Phrase
CP	Complementizer Phrase
D	determiner
DegE	Degree Expression
DO	direct object
DP	Determiner Phrase
DPrel	Relative Determiner Phrase
Drel	relative determiner/pronoun
D-structure	deep structure

e	empty
E	Expression
E/CSR	Emphatic/Contrastive Stress Rule
EPP	Extended Projection Principle
EvaluativeP	Evaluative Phrase
F	functional head
[F]	focus (diacritic used to mark focused elements)
Fin	finiteness head
FinP	Finiteness Phrase
Foc	focus head
[foc]	focus feature
FocP	Focus Phrase
ForceP	Force Phrase
FP	Functional Projection (unspecified)
FPR	Focus Prominence Rule
I	inflection
IntP/ip	Intonational Phrase
IO	indirect object
IP	Inflection Phrase
LCA	Linear Correspondence Axiom
LP	Lexical Projection
N	noun *or* nominal
Nom-P	Nominative Phrase
NP	Noun Phrase
NSR	Nuclear Stress Rule
O	object
Op	operator
P	Phrase
[P] feature	EPP-feature
p-movement	prosodically motivated movement
PF	Phonological Form
PP	Prepositional Phrase
Q	quantifier/question
QP	Quantificational Phrase, Question Phrase
QR	Quantifier Raising

REL/rel	relative
RC	relative clause
RRC	Restrictive Relative Clause
S	subject/sentence
ScalW	scalar word
S-NSR	Nuclear Stress Rule (sensitive to selectional ordering)
Spec	specifier
S-structure	surface structure
t	trace
T	tense
Top	topic head/feature
TopP	Topic Phrase
TP	Tense Phrase
v	light verb ('little v')
V	verb
Voc	vocative
vP	Light Verb Phrase ('little vP')
Σ-structure	sigma structure
VP	Verb Phrase
wh-	*who, which, what, why, when*
X	unspecified head
XP	unspecified Phrase

Abbreviations used in the glosses:

1	first person
2	second person
3	third person
ACC	accusative case
C	complementizer
CL	clitic
COND	conditional
EXPL	expletive
F	feminine
FUT	future tense
GEN	genitive
GER	gerundive

IMP	imperative
INF	infinitive
LIV	living entity
M	masculine
N	neuter
NOM	nominative
NR	nominalizing particle
PERF	perfect tense
PL	plural
PPRF	pluperfect tense
PREP	preposition
PRS	present tense
PTCP	participle
PTL	particle
SBJV	subjunctive mood
SG	singular
SPC	specific
SR	subordinating particle
WEAK	weak inflection

Abbreviations denoting corpora:

CETEMP	*CETEMPúblico: A large corpus of Portuguese newspaper language* (Rocha and Santos 2000)
COCA	*Corpus of Contemporary American English* (Davies 2008–)
C-ORAL-ROM	*Corpus of Spoken Portuguese* (Bacelar do Nascimento, Gonçalves, Veloso, Antunes, Barreto, and Amaro 2005)
CORDIAL-SIN	*Syntax-oriented Corpus of Portuguese Dialects* (Martins, coord., 2000–10)
CP	*Corpus of Portuguese* (Davies and Ferreira 2006–)
CRPC	*Reference Corpus of Contemporary Portuguese* (Bacelar do Nascimento 2000)
DCMP	*Digital Corpus of Medieval Portuguese* (Xavier, coord., 1993–)
PPCEME	*The Penn-Helsinki Parsed Corpus of Early Modern English* (Kroch, Santorini, and Delfs 2004)
PPCMBE	*The Penn Parsed Corpus of Modern British English* (Kroch, Santorini, and Diertani 2010)
P.S.	*P.S. Post Scriptum: A Digital Archive of Ordinary Writing (Early Modern Portugal and Spain)* (CLUL, ed., 2014)
TYC	*Tycho Brahe Parsed Corpus of Historical Portuguese* (Galves and Faria 2010)

1

Introduction

Chapter 1 presents a summary of the book (see §1.1) and details the data and methods used (§1.2). It also addresses the theoretical framework that underlies the research (§1.3).

1.1 Overview of the book

This book sheds light on language variation and change from a generative syntactic perspective, based on a case study of relative clauses in Portuguese and other languages. Concretely, it offers a comparative account of three linguistic phenomena documented in the synchrony and diachrony of Portuguese: remnant-internal relativization; extraposition of restrictive relative clauses (RRCs); and appositive relativization.

The research methodology adopted involves comparative syntax (see Cinque and Kayne eds. 2005, among others), both in the diachronic and the synchronic dimensions: contemporary European Portuguese (CEP) is systematically compared with earlier stages of Portuguese; moreover, Portuguese is compared with other languages, in particular Latin, English, Dutch, and Italian.

Some interesting results emerge out of these comparisons. As far the diachrony of Portuguese is concerned, I propose that the loss of IP-scrambling after the sixteenth century (Martins 2002) gives rise to a series of changes in the syntax of extraposition and relativization, which ultimately lead to the reduction of the patterns of nominal discontinuity available in the language. The raising analysis of relative clauses, the stranding analysis of extraposition (Kayne 1994), and the specifying coordination analysis (De Vries 2002, 2006b) proved to be central to the understanding of these phenomena. Against this theoretical background, I propose that the loss of IP-scrambling, interpreted as the loss of the Attract-all-F EPP-feature optionally associated with the AgrS head (Martins 2002), gives rise to the loss of extraposition generated by the specifying coordination plus ellipsis structure. In turn, these two earlier changes originate the loss of *o qual*-ARCs generated by the specifying coordination structure.

Portuguese Relative Clauses in Synchrony and Diachrony. First Edition. Adriana Cardoso.
© Adriana Cardoso 2017. First published in 2017 by Oxford University Press.

Moreover, I provide evidence that a change parallel to that found at the clausal level (i.e. the loss of IP-scrambling) might also have affected the DP-level. In line with Poletto (2014), I hypothesize that PP-complements/modifiers of the noun cease to target a higher specifier position within the DP, which prevents them from undergoing other potential movements out of the DP.

The present research also contributes to the theoretical debate on the structural analysis of relativization and extraposition. Two important findings are (1) that competing theoretical analyses need not be either false or true universally, but can be instrumental in explaining language variation (both diachronically and synchronically), and (2) that languages (and different stages of the same language) vary according to whether they allow extraposition and relativization to be derived from specifying coordination.

The book is organized around the three linguistic phenomena aforementioned: remnant-internal relativization (Ch. 2); extraposition of RRCs (Ch. 3); and appositive relativization (Ch. 4).

Chapter 2 provides a comprehensive analysis of RRCs involving noun phrase discontinuity. In this configuration (referred to as *remnant-internal relativization*), an element that is thematically dependent on the head noun (either as a complement or as a modifier) does not appear adjacent to it but rather in a position internal to the relative clause, as illustrated in (1)–(4), from earlier stages of Portuguese.

(1) <u>Casos</u>   que Adamastor contou <u>futuros</u>
     cases.M.PL that A.   told   future.M.PL
     'future events that Adamastor foresaw' (16th c., from Lausberg 1967/1972: §331)

(2) <u>os livros</u> que eu compus <u>da   philosaphia</u>
     the books that I wrote of.the philosophy
     'the books of philosophy that I wrote' (15th c., from Martins 2004: 503)

(3) que   muyto conforto tomava com os tres paos do   leito, por
     because much comfort had.3SG with the three sticks of.the bed for
     a <u>senificança</u> que <u>deles</u> lhe   dissera o bom homem da   barca
     the meaning   that of.them him.CL tell.PPRF the good man of.the boat
     'because he felt very good about the three sticks of the bed because of the meaning that the good man of the boat said they had' (13th c. [transmitted by a 16th-c. MS], Martins, Pereira, and Cardoso 2013–15)

(4) e <u>qualquer</u> que <u>de nos</u> primeiro morer
     and any   that of us first   die.FUT.SBJV
     'and whoever of us first die' (13th c., Martins 2001: 344)

In (1) and (2) the modifier/complement surfaces in the rightmost position of the noun phrase. For this reason, it can be structurally analyzed as occurring either in a position internal to the relative clause or in an external position as a second modifier following the relative clause. However, the fact that the modifier/complement may occur in other positions than the rightmost one (see (3)–(4)) indicates that it is internally merged.

Based on this evidence, I argue that the analysis of remnant-internal relativization is of particular interest from the theoretical and diachronic point of view. Theoretically I submit that it can illuminate the long-standing debate between the right adjunction analysis of RRCs (originally proposed by Ross 1967, Chomsky 1977, and Jackendoff 1977) and the raising analysis of RRCs (originally proposed by Schachter 1973 and Vergnaud 1974, 1985, and more recently revived by Kayne 1994, Bianchi 1999, and De Vries 2002), providing evidence in favor of the latter. There are two main theoretical reasons that support this claim: First, if the head and its modifier/complement were base-generated together in an relative clause external position (as proposed by the right adjunction analysis), the pattern in (3)–(4) could not be derived as it would require lowering the modifier/complement to a non-c-commanding position (Fiengo 1977). Secondly, if the head and its modifier/complement were generated separately (the head being CP-external—as proposed by the adjunction analysis—and the modifier/complement being CP-internal), the semantic dependency between the head and its modifier/complement (requiring that these elements be in a structural relation at some point of the derivation) would not be satisfied.

By contrast, there is a natural explanation for remnant-internal relativization if the head noun and its modifier/complement are merged together in the relativization site, as proposed by the raising analysis. The fact that the modifier/complement enters into a local relation with the head noun at some point of the derivation suffices to explain why, under certain circumstances, the modifier/complement is not adjacent to the head noun and instead shows up in a more embedded position.

From a diachronic point of view, I show that remnant-internal relativization is possible in CEP, but only with the modifier/complement in the rightmost position of the noun phrase (as in (2)); the pattern with the modifier/complement in the left periphery of the RRC (as in (3)–(4)) is excluded. The tentative hypothesis I put forward to explain this contrast is that there was an independent syntactic change in the history of Portuguese that affected the movement operations available within the DP domain and, as a consequence, the word order patterns allowed in remnant-internal relativization.

In Chapter 3 I investigate a specific change that took place in the history of Portuguese involving the extraposition of RRCs. Although this phenomenon has been a neglected domain in the literature on Portuguese (in both the synchronic and the diachronic dimensions), I show that it raises some challenging questions for linguistic theory in general and for the study of syntactic change in particular.

From a descriptive stance, I identify three contrasting properties of RRC-extraposition: (1) the definiteness effect; (2) extraposition from pre-verbal positions; and (3) extraposition from prepositional phrases. On the basis of comparative evidence, I show that earlier stages of Portuguese contrast with CEP in respect of the properties of RRC-extraposition, being to a large extent Germanic-like.

Based on the contrasts identified, I claim that the variation found in extraposition is not compatible with a uniform approach to the phenomenon. In particular, I propose that RRC-extraposition may involve two different structures: specifying coordination plus ellipsis (De Vries 2002) and VP-internal stranding (Kayne 1994), and that languages and different stages of the same language may diverge with respect to the structures they display.

In the diachronic dimension, I claim that RRC-extraposition in earlier stages of Portuguese is generated by the specifying coordination plus ellipsis structure (and possibly also by VP-internal stranding), whereas in CEP it only involves VP-internal stranding.

In a cross-linguistic perspective, I suggest that there are at least two types of language. Type-I languages do not generate RRC-extraposition by specifying coordination plus ellipsis (e.g. CEP and possibly Italian, Spanish, and French). Type-II languages generate extraposition by specifying coordination plus ellipsis (e.g. English and Dutch). Type-I languages do not have extraposition derived from specifying coordination plus ellipsis and generate RRC-extraposition by stranding, whereas Type-II languages allow for extraposition derived from specifying coordination plus ellipsis and might also make use of the stranding structure to derive extraposition.

Chapter 4 deals with the syntax of appositive relative clauses (ARCs). In line with Cinque (1982, 2008) and Smits (1988), I argue that ARCs do not constitute a uniform syntactic type. This claim is supported by the study of a syntactic change that took place within the history of Portuguese, involving ARCs introduced by the complex relative pronoun *o qual* 'the which' (lit.). The investigation of this micro-variation demonstrates that the syntactic properties of *o qual*-appositives have changed over time, namely with respect to: (1) the possibility of having an additional internal head; (2) restrictions on extraposition; (3) restrictions on pied-piping; (4) the possibility of taking clausal antecedents and (5) split antecedents; (6) coordination of the wh-pronoun with another DP; (7) illocutionary force; and (8) the presence of a spelled-out coordinator. To account for these contrasts, I propose that *o qual*-ARCs in CEP involve the head raising analysis (Kayne 1994, Bianchi 1999), whereas in earlier stages of Portuguese they involve the specifying coordination analysis (De Vries 2006b). The dual approach to the phenomenon straightforwardly derives the variation in the syntax of appositive relativization found within a language and across languages, both in the synchronic and diachronic dimensions.

1.2 Data and methods

Broadly, the research presented in the book involved two main steps: data collection (see §1.2.1) and formal analysis (see §1.2.2.). The conventions adopted for data presentation are described in §1.2.3.

1.2.1 Data collection

In the studies offered in the book, I adopt a comparative perspective, contrasting the behavior of different languages and different stages of the same language with respect to some aspects of the syntax of relativization. Such an approach required the collection of data from different languages and periods, namely from historical Portuguese, CEP, and other languages.

For earlier stages of Portuguese, given the limitations of the resources available,[1] a small corpus of texts was selected for systematic syntactic analysis. This corpus has approximately 140,000 words and contains 218 notarial documents edited by Martins (2001), produced mostly between the second half of the thirteenth century and the second half of the sixteenth century. Following a corpus-driven methodology, without predefined search structures (Tognini-Bonelli 2001), I manually extracted all the relative clauses in the corpus. This process resulted in a sample of *c*.4,000 relative clauses, which were stored in a database and qualitatively analyzed.

On the basis of this analysis, the phenomena to be studied were selected according to three main principles: (1) the contrasting properties of the relevant structures in earlier stages of Portuguese with respect to CEP; (2) the novelty of the phenomena (i.e. phenomena not yet reported/explored in the literature); and (3) the theoretical relevance of the phenomena. The adoption of a corpus-driven methodology was rewarding in this first phase; a variety of constructions (or properties of the constructions) were found that have not been reported in the grammars and studies of the history of Portuguese.

Once the study topics were selected, a corpus-based methodology was adopted, which involves the selection of particular examples for specific and predetermined purposes (Tognini-Bonelli 2001). Hence, besides the collection of data from

---

[1] At the time the research was conducted (2006–10), there were three important digital corpora available for the study of earlier stages of Portuguese: *Tycho Brahe Parsed Corpus of Historical Portuguese* (Galves and Faria, 2010); *Digital Corpus of Medieval Portuguese* (Xavier, coord., 1993–); and *Unknown Letters*, which later gave rise to the *P.S. Post Scriptum: A Digital Archive of Ordinary Writing (Early Modern Portugal and Spain)* project (CLUL, ed., 2014). However, with the exception of the *Tycho Brahe Parsed Corpus of Historical Portuguese*, which contained eleven syntactically annotated texts, no other texts were available for syntactic search.

grammars and studies on the history of Portuguese, I inspected other sources in order to: (1) document specific phenomena unattested in Martins (2001); (2) broaden the variety of text-types documenting a specific phenomenon; and (3) cover the period from the second half of the sixteenth century to the nineteenth century. Table 1.1 provides a list of the additional sources considered for earlier stages of Portuguese. The texts correspond to different genres and registers and they date from different periods.

TABLE 1.1 **Additional primary sources for earlier stages of Portuguese**

	Corpus/Edition	Reference
13th–16th (1st half) c.	*Tycho Brahe Parsed Corpus of Historical Portuguese (TYC)*	Galves and Faria (2010)
	Digital Corpus of Medieval Portuguese (DCMP)	Xavier (coord., 1993–)
	Crónica do Conde D. Pedro de Meneses	Brocardo (1997)
	Livro de Linhagens do Conde D. Pedro	Brocardo (2006)
	Demanda do Santo Graal[2]	Piel and Nunes (1988)
	Livro de José de Arimateia	Castro (1984)
	Livro dos Ofícios	Piel (1948)
	Crónica de D. Fernando	Macchi (1975)
	Gil Vicente: todas as obras	Camões (ed., 1999)
16th (2nd half)– 19th c.	*Tycho Brahe Parsed Corpus of Historical Portuguese (TYC)*	Galves and Faria (2010)
	P.S. Post Scriptum: A Digital Archive of Ordinary Writing (P.S.)	CLUL (ed., 2014)
	Corpus do Português (CP)	Davies and Ferreira (2006–)
	Os Autos do Processo de Vieira na Inquisição	Muhana (1995)
	Documentos para a História da Inquisição em Portugal	Pereira (1987)
	Inquisição de Évora: dos Primórdios a 1668	Coelho (1987)

---

[2] *Demanda do Santo Graal* is a 15th-century copy of a lost Portuguese translation, from the 13th century, of the last section of the Post-Vulgate *Roman du Graal* (see Castro 1993; Martins 2013). *Livro de José de Arimateia* is a 16th-century copy of a lost Portuguese translation, also from the 13th century, of the first section (see Castro 1983; Neto 2001). Parsed versions of *Demanda do Santo Graal* in the edition of Neto (2012–15), and *José de Arimateia* in the edition of Castro (1984), have in the meantime been developed by Martins, Pereira, and Cardoso (2014–15, 2013–15 respectively). Because these versions are available online, I will use them for reference purposes.

TABLE 1.2 **Additional sources for contemporary European Portuguese**

Corpus/Edition	Reference
CETEMPúblico: A large corpus of Portuguese newspaper language (*CETEMP*)	Rocha and Santos (2000)
Reference Corpus of Contemporary Portuguese (*CRPC*)	Bacelar do Nascimento (2000)
Corpus of Spoken Portuguese (*C-ORAL-ROM*)	Bacelar do Nascimento et al. (2005)
Syntax-oriented Corpus of Portuguese Dialects (*CORDIAL-SIN*)	Martins (coord., 2000–2010)

TABLE 1.3 **Additional sources for contemporary and historical English**

Corpus/Edition	Reference
Corpus of Contemporary American English (*COCA*)	Davies (2008–)
Penn Parsed Corpus of Modern British English (*PPCMBE*)	Kroch, Santorini, and Diertani (2010)
Penn-Helsinki Parsed Corpus of Early Modern English (*PPCEME*)	Kroch, Santorini, and Delfs (2004)

As the present research adopts a comparative perspective (Cinque and Kayne eds. 2005, among others), additional evidence was collected to show how different languages (or different stages of the same language) behave with respect to the phenomena under analysis. Therefore, I systematically compared earlier stages of Portuguese with CEP as regards the study topics. The empirical evidence for CEP is based on my own linguistic intuitions, intuitions from other speakers, corpora, and data available in grammars and studies on Portuguese syntax. In addition, following a corpus-based methodology, I searched for specific aspects related to the syntax of relativization in corpora of oral and written texts (Table 1.2).

Moreover, I systematically compared Portuguese with other languages, in particular Latin, English, Dutch, and Italian. To that end, I collected empirical data from grammars and studies on the syntax of relativization. As for contemporary and historical English, I additionally inspected the corpora listed in Table 1.3.

1.2.2 *Formal analysis*

On the basis of the data collected, the relevant inter- and intra-linguistic contrasts were identified and a formal account was developed, which is built on generative syntax and on the theories that combine language change with language acquisition. See §1.3 for an introduction to the relevant framework.

1.2.3 Transcription and reference conventions

For ease of reading, the conventions adopted by some editors in text transcription have been simplified, that is: (1) parentheses and italics that indicate the expansion of abbreviations are eliminated; (2) the indication of line breaks and the *hyphen* sign (which indicates the division of a word at the end of a line) are removed; and (3) the tildes and the superscript marks (similar to an acute accent) that editors transcribe after a letter appear above the letter.

The data excerpts are drawn from primary and secondary sources. Primary sources are referenced by the corpus abbreviation or by the author–date system (in the case of individual editions), and the full reference is provided in the reference list at the end of the book ("Primary sources"). In the case of manuscripts, the source is referenced by the place-name and by the name of the archive. If other primary sources are used, the specific kind of source is identified (e.g. TV-show, newspaper) and no reference is provided in the reference list. Secondary sources (e.g. grammars and other studies) are referenced by the author–date system and the full reference is provided in the reference list ("Secondary sources").

The examples provided in the book may be complemented with further information: (1) historical data have indication of the century of the text; and (2) non-English examples are followed by a word-for-word gloss with the relevant morphological information and by the English translation.

1.3 Theoretical framework

This section outlines the theoretical framework that underlies the studies presented in the book, considering: (1) the theory of grammar (§1.3.1); (2) the syntax of relative clauses (§1.3.2); (3) information structure (§1.3.3); and (4) the theory of language change (§1.3.4). Emphasis is given to the aspects that directly concern the study topics. More specific implementations are presented in later chapters as they become relevant for a particular phenomenon.

1.3.1 Theory of grammar

The theory of grammar adopted in the book broadly falls within the premises of the generative Principles-and-Parameters approach to the study of human language (Chomsky 1981), under its Minimalist version (Chomsky 1993, 1995, and subsequent work). It is also inspired by the new insights deriving from Kayne's (1994) antisymmetry theory.

1.3.1.1 The architecture of grammar   The general trend in generative grammar is to adopt a model of grammar represented by the shape of an inverted-Y: the so-called Y- or T-model (see (5)). Under this view, the computational system accesses the lexical items[3] and builds the syntactic structures through the operation Merge.[4] At the point at which the system employs the operation Spell Out, the computation is split into two parts—Phonological Form (PF) and Logical Form (LF)—which correspond to interface levels that provide instructions to the phonological module and to the interpretative system, respectively.

(5) Architecture of grammar (Y/T-model)

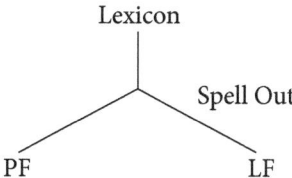

Some authors argue that the classical Y/T-model in (5) needs to be changed in order to account for some interface phenomena, such as the relationship between focus, word order, and nuclear stress.[5] However, despite the prolific research in this field, to date there is still much debate on the way that syntax relates to PF and LF. Moreover, it is still not clear how to integrate information structure in the classical Y/T-model.

1.3.1.2 Phrase structure   In the book the hierarchical phrasal organization is represented either by tree diagrams (as in (6)) or by labeled brackets (as in (7)). The crucial relations are stated in the simple terms of the X′ (or X-bar) notation. Structures of the form in (6)–(7) are composed of a head (X), which takes ZP as its complement and YP as its specifier. Besides the head X, the structure involves three maximal projections (or phrases)—XP, YP, and ZP—and an intermediate projection—X′.

---

[3] The lexical items may correspond to words, morphemes, or submorphemic units, depending on the theory adopted.

[4] Chomsky (2001) distinguishes between External and Internal Merge. External Merge takes two distinct objects and combines them, whereas in Internal Merge one of the objects is a subpart of the other. The latter operation is more frequently called Move.

[5] For alternative models, see Jackendoff (1997) and Zubizarreta (1998), among others. Broadly, Jackendoff (1997) proposes a radical change in the architecture of grammar, postulating a "parallel" model of grammar where all the modules create their own derivations in a parallel fashion, the articulation between the modules being established by some correspondence rules. Zubizarreta (1998), in turn, proposes a change in the classic Y/T-model, including an earlier point in the derivation where the structure involves a single phrase marker (Σ-structure) and a post-LF level (Assertion Structure) where the focus-presupposition partitioning is encoded.

(6)      (7) [$_{XP}$ YP [$_{X'}$ X ZP]]

1.3.1.3 Linear order   The most famous algorithm to derive linear order from the hierarchical structures is the Kayne's (1994) *Linear Correspondence Axiom* (LCA), which states that asymmetric c-command imposes a linear ordering of terminal elements.

The LCA imposes severe restrictions on the syntactic structure, in particular, (1) the impossibility of right-hand adjunction; (2) the impossibility of rightward movement; (3) strict binary branching; and (4) the specifier-head-complement universal order.

I adopt the restrictions in (1)–(4) in the comparative analysis developed for relative clauses. However, given that no systematic LCA-compatible analysis has been developed for scrambling in CEP, I will have to stick to the specifier/adjunct distinction along with the possibility of multiple specifiers and adjuncts (Chomsky 1995: 340) in order to accommodate the analyses developed for middle/short scrambling (J. Costa 1998, 2004a; Martins 2002; Costa and Martins 2009) and VP-modifiers (J. Costa 2004a,b) in CEP—at least until an analysis consistent with LCA is developed for these phenomena.

1.3.1.4 Clause structure   The structure of the clause is represented with a tripartite structure, including a Verb Phrase (VP), an Inflection Phrase (IP), and a Complementizer Phrase (CP), as in (8).

(8)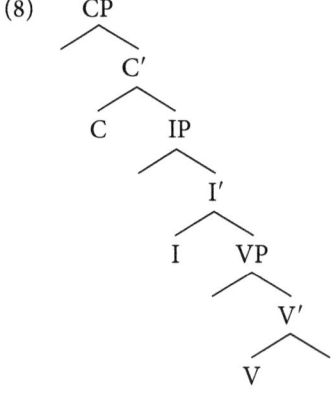

The VP is headed by a verb. For ease of exposition, I represent it by default with a single shell, as in (8); I make use of the so-called double VP-shell[6] only to represent the double complement construction.

The IP is headed by inflection, a cover term that encompasses functional categories associated with the verb (e.g. tense, agreement, aspect). Although the IP space has been claimed to involve more than one functional projection (Pollock 1989; Belletti 1990; Cinque 1999; among others), I represent it by default with a single inflection projection (IP),[7] except when considering analyses developed by other authors (e.g. J. Costa's 2004a and Stjepanović's 2007 representation of the IP space, which includes a TP immediately dominated by the AgrSP projection; see §3.5.1.3a)).

Following Rizzi (1997), the CP level is taken to involve several functional projections (see the template in (9), where the asterisk means that the projection is recursive). It is delimited by a Force Phrase (ForceP), which encodes the illocutionary force of the clause, and a Finiteness Phrase (FinP), which defines the finite/non-finite status of the clause; in between FinP and ForceP there are some functional projections—a Topic Phrase (TopP) and a Focus Phrase (FocP)—which host wh-elements, topics, and foci.

(9)   [$_{ForceP}$ [$_{TopP}*$ [$_{FocP}$ [$_{TopP}*$ [$_{FinP}$ [$_{IP}$]]]]]]

In the book I adopt the single CP projection by default; a split representation of the CP level is used only when a topic and/or a focalized element is involved in the structure.

1.3.1.5 Movement and features   An important property of human languages is that linguistic expressions may surface in a position distinct from their first merged position, that is, they appear to have been moved. Under Minimalist assumptions, movement (or Internal Merge) is driven by features (i.e. linguistic properties).

Features can be classified according to different criteria. Cut one way, there are phonological, semantic, and formal features (Chomsky 1995: 230).[8] Phonological and semantic features are relevant for the articulatory-phonetic system and for the conceptual-intentional system, respectively; formal features correspond to the set of

---

[6] According to the double VP shell approach, the verb phrase consists of a lower lexical verb phrase (VP) and a higher light verb phrase (*v*P) (Larson 1988, 1990, among others).

[7] In the spirit of Chomsky (1995), Bošković (1999), and Martins (2002), I assume that the inflection head can attract multiple specifiers.

[8] Taking an example from Chomsky (1995: 230), the lexical entry for *airplane* contains three collections of features: phonological features (e.g. begins with a vowel); semantic features (e.g. artifact); and formal features (e.g. nominal).

features that function in the computation, excluding the phonological and purely semantic features.

In earlier Minimalism, movement takes place when a formal feature needs to enter into a checking relation with a feature of the same sort. Two options are available, depending on feature's strength: weak features involve pure feature movement, whereas strong features involve movement of a full category. More recently, Chomsky (2000) adopts a different approach, according to which movement is triggered by a specific feature (EPP). If a head is associated with the EPP-feature, its specifier position needs to be overtly filled.

Another important distinction among formal features concerns their interpretability in LF: interpretable features (e.g. categorial features, phi-features of nouns) have effect on the interpretation and therefore remain accessible to the computation and visible in LF; uninterpretable features (e.g. Case, agreement features of the verb) have no effect on the interpretation and therefore must be eliminated for convergence in LF (Chomsky 1995: 277).

1.3.2 *Syntax of relative clauses*

After some preliminaries (§1.3.2.1), I present the definition of *relative clause* adopted in the book (§1.3.2.2) and the restrictive/appositive dichotomy (§1.3.2.3). Then I briefly outline the core competing analyses proposed in the literature to account for the syntax of RRCs (§1.3.2.4) and ARCs (§1.3.2.5), placing emphasis on the approaches implemented in the book (i.e. the *raising analysis* and the *specifying coordination analysis*).

1.3.2.1 *Preliminaries* Perhaps one of the most relevant contributions of the Principles and Parameters model (Chomsky 1981) has been the rejection of the view that a language consists of rules for forming grammatical constructions (e.g. relative clauses and passives). As Chomsky (1995: 5–6) states:

The P&P [Principles and Parameters] approach held that languages have no rules in anything like the familiar sense, and no theoretically significant grammatical constructions except as taxonomic artifacts. There are universal principles and a finite array of options as to how they apply (parameters), but no language-particular rules and no grammatical constructions of the traditional sort within or across languages.

This move is crucial for the development of generative syntax. It asserts that the notion of *construction*,[9] which is used in traditional grammar (and in earlier periods

---

[9] See Schönefeld (2006), where the notion of "construction" is examined from a number of different theoretical perspectives. In this respect, it is worth mentioning that there are many theories that diverge radically from the generative view presented here. This is, for instance, the case as regards the Construction

of the generative grammar) to refer to clause types (among other syntactic patterns), can be used non-technically to refer to a variety of apparently related structures but has no theoretical relevance.

In view of the new paradigm, the term *relative clause* is used in this book as a mere descriptive label with no explanatory force. Similarly, the view that relative clauses (and other "constructions") involve uniform underlying structure and movement is rejected. Indeed this ideal, which is still pursued in many generative studies, can rather be taken as a revival of the traditional concept of *construction*.

1.3.2.2 Definition of relative clause   The concept of *relative clause* is difficult to characterize, given the diversity of structures traditionally grouped under this label. As a working definition, I adopt De Vries' (2002: 14) proposal, which defines relative clauses as having the properties in (10).

(10)   Defining properties of relative clauses
    a. A relative clause is subordinated.
    b. A relative clause is connected to surrounding material by a pivot constituent.

In the context of (10b), the term *pivot* refers to a constituent that is semantically shared by the matrix clause and the relative clause.

1.3.2.3 The restrictive/appositive dichotomy   Much of the traditional and generative literature has assumed that relative clauses can be semantically classified as *restrictives* or *appositives*. RRCs are interpreted intersectively, that is, as restricting the denotation of the antecedent. ARCs are interpreted as providing additional information about the antecedent. This is illustrated in (11). In the RRC in (11a), there is another potential group of students that did not participate in the research, whereas in the ARC in (11b), there is only one group of students in the domain of discourse and no contrast with other students.[10]

(11)   a. The students who participated in the research showed improvement in this area.
    b. The students, who participated in the research, showed improvement in this area.

Grammar model, pursued by a growing number of researchers (Ivan Sag, Charles Fillmore, and William Croft, among others).

[10] In recent studies, there seems to be a growing consensus that not all relative clauses fit the traditional restrictive/appositive dichotomy. Some authors (Carlson 1977; Heim 1987; Grosu and Landman 1998; among others) have identified a "third type" of relative clause: the so-called *degree* (or *amount*) *relative*. For more details on degree relatives, see §1.3.2.4B(e).

1.3.2.4 Syntax of restrictive relative clauses   Much of the debate on the syntax of RRCs has centered on the contrast between the *adjunction analysis* and the *raising analysis*, which are schematically represented in (12).

(12)   a. The book [ø$_i$ I read t$_i$] [adjunction analysis]
         b. The [book$_i$ I read t$_i$] (*raising analysis*)

The major difference is that the head noun *book* is generated in the matrix clause in the adjunction analysis (see (12a)), but it is raised from within the relative in the raising analysis (see (12b)). This is why these approaches are often referred to as, respectively, *head external analysis* and *head internal analysis* (or *promotion analysis*).[11]

A. Adjunction analysis

The development of the adjunction analysis goes back to Ross (1967), Chomsky (1977), and Jackendoff (1977). For the current exposition, I consider the version of the adjunction analysis proposed by Demirdache (1991), according to which the RRCs are right-adjoined to the Noun Phrase (NP) projection (see (13)).[12] The head noun originates outside of the RRC, and the relative CP involves the A′-movement of a relative operator, which is linked to the head-NP via predication, semantically interpreted as intersective modification.

(13)   [$_{DP}$ the [$_{NP}$ [$_{NP}$ book]$_i$ [$_{CP}$ Op$_i$ I read t$_i$]]]

Two aspects of the adjunction analysis are worth emphasizing: (1) the head is not directly represented in the relative clause; and (2) the relative clause is c-commanded by the D head.

---

[11] An alternative approach to the syntax of RRCs is the so-called *matching analysis*, which is originally proposed by Lees (1960, 1961), and Chomsky (1965), and, more recently, extended in Sauerland (1998, 2003), Cresti (2000), and Citko (2001), among others. In the matching analysis, two heads are involved in an RRC: (1) one head is generated in the matrix (external head); and (2) the other is generated in a position internal to the relative clause (internal head). The internal head is deleted under identity with the external head, as sketched below:

the [book] [$_{CP}$ [Op/which ~~book~~]$_i$ I read t$_i$]

The matching analysis can be taken as a compromise between the adjunction and the raising analyses and, as a consequence, it involves some pros and cons of both approaches (see Bhatt 2002 for a detailed criticism). For this reason, and to keep the discussion simpler, I limit the treatment in this book to the adjunction analysis and raising analysis.

[12] The adjunction analysis is also proposed for ARCs (see §1.3.2.5). The difference concerns the level of attachment: in present-day syntax, RRCs may be viewed as adjoined to the NP level, whereas ARCs are attached to the Determiner Phrase (DP) level.

B. Raising analysis

The raising analysis was originally proposed by Schachter (1973) and Vergnaud (1974, 1985). It was later revived by Kayne (1994), who combines head raising with the D-complement hypothesis, according to which the relative clause is the complement of the outer determiner.[13]

In this book I adopt the version of the raising analysis proposed by Kayne (1994) with some of the implementations developed by Bianchi (1999) and De Vries (2002). Concretely, I assume that the head NP (i.e. the antecedent) of an RRC originates at the relativization site inside the subordinate clause and then raises to the left edge. The relative clause itself is generated as the complement of the so-called external determiner, with which the head NP may associate after raising. A relative pronoun or operator is then analyzed as a *relative determiner* originally belonging to the internal head NP. As represented in (14), there are normally two movement steps: movement of the operator phrase DP_{rel} to the CP domain, and subsequent movement of the head NP to the left of D_{rel}.

(14) $[_{DP}$ D $[_{CP}$ $[_{DP_{rel}}$ NP_j $[D_{rel}$ $t_j]]_i$ C $[_{IP}...t_i]]]$
     e.g.   the   book   which   I read

If no relative pronoun is present, I take the relative clause to involve the same structure as (14). In this case, however, D_{rel} is not spelled out and the complementizer *que* 'that', if present, occupies the C position (see (15)).

(15) $[_{DP}$ D $[_{CP}$ $[_{DP_{rel}}$ NP_j $[D_{rel}$ $t_j]]_i$ C $[_{IP}...t_i]]]$
     e.g.   the   book   that I read
          the   book   I read

For the subsequent movement of the head NP to the left of D_{rel}, I adopt Bianchi's (1999) proposal, according to which the external D bears a strong N-feature that needs to be checked by a [+N] category. Because the CP category itself (the complement of D) has no such feature, the head NP inside CP must be moved to a position governed by (or in the minimal domain of) the external D.

For the landing site of this movement, I take the head NP to be moved to [Spec, DP_{rel}] in sentences such as (14). However, when DP_{rel} is embedded in another constituent and this constituent is dragged along with D_{rel} to the CP domain (i.e. when pied-piping is involved), I assume that the head NP moves to the highest

---

[13] It is worth noting that Kayne (1994) works within an antisymmetric framework of syntax that does not permit right-adjunction; hence, the adjunction analysis of relative clauses is not an option in his framework (see §1.3.1.3).

specifier position within the pied-piped constituent (Kayne 1994, De Vries 2006a). See, for instance, (16), which involves pied-piping of a PP to the CP domain.

(16) $[_{DP}$ D $[_{CP}$ $[_{PP}$ NP$_i$ $[_{P'}$ P $[_{DP_{rel}}$ D$_{rel}$ t$_i$]]]$_k$ C $[_{IP}$ t$_k$]]]
      the   bed   in   which   he sleeps

The strongest arguments adduced in the literature in favor of the raising analysis are summarized in (a) to (g) below. For further discussion of arguments and counter-arguments regarding this approach, see Bianchi (1999), Alexiadou, Law, Meinunger, and Wilder (2000), De Vries (2002), Bhatt (2002), Salzmann (2006), and discussions in Borsley (1997) and Bianchi (2000).

(a) Binding theory

Reconstruction is originally proposed in the Government and Binding Theory as a process that occurs in the mapping from S-structure to LF, moving some constituents back to their D-structure positions.[14] It has been considered as a reliable diagnosis for movement because a constituent that has undergone movement behaves as if it were in the position occupied before movement at the level of computation at which binding principles apply. These facts can be observed, for example, in interrogative wh-movement. In (17a) the anaphor *himself* has to be c-commanded by its antecedent *John*, and consequently it behaves as if it were in its base position. In (17b) *John* is interpreted in its base position, the sentence being ruled out as a violation of Principle C of the binding theory.

(17)   a. Which picture of himself$_i$ did John$_i$ buy t?
      b. *Which picture of John$_i$ did he$_i$ buy t?

Based on the idea that reconstruction effects can be a diagnosis for movement, the reconstruction of the relative head has been widely discussed by proponents and opponents of the raising analysis. One traditional argument in favor of this approach is the presence of reconstruction effects in sentences like (18).

(18)   [The portrait of himself$_i$ that John$_i$ painted t] was extremely flattering.

The adjunction analysis makes the wrong predictions about (18): if the head is base-generated in a relative clause external position, the anaphor *himself* cannot be bound by *John*; hence (18) should be ungrammatical, in violation of Principle A of the binding theory.

---

[14] In the terms *D-structure* and *S-structure*, the letters *D* and *S* are originally associated with 'Deep' and 'Surface'.

In contrast, the pattern of grammaticality of (18) is explained under the raising analysis. Because the head is base-generated in a position internal to the relative clause, the anaphor embedded in the head can be reconstructed in its base position and, consequently, be bound by the subject of the relative clause.[15]

(b) Quantifier binding

Quantifier binding requires that a quantificational noun phrase c-commands a bound pronominal. To test quantifier binding in relative clauses, the relevant configuration involves a pronoun embedded in the head bound by a quantifier inside the relative clause, as in (19), from English, and (20), from Italian.

(19) The picture of his$_i$ mother that every soldier$_i$ kept t wrapped in a sock was not much use to him. (Salzmann 2006: 22)

(20) La parte del suo$_i$ stipendio che ho   anticipato t ad ogni impiegato$_i$
      the part of his salary   that have.1SG advanced   to every clerk
      verrà   sottratta dalla   busta paga
      come.FUT deducted from.the payslip
      'The part of his salary that I paid in advance to every clerk will be deducted from the pay-sheet.' (Bianchi 1999: 124)

On the assumption that a pronoun cannot incidentally co-refer with a quantified expression, quantifier binding in (19)–(20) requires that the pronouns *his* and *suo* 'his' be in the gap position of the relative clause at the relevant level.

The appropriate configuration is obtained by the raising analysis: the head is base-generated inside the relative clause and, as a result, can be interpreted in its trace position in LF. Such an explanation is not, however, available for the adjunction

---

[15] According to Cecchetto (2005), when a transitive noun such as *picture* is used in these tests, the anaphor can be bound by an NP-internal PRO that sits in the subject position of the NP (Giorgi and Longobardi 1991). Therefore in sentences like (i), the absence of Principle A violation is not a case of reconstruction because the position in which *himself* occurs is c-commanded by a suitable antecedent for *himself* (PRO).

(i) [$_{DP}$ the [$_{NP}$ PRO$_i$ picture of himself$_i$] [that John$_i$ likes *e* most]] (was never on display) (Cecchetto 2005: 16)

However, Cecchetto (2005) notes that the same effect appears if, as in (ii), from Italian, an unaccusative noun like *naufragio* 'shipwreck' is involved. Because in this case no internal PRO is available, the absence of Principle A violation indicates that reconstruction is at stake.

(ii) Il [naufragio della propria$_i$ nave] [che Gianni$_i$ teme *e*] è quello che può avvenire
      the shipwreck of.the own   ship   that G.   fears is that   that can happen.INF
      durante la   regata principale
      during the regatta main
      'The shipwreck of his own ship that Gianni fears is the one that can happen during the main regatta.'
      (Cecchetto 2005: 18; gloss and translation mine)

analysis; in this case, the head cannot be interpreted in a position inside the relative clause because it is externally generated.

(c) Scope assignment

The head of a relative clause can be reconstructed for the purposes of scope assignment (Salzmann 2006, among others). Consider, for instance, the sentence in (21), which can have a distributive reading or a wide-scope reading. In the distributive reading, each doctor will examine a different set of two patients that every doctor examines; in the wide-scope reading, all doctors examine the same two patients. Crucially, the distributive reading is only possible if the numeral is reconstructed under the scope of the universal quantifier.

(21)   I called the two patients that every doctor will examine t tomorrow (Salzmann 2006: 22)

In the raising analysis, this requirement is fulfilled because the head can be reconstructed in its base position, under the scope of the subject of the relative clause. This is not possible under the adjunction analysis: the head originates outside the relative clause and therefore cannot reconstruct to a relative clause internal position.

(d) Idioms

The argument from idiom chunks (or collocations) is based on configurations like (22), where the direct object of an idiom (i.e. *headway*) is relativized.

(22)   The headway that we made was satisfactory. (attributed to Brame 1968 MS, cited in Schachter 1973: 31)

The basic idea is that the verb and the object form a fixed expression with a special meaning, which can be derived only if the verb and the object are merged together (Schachter 1973; Vergnaud 1974; Chomsky 1993; Bianchi 1999; Bhatt 2002; among others).

In the raising analysis, the conditions on the adjacency of the parts of the idiom are met in LF: *headway* is generated as the complement of *made* within the relative clause; hence it can be reconstructed in its base position. In the adjunction analysis, the grammaticality of (22) is unexpected: the verb and the head are not merged together and therefore cannot become adjacent in LF via reconstruction.

(e) Degree relatives

It has been argued in the literature that some relative clauses do not fit in the traditional appositive/restrictive dichotomy. A case in point concerns the so-called *degree* (or *amount*) *relatives*, which differ from the traditional types in a number of ways, including their semantics (Carlson 1977; Grosu and Landman 1998; among others). In (23), for instance, the relative clause refers to the amount of wine, rather than to the fact that there was wine in the bottle; in fact it can be paraphrased as (*Mary drank*) **all** *the wine in the bottle*.

(23)   Mary drank the wine that there was in the bottle.

To derive the amount reading of degree relatives, Grosu and Landman (1998) assume that: (1) the head of the relative clause is interpreted in a CP internal position; and (2) an operation of maximalization takes place within the relative clause.

The raising analysis derives straightforwardly the amount reading, because the head is reconstructed inside the relative clause and the abstraction is over a degree variable. The same effect cannot, however, be obtained under the adjunction analysis because the head is merged CP-externally.

(f) The interpretation of adjectival modifiers

Bhatt (2002) argues that certain adjectival modifiers associated with the head noun can be interpreted in a CP internal position. Sentence (24), for instance, is ambiguous between a high and a low reading of the adjective *first*. In the high reading, the order in which the books were actually written is irrelevant; what matters is the order in which John names the books. In the low reading, the order of John's naming it is irrelevant and what matters is the order in which the books were written.

(24)   The first book that John said that Tolstoy had written. (Bhatt 2002: 57)

Bhatt (2002) shows that the low reading[16] of the adjective can be derived if the head and its modifier are reconstructed inside the relative clause. This is possible under the raising analysis because the head and its modifier originate inside the relative clause and undergo leftward movement. This not, however, an option in the adjunction analysis because the head is not directly represented inside the relative clause.

(g) Head-internal relatives

From a cross-linguistic perspective, there is wide variation in the relative position of the head with respect to the relative clause. On the basis of this criterion, three main syntactic types are identified: (1) post-nominal or head-initial relative clauses (see (25), from English); (2) pre-nominal or head-final relative clause (see (26), from Mandarin Chinese); and (3) circum-nominal or head-internal relative clauses (see (27), from Dagbani, a Gur language spoken in Ghana).[17]

(25)   The book that you gave me was very interesting.

---

[16] The high reading is not crucial for Bhatt's argument because it can also be derived by a non-raising structure (namely by merging the adjectival modifier outside the relative CP).

[17] Post-nominal and pre-nominal relative clauses are sometimes grouped together under the label *head-external relative clauses* (as opposed to *head-internal relative clauses*).

(26) Wǒ bǎ nǐ gěi wǒ de shū diūdiào-le.
      I   ACC you give I   NR book loose-PERF
      'I have lost the book that you gave me.' (Lehmann 1984, cited in De Vries
      2002: 16)

(27) A mi [o nə ti saan-so   ləgri] la.
      you know he SR give stranger SPC/LIV money PTL
      'You know the stranger to whom he gave the money.' (Lehmann 1984, cited in
      De Vries 2002: 16)

The existence of head-internal relative clauses has been taken as a strong argument in
favor of the raising analysis (Bianchi 1999: 61ff.; De Vries 2002: 77, 135ff.). The head-
internal relatives involve a nominalized sentence that modifies a nominal (overt or
not) internal to the sentence (Culy 1990), as depicted in (28) (the head noun and the
determiner are in bold face).

(28) [$_{DP}$ [$_{CP}$...N...] (**D**)] (De Vries 2002: 136)

The fact that in (28) the head surfaces in the argument position inside the relative
clause has led some proponents of the raising analysis to postulate the same base
position for the head in head-external relative clauses. In accordance with the
principle that derivations are uniform, head-external and head-internal relative
clauses would then involve the same derivation. The only extra assumption would
be that head-internal relative clauses involve covert (and not overt) movement of
the head in LF.

This hypothesis is not, however, available in the adjunction analysis because the
head is generated outside the relative clause. Under this approach, head-internal and
head-external relatives must involve two completely different derivational stories.

1.3.2.5 Syntax of appositive relative clauses Syntactic analyses of ARCs differ in the
relationship established between the antecedent and the relative clause, being classified as *orphanage analysis* or *constituency analysis*[18] (see De Vries 2006b and Arnold
2007 for an overview).

For the sake of concreteness, Table 1.4 shows how the main analyses of ARCs
proposed in the literature fall within this bipartite classification.

A. Orphanage analyses vs. constituency analyses

The central plank of the orphanage analyses is that the ARC and the antecedent are
generated separately. Two variants of this approach can be identified: *radical orphanage analyses* and *non-radical orphanage analyses*.

---

[18] The orphanage/constituency dichotomy corresponds to what Emonds (1979) calls the *Main Clause
Hypothesis* and the *Subordinate Clause Hypothesis*.

TABLE 1.4 **Appositive relatives: Orphanage analyses vs. constituency analyses**

Type	Subtype	Authors (e.g.)
Orphanage analyses	Radical orphanage analyses	Safir (1986) Fabb (1990) Espinal (1991)
	Non-radical orphanage analyses	Ross (1967) Emonds (1979) Demirdache (1991)
Constituency analyses	Adjunction analyses	Jackendoff (1977) Perzanowski (1980)
	Head raising analyses	Vergnaud (1974) Kayne (1994) Bianchi (1999)
	Coordination analyses	Koster (1995, 2000) De Vries (2002, 2006b)

Radical orphanage analyses propose that there is no syntactic link between the relative clause and the sentence containing the antecedent at any level of syntactic representation. For instance, Fabb (1990), one of the proponents of this approach, claims that ARCs do not enter any syntactic relation with the matrix (such as modification, specification, or theta-assignment). This fact is illustrated in (29), from Fabb (1990: 61).

(29)

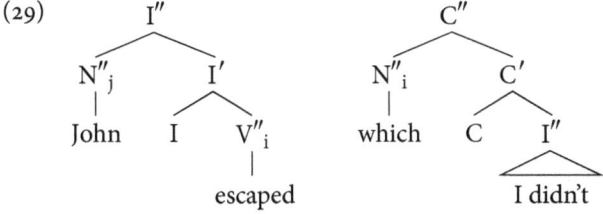

According to this approach, there is no syntactic link between the relative CP and the sentence *John escaped*. Other than some pragmatic notion of *aboutness*, the only relation established is between the antecedent and the relative pronoun. This relationship involves the sharing of the same referential index (see index i in (29)), a condition that is satisfied at the level of discourse structure rather than in the syntax. The adjacency between the ARC and the antecedent is then derived only at the discourse level.

In contrast, non-radical orphanage analyses propose that the antecedent and the ARC are generated separately in the syntax; the ARC, however, is part of the syntactic structure of the matrix clause at some syntactic level. Emonds (1979), one of the proponents of this approach, suggests that ARCs are derived from underlying conjoined clauses. The adjacency between the antecedent and the relative clause is derived from extraposition (interpreted as rightward movement) of the intervening material. The derivation of a sentence such as *The girl, who is my friend, is late* can then be represented as in (30).[19]

(30)   a.   b.

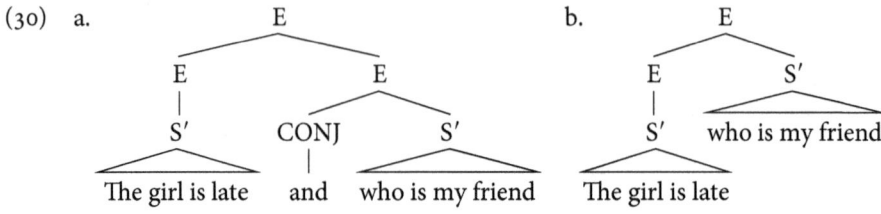

c.

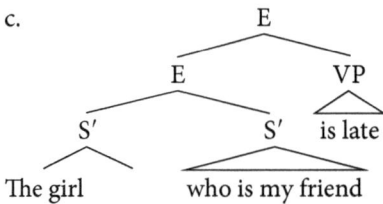

Under this account, the derivation involves three main steps: (1) at D-Structure, two main clauses are conjoined (see (30a)); (2) the conjunction *and* is deleted, and the relative is directly attached to E (see (30b)); (3) finally, the constituent that intervenes between the antecedent and the ARC (a VP in (30)) undergoes rightward movement, right-adjoining to the main clause (see (30c)).

At the opposite extreme, constituency analyses claim that the antecedent and the ARC form a constituent. The standard account corresponds to the *adjunction analysis*, which takes the ARC to be adjoined to the antecedent (Ross 1967; Chomsky 1977; Jackendoff 1977). In present-day syntax it is assumed that ARCs are attached to the DP-level, as depicted in (31) (Demirdache 1991: 109, among others).[20]

[19] For ease of exposition, I present the representation of Emonds' analysis given in Demirdache (1991: 104). In this representation, E stands for 'Expression', the highest category in a sentence, which cannot be subordinated.

[20] The adjunction analysis is also proposed to account for the syntax of RRCs. See §1.3.2.4A for more details.

(31)

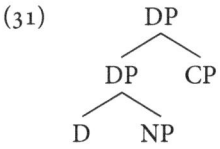

Another structure that qualifies as constituency analysis is the *raising analysis*. Kayne (1994) and Bianchi (1999) propose that ARCs are derived via the head raising, just like RRCs (see §1.3.2.4B). To account for the scope-related contrasts between RRCs and ARCs, they hypothesize that ARCs involve covert remnant movement (at LF) of the relative IP to the specifier position of the external determiner D, where it is no longer in the scope of either D or the head NP (see (32)).

(32)   [$_{DP}$ [$_{IP}$ I read t$_{DP}$] [$_{D'}$ this [$_{CP}$ book which t$_{IP}$]]] (*LF*)

The *coordination analysis*, proposed by Koster (1995, 2000) and De Vries (2002, 2006b), also falls under the umbrella of the constituency analyses. The basic assumption is that the ARC is coordinated to the antecedent, as schematically represented in (33).

(33)

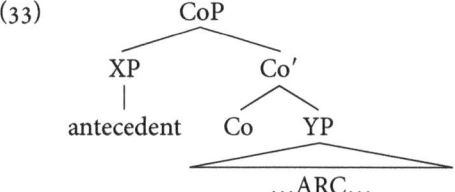

The scheme in (33) is implemented in different ways. For Koster (1995, 2000), YP=CP; consequently, ARCs usually involve unbalanced coordination (because XP can correspond to DP, AP, PP, VP, IP). For De Vries (2002, 2006b), YP=DP; therefore ARCs with nominal antecedents always involve balanced coordination. Interestingly, the *specifying coordination analysis* proposed by De Vries also involves raising, as an abstract D in the second conjunct takes the relative clause as its complement; this corresponds to a raising style configuration of a full relative construction (i.e. a DP containing a relative clause), as shown in (34). The most interesting aspect of De Vries's analysis is that an ARC is in fact an RRC in apposition to the overt antecedent.

(34)   [$_{CoP}$ DP Co [$_{DP}$ D [$_{CP}$ NP$_i$ [$_{Drel}$ t$_i$]$_k$ C [$_{IP}$ t$_k$...]]]]
          e.g. Jack,   ø   ø   who ø   lives in Paris,

Given that the specifying coordination and the raising analyses of ARCs are crucial for the developments in this book, §§1.3.2.5B and 1.3.2.5C detail the specific implementations of these approaches.

B. Specifying coordination analysis

(a) A coordination account of apposition

De Vries (2006b) argues that appositional constructions involve a coordinating relationship between the anchor and the apposition. More recently, Heringa (2007, 2012) makes the same claim.[21]

There are at least three arguments that support this view.[22] First, a coordinator may occasionally show up in appositions. This is illustrated in (35), from Heringa (2007: 69).

(35) a. The United States of America, or America for short...
      b. You could cut the atmosphere with a knife, and a blunt knife at that.
      c. John is interested in science, but especially linguistics.

The connection between the anchor and the apposition can also be made explicit by apposition markers such as *that is (to say)*, *namely*, or *for example*. What these elements have in common is that they are specifying phrases, that is, elements that introduce a DP that adds information to the anchor.

Second, similarly to coordinate structures, appositions may combine more than two elements, as shown in (36).

(36) a. John, Mary's boyfriend, a doctor, is a linguistic celebrity.
      b. John, Mary and Peter went to the store. (both Heringa 2007: 70)

Finally, coordination may operate at the sentence level or at a lower level, and there are clear indications that apposition operates at the two different levels at once. According to Potts (2007), appositions consist of two separate propositions, with independent truth values. Under this view, the propositions corresponding to (37) can be described as in (38).

(37) John, a nice guy, lives in Portugal.

(38) a. John lives in Portugal.
      b. John is a nice guy.

The independence of truth values of each proposition becomes intuitively clear from two possible reactions to (37), which are given at (39).

(39) a. No, he does not.
      b. Well yes, but he is not a nice person. (both adapted from Heringa 2007: 70)

---

[21] Other authors have highlighted the parallel between coordination and appositive constructions. For example, Quirk, Greenbaum, Leech, and Svartvik (1985: 1301–2) state that, "Apposition resembles coordination in that not only do coordinate constructions also involve the linking of units of the same rank, but the central coordinators *and* and *or* may themselves occasionally be used as explicit markers of apposition."

[22] These arguments are from Heringa (2007).

But appositions also operate at a lower constituent level. Evidence for this claim comes, for instance, from case marking in Latin.[23] Just as conjuncts exhibit the same case marking, appositions typically get the same case as the anchor, as illustrated in (40).

(40) uoluptates,   blandissimae   dominae,   maiores partes animi
     pleasures.NOM most.alluring.NOM mistresses.NOM greater parts of.soul
     a   uirtute detorquent
     from virtue divert
     'pleasures, most alluring mistresses, divert the greater parts of the soul from virtue' (1st c. BC, from Cardoso and De Vries 2010: 24)

For more arguments on treating appositional constructions in terms of coordination, see De Vries (2006b) and Heringa (2007, 2012). For now, it is sufficient to point out that appositions can be analyzed as a special type of coordination. Such a hypothesis implies that there are (at least) four semantic types of coordination, which are illustrated in (41).

(41) a. the Netherlands and Belgium (*additive*)
      b. the Netherlands or Belgium (*disjunctive*)
      c. not the Netherlands, but Belgium (*adversative*)
      d. the Netherlands, or Holland (*specifying*) (all Heringa 2012: 556)

The main difference between the traditional types of coordination and the type involved in appositional constructions is semantic. Whereas the conjuncts denote two different entities in (41a) to (41c), they refer to one and the same entity in (41d). In the latter case, the second conjunct specifies (i.e. gives more information about) the anchor. It is precisely this relationship that is dubbed *specifying coordination*.

In syntactic terms, however, the different types of coordination involve the same structure. Following Kayne (1994) and Johannessen (1998), De Vries (2006b) represents coordination as [$_{CoP}$ XP [$_{Co'}$ YP]]. Concretely, the author assumes that appositions involve a coordination phrase (CoP), with a coordinator as the head and with the two conjuncts as the specifier and complement of this head, as demonstrated in (42).[24]

---

[23] It is worth noting that in specific configurations some languages resort to a default case in appositions. For more details on this topic, see Cardoso and De Vries (2010).

[24] The structure in (42) involves a semantically specialized abstract head that establishes an asymmetric relationship of specification between the two conjuncts. De Vries (2006b) symbolically represents this relator by an ampersand plus a colon (&:). In this book, I simply make use of the more general notation *Co* for coordinating head.

(42) $[_{CoP} [_{DP} \text{anchor}] [_{Co} [_{DP} \text{apposition}]]]$
     e.g.   John,   a nice guy

The coordinating head is often phonologically null, but, as already mentioned, it can also be made overt by a specifying phrase.

(b) A coordination account of appositive relatives

According to De Vries (2006b), the ARC also involves specifying coordination. Concretely, the ARC is taken as a complex apposition that is coordinated with the antecedent, as depicted in (43).

(43) $[_{CoP} [_{DP} \text{antecedent}] [_{Co} [_{DP} \text{D} [_{CP} \text{ARC}]]]]$

The abstract coordinator involved is semantically specialized; it constitutes a relationship of specification between the two DP conjuncts. Within the second conjunct, the relative clause is the complement of D; this corresponds to a raising-style configuration of a full relative construction (i.e. a DP containing a relative clause). Given that the second conjunct normally does not contain an overt antecedent itself, the relative clause behaves as a semi-free relative clause in apposition to the visible antecedent. Thus, (44a) is analyzed roughly in the same manner as (44b).

(44) a. Jack, who lives in Paris
      b. Jack: person who lives in Paris

The structural representation of (44a) is displayed in (45).

(45) $[_{CoP} \text{DP Co} [_{DP} \text{D} [_{CP} \text{NP}_i [_{Drel} t_i]_k \text{C} [_{IP} t_k...]]]]$
     e.g.   Jack,   ø   ø   who   ø lives in Paris

Regular ARCs as in (45) involve balanced coordination because the conjuncts have equal category (i.e. both are DPs). The determiner heading the second conjunct (possibly together with the raised abstract head NP) can be considered a pronoun that behaves in a similar way to an E-type pronoun requiring co-reference with some objects (Evans 1980).[25] Therefore, the null pronoun is able to pick up an appropriate antecedent without requiring any particular syntactic configuration, similarly to how definite anaphoric or demonstrative pronouns refer to a phrase across discourse. The range of possibilities is constrained, however, by the semantics of the specifying coordination, which requires that the second conjunct give additional information to the phrase in the first conjunct. This is why the null pronoun cannot take as its antecedent a phrase outside the first conjunct.[26]

---

[25] For the E-type character of the referential link between (regular) ARCs and the antecedent, see also Del Gobbo (2008).
[26] In §4.5.3, I introduce a minor change in the structure in (45) with respect to the position of the abstract NP head in the second conjunct. Until then, I will make use of the structure in (45).

However, if the first conjunct is not a DP (as in the case of ARCs with a clausal antecedent), the coordination is syntactically unbalanced. De Vries (2006b) argues that in these cases the external D heading the second conjunct (possibly together with the raised abstract head NP) refers to the XP in the first conjunct, so that the two conjuncts are functionally equivalent. According to De Vries, this is possible because a pronoun, in principle, can refer to any syntactic category. He additionally notes that ARCs with a non-DP antecedent are less common than those ARCs with DP antecedent (Lehmann 1984: 277), which is in line with his proposal given that syntactically unbalanced coordination is more marked than balanced coordination in general.

(c) Some properties of appositive relatives derived

The coordinate-style account offers a natural explanation for the interpretative properties of ARCs. For the sake of illustration, I will consider three of these properties in some detail: (1) the scope of the determiner; (2) the lack of reconstruction effects; and (3) the opacity for binding. For a detailed presentation of how the specifying coordination analysis derives other properties of ARCs, see De Vries (2006b).

(i) Scope of the determiner

ARCs, in contrast to RRCs, are not within the scope of the determiner/quantifier that belongs to the antecedent; see (46).

(46)   a. the students that passed the exam (*RRC*)
         b. the students, who passed the exam (*ARC*)

In (46a), the determiner *the* takes scope over the noun and the relative clause; from the interpretative point of view, it implies that there is a group of students that did not pass the exam. In contrast, in (46b), the determiner *the* takes scope over only the noun; consequently, it refers to all the students regardless of whether they passed the exam.

Now compare the representations in (47a) and (47b), which involve the raising analysis and the specifying coordination analysis, respectively. For the sake of clarity, the visible antecedent is underlined in both structures.

(47)   a. [$_{DP}$ $\underline{D}$ [$_{CP}$ $\underline{NP}$...relative IP]]   (*RRC*)
         b. [$_{CoP}$ [$_{DP}$ $\underline{D\ NP}$] [Co [$_{DP}$...relative IP]]] (*ARC*)

Clearly, the relevant D in (47a) c-commands the head NP and the relative clause, but the antecedent D (and also N) in (47b) does not c-command the relative clause because of the coordination structure; both elements are embedded inside the first conjunct. Following the standard assumption that scope is dependent on c-command, the scopal difference between RRCs and ARCs is derived.

(ii) Reconstruction effects

RRCs and ARCs behave differently with respect to reconstruction effects. For instance, some idiomatic expressions allow the relativization of the idiomatic object in RRCs but not in ARCs, as shown in (48).

(48) a. The horrible face that Harry made at Peter scared him. (*RRC*)
      b. *The horrible face, which Harry made at Peter, scared him. (*ARC*)
         (both Emonds 1979: 233)

In the raising analysis, the head is base-generated inside the relative clause; hence, it can be reconstructed in that position. Following the assumption that the constituents of the idiomatic expression must be adjacent in the LF representation, the grammaticality of (48a) follows. In the specifying coordination analysis, although there is raising of the (abstract, pronominal) head NP within the second conjunct, the visible antecedent is base-generated in the first conjunct. There is no movement chain between the antecedent and the position of the gap inside the relative CP; thus, the constituents of the idiomatic expression cannot reconstruct in a position internal to the relative clause.

(iii) Opacity for binding

Pronoun-binding by a quantifier is possible if the pronoun surfaces in an RRC but not in an ARC; see (49).

(49) a. I gave every assistant$_i$ who loved his$_i$ uniform a new one. (*RRC*)
      b. *I gave every assistant$_j$, who loved his$_j$ uniform, a new one. (*ARC*) (both Emonds 1979: 236)

In the raising analysis, the grammaticality of (49a) is derived from the fact that the antecedent c-commands the pronoun inside the relative clause. In the specifying coordination analysis, such a relationship cannot be established because second conjuncts are *invisible* for the higher context in terms of c-command (De Vries 2005).[27]

(d) The expansion of the specifying coordination analysis

One of the most promising aspects of the specifying coordination analysis is that it accounts not only for the syntax of ARCs but also for a wide range of appositive structures. According to Cardoso and De Vries (2010), differences lie primarily in

---

[27] In the contexts involving a pronoun that might potentially be bound by material higher up in the matrix (as in (ii)), the same reasoning applies, i.e. the pronoun cannot be bound because second conjuncts are shielded from c-command relationships.

(i)   Everyone$_i$ spoke about the museum that he$_i$ had visited. [RRC]

(ii) *Everyone$_i$ spoke about the Millennium Dome, which he$_i$ had visited. [ARC] (De Vries 2006b: 256)

the choice of which elements are spelled out and in their respective positions. In this section, I summarize the main findings of this proposal, showing that the specifying coordination analysis straightforwardly derives a wide range of appositive structures.

(i) Predictions of the specifying coordination analysis

It is uncontroversially accepted that RRCs exhibit variation in the choice of elements that can be spelled out in the CP domain. As shown in (50), the sources of variation include the presence/absence of an overt relative pronoun D_{rel} and the presence/absence of an overt complementizer C.

(50) a. the girl whom I saw
      b. the girl that I saw
      c. the girl I saw

According to Cardoso and De Vries (2010), additional sources of variation in RRCs include the presence/absence of an overt head noun, the presence/absence of an overt external determiner, and the position of the head NP. This yields the difference between fully headed, semi-free, free, and internally headed free relative clauses (see (51)).

(51) a. the pirate who Jack admires   (*headed relative*)
      b. he/those/someone/the one who Jack admires (*semi-free relative*)
      c. who Jack admires; what Jack did   (*free relative*)
      d. whichever man Jack admires   (*internally headed free relative*)
         (all Cardoso and De Vries 2010: 7)

If the specifying coordination analysis of ARCs involves a complete RRC in the second conjunct, the same type of variation is expected to occur in appositive constructions. More precisely, variation is expected to be found with respect to the items listed in (52).

(52) Sources of variation in appositive constructions
      a. the presence/absence of an overt relative pronoun D_{rel}
      b. the presence/absence of an overt complementizer C
      c. the presence/absence of an overt (additional) external D
      d. the presence/absence of an overt (additional) head NP
      e. the position of the additional head NP, if present

As will become clear, these predictions are confirmed by the existence of various appositive construction types.

(ii) Overview of the construction types

Cardoso and De Vries (2010) show that the predicted patterns are attested in the synchronic and diachronic dimensions. Example (53) outlines some of the relevant possibilities; for ease of exposition, they are illustrated with English words, and only overt elements are indicated.

(53)   a. DP, C...   Jack, that is my best friend
       b. DP, D_{rel}...   Jack, who is my best friend
       c. DP, D C...   Jack, he that is my best friend
       d. DP, D D_{rel}...   Jack, he who is my best friend
       e. DP, NP D_{rel}...   Jack, man who is my best friend
       f. DP, NP C...   Jack, man that is my best friend
       g. DP, D NP C...   Jack, the man that is my best friend
       h. DP, D NP D_{rel}...   Jack, the man who is my best friend
       i. DP, D_{rel} NP...   Jack, which man is my best friend
       j. DP,...   Jack, my best friend (all Cardoso and De Vries 2010: 7)

The patterns in (53) can be grouped together into five categories: regular appositive relatives (see (53a–b)); semi-free appositive relatives (see (53c–d)); appositive relatives with an additional external head (see (53e–h)); appositive relatives with an additional internal head (see (53i)); and regular apposition (see (53j)). Each of these patterns is briefly presented in turn.

In the *regular appositive relatives*, the D and NP remain silent, but D_{rel} or C can be spelled out. The choice between D_{rel} and C seems to be subject to minor parametric choices. For instance, in Italian, the appositive relative can be introduced by a complementizer (see (54a)); whereas in English, this option is not available: appositive relatives must be introduced by a relative pronoun D_{rel} (see (54b)). The two different possibilities are represented in (55).

(54)   a. Inviterò   anche Giorgio, che abita qui vicino.
          invite.FUT.1SG also G.   that lives here close
          'I will also invite Giorgio, who lives nearby.' (Cinque 2008: 100, gloss and
          translation mine)

       b. Jack, who is my best friend...

(55)   [$_{CoP}$ DP   Co [$_{DP}$ D [$_{CP}$ NP$_i$ [$_{Drel}$ t$_i$]$_k$ C [$_{IP}$ t$_k$...]]]]
       e.g.   Giorgio,   ø   ø   ø   che abita qui vicino
                Jack,   ø   ø   who   ø   is my best friend

The *semi-free appositive relatives*[28] exhibit an additional D element (possibly combined with a light noun) that can be spelled out as an article or pronoun. There is

---

[28] Semi-free relatives (also called light-headed or false free relatives) are a variant of regular RRCs. The main difference concerns the nature of the head NP. Regular RRCs have an overt, full nominal head. In contrast, in semi-free relatives, the external determiner is spelled out in the form of a pronoun or article, and the nominal head remains abstract or can be considered to be part of the pronoun or pronominal complex.

cross-linguistic variation with respect to the light elements that can introduce semi-free relatives (Lehmann 1984; Smits 1988; Rebuschi 2001). For instance, CEP allows for a definite article, as in (56a), but not for a personal pronoun. In English, however, the light element can be a personal pronoun, as in (56b), but not a definite article. Notice additionally that Portuguese uses a complementizer[29] and English a relative pronoun.

(56) a. A   Ana e   a   Maria, as   que ganharam uma bolsa de estudo,
          the A. and the M.   the.F.PL that won   a   grant of study
          acabaram de   entrar na   sala.
          have.just DE.PREP enter.INF in.the room
          'Ana and Maria, the ones who won the grant, have just entered the room.'
          (Alexandre 2000: 30)

      b. Jack, he who is my best friend

The structural representation of the sentences in (56) is given in (57).

(57) $[_{CoP}$ DP   Co $[_{DP}$ D $[_{CP}$ NP$_i$ $[_{DP_{rel}}$ D$_{rel}$ t$_i]_k$ C $[_{IP}$...t$_k$...]]]]
      e.g. A A. e a M.,   as   ø   ø   que ganharam uma bolsa
            Jack,   he   ø   who   ø   is my best friend

The *appositive relatives with an additional external head* have an additional full NP (the additional external head) that is left peripheral within the embedded clause. The additional external head may be preceded by an external D and/or followed by an internal D$_{rel}$ and/or C. Two of the possible combinations are illustrated in (58a), from CEP, and (58b), from English. In these examples the additional external head corresponds to the NP *viagem* 'trip' and *man*, respectively.

The result is a semantically (and often morphologically) light antecedent. This is different from true free relatives, where there is no external element whatsoever (Cardoso and De Vries 2010).

[29] There is no consensus in the literature regarding the status of the Portuguese *que* 'that' in relative clauses. Traditional grammar analyzes the *que* as a relative pronoun comparable to *quem* 'who'. However, it has been claimed that there are good reasons for identifying this *que* with the complementizer that introduces other subordinate clauses (Brito 1991; Brito 1995; Brito and Duarte 2003). This analysis has, however, been recently challenged by Kato and Nunes (2009), who claim that when introducing relative clauses, *que* is always a relative pronoun and that the *que/quem* alternation can be derived in the morphological component.

I will not go into this discussion here. Following Brito (1991, 1995), and Brito and Duarte (2003), I simply assume that *que* can be analyzed as a complementizer when introducing subject and object relative clauses.

(58) a. Vínhamos de   viagem, viagem que acabava na   Avenida da
          were.1PL   DE.PREP trip   trip   that finished in.the A.   d.
          Liberdade.
          L.
          'We were coming on a trip, a trip that would finish in Avenida da
          Liberdade.'
      b. Jack, the man who is my best friend

Again, notice that Portuguese uses a complementizer, and English uses a relative pronoun. These two options are illustrated in (59).

(59) [$_{CoP}$ DP   Co [$_{DP}$ D [$_{CP}$ NP$_i$ [$_{Drel}$ t$_i$]$_k$ C   [$_{IP}$...t$_k$...]]]]
      e.g. viagem,   ø   viagem ø   que acabava na Avenida...,
            Jack,   the   man   who   ø   is my best friend,

The *appositive relatives with an additional internal head* involve an additional full NP (the internal head) c-commanded by a dependent relative pronoun D$_{rel}$. See, for instance, example (60), where the additional internal head corresponds to the NP *faithful animal*, with its structural representation displayed in (61).

(60) My dog, which faithful animal has guarded me for years, died last week. (Smits
      1988: 287)

(61)   [$_{CoP}$ DP   Co [$_{DP}$ D [$_{CP}$ [$_{Drel}$ NP]$_k$ C [$_{IP}$...t$_k$...]]]]
      e.g.   My dog,   ø   which faithful animal ø has guarded me...

The *regular apposition*[30] might be a simple DP that is linked to the antecedent (i.e. the anchor) by means of specifying coordination. However, there are indications that there is an (implicit) clausal structure in appositional constructions as well.

Cardoso and De Vries (2010), in line with O'Connor (2008) and Heringa (2007, 2012), show that this hypothesis is corroborated by several facts. First, all types of adverbs, including sentential and even speech act adverbs, can be used in appositions; see (62), from English, and (63), from CEP.

(62) a. Norman Jones, *then* a student, wrote several bestsellers. (Quirk, Greenbaum,
          Leech, and Svartvik 1985: 1314)
      b. Keith, *once* a drug addict, now leads a rehabilitation centre. (Heringa 2012:
          558)
      c. Racial profiling, *unfortunately* a frequent occurrence in American society,
          must be stopped. (O'Connor 2008: 97)
      d. This book, *frankly* not my favourite, won a prize. (Heringa 2012: 559)

---

[30] Here, I focus the discussion on attributive appositions. For more details on the analysis of identifying appositions, see Cardoso and De Vries (2010).

(63)   George W. Bush, *então* o   'homem mais poderoso da   terra'
       G.   W. B.   then the man   more powerful of.the earth
       'George W. Bush, then the most powerful man on the earth' (Official site of
       Mário Soares foundation)

Second, the tense, modality, and illocutionary force of the secondary proposition may differ from that of the primary one, as can be observed in (64).

(64)   Should Jane, once the best doctor in town, marry John?
       a. Should Jane marry John?
       b. Jane was once the best doctor in town. (both Cardoso and De Vries 2010: 16)

Third, a subordinator may show up in appositions; see (65) in English and (66) in CEP.

(65)   a. John, *though* no longer a coward, was still a weakling. (Wulf Sachs, *Black Hamlet*, 1937)
       b. The victim, *whether* a nice person or not, has to be helped. (Heringa 2012: 561)

(66)   O Belenenses, *embora* vencedor da   jornada anterior,   não está no
       the B.   although winner of.the round   preceding not is   in.the
       melhor da   sua forma individual e   colectiva.
       best   of.the its form individual and collective
       'Belenenses, although winner of the preceding round, is not in its best individual and collective form.' (*CETEMP*)

Finally, regular appositions may apparently involve wh-movement. Consider, for instance, (67) from CEP. Here, the DP *quatro das quais* lit. 'four of.the which', a partitive construction, is apparently pied-piped along with the relative pronoun to the CP domain.

(67)   Com a   sua prisão   já   são cinco as pessoas detidas no
       with the his imprisonment already are five the people arrested in.the
       âmbito do   processo Lasa e   Zabala, [DP quatro das   quais]
       context of.the case   L.   and Z.   four of.the which
       comandos e   militares   da   guarda.
       commandos and military.men of.the guard
       'With his detention, there are already five people arrested in the Lasa and Zabala case, four of whom (are) commandos and men of the military guard.' (*CRPC*)

This evidence points to the conclusion that regular appositions contain a more extensive functional structure than has hitherto been assumed. As Cardoso and De Vries (2010) suggest, the fact that regular appositions have their own tense, possibly modified by adverbs, suggests that at least IP is projected in the structure. Moreover, the eventual presence of a subordinator, the independent illocutionary force, and the movement of a wh-constituent indicate that CP is also projected.

In this line, the main idea of Cardoso and De Vries' (2010) approach is that regular appositions (e.g. *Frank, a nice guy*) and regular appositive relatives (e.g. *Frank, who is a nice guy*) involve the structure in (68).[31] The difference is that, in the regular apposition, not only the CP domain but also the verbal part of the predicate, which corresponds to an abstract copula, is silent.

(68) $[_{CoP}$ DP $[Co [_{DP2}$ D $[_{CP}$ NP$_i$ $[$ D$_{rel}$ t$_i]_k$ C $[_{IP}$ t$_k$ BE...$]]]]]$
      e.g. John,   ø   ø   ø   ø   ø my best friend,

The existence of such a null copula (or zero copula) in this structure is not particularly surprising because it has been observed in many languages that copulas can be omitted (for a cross-linguistic overview, see Stassen 2008). In CEP, for instance, the omission of the copula is allowed for at least some syntactic environments. Matos (2003) reports that the copula can be omitted from some dependent clauses, as in (69) and (70).[32]

(69) O cargo   pode-lhe   ser   atribuído desde que [–] compatível com as
      the position can-him.CL be.INF given   as.long.as   compatible with the
      funções que actualmente exerce.
      duties that currently   carries.out
      'The position may be given to him, as long as it is compatible with the duties
      that he currently performs.' (Matos 2003: 875)

(70) Embora [–] cansada, a   Maria dispunha-se   a acabar   o   trabalho
      although tired   the M.   was.willing-SE.CL to finish.INF the assignment
      antes de   se   ir   deitar.
      before DE.PREP SE.CL go.INF lay.INF
      'Although Maria was tired, she was available to finish the assignment before
      going to bed.' (Matos 2003: 875)

The omission of the copula also occurs in non-standard varieties of Portuguese: see (71)–(73), which involve, respectively, a passive, a cleft, and a modal auxiliary.

---

[31] Other authors have suggested a relationship between appositions and appositive relatives; for earlier ideas, see Smith (1964); Delorme and Dougherty (1972); Halitsky (1974); Klein (1977). Quirk, Greenbaum, Leech, and Svartvik (1985: 1314), for instance, suggest that a regular appositions, such as that in *The two men, one a Norwegian and the other a Dane*, may involve a reduced relative clause: *The two men, one (of whom was) a Norwegian and the other (of whom was) a Dane.*

[32] The null copula is represented by the symbol [–].

(71) INQ Às vezes até é assim de tijolo, não é?
      'Interviewer: Sometimes they are made out of brick, aren't they?'
      INF Pois. Muitas [–] feitas de tijolo; e   outras são feitas só   no
      ±Yes. Many   made of brick and others are made only in.the
      summer
      verão
      'Informant: Yes. Many are made out of brick; others are made only in the
      summer.' (*CORDIAL-SIN*)

(72) E   depois essa água que ficava   dessa cera escaldada [–] que
      and then that water that remained of.that wax heated   that
      fazia-se   os rebolos
      made-SE.CL the ±balls
      'And then it was from the remaining water of the heated wax that the balls
      were made.' (*CORDIAL-SIN*)

(73) Pode   [–] que eu esteja   enganado!
      can.3SG   that I be.SBJV wrong
      'It can be that I am wrong!' (*CORDIAL-SIN*)

The same is true of earlier stages of Portuguese. Examples (74)–(75) illustrate contexts
in which the copula is omitted in clefts.

(74) o   que lhe   poco diser [–] que nunca em minha vida não vi
      the that to.you.CL can say.INF   that never in my   life not saw.1SG
      nem ovi   o   que aqui te   visto e   ovisto
      nor heard the that here have.1SG seen and heard
      'what I can tell you is that I have never seen nor heard in my life what I have
      been seeing and hearing here' (19th c., *P.S.*)

(75) o que peco   a VSa   [–]que faca   a ismola de
      what ask.1SG to Your.Excellency   that make.SBJV the favor DE.PREP
      pedir ao   Senhor Intendente que me   mande   na   segunda feira
      ask.INF to.the Superintendent   that me.CL send.SBVJ on.the Monday
      para baixo
      to   downwards
      'what I ask you, Your Excellency, is that you do me a favor and ask the
      Superintendent to send me to the south on Monday.' (19th c., *P.S.*)

As for the representation of the anchor in the copular sentence, Cardoso and De
Vries (2010) propose that the subject of the embedded clause is the additional
external D in (68) (possibly with an incorporated N). Recall that these elements are
also silent in some of the appositional structures already discussed, for instance, in
regular ARCs.

To conclude, Cardoso and De Vries (2010) show that (attributive) appositions involve an implicit relative copular clause. Given the similarities between regular appositions and the complex appositional structures already analyzed, they claim that the same structure can be realized in a number of ways; see (76). The differences lie primarily in the choice of which elements are spelled out and in the respective positions of these elements.

(76) $[_{CoP} [_{DP_1}$ anchor$] [Co [_{DP_2}$ D $[_{CP}$ NP$_i$ $[_{Drel}$ t$_i]_k$ C $[_{IP}$ t$_k$ BE predicate$]]]]]$

Jack					a nice guy
Jack			who	is	a nice guy
Jack	he		who	is	a nice guy
Jack	the	one	who	is	a nice guy
Jack	some	one	who	is	a nice guy

(Cardoso and De Vries 2010: 17)

C. The raising analysis

Kayne (1994) extends the raising analysis to ARCs and proposes that ARCs differ from RRCs only at the level of LF. In his view, the non-restrictive interpretation results from LF-movement of the relative IP to the specifier position of the determiner, where it is no longer in the scope of the external D (see (77)).[33]

(77)   a. $[_{DP}$ D $[_{CP} [_{DP_{rel}}$ NP$_j$ $[_{Drel}$ t$_j]_i]$ C $[_{IP}$...t$_i]]]$ (*pre-LF*)
       b. $[_{DP}$ IP $[_{DP}$ D $[_{CP} [_{DP_{rel}}$ NP $[_{Drel}$ t$_{NP}]]$ C t$_{IP}]]]$ (*LF*)

From this approach, it follows that all differences found between RRCs and ARCs generated by the raising analysis are determined by the different derivation in LF.

(a) Some properties of appositive relatives derived

In this section, I demonstrate how the raising analysis derives some interpretative properties of ARCs, namely the scope of the determiner and the lack of reconstruction effects. For more arguments, see Kayne (1994) and Bianchi (1999).

(i) Scope of the determiner

RRCs differ from ARCs in that only the former are in the scope of the external D (see (47)). This contrast can be easily derived under the raising analysis. Clearly, the external D in the configuration in (77a) c-commands the relative clause. The same does not hold, however, for the appositive configuration in (77b); after LF-movement, the IP of the ARC is no longer c-commanded by the external D.

---

[33]   According to Kayne (1994), the movement of IP to the specifier position of D is overt in pre-nominal (or head-final) relatives (see §1.3.2.4B(g)).

(ii) Idioms

ARCs differ from RRCs in that they do not allow reconstruction of the head. This property can explain the impossibility of having the object of an idiom chunk relativized (see (78)),[34] under the assumption that the interpretation of idiomatic expressions requires the adjacency of its syntactic constituents in LF.[35]

(78)   *That headway, which the students made last week, was phenomenal. (Bianchi 1999: 125).

The lack of reconstruction effects in ARCs is initially unexpected under an analysis that combines head raising with covert IP-movement; the head, being generated inside the relative clause, should in principle be able to reconstruct in a position internal to the relative clause. However, as Alexiadou, Law, Meinunger, and Wilder (2000: 32) note, head raising only opens the possibility for the reconstruction from the head; it does not force it. The lack of reconstruction effects can be consistent with head raising if independent principles ensure that the head cannot reconstruct in ARCs.

An analysis along these lines is put forth by Bianchi (1999), who suggests that the relativization of the idiomatic object in ARCs involves a structure like (79).

(79)   LF: $[_{DP} [_{IP}$ we made $t_i] [_{DP}$ the $[_{CP} [_{DP} [_{NP}$ headway$] [_{DP}$ which $t_{NP}]]_i$ $[_{CP}$ C $t_{IP}]]]]$ (adapted from Bianchi 1999: 148)

Bianchi argues that if the head were reconstructed within IP, the c-command domain of the external determiner would be empty in LF because it would not contain any variable to be bound by it. This would be an instance of vacuous quantification, and it would be ruled out by the Full Interpretation Principle.

(iii) Opacity for binding

Pronoun-binding by a quantifier is possible if the pronoun surfaces in an RRC but not in an ARC; see (80) (repeated from (49)).

(80)   a. I gave every assistant$_i$ who loved his$_i$ uniform a new one. (*RRC*)
       b. *I gave every assistant$_i$, who loved his$_i$ uniform, a new one. (*ARC*) (both Emonds 1979: 236)

The opacity for binding in ARCs can be explained by assuming that, after LF-movement, the IP of the ARC (where the pronoun is placed) is no longer c-commanded by the quantifier.

---

[34] See also example (48b).
[35] For a alternative explanation of the ungrammaticality in (78), see Cinque (1990).

For the contexts involving a pronoun that might potentially be bound by material higher up in the matrix (as in (81b), repeated from n. 27), Kayne (1994: 163–4 n. 69) and Bianchi (1999: 152–3) suggest that IP is moved further out of DP_{rel}, "to a topic-like position of matrix clause, where it is not c-commanded by any matrix binder" (Bianchi 1999: 152).

(81) a. Everyone$_i$ spoke about the museum that he$_i$ had visited. (*RRC*)
      b. *Everyone$_i$ spoke about the Millennium Dome, which he$_i$ had visited. (*ARC*) (both De Vries 2006b: 256)

1.3.3 Information structure

Information structure can be regarded as a phenomenon of information packaging that responds to the immediate communicative needs of interlocutors (Chafe 1976, cited in Krifka 2007). It is generally taken to interact not only with syntax but also with other grammatical domains, such as interpretation, intonation, and morphology (Erteschik-Shir 2007).

According to Lambrecht (1994: 5–6), information structure involves the analysis of four major categories: propositional information; identifiability and activation; topic; and focus. The present book only explicitly addresses two of these categories: topic and focus. Because the terminology associated with these two concepts is notoriously varied, in the present section I clarify the use of these terms, introducing some theoretical details that are crucial for the argument developed in the book.

1.3.3.1 Focus   The term *focus* has been used in the literature with many different meanings and labels (e.g. information focus, presentational focus, contrastive focus, restrictive focus, exhaustive focus, identification focus) (see Cruschina 2011 for an overview). Although it can be classified in different ways, this book only deals with two main distinctions: (1) broad focus vs. narrow focus and (2) information focus vs. contrastive focus.

The distinction between broad and narrow focus is based on the scope of focus. Broad information focus (also known as sentential focus or unmarked focus) is used to refer to contexts in which the focus is assigned to the whole sentence. Narrow information focus refers to contexts in which only part of the sentence is assigned focus.

Another important distinction concerns the contrast between information focus and contrastive focus. Information focus (also known as semantic focus or presentational focus) signals distinctions between shared and new information (Enkvist 1980). It represents new information related to what has been called a topic, presupposition, background, or common ground. A typical test used to identify information focus is a question–answer pair, where the focused constituent of the answer replaces the wh-word in the question (J. Costa 1998, 2004a, among others).

For illustrations, see examples (82)–(83), from CEP (the wh-expression in the question and the focused constituent in the answer are marked in bold).

(82) Sentence-focus (broad focus)
  A: a. **O que** é que aconteceu?
    'What happened?'

  B: b. O João **partiu a** **janela.**
    the J. broke the window
    'João broke the window.' (J. Costa 2004a: 79)

(83) Object focused (narrow focus)
  A: a. **O que** é que o Paulo partiu?
    'What did Paulo break?'

  B: b. O Paulo partiu **a** **janela.**
    the P. broke the window
    'Paulo broke the window.' (J. Costa 2004a: 79)

Contrastive focus (also known as identificational focus) is commonly defined as evoking a suitable set of alternatives from which a subset is chosen (Chafe 1976; Rooth 1985, 1992). Some authors also define it on the basis of semantic features, such as exhaustiveness (É. Kiss 1998, among others). In this book and in Zimmermann (2007), contrastive focus is taken as a discourse-pragmatic phenomenon related to "the speaker's assumptions about what the hearer considers to be likely or unlikely, introducing a certain degree of subjectivity" (Zimmermann 2007: 148). This definition has a broader scope because it includes not only the concepts of contrast and exhaustivity but also the more general concept of emphasis.[36] In order to highlight the different values covered by the label, I henceforth adopt the term *emphatic/ contrastive focus*.

Languages may resort to different strategies of emphatic/contrastive focus marking, namely intonation contour, syntactic movement, particular syntactic structures (e.g. clefts), focus-sensitive particles, and morphological markers. In CEP, I assume that emphatic/contrastive focus can be expressed by:[37] (1) prosodic prominence alone (see (84)); (2) contrastive focus movement (see (85)); (3) specific syntactic constructions (e.g. clefts); and (4) focus-sensitive particles (e.g. *só* 'only') (see (86)). Note that both syntactic (see (85)–(86)) and lexical (see (87)) strategies co-occur with prosodic marking.

---

[36] For an overview of the different values that can be associated to the concept of contrastive focus, see Cruschina (2011).

[37] In examples (84)–(94) the emphatic/contrastive focus is indicated by small caps.

(84)   Partimos DIA VINTE de abril.
        leave.1PL day twenty of April
        'We leave on April 20 (and not on April 21).'

(85)   COM ESTAS PALAVRAS me   despeço.
        with these words   me.CL say.goodbye.1SG
        'It is with these words that I say goodbye.'

(86)   É COM ESTAS PALAVRAS que me   despeço.
        is with these words   that me.CL say.goodbye.1SG
        'It is with these words that I say goodbye.'

(87)   SÓ OS MEUS AMIGOS percebem o   que quero   dizer.
        only the my   friends understand the that want.1SG say.INF
        'Only my friends understand what I mean.'

Note, however, that there is no consensus in the literature as to the availability of contrastive focus movement in CEP (see (85)). Martins (1994 and forthcoming) contends that focus movement is available in present-day Portuguese, while J. Costa (1998) argues that focus movement is ungrammatical (see also Ambar 1992, 1999; Barbosa 1995; Duarte 1987, 1997).

More recently, Costa and Martins (2011) propose a conciliatory approach by claiming that the lack of consensus in this matter is a consequence of the variation across speakers. Concretely, they suggest that two different grammars coexist in CEP: "One grammar is less restrictive regarding the array of constituents that can be fronted. The other grammar only allows fronting of deictics or constituents containing them" (Costa and Martins 2011: 217).

Examples (88)[B] and (89) are provided in Costa and Martins (2011) to illustrate the emphatic/contrastive fronted focus in main clauses; note that these examples are allowed in both grammars.

(88)   [A] Estás cansada. Vai   passar   uns dias na   praia.
            are.2SG tired.   go.IMP.2SG spend.INF some days in.the beach
            'You're tired! Go spend some days at the beach.'

        [B] ISSO queria eu.
            that wanted I
            'That's what I wanted.' (Costa and Martins 2011: 232)

(89)   A retórica é a   maior arma   dos   políticos.
        the rhetoric is the biggest weapon of.the politicians
        COM ELA se   elevam, COM ELA se   desgraçam.
        with it SE.CL raise.3PL with it   SE.CL disgrace.3PL
        'Rhetoric is the politicians' greatest weapon. It is with it they elevate
        themselves, it is with it they fall in disgrace.' (Costa and Martins 2011: 233)

Evidence for contrastive focus fronting comes from the syntactic and interpretational tests provided by Costa and Martins (2011) to distinguish contrastive focus fronting from topicalization.[38] Under this proposal, *isso* 'that' in (88)[B] is contrastively focused; evidence for this analysis comes from (1) the cleft-like interpretation, which is made visible in the relevant paraphrase; (2) the subject–verb inversion (*queria eu* 'wanted I'); and (3) the incompatibility with quantifier floating (*Isso tudo queria eu/*Isso queria eu tudo*, 'It's all this what I wanted'). The example (89), in turn, displays contrastive focus fronting of the PP *com ela* ('with it'), which is confirmed by (1) the cleft-like interpretation in the relevant paraphrase; (2) the proclisis configuration (*se elevam*, 'SE.CL raise.3PL') and the impossibility of having the PP topicalized (**Com ela, elevam-se*, lit. 'With it, they elevate themselves'; **Com ela, desgraçam-se*, lit. 'With it, they fall in disgrace').

The same fronting phenomenon holds true for embedded clauses in CEP. Costa and Martins (2011) provide a few examples of contrastive focus-fronting in embedded clauses, namely in an embedded declarative clause (see (90)) and in a relative clause (see (91)).

(90) Digo-te   que ISSO queria eu.
      say.1SG-you.CL that that wanted I
      'I tell you: that's what I wanted.' (Costa and Martins 2011: 234)

(91) um discurso redutor e   pessimista que NADA   tem contribuído
      a   discourse reductive and pessimistic that nothing has contributed
      para a   melhoria   do   clima   escolar
      to   the improvement of.the atmosphere of.schools
      '[They launch in the media] a reductive and pessimistic rhetoric that has contributed nothing to the improvement of the atmosphere in schools.' (Costa and Martins 2011: 222; gloss and translation mine)

More examples of focus fronting are provided in (92)–(94), which involve an embedded declarative clause (see (92)), an adverbial clause (see (93)), and a relative clause (see (94)).

(92) A   continuar   assim, é certo   que NOVOS HORIZONTES se
      A.PREP continue.INF as.such is certain that new   horizons   SE.CL
      lhe   vão abrir.
      him.CL go open.INF
      'If things continue this way, it is certain that new horizons will open up to him.' (*CETEMP*)

---

[38] Costa and Martins (2011) suggest seven syntactic and interpretational tests to distinguish contrastive focus fronting from topicalization, namely: (1) cleft-like interpretation; (2) clitic placement; (3) sensitivity to referential properties of fronted constituents; (4) subject-verb inversion; (5) PP-preposing (when the PP is the complement of certain existential and light verbs); (6) quantifier floating; and (7) relative clause extraposition.

(93)   Mas, se DE ALGUMA COISA nos   serve a   experiência e   a   história,
       but if of some   thing us.CL bring the experience and the history
       é justamente para não repetir   os   mesmos erros.
       is precisely   to   not repeat.INF the same   mistakes
       'But if experience and history can teach us anything, it is precisely not to repeat
       the same mistakes.' (from a political speech, *Jornal i* newspaper)

(94)   pode   'escolher' o   clube que MELHORES CONDIÇÕES lhe
       can.3SG choose.INF the club   that better   conditions him.CL
       ofereça
       offer.SBJV
       'he can choose the club that offers him better terms' (from the news website
       Notícias ao Minuto)

Evidence for contrastive focus fronting in the embedded declarative clause provided in (92) comes from: (1) the proclisis configuration displayed both in (92) and in a corresponding main clause (*Neste cenário, novos horizontes se (lhe) vão abrir*, lit. 'In this scenario, new horizons SE.CL him.CL will open.'); and (2) the compatibility with relative clause extraposition (*É certo que novos horizontes se (lhe) vão abrir que podem contribuir para a resolução do problema*, lit. 'It is certain that new horizons will open up to him which may contribute to solving the problem').[39]

As for the conditional clause in (93), the evidence for PP fronting is found in (1) the proclisis configuration displayed both in (93) and in the corresponding main clause (*De alguma coisa nos serve a experiência e a história.*, lit. 'Something us.CL bring the experience and the history.'); (2) the subject inversion; and (3) the impossibility of having the PP *de alguma coisa* 'of something' topicalized (**se de alguma coisa, serve-nos a experiência e a história*, lit. 'if something, brings us the experience and the history').

Finally, in the relative clause in (94), *melhores condições* 'better conditions' is contrastively focused, which can be confirmed by the proclisis configuration displayed in a corresponding main clause (*Melhores condições lhe oferecem os clubes portugueses*, lit 'Better conditions him.CL offer the Portuguese clubs').

1.3.3.2 Focus and prosody   Several authors have proposed that prosody plays an important role in the identification of focus in CEP (J. Costa 1998, 2004a; Frota 1998, 2002; among others). In this book I adopt Zubizarreta's (1998, 1999) view of the

---

[39] Note that in (92) *novos horizontes* 'new horizons' is the subject of the verb *abrir* 'open'; however, it does not occupy the subject position, because relative clause extraposition from a pre-verbal subject is not allowed in CEP (see Ch. 3 for more details).

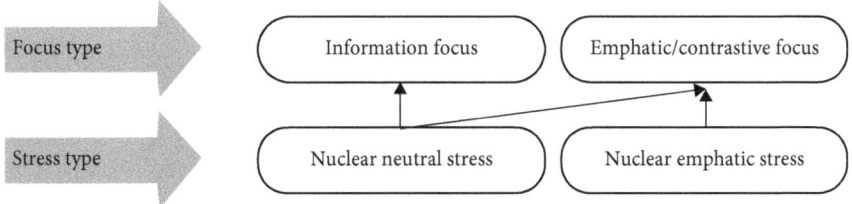

FIGURE 1.1 Relationship between focus and prosody. Diagram based on Zubizarreta (1998, 1999).

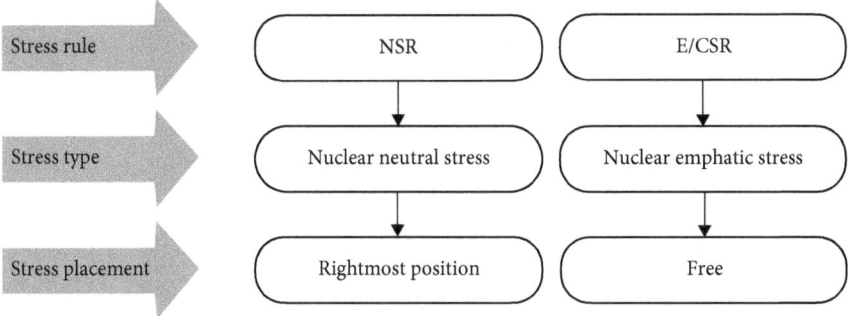

FIGURE 1.2 Effects of stress rules on stress placement. Diagram based on Zubizarreta (1999).

relationship between prosodic prominence and focus, which can be schematically represented as in Figure 1.1.

Starting with a slightly impressionistic generalization, the crucial factor seems to be that a focused constituent always carries the nuclear stress. However, there is no one-to-one correlation between the subtypes of focus and the subtypes of stress: information focus is identified by neutral stress, whereas emphatic/contrastive focus may be identified by either emphatic or neutral stress (Zubizarreta 1999: 4229 n. 16 and 4242 n. 27).[40]

Neutral and emphatic stresses are, in turn, assigned by different rules, which impact on stress placement. As shown in Figure 1.2, the Nuclear Stress Rule (NSR) (see (95)), assigns prominence to the rightmost/lowest sentential constituent, whereas the Emphatic/Contrastive Stress Rule (E/CSR) (see (96)) assigns prominence to any position.[41]

---

[40] In CEP the ambiguity between information focus and emphatic/contrastive focus can only arise if the focused constituent is rightmost. Following Frota (1998, 2002, and other related work), I propose that the aforementioned ambiguity is eliminated by differences in peak alignment (or choice of pitch accent) (see §2.4.2.2A for further details).

[41] In Ch. 2, I show that this generalization only applies to corrective contexts, i.e. contexts which aim to set right a poorly transmitted or wrongly received part of a message. In this case, the emphatic stress can fall on any item: a phrase (as in (ib)), a word (as in (iib)), or even an individual syllable of a word, as in

(95)   Nuclear Stress Rule (NSR)[42]
Given two sisters Ci and Cj, the one lower in the asymmetric c-command ordering is more prominent. (Zubizarreta 1998: 19)

(96)   Emphatic/Contrastive Stress Rule (E/CSR)
A word with contrastive stress must be dominated by every F[ocus]-marked constituent in the phrase. (Zubizarreta 1998: 45)

In addition, Zubizarreta (1998) proposes the *focus prominence rule* in (97), which aims to capture the relationship between the focus-structure of a sentence and its prosody. The idea is that the focused elements in a sentence are marked with a feature [+F], whereas the presupposed ones are marked with a feature [−F]. The rule in (97) dictates that the nuclear stress must target an [+F]-element.

(97)   Focus Prominence Rule (FPR)
Given two sister nodes C_i (marked [+F]) and C_j (marked [−F]), C_i is more prominent than C_j. (Zubizarreta 1998: 21)

The coexistence of the FPR and E/CSR in the grammar does not produce any conflict: because the E/CSR assigns emphatic/contrastive stress to any element, no principle prevents an [+F]-element from receiving it.

Some conflicts may arise, however, between the FPR and the NSR. The FPR may force the stress on a non-final position, whereas the NSR requires the stress to fall on the rightmost clausal position. According to Zubizarreta (1998), languages seem to vary in the way they resolve this conflict. In languages such as English and French,

---

I said DEfensive, not OFfensive (example from Enkvist 1980: 135). For details on non-corrective contexts see §2.4.2.2.

(i)   [A] a. O   rapaz de olhos azuis é   bonito.
         the boy   of eyes   blue   is handsome
         'The boy with blue eyes is handsome.'

      [B] b. O   rapaz DE OLHOS VERDES é   bonito.
         the boy   of eyes   green   is handsome
         'The boy with green eyes is handsome (the one with blue eyes is absolutely stunning!)'

(ii) [A] a. Vamos para Paris.
         go.1PL to   P.
         'We are going to Paris (± and staying there for a while).'

      [B] b. Vamos A Paris.
         go.1PL to P.
         'We are going to Paris (± and coming back soon).'

[42] Actually, this rule consists of two parts: one sensitive to asymmetric c-command relations (C-NSR) and the other sensitive to selectional ordering (S-NSR). Languages differ in the way in which the NSR applies; both C-NSR and S-NSR are active in German and English, but only C-NSR is active in languages such as Spanish, Italian, and Portuguese. In (95) I transcribe only the part of the NSR that is relevant to CEP.

defocalized [–F] elements are treated as extrametrical in the sense that they are skipped by the NSR. Other languages (such as Spanish and Italian) employ prosodically motivated movement (p-movement), which moves the post-focal [–F] elements out of the rightmost clausal position. Then, the NSR applies and puts the stress on the sentence-final position.

1.3.3.3 Topic   Most authors define the concept of topic in relation to the concept of comment; the topic is what the sentence is about, whereas the comment is what is said about the topic. However, there seems to be no consensus in the literature as to what topic really is. Kuroda (2005) identifies three main views on this concept in the literature, according to which topic is taken as (1) a syntactic concept, referring to a constituent that is placed at the sentential left periphery; (2) a discourse-theoretical concept, referring to a constituent that expresses old information in the organization of the discourse; (3) a semantic concept, referring to a constituent that expresses an aboutness relation; it can be familiar or recognizable or presupposed or part of the common ground, but need not be old information.

These views on topic do not correspond to actual theories, but rather to different dimensions of the concept. What usually happens is that linguists have a preferred dimension that they focus on, without denying the relevance of the other dimensions (Henk 2010).

In the literature, a distinction is also made between a marked topic and a non-marked topic (Duarte 1987, 1997, and subsequent work, among others). In subject-prominent languages such as CEP, a topic is non-marked if it has the grammatical function of the subject (as in (98b)). A topic is marked if it does not have the grammatical function of the subject (as in (99)), where the topic is the complement of the verb).

(98)   A: a. Porque é que estás tão bem-disposto?
              'Why are you in such a good mood?'
       B: b. A   Cristina já   chegou.
              the C.   already arrived
              'Cristina has arrived already.'

(99)   Na   Cristina, eu nunca mais confio.
       in.the C.   I never more trust.1SG
       'I will never trust Cristina again.'

In the present book, a semantic definition of topic is adopted as a way of rejecting the traditional idea that topic expresses old information (see Reinhart 1982; Kuroda 2005; Krifka 2007; among others). Evidence in support of rejecting this idea comes from sentences such as (98b), where the subject *a Cristina* is contained in the focus domain (because the whole sentence is assigned broad information focus). Nevertheless, *a Cristina* is interpreted as the topic of the sentence because it expresses an aboutness relation (i.e., what the sentence is about).[43] In this sense, a topic must be familiar, recognizable, or presupposed, but does not need to be old information.

Another tendency in the literature has been to emphasize the logical function of topic (Duarte 1987, 1997; Kuroda 2005; Martins 1994 and forthcoming). According to this view, a topic is taken to foreground an individual or class as the subject of the predication, occurring in sentences that express categorical/predicational judgments.[44] A sentence without a topic expresses a thetic/descriptive judgment.

The logical view on topics is of particular relevance to the present book, as it seems to play an important role in explaining some word-order facts in CEP. For instance, broad information-focus sentences with a post-verbal subject always express a thetic/descriptive judgment (i.e. the subject is always non-topic).

(100)   Chegou o   João.
         arrived the J.
         'João arrived.'

Broad information-focus sentences with a pre-verbal subject are ambiguous (Martins forthcoming), as they can express either a categorical or a thetic judgment[45] (see (101)). The idea underlying this proposal is that when stage-level predicates (such as *chegar* 'arrive') are involved, the "apprehension" of a situation is rooted in visual, auditory, or sensorial perception. Therefore, a thetic/descriptive judgment is available only if the speaker is able to perceptually observe the situation.

(101)   O   teu pai já   chegou.
         the your father already arrived
         'Your father has arrived.'
         √ Reading 1: *(thetic)* Your father has arrived already (here, at ours, for dinner).
         √ Reading 2: *(categorical)* Your father has arrived already (back at his home).
         (Martins forthcoming)

---

[43] In characterizing discourse contexts similar to (98), Gécseg (2006, cited in Henk 2010: 7) proposes that a sentence like (98b) pragmatically asserts something about the speaker by means of a proposition that logically or semantically asserts something about the subject.

[44] In what might be called a *theory of judgments*, a judgment can be considered a cognitive act expressed by the utterance of a sentence (Kuroda 1992: 20). There are two types of judgment: categorical judgment and thetic judgment (as proposed by F. Brentano and A. Marty). Following Kuroda (2005), a categorical judgment can be defined as "a cognitive act of attributing a predicate to a subject, a predication of the form conforming to the classical Aristotelian logic" (Kuroda 2005: 25). In turn, a thetic judgment is grounded on perception: "A thetic judgment is a representation of a perceptually apprehended real, recalled, or imagined situation" (Kuroda 2005: 29–30).

[45] Note that previous studies on CEP (see Duarte 1997; Martins 1994; among others) generally assume that broad information-focus sentences with pre-verbal subjects always express categorical judgments.

As Readings 1 and 2 show, a broad information-focus sentence involving a pre-verbal subject may express two different types of judgment: a categorical judgment, if the arrival stays outside the visual, auditory, or sensorial reach of the speaker (Reading 2) or a thetic judgment, if the speaker perceptually observes the situation (Reading 1).

Therefore, it is possible to conclude that the pre-verbal subject position in CEP (i.e. [Spec, IP])[46] is an ambiguous one: it can be filled by topic elements (i.e. the subject of predication in sentences expressing categorical judgments), but it can also be filled by non-topic elements (i.e. the subject of a sentence expressing thetic/descriptive judgments). On the other hand, the post-verbal position of the subject is non-ambiguous, as it is occupied by non-topic elements (occurring in sentences that express thetic judgments).

1.3.3.4 Topicalization and focalization   A last terminological note is in order regarding the use of the terms *topicalization* and *focalization*. *Topicalization* has been traditionally used in the generative literature to refer to the movement of a constituent to the left periphery of the sentence. According to this view, topicalization occurs in sentences expressing a topic-comment articulation or a focus-presupposition articulation. For an illustration, see the contrast in (102), from Rizzi (1997: 285).

(102) a. Your book, you should give t to Paul (not to Bill) (*topic-comment articulation*)
       b. YOUR BOOK you should give t to Paul (not mine) (*focus-presupposition articulation*)

In the late 1990s, a terminological shift occurred that reflects the emergence of the cartographic analysis proposed by Rizzi (1997). Within this approach, a clear distinction is made between sentences such as (102a) and (102b), because preposed topics and preposed foci are taken to occupy different positions in the split-CP. As a consequence, *topicalization* starts to designate topic-comment structures alone, whereas *focalization* refers to focus-presupposition structures.

This terminological shift also clarifies the status of preposed constituents in Romance languages. Generally, Romance languages express the topic-comment articulation with the construction that Cinque (1990) has called *clitic left dislocation*,

---

[46] There are two competing proposals for the syntactic analysis of pre-verbal subjects in CEP: J. Costa (2001, 2004a) and Costa and Duarte (2002) claim that pre-verbal subjects A–move to the specifier of IP, whereas Barbosa (1995, 2000, 2009) claims that subjects are base-generated in a left-dislocated position (as adjuncts to CP/IP). The two hypotheses are sketched in (i) and (ii), respectively. In this book, I assume that pre-verbal subjects in CEP are in [Spec, IP].

(i)   [$_{IP}$ S V [$_{VP}$ t$_S$ t$_V$]]
(ii) [$_{IP/CP}$ S [$_{IP/CP}$ V [$_{VP}$ *pro* t$_V$]]]

involving a resumptive clitic co-referential to the topic. As Duarte (1987, 1997, and subsequent work) shows, CEP has a special behavior in this respect because the topic-comment articulation may also involve a topic that is syntactically connected with an empty category inside the comment (as in the English example in (102a)). Hence, in CEP, clitic left dislocation coexists with topicalization,[47] as illustrated in (103a) and (103b).

(103) a. Esse livro, ainda não li   t.   (*topicalization*)
           that book yet   not read
           'I have not read that book yet.'

        b. Esse livro, ainda não o   li   (*clitic left dislocation*)
           that book yet   not it.CL read
           'I have not read that book yet.'

The focus-presupposition articulation is expressed in some Romance languages by a preposed contrastive focus in a construction called focalization (which was also called topicalization before the terminological split). Such a construction has been reported for Italian (Cinque 1990), Spanish (Zubizarreta 1999), Catalan (Sòla 1992), and for CEP (see §1.3.3.1). A case in point is provided in (104) (repeated from (85)).

(104) COM ESTAS PALAVRAS me   despeço.   (*focalization*)
      with these   words   me.CL say.goodbye.1SG
      'It is with these words that I say goodbye.'

Interestingly, contemporary languages seem to feature a correlation between punctuation and the two constructions under consideration. In particular, the use of a comma after the preposed constituent usually acts as a signal of the topic-comment structure and, concomitantly, as an orthographic means of excluding the focus-presupposition reading.

The present book adopts the terminology used in the cartographic approach. The term *topicalization* is used to refer to the construction in (103a), in which a topic is syntactically connected with an empty category inside the comment. The term *focalization* (also referred to as *contrastive focus fronting*) is used to refer to constructions such as (104), where the preposed constituent is a contrastive focus.

1.3.4 Language change

The interpretation and explanation of grammatical changes is developed within the model proposed by Lightfoot (Lightfoot 1991, 1999, and subsequent work), but it also benefits from insights of the competing grammars hypothesis developed by Kroch (1989, 1994, 2001), Pintzuk (1991), and Santorini (1992).

---

[47] The construction in (103a) is also referred to in the literature as *English-type topicalization*.

Lightfoot's model associates diachronic change with language acquisition. Grammars are regarded as mental organs (represented in the mind of the speaker) and not as social entities (codifying the data presented in a particular period). Following the Chomskian view of language acquisition, it is assumed that children are born with a universal grammar (a set of linguistic principles common to all languages) and that, when exposed to primary linguistic data (crucial experiences, what the children hear), they develop a specific grammar. Grammatical change consists of an abrupt grammatical reanalysis by new generation of speakers. That is, a language learner, on the basis of primary linguistic data, abduces a grammar that differs in one or more respects from that of previous generations. Lightfoot's model can therefore be seen as a synchronic approach to language change, according to which changes have local causes, and are not driven by diachronic generalizations about language change.

A different view on grammatical change is offered by the synchronic grammatical competition hypothesis developed by Kroch (1989, 1994, 2001), Pintzuk (1991), and Santorini (1992). This approach shares the view that language acquisition and language change are closely connected, but it proposes that the process of change begins in the learner's grammar and not with gradual changes in the frequency of different linguistic forms. Under this hypothesis, a grammatical change is caused by an inaccuracy in language transmission and it progresses gradually by means of grammatical competition within the grammars of individual speakers until one of the alternatives is driven out of language. Working within a quantitative model of variation and change, Kroch (1989) formulates the *Constant Rate Effect*, according to which "when one grammatical option replaces another with which it is in competition across a set of linguistic contexts, the rate of replacement, properly measured, is the same in all of them" (Kroch 1989: 200). This proposal has been crucial to the development of quantitative approaches to language variation and change.

Finally, the parametric theory of variation (see Holmberg and Roberts 2010; Biberauer, Holmberg, Roberts and Sheehan 2010, among others), although not formally implemented in this book, provided an important conceptual background to the comparative view adopted here.

2

Remnant-internal relativization

2.1 Introduction

In the syntactic literature, the notion of a phrase is used to refer to a group of words that behave syntactically (and semantically) as a single unit. More often than not, the elements that make up a phrase are continuous, that is, they involve words that appear next to one another. However, phrases may also surface in a discontinuous manner, split up into two or more parts. This can be observed in different phrase types (e.g. noun phrases, prepositional phrases) and different linguistic environments, as shown in (105)–(108), from Croatian, French, Russian, and Dutch, respectively.

(105) Knjige mi je Marija zanimljive preporucila.
      books me has M. interesting recommended
      'Mary has recommended interesting books to me.' (Fanselow and Ćavar 2002: 66)

(106) Combien as-tu lu de livres?
      how.many have-you read of books
      'How many books have you read?' (Butler and Mathieu 2004: 2)

(107) v kakoj on poedet gorod?
      to which he go.FUT town
      'To which town will he go?' (Fanselow and Féry 2006: 70)

(108) Wat heb je voor boeken gekocht?
      what have you for books bought
      'Which kind of books have you bought?' (Mark de Vries, p.c.)

Phrasal discontinuity has been documented in various studies (Corver 1990; Devine and Stephens 1999; Fanselow and Ćavar 2002; Butler and Mathieu 2004; Fanselow and Féry 2006; Kariaeva 2009; Ledgeway forthcoming; among others) and has been approached from the syntactic, semantic, pragmatic, and prosodic points of view. Of particular interest here is the idea, put forth by Fanselow and

Portuguese Relative Clauses in Synchrony and Diachrony. First Edition. Adriana Cardoso.
© Adriana Cardoso 2017. First published in 2017 by Oxford University Press.

Ćavar (2002: 69), that discontinuous noun phrases arise only in the context of operator movement. This generalization accounts for the typical cases reported in the literature, which involve focus/topic movement (see (105), from Croatian) and interrogative wh-movement (see (106)–(108), from French, Russian, and Dutch, respectively).

However, Fanselow and Ćavar's generalization also predicts that discontinuous noun phrases may also surface in relative clauses. In the present chapter, I show that this prediction is correct: in earlier stages of Portuguese (and Latin), discontinuous noun phrases may arise in RRCs, a phenomenon that I dub *remnant-internal relativization*. In this configuration, an element that is thematically dependent on the head noun (either as a complement or as a modifier) does not appear adjacent to it but rather in a position internal to the relative clause, as illustrated schematically in (109). Example a., which involves adjacency between the head noun and its modifier/complement, displays the regular word order (in head-initial relative clauses); example b., which does not involve adjacency between these elements, displays remnant-internal relativization.

(109)   a. (D) N modifier/complement [$_{CP_{rel}}$...]
         b. <u>(D) N</u> [$_{CP_{rel}}$...<u>modifier/complement</u>...]

Some concrete instances of remnant-internal relativization are given in (110)–(111), from Latin and earlier stages of Portuguese, respectively. These examples display phrasal discontinuity between the head noun and the adjectival modifier (see (110)) and the head noun and its PP complement (see (111)).

(110)   Inter   jocos quos   inconditos jaciunt
        amidst jests which rude   utter.3PL
        'Amidst the rude jests which they utter' (1st c. BC–1st c. AD, from Zumpt 1832: 237)

(111)   que   muyto conforto tomava com os tres paos do   leito, por
        because much comfort had.3SG with the three sticks of.the bed   by
        a   senificança que <u>deles</u>   lhe   dissera o   bom homem da   barca
        the meaning   that of.them him.CL tell.PPRF the good man   of.the boat
        'because he felt very good about the three sticks of the bed because of the
        meaning that the good man of the boat said they had' (13th c. [transmitted by
        a 16th-c. MS], Martins, Pereira, and Cardoso 2013–15)

This chapter has three specific aims: (1) to provide a comprehensive description of remnant-internal relativization, showing that it fits in with the more general phenomenon of phrasal discontinuity; (2) to demonstrate that remnant-internal relativization can be added to the arguments adduced in the literature in favor of the raising analysis of RRCs; and (3) to provide a tentative explanation for the contrasting properties of remnant-internal relativization in earlier stages of Portuguese and CEP. The empirical data are mainly drawn from Portuguese and Latin, but other languages are considered (e.g. French and Italian).

The remainder of chapter is organized as follows. Before discussing the syntax of remnant-internal relativization, I provide some background information regarding noun phrase discontinuity (see §2.2). With these preliminaries in mind, I focus on the study of remnant-internal relativization (see §2.3), presenting an analysis of the phenomenon in terms of a version of the copy theory of movement on the PF side proposed by Bošković and Nunes (2007) (based on previous work by Bošković 2001, 2002, 2004a,b, and Nunes 1999, 2004) (see §2.4). In §2.5, I show that CEP contrasts with earlier stages of Portuguese with respect to the properties of remnant-internal relativization, offering a tentative explanation for the observed contrast. Finally, §2.6 summarizes the chapter.

2.2 Noun phrase discontinuity

This section is devoted to the phenomenon of noun phrase discontinuity. It starts by introducing the core properties of discontinuous noun phrases (see §2.2.1). Then, it provides an overview of empirical data from Latin and earlier stages of Portuguese (see §2.2.2). Finally, it outlines the competing analyses available in the literature to account for noun phrase discontinuity (see §2.2.3).

2.2.1 Core properties

The term *discontinuous noun phrase* (or split noun phrase)[1] is used in the book to cover any interrupted sequence of elements in a noun phrase that would normally surface in a continuous manner. On the basis of Fanselow and Ćavar (2002) and Fanselow and Féry (2006), I identified five core properties of discontinuous noun phrases, which are listed in (1)–(4).

(1) *Order of the split parts* Discontinuous noun phrases can retain the order of elements found in the continuous counterpart (*simple splits* or *pull-splits*) or can invert this order (*inverted splits*) (Fanselow and Ćavar 2002: 68). This is illustrated in (112b) and (112c), from Ukrainian:

---

[1] Other terms used in literature on discontinuous noun phrases are: *partial fronting, incomplete category fronting, left branch extraction*, and *hyperbaton*.

(112)　a. Marija maje　bahato krisel.
　　　　　M.　　has.got many　chairs.GEN.PL
　　　　　'Mary has got many chairs.'

　　　　b. Bahato maje Marija krisel [simple split or pull-split]

　　　　c. Krisel Marija maje bahato [inverted split] (all Fanselow and Féry 2006: 5)

(2) *Prosody*　The contrast between simple and inverted splits tends to correlate with a prosodic distinction: simple splits tend to be cohesive (i.e. the two parts of the split are integrated into a single intonation phrase), whereas inverted splits tend to be non-cohesive (i.e. the two parts of the split are separated into two intonation phrases) (Fanselow and Féry 2006).

(3) *Number of the split parts*　Discontinuous noun phrases can stretch across more than two discontinuous (or split) parts. A case of tripartite discontinuity is given in (113), from Ukrainian:

(113)　a. Ivan　kupyv duže velyku　　　mašynu.
　　　　　I.NOM bought very　big.F.SG.ACC car.F.SG.ACC
　　　　　'John bought a very big car.'

　　　　b. Duže Ivan　velyku　　　kupyv　mašynu.
　　　　　very I.NOM big.F.SG.ACC bought car.F.SG.ACC
　　　　　'Ivan bought a VERY BIG car.' (both Kariaeva 2009: 207)

(4) *Syntactic environment*　Discontinuous noun phrases arise in the context of operator movement only (Fanselow and Ćavar 2002: 69),[2] namely in interrogative wh-movement, as in (106) (repeated here as (114)), or in focus/topic movement, as in (105) (repeated here as (115)).

(114)　Combien　as-tu　　lu　de livres?
　　　　how.many have-you read of books
　　　　'How many books have you read?' (Butler and Mathieu 2004: 2)

---

[2] There is no consensus in the literature regarding the relation that can be established between the parts of the discontinuous noun phrases. While for Fanselow and Ćavar (2002: 69), the parts of the splits necessarily establish an operator–variable relation, for Kariaeva (2009) they can simply stand in an agreement relation, as in the sentence below, from Ukrainian:

Ivan　červonu　　kupyv　mašynu
I.NOM red.F.SG.ACC bought car.F.SG.ACC
'Ivan bought a RED car.' (Kariaeva 2009: 70)

(115) Knijge mi je   Marija zanimljive preporucila.
       books me has   M.   interesting recommended
       'Mary has recommended interesting books to me.' (Fanselow and Ćavar
       2002: 66)

On the areal distribution of discontinuous noun phrases, studies of other languages
and cross-linguistic systematizations have yielded evidence for the idea that discontinuous phrases are frequently found in the world's languages, although they are
quite uncommon in Western European languages (Fanselow and Féry 2006). This
situation changes radically when other European languages are considered. As
Fanselow and Féry (2006: 9) put it: "In Europe, the situation changes dramatically
when one crosses the river Rhine or the Isonzo: one enters 'split country', which
extends to the Pacific Ocean." In this area, discontinuous noun phrases are reported
to occur, for instance, in the "Eastern" Germanic languages (Dutch, German, Swedish),
Romanian, all Slavic languages, the Baltic languages Lithuanian and Latvian, the
Finno-Ugric languages, Albanian, Ancient and Modern Greek, and the Altaic
languages.

2.2.2 Empirical evidence from Latin and earlier stages of Portuguese

Pinkster (2005) and Devine and Stephens (2006), among others, report that discontinuous noun phrases are frequently attested from the earliest Latin texts until Late
Latin.[3] This is illustrated, for instance, in the contrast given in (116): in (116a) the
phrase *legiones novas* 'two legions' is continuous, whereas in (116b) the phrase *duas
legiones novas* 'two new legions' is split into two parts.

(116) a. Facite   hoc meum consilium legiones novas non improbare.
          suppose.IMP this my   policy   legions new   not reject.INF
          'Suppose that the new legions do not reject my policy.'

       b. Caesar duas legiones in   citeriore Gallia novas conscripsit.
          Caesar two legions into Hither   Gaul   new   enrolled
          'Caesar enrolled two new legions in Hither Gaul.' (both 1st c. BC, from
          Devine and Stephens 2006: 531; glosses mine)

According to Devine and Stephens (2006), the discontinuous noun phrase in (116b)
arises in the context of scrambling: *duas legiones* 'two legions' has been scrambled,

---

[3] In Latin, the operation of "splitting" arises not only in noun phrases but also in such constituents as
prepositional phrases and conjuncts. Given the limited scope of this study, I will focus only on the
occurrence of discontinuous noun phrases, paying special attention to those involving discontinuity
between the noun and a post-nominal modifier or complement.

leaving the modifier *novas* 'new' in a focus position. The same phenomenon can be found in sentences involving topicalization, as in (117); here, the noun *vinaceos* 'dregs' has raised to a topic position to the left of the frequency adverb *cotidie* 'daily', stranding the adjective *recentis* 'fresh'.

(117) Vinaceos cotidie recentis succernito.
   dregs daily fresh sift.IMP.FUT.2SG
   'Sift the fresh dregs daily.' (2nd c. BC, from Devine and Stephens 2006: 531; gloss mine)

Interestingly, Devine and Stephens (2006) also report the occurrence of discontinuous noun phrases in interrogative wh-contexts. Consider, for instance, example (118), where the wh-expression *quod supplicium* 'what punishment' is split into two parts: the wh-pronoun occurs in the left periphery of the clause, and the noun *supplicium* 'punishment' appears in the rightmost sentential position.

(118) quod tandem excogitabitur in eum supplicium...?
   what then be.thought.up.FUT in him punishment
   'what punishment, I ask you, will be thought up for the man...?' (1st c. BC, from Devine and Stephens 2006: 584; gloss mine)

Although discontinuous noun phrases are frequently attested from the earliest until Late Latin texts, this situation changed quite drastically in the development from Latin to Romance languages. Western European Romance languages are often characterized as not allowing discontinuous noun phrases or by allowing them only in a very restricted way (Pinkster 2005; Fanselow and Féry 2006; Ledgeway forthcoming).

Importantly, some exceptions to this generalization have been reported in the literature. Pinkster (2005) refers to the occurrence of discontinuous noun phrases in Old French (see (119)). Butler and Mathieu (2004) take the French construction in (120) (repeated from (106))[4] as involving a discontinuous noun phrase.

(119) la hautece   i sera tote de mon empire
   the high.ranking.people there be.FUT all of my empire
   'all the high-ranking people of my empire will be there' (13th c., from Pinkster 2005: 5; gloss mine)

(120) Combien as-tu lu de livres?[5]
   how.many have-you read of books
   'How many books have you read?' (Butler and Mathieu 2004: 2)

---

[4] For a different analysis of the French construction in (120), see Fanselow and Féry (2006).
[5] The canonical word order of the sentence in (120) is: *Combien de livres as-tu lus?*

Similar facts have been documented for earlier stages of Portuguese. Martins (2004) shows that discontinuous noun phrases are attested in earlier stages of Portuguese.[6] Some of the examples cited in her paper are given in (121)–(123).

(121) Noticia fecit pelagio romeu de fiadores.
       notitia made P.   R.   of guarantors
       'Pelagio Romeu made a *notitia* of guarantors.' (12th c., from Martins
       2004: 501)

(122) Boscadas as rrazoões dos   que livros fezerom desta estoria
       found   the reasons of.the that books did   of.this story
       'Found the reasons of the ones that made books of this story...(Once the
       reasons of the ones that wrote this story are found...)' (15th c., from Martins
       2004: 503)

(123) Em que nos mostra esta rregla que fame   ham da.   palavra de Deus
       in that us.CL shows this rule that hunger have of.the word   of God
       aquelles que desejam de   a   ouujr.
       those   that want   DE.PREP it.CL listen.INF
       'This rule shows us that those who want to listen to God's word have hunger
       for it.' (15th c., from Martins 2004: 503)

In (121)–(123) the discontinuous noun phrases correspond to the sequence: head noun...PP, but this is not necessarily so. The head noun in the first split part may be associated with other elements, such as an adjective (see *ma* 'bad' in (124)) or a determiner (see *outros* 'other' in (125)). Moreover, the constituent in the second split part can be a PP, as in (121)–(124), or an adjective, as in (125).

(124) diz que se deus o   matar   de fome que ma bocado a   deus
       says that if god him.CL kill.FUT.SBJV of hunger that bad piece   have god
       de comer dele
       to eat.INF of.him
       'he says that if God kills him by hunger, God will eat a bad piece of him
       (= God will go through a hard time with him)' (17th c., *P.S.*)

(125) Outros   fauores   se   lhe   tem feito estraordinarios.
       other.M.PL favors.M.PL SE.CL him.CL has done extraordinary.M.PL
       'Other extraordinary favors have been done for him.' (17th c., Coelho
       1987: 192)

---

[6] To be more precise, Martins (2004) also reports the possibility of finding discontinuous noun phrases in CEP under some restricted constructions. I return to this issue in §2.5.

Just as was observed for Latin, discontinuous noun phrases in earlier stages of Portuguese can also arise in interrogative wh-movement contexts, as illustrated in (126)–(127).

(126) a. <u>que origem</u> lhe   havemos de   dar   <u>mais nobre?</u>
        what origin   him.CL have.1PL DE.PREP give.INF more noble
        'what more noble origin shall we give him?'

     b. <u>que susto ou que dano</u>   nos   pode vir   <u>maior?</u>
        what fright or what damage us.CL can   come.INF bigger
        'what bigger fright or damage could be done to us?' (both 18th c., *TYC*)

(127) a. <u>Quantas</u>   <u>castas</u> há   de nomes?
        how.many types   has of nouns
        'How many types of nouns are there?'

     b. <u>Quantas</u>   <u>figuras</u> há   de Dicção?
        how.many figures has of diction
        'How many figures of diction are there?' (both 18th c., *TYC*)

2.2.3 *Competing analyses*

Much of the debate on the syntax of discontinuous noun phrases has centered on the contrast between movement and base-generation analyses. The main assumptions underlying these proposals are outlined in §§2.2.3.1 and 2.2.3.2, respectively.

2.2.3.1 Movement analyses The movement analyses of discontinuous noun phrases can be grouped together into four main types: (A) simple movement analyses; (B) regeneration; (C) remnant movement; and (D) distributed deletion. These types are listed and discussed in turn in the following subsections.[7]

A. Simple movement analyses

Simple movement analyses posit that discontinuous noun phrases are derived from extraction of an element X out of a constituent Y (van Riemsdijk 1989, among others). In the early period of generative syntax, these movement-based approaches faced a serious problem because they seem to go against the generalization that movement can only apply to maximal or minimal projections. Relevant empirical evidence comes from sentences as in (128), from German, which show that any segment of *keine interessanten neuen Bücher* can be extracted. Under the

---

[7] In the present section I closely follow Fanselow and Ćavar's (2002) criticism of movement-based analyses.

assumption that noun phrases involve only one maximal projection (NP), the part of the discontinuous noun phrase that undergoes movement in (128c–d) only forms a submaximal N′-projection and therefore should not be able to undergo movement.

(128) a. Sie hat keine interessanten neuen Bücher gekannt.
       she has no   interesting   new   books   known
       'She did not know any interesting new books.'

   b. [Bücher]$_i$ that sie [keine interessanten neuen t$_i$] gekannt.

   c. [Neue Bücher]$_i$ hat sie [keine interessanten t$_i$] gekannt.

   d. [Interessanten neue Bücher]$_i$ hat sie [keine t$_i$] gekannt.

   e. [Keine interessanten neue Bücher]$_i$ hat sie t$_i$ gekannt. (all Fanselow and Ćavar 2002: 70)

Research in the late 1980s and the 1990s on the structure of the noun phrase and its similarities with the structure of clauses (Abney 1987) provides a new way of looking at the movement analysis of discontinuous noun phrases. One important development is the proposal that discontinuous noun phrases may involve the movement of different functional projections of the noun phrase. Under this view, the elaborate syntactic structure of the noun phrase in (128) would look like (129), and the problem mentioned above could easily be solved: discontinuous noun phrases involve the leftward movement of different functional projections within the noun phrase.

(129) [$_{DP}$ [$_D$ keine] [$_{AGR-A1-P}$ [$_{AP}$ interessanten] [[$_{AGR-A1}$ e] [$_{AGR-A2-P}$ [$_{AP}$ neuen] [[$_{AGR-A2}$ e] [$_{Nom-P}$ Bücher]]]]]] (Fanselow and Ćavar 2002: 70)

Despite this welcome development, other problems for the simple movement analyses are reported in the literature, namely (1) the movement of non-constituents; (2) imperfect splits; (3) morphological adjustments; and (4) movement across islands (see Fanselow and Ćavar 2002 for an overview).

   The movement of non-constituents is a problem in accounting for simple (or pull) splits, as in (130), from Croatian. Simple movement analyses cannot generate sentences like (130) because there is no constituent that includes the preposition and the determiner but excludes the noun that could be moved to the left to form a discontinuous noun phrase.

(130) <u>Na kakav</u>   je Ivan <u>krov</u> skocio?
       on what.kind has I.   roof jumped
       'On what kind of roof has Ivan jumped?' (Fanselow and Ćavar 2002: 71)

Another problem faced by the simple movement analyses concerns the existence of imperfect splits, that is, discontinuous noun phrases that have no well-formed source in a movement account. This is the case of preposition doubling exemplified in (131), from German, where the preposition heading the PP appears in both parts of an inverted split.

(131) In Schlössern habe ich noch in keinen gewohnt
       in castles   have I yet in no   lived
       'I have not yet lived in any castles.' (Fanselow and Ćavar 2002: 69)

The same phenomenon can be observed in the so-called determiner spreading found in Modern Greek. In this construction, the determiner may show up only in the first part of the discontinuous noun phrase (see (132a)) or in both parts (see (132b)), depending on the dialect/register (Mathieu and Sitaridou 2005).

(132) a. To   KOKINO   agorase forema.
           the.ACC.N.SG red.ACC.N.SG bought dress.ACC.N.SG
       b. To   KOKINO   agorase to   forema.
           the.ACC.N.SG red.ACC.N.SG bought the.ACC.N.SG dress.ACC.N.SG
           'She bought the RED dress (not the blue one).' (both Mathieu and
           Sitaridou 2005: 240)

It is widely recognized in the literature that the phenomena of preposition doubling and determiner spreading are a problem for the simple movement account because there is not enough space in a single continuous phrase for the material occurring in the two discontinuous parts.

A third problem with the simple movement analysis concerns the so-called morphological adjustments (Fanselow and Féry 2006). This term refers to a surprising property of discontinuous noun phrases: the parts of a discontinuous noun phrase can take morphologically different shapes than in their continuous counterpart (see (133)–(134), from German).

(133) a. Er hat kein   Geld.
           he has no.WEAK money
           'He has no money.'
       b. Er hat keines
           he has no.STRONG (both Fanselow and Féry 2006: 55)

(134) a. Er hat kein   Geld.
           he has no.WEAK money
       b. Geld   hat er keines
           money has he no.STRONG (both Fanselow and Féry 2006: 55)

In German, the morphological shapes of quantifiers and adjectives are dependent on the presence of a noun. If a noun is present, as in (133a), the negative quantifier *kein* bears a weak inflection; if a noun is not present, as in (133b), it obligatorily carries a strong inflection. As can be seen in (134b), when a split noun phrase is involved, the quantifier *kein* obligatorily bears a strong inflection. This seems to militate against a simple movement approach in that the two parts inflect as if they were independent noun phrases.

A fourth problem is that discontinuous noun phrases are insensitive to some island constraints (Fanselow and Ćavar 2002). For instance, in German, subjects (of non-unaccusative verbs, at least) are generally islands for extraction (see (135a)), but they can nevertheless be split up (see (135b)).

(135) a. *<u>An Maria</u> haben mir <u>keine Briefe</u> gefallen.
            to M.   have me no   letters pleased
            'No letters to Mary have pleased me.'

       b. <u>Briefe an Maria</u> gefallen mir <u>keine</u>
          letters to M.   please   me no
          'As for letters to Mary, they do not please me.' (both Fanselow and Ćavar 2002: 72)

Different solutions have been proposed in the literature to circumvent these problems, namely: (1) regeneration; (2) remnant movement; and (3) distributed deletion. As becomes clear in §2.2.3.1B–D, some of these approaches are better equipped than others to handle the different problems. This can be explained, at least to some extent, by the fact that some of them were originally conceived as solutions to different, very specific phenomena.

B. Regeneration

Van Riemsdijk (1989) proposes to account for some of the properties of discontinuous noun phrases by means of a process he refers to as *regeneration*. The core of his proposal is that the movement of X′ projections is not precluded in principle. Hence, what makes X′ movement rare is not a restriction on Move α, but rather a well-formedness condition that applies to the S-structure, which disallows any X′ not dominated by its maximal projection node. Some languages simply ban this configuration at the S-structure level, whereas other languages may resort to a mechanism of repair that allows the regeneration of the missing structure and, in some cases, even the relexicalization of the regenerated structures, as illustrated in (136).

(136)   a. Regeneration: $[_{CP} [_{N'}]_i] [_{C'}... \Rightarrow [_{CP} [_{NP} [_{N'}]_i] [_{C'}...$
        b. Relexicalization: $[_{CP} [_{NP} \text{determiner} [_{N'}]] [_{C'}...$

This approach straightforwardly explains two of the problematic properties of discontinuous noun phrases mentioned above: the possibility of moving X′ projections is linked to the availability of regeneration (see (136a)), whereas the existence of imperfect splits (e.g. determiner spreading) is correlated with the process of relexicalization (see (136b)). As Hoof (2005) notes, this approach is also able to derive morphological adjustments by assuming that the Spell Out of the strong/weak inflection is not caused by a specific lexical-grammatical feature but is instead postponed until the movement of the first part of the split takes place.

However, the regeneration analysis also has its flaws. First, it fails to account for the movement of non-constituents (as in (130)) and for movement across islands. Second, the mechanism of regeneration has been criticized on independent grounds for introducing unnecessary complications to the movement analysis (Fanselow and Ćavar 2002).

C. Remnant movement

An alternative approach to the syntax of discontinuous noun phrases that deserves special attention is the remnant movement analysis. The normal instantiation of remnant movement starts with the movement of an element X out of a constituent. Then, the whole constituent, which contains the trace of X, rises to its designated position, as is depicted in (137).

(137) $[_{YP}...Y...t_i]_j...X_i \, t_j$

Androutsopoulou (1997) proposes an analysis along these lines for the discontinuous adjectival construction in Modern Greek (see (138b)).

(138)   a.   Idha   to   forema   (to) kokino.
           saw.1SG the dress   the red
           'I saw the red dress.'

        b.   <u>To   KOKINO</u> idha   (to)   forema
           the red   saw.1SG the   dress
           'I saw the RED dress.' (both Androutsopulou 1997, cited in Butler and Mathieu 2004: 174)

Under this approach, the nominal first rises to the specifier position of a Clitic Voice Phrase, which functions as the clause internal topic position and then the whole complex containing the trace of the nominal moves to the specifier of FocP in the left periphery of the clause. For other attempts to explain discontinuous constructions in terms of remnant movement, see Sekerina (1999) for Russian; Franks and Progovac (1994) and Bašić (2004) for Serbo-Croatian.

A welcome result of the remnant movement analysis is that it straightforwardly explains why a non-constituent appears to undergo movement. However, this approach faces serious problems in explaining other properties of discontinuous noun phrases, namely, the repetition of phonetic material in imperfect splits, the occurrence of morphological adjustments, and the possibility of having discontinuous noun phrases that disregard standard islands for movement (see Fanselow and Ćavar 2002 for further details).

D. Distributed deletion

Assuming the copy theory of movement (Chomsky 1995), according to which moved elements leave copies behind that are subsequently deleted, Fanselow and Ćavar (2002) argue that discontinuous noun phrases are best analyzed in terms of distributed deletion. According to this proposal, splits do not involve the extraction of an element from a constituent. Instead, a complete noun phrase is copied to the left and the splitting results from the fact that the deletion operation may partially affect both the upstairs and the downstairs copies of the moved constituent.

In a nutshell, the deletion operation works as follows. First, the relevant noun phrase undergoes leftward movement, leaving a copy behind. The copies are then each deleted at PF, as illustrated in (139). If the lower copy is completely deleted, a continuous noun phrase shows up (see (139c)); if one element is deleted in the higher copy and the other is deleted in the lower copy, a discontinuous noun phrase emerges (see (139d)). See Fanselow and Ćavar (2002) for further details.[8]

(139) a. hat er keine Bücher gelesen
          has he no   books read
          (*copying the noun phrase* ⇒)

       b. keine Bücher hat er keine Bücher gelesen
          (*full deletion of lower copy (continuous noun phrase)* ⇒)

       c. keine Bücher hat er ~~keine~~ ~~Bücher~~ gelesen
          (*partial deletion in both copies—discontinuous noun phrase* ⇒)

       d. ~~keine~~ Bücher hat er keine ~~Bücher~~ gelesen. (all Fanselow and
          Ćavar 2002: 84)

According to Fanselow and Ćavar (2002), it is the pragmatic structure that determines the occurrence of (dis)continuous noun phrases. Continuous noun phrases emerge when the noun phrase is linked only to one feature. This is the case of the continuous noun phrase in (139c), which is associated with a +TOP feature. On the other hand, discontinuous noun phrases emerge when the noun phrase is linked at least to two different pragmatic features that cannot be checked in the same structural position. This is the case of (139d), where the first part of the split bears a +TOP feature, whereas the second part bears a +FOC feature (which, under Fanselow and Ćavar's proposal, is checked in a specific lower focus position).

In more concrete terms, what this means is that discontinuous noun phrases involve two instances of movement, schematically represented in (140). The heads H^p and H^q have two different semantic or pragmatic features (p, q) and attract a phrase bearing the corresponding feature.

---

[8] It is worth noting here that the partial deletion of copies (also known as *scattered deletion*) has been independently argued for in the literature. For further details, see Bošković and Nunes (2007), Bošković (2001), Nunes (1999), and Wilder (1995), among others. I return to this issue in §2.4.1.

(140) a. $[_{H^P}...[H^q...[_{XP} a^P [b c]^q]]]$

  b. $[[_{XP} a^P [b c]^q] [_{H^P}...[[_{XP} a^P [b c]^q] [H^q...[_{XP} a^P [b c]^q]]]]]$ (both Fanselow and Ćavar 2002: 85)

Assuming that the phonetic realization of copies is regulated by the Spell Out Principle in (141), the structure of split topicalization in (139d) would then look like (142) (where q corresponds to a +TOP feature and p to a +FOC feature).

(141) Spell Out Principle:

  Suppose $C = <C_1, C_2>$ is formed because a strong feature of H has attracted XP and suppose that H checks the operator features $f_1...f_k$ of XP. Then the categories bearing $f_1...f_k$ must be spelt out in C_1.

(142) $[[_{XP} a^P [b]^q] [H^q...[[_{XP} a^P \cancel{[b]}^q] [_{H^P}...[_{\cancel{XP}} a^P \cancel{[b]^q}]]]]]$

Distributed deletion has many advantages over the movement-based approaches considered thus far. First, it explains the apparent movement of non-constituents illustrated in (143) (repeated from (130)). Under distributed deletion, it is the whole PP (*na kakav krov*) that undergoes leftward movement; hence, what looks like the movement of non-constituents is in fact the result of partial phonological deletion of different copies.

(143) <u>Na kakav</u>   je   Ivan <u>krov</u> skocio?
  on what.kind has I.   roof jumped
  'On what kind of roof has Ivan jumped?' (Fanselow and Ćavar 2002: 71)

Second, imperfect splits, such as the preposition doubling exemplified in (144) (repeated from (131)), can be derived by assuming that it is the whole PP that undergoes movement, leaving a copy behind. Then, if the language tolerates multiple realizations of the same element, the deletion process removes portions of the phrases in the copy relation.

(144) <u>In Schlössern</u> habe ich noch <u>in keinen</u> gewohnt.
  in castles   have I yet   in no   lived
  'I have not yet lived in any castles.' (Fanselow and Ćavar 2002: 69)

Third, morphological adjustments as in (145) (repeated from (134)) can be derived from distributed deletion if one assumes that the morphological shape of the determiner or adjective is determined after copying and deletion.

(145) a. Er hat kein   Geld.
    he has no.WEAK money

  b. <u>Geld</u>   hat Er <u>keines</u>
    money has he no.STRONG (both Fanselow and Féry 2006: 55)

According to Fanselow and Ćavar (2002), the morphemes are merged into a syntactic representation as abstract entities and, when spelled out, they must meet the lexical and morphological well-formedness conditions for DPs. This explains why the quantifier *kein* bears a strong inflection in (145b), but not in (145a). Each part of the discontinuous noun phrase is dominated by the DP node and therefore must obey the well-formedness conditions for noun phrases in German.[9] In (145a), the negative quantifier carries a weak inflection because the noun phrase *kein Geld* 'no money' contains a noun; in (145b) the quantifier in the second split part carries a strong inflection because, after copying and deletion, the noun phrase does not contain a noun.

Finally, discontinuous noun phrase formation does not respect islands because it does not involve extraction out of a noun phrase; it is the whole constituent that undergoes leftward movement.

As this brief discussion shows, the deletion analysis is better equipped to handle the problems raised above than are the other movement-based approaches. This fact follows from the less constrained nature of the movement (not involving extraction of the noun phase) and from the mechanism of partial deletion. However, it should be noted that distributed deletion is subject to the problem of overgeneration. Some authors, including Bošković (2005) and Kariaeva (2009), point out that an item can, in principle, be spelled out in any location where the copy of a constituent appears. Therefore, additional conditions have to be imposed on the deletion operation in order to constrain the application of the distributed deletion, blocking derivations such as (146a,b).

(146) a. *The ~~students~~ were arrested ~~the~~ students.
       b. *~~The~~ students were arrested the ~~students~~.
       c. The students were arrested ~~the students~~. (all Bošković 2005: 14)

2.2.3.2 Base-generation analyses   Base-generation analyses claim that the parts of a discontinuous noun phrase are merged independently of each other in different slots of the sentence (Hale 1983; Jelinek 1984; Fanselow 1988). Along with this hypothesis, a number of different proposals have been made in the literature.

In the original version developed by Hale (1983) and Jelinek (1984) for Australian languages like Warlpiri, none of the parts of a discontinuous noun phrase figure as an argument in the sentence. Rather, the true argument is the (possibly phonologically empty) pronominal clitic on the predicate, while the discontinuous noun phrase parts are adjunct modifiers of this argument position.

---

[9] As already mentioned, these conditions dictate that: (1) if a noun is present, the negative quantifier *kein* bears weak inflection; (2) if a noun is not present, the negative quantifier must carry strong inflection.

In Fanselow's (1988) account of split topicalization in German, one part of the discontinuous noun phrase is merged as a verbal argument, while the other part might originate as a modifying adjunct and move to the topic position later or be generated there directly.

Under Kariaeva's (2009) approach to discontinuous constituents with an adjectival part in Ukrainian and Greek, the adjectival modifier is base-generated in the location in which it is spelled out, either as an adjunct inside the noun phrase (deriving a continuous noun phrase) or as an adjunct inside the VP (deriving a discontinuous noun phrase).

The advantages of a base-generation analysis are clear. First, the problem of the movement of a non-constituent simply does not arise because discontinuity is not derived from movement. Secondly, imperfect splits, such as preposition doubling, can be derived by assuming that a preposition shows up in two PPs generated independently of each other. Finally, morphological adjustments do not constitute a problem given that the different parts of the split can be generated with different morphologies.

However, the base-generation analysis also faces serious difficulties. The first difficulty concerns the fact that discontinuous noun phrases are sensitive to some island effects. As Ott (2009) notes, if it is true that discontinuous noun phrases are insensitive to certain island constraints (as is the case of the subjects of transitive verbs), it is also true that they respect other island types, such as the Complex-NP Constraint (see (147)), the Adjunct-Island Condition (see (148)), and the Coordinate Structure Constraint (see (149)).

(147) *Bücher$_i$ habe ich [NP eine Geschichte dass sie [keine t$_i$] liest] gehört.
      books have I   a   story   that she no   reads heard
      'I have heard a story that she does not read any books.' (Ott 2009: 66)

(148) *Bücher$_i$ ist sie schon oft   nachhause gegangen.
      books   is she already often home   went
      [bevor sie [welche t$_i$] gelesen hat]
      before she   some   read   has
      'She often went home before reading some books.' (Ott 2009: 67)

(149) *Bücher hat sie bisher [nur wenige t$_i$ und Zeitschriften] gelesen
      books has she so.far only few   and magazines   read
      'So far, she has only read few books and magazines' (Ott 2009: 67)

An additional argument that militates against the base-generation analysis is the preservation of the noun-phrase internal order (van Riemsdijk 1989, cited in Ott 2009). In German, the adjective ordering illustrated in (150a) is unmarked, whereas the order in (150b) is only acceptable with a strong focal stress on the preposed adjective. Crucially, if the noun phrase *schnelle amerikanische Autos* is split-topicalized, the order among the adjectives must be preserved (see (151)). As Ott (2009) concludes, this means that in some sense the two parts of the split are merged together and then split apart.

(150) a. Hans mag schnelle amerikanische Autos.
          H.   likes fast   American   cars
          'Hans likes American fast cars.'

      b. ??Hans mag amerikanische schnelle Autos.
            H.   likes American   fast   cars (both Ott 2009: 67)

(151) a. [Amerikanische Autos]$_i$ mag Hans nur [schnelle t$_i$].
          American   cars   likes H.   only   fast
          'Hans only likes American fast cars.'

      b. ??[Schnelle Autos]$_i$ mag Hans nur [amerikanische t$_i$]
          fast   cars   likes Hans only   American (both Ott 2009: 67)

Besides the objections already raised in the literature, additional objections can be brought against the base-generation analysis. First, under this approach, discontinuous noun phrases are not derived from continuous noun phrases. Instead, continuous and discontinuous noun phrases involve two different derivations, a fact that can be seen as a drawback for those who are committed to a transformational view of grammar. Secondly, it is standardly assumed (at least in transformational-generative approaches to grammar) that topicalization, focalization, and questions involve the movement of the fronted/preposed element. This constituent is typically the first part of the discontinuous phrase; hence it seems intuitively unnatural to assume that this first part of the split is base-generated in the Spell Out position. Thirdly, if the parts of the split can be merged independently of each other, the question arises of how to constrain the merge positions of the fragments. At least for some languages, it seems clear that the parts of the split cannot be freely merged. Finally, under base-generation analysis, it is not clear how to derive the semantic dependency (and, in some cases, the selectional relation) established between the discontinuous parts.

2.3 Remnant-internal relativization

To my knowledge, the term *remnant-internal relativization* has not been previously introduced in the literature. It is proposed here to describe RRCs where an element that is thematically dependent on the head noun (either as a complement or as a modifier) does not appear adjacent to it but rather in a relative clause internal position. This is illustrated schematically in (152) (repeated from (109)).

(152) a. (D) N modifier/complement [_{CPrel}...]
      b. <u>(D) N</u> [_{CPrel}...<u>modifier/complement</u>...]

The fact that relative clauses may generate discontinuous noun phrases has scarcely been noted in the literature. Pinkster (2005) reports that noun phrase discontinuity may arise in relativization constructions, as in (153), from Latin:

(153) mittit   rogatum <u>vasa</u>   ea   quae <u>pulcherrima</u>   apud eum viderat.
       sent.3SG ask.PTCP vessels the which most.beautiful at   him see.PPRF
       'he sent to ask for the loan of the most beautiful vessels he had seen at his
       house.' (1st c. BC, from Pinkster 2005: 2; gloss mine)

Some Latin grammars also mention this possibility: "The relative sometimes takes an adjective after it, which properly belongs to the antecedent" (Zumpt 1832: 237), and "The Relative Clause frequently attracts into itself an Adjective belonging to the antecedent, especially if that Adjective is a Superlative" (Hale and Buck 1966: 157).

The lack of more studies reporting remnant-internal relativization may in part explain why the theoretical impact of this phenomenon remains unexplored. I only found one vague allusion to this fact in a footnote of Fanselow and Féry (2006):

In Old Occitan, relative clause formation leads to discontinuity (see Pinkster 2005). Depending on one's theory of relative clause formation, this construction (exemplified below) would also involve a discontinuous noun phrase.

  <u>la justicia</u>   que   <u>grant</u> áig   a mandar (Old Occitan)
  the legal.power   which great have.1SG to dispose
  'The great legal power which I have at my disposal' (Fanselow and Féry 2006: 7; gloss and
  underlining mine)

2.3.1 Core properties

On the basis of the empirical data of earlier stages of Portuguese inspected thus far, remnant-internal relativization can be characterized in terms of six core properties, displayed in (i)–(vi).

(i) *Syntactic type of relative clause*   Remnant-internal relativization involves postnominal RRCs, that is, relative clauses with the *head + relative clause* order.

(ii) *Number of the split parts*   Remnant-internal relativization involves bipartite discontinuity, that is, two discontinuous parts.

(iii) *Order of the split parts*   Remnant-internal relativization involves simple (or pull-)splits, that is, splits that retain the order of elements found in the continuous counterpart (Fanselow and Ćavar 2002). This is illustrated in (154).[10]

(154) a. <u>os livros</u> que eu compus <u>da   philosaphia</u>
the books that I   wrote   of.the philosophy
'the books of philosophy that I wrote' (15th c., from Martins 2004: 503)

  b. os livros da   philosaphia que eu compus
the books of.the philosophy that I   wrote

(iv) *Elements in the first split part*   In the first split part, the head noun may appear alone (see (155)) or associated with other elements, such as a definite article (see (154a), (156)), an indefinite article (see (157)), or an adjectival modifier (see (158)). A quantifier used as a pronoun may also appear alone in the first split part (cf. *qualquer* 'any' in (159)).

(155) <u>Casos</u>   que Adamastor contou <u>futuros</u>
cases.M.PL that A.   told   future.M.PL
'(the) future events that Adamastor foresaw' (16th c., from Lausberg 1967/1972: §331)

(156) que   muyto conforto tomava com os tres paos do   leito, por
because much   comfort had.3SG with the three sticks of.the bed   for
a   senificança que <u>deles</u>   lhe   dissera o bom homem da   barca
the meaning   that of.them him.CL tell.PPRF the good man   of.the boat
'because he felt very good about the three sticks of the bed because of the meaning that the good man of the boat said that they had' (13th c. [transmitted by a 16th-c. MS], Martins, Pereira, and Cardoso, 2013–15)

(157) e   pasarã   <u>huũ rrio</u> que perhy   core <u>dagoa   doce</u>
and crossed.3PL a   river that through.there flows of.water sweet
'and they crossed a river of sweet water that flows through there' (15th c., from Martins 2004: 503)

---

[10] The sequence given in (154b) is not attested in Old Portuguese texts with the exact words that parallel the example (154a). However, because the construction is well attested in all periods of the history of Portuguese, I constructed the example in (154b) to make the contrast clearer.

(158) da   qual cousa ellas dizem que som hisentas e   que nũca a
      from.the which thing they say   that are   free   and that never it.CL
      pagarõ per príuelegio antigo que tẽem   do   papa
      paid.3PL by privilege old   that have.3PL from.the pope
      'as for it, they say that they never paid it because they have an old privilege
      from the pope' (15th c., Martins 2001: 483)

(159) e   qualquer que de nos primeiro morer
      and any   that of us first   die.FUT.SBJV
      'and whoever of us first die' (13th c., Martins 2001: 344)

(v) *Elements in the second split part* The second split part can be an adjectival
modifier (see (155)) or a PP. The PP can be either modifier (see (157)) or complement of the noun (as in (160) and (161)).[11]

(160) eram   sobrinhas da   molher que faleseo de lamsarote rodrigues
      were.3PL nieces   of.the wife   that died   of L.   R.
      'they were nieces of the wife of Lamsarote Rodrigues who died' (17th c.,
      Coelho 1987: 124)

(161) comoeu me   encontro num estado miseravel pell a falta que há
      as   I myself.CL am   in.a state miserable by.the lack that has
      do   vinho
      of.the wine
      'as I am in a miserable state by the lack of wine that is there (= because of the
      wine shortage)' (19th c., *P.S.*)

(vi) *Position of the second split part* The second split part may surface in the
rightmost position of the clause (see (157)–(161)) or in a non-final position, following the relativizer, as in (156), (159), and (162)–(165).

(162) e   esto por prool e   verdade de hũa Licença que
      and this by favor and truth   of a   license that
      do   dito   senhor pera ello tenho
      from.the mentioned man   for that have.1SG
      'and (I wrote this document) under the benefit and truth of a license
      from the aforementioned man that I have to (make) it' (16th c., Martins
      2001: 557)

---

[11] In (160), *molher* 'wife' is a relational name, and in (161), *falta* 'lack' is a deverbal noun derived from
the verb *faltar* 'to lack.'

(163) e   o   deradeiro que delas   fiquar   posa   amte de sua morte
       and the   last   that of.them stay.FUT.SBJV can.SBJV before of his death
       nomear   a   terceira
       appoint.INF the third
       'and the last of them that stays alive can appoint the third (person) before his
       death' (16th c., Martins 2001: 547)

(164) Nas   bombas que de fogo estão queimando
       in.the bombs that of fire are   burning.GER
       '(the Cyclops' art is shown) in the bombs of fire that (they) are burning' (16th
       c., Pimpão 1972/2000: 73)

(165) quando alevantárão Hum   por seu   capitão, que peregrino   Fingio.3SG
       when   chose.3PL   a.M.SG by their captain that foreigner.M.SG pretended
       na   cerva espirito divino
       in.the doe   spirit   divine
       'when they chose for captain a foreigner who pretended that there was divine
       spirit in his doe' (16th c., from Dias 1933/1970: §462)

2.3.2 Information structure

It has been observed in the literature that the members of discontinuous noun
phrases differ in their information structure status, a property that Predolac (2009)
refers to as *split information structure*.

The same seems to be true of the instances of remnant-internal relativization
attested in earlier stages of Portuguese. Indeed, in neutral declarative sentences
displaying broad information focus, remnant-internal relativization emerges when
the modifier/complement is assigned emphatic/contrastive focus, in the sense of
Zimmermann (2007) (see §1.3.3.1).

This interpretation is available if the second split part appears in either a non-final
or a final clausal position. When the modifier/complement appears in a non-final
position, as in (166), it is interpreted as an identificational focus (in the sense of
É. Kiss 1998). For instance, in (166) *do dito senhor* 'of the aforementioned man' is
interpreted as an identificational focus as it presupposes a set of relevant entities for
which the predicate can hold and exhaustively identifies the proper subset of this
set for which the predicate actually holds. Example (166) can thus be paraphrased
as in (167).

(166) e   esto por prool e   verdade de hũa Licença que
       and this by favor and truth   of a license that
       do   dito   senhor pera ello tenho
       from.the mentioned man   for that have.1SG
       'and (I wrote this document) under the benefit and truth of a license from the
       aforementioned man that I have to (make) it' (16th c., Martins 2001: 557)

(167) Of a set of relevant licenses it is true for the license from the aforementioned man (and no other) that I have it.

If the second split part surfaces in the rightmost position, various meaning facets of emphatic/contrastive focus related to different syntactic environments may be available. The notion of contrastiveness may be expressed in overtly contrastive statements, as in (168). In this case, the focused constituent *(livros) da philosaphia* '(books) of philosophy' explicitly contrasts with *(obras minhas) que som fundadas sobre bem falar* '(writings of mine) on the art of speaking'. It is clear, then, that the paragraph context explicitly indicates the existence of a contextually salient set of alternatives.

(168) Por a qual cousa aficadamente te amoesto, meu Ciceram, que nom soomente
       aquelas obras minhas que som fundadas sobre bem falar, mas ainda
       os   livros que eu compus da   philosaphia,
       the books   that I   wrote   of.the philosophy
       que som ja iguaaes a elas, tu os leas com boa deligencia.
       'This is why I strongly urge you, my dear Cicero, to read with care
       not only my writings on the art of speaking well, but also the books
       that I wrote on philosophy, which are now about as extensive.'
       (15th c., Piel 1948: 8)

However, the emphatic/contrastive focus in the rightmost position can also be interpreted as an identificational focus. The exhaustive interpretation associated with *das suas qujntãas e casaaes* 'of their farms and hamlets' in (169) is evident upon the paraphrase in (170).

(169) E   aos   prazos   que as Egreias e   Moesteiros qujserem
       and to.the contracts that the churches and monasteries want.FUT.SBJV
       ffazer   das   suas qujntãas e   casaaes
       make.INF of.the their farms   and hamlets
       '(and give authority) to the contracts that the churches and the monasteries
       may make on their farms and hamlets' (15th c., Martins 2001: 265)

(170) Of the set of the relevant things that a church or a monastery may grant, legal authority should be given to the contracts made on their farms and hamlets, and nothing else.

Moreover, the emphatic/contrastive focus may simply signal the speaker-oriented emphasis, that is, the relative weight that the speaker/writer wants to attach to a particular element in the sentence (Enkvist 1980: 135). In this sense, it adds a surplus value to the interpretation, "not at the level of the proposition, but of speech modality or a metalinguistic level, where information stemming from the speaker coordinates becomes relevant" (Remberger 2010: 5). A case in point is provided in (171), where the writer emphasizes the sort of "shortage" that leads him to such a miserable state without referring (implicitly or explicitly) to any other type of "shortage".

(171)   como eu me   encontro num estado miseravel pella <u>falta</u> que há
         as   I   myself.CL am   in.a state   miserable by.the lack that has
         do   vinho
         of.the wine
         'as I am in a miserable state by the lack of wine that is there (= because of the
         wine shortage)' (19th c. MS, Portugal, District Archive of Bragança)

2.3.3 Word order

There is a clear impact of information structure on the word order patterns
found in remnant-internal relativization. As observed in §2.3.1, the second
split part may surface: (1) in the rightmost position of the clause, as in (172)
(partially repeated from (168)); or (2) in a non-final position, following the
relativizer, as in (173) (partially repeated from (166)). Moreover, §2.3 shows
that the second split part is interpreted as an emphatic/contrastive focus in both
word order patterns.

(172)   os <u>livros</u> que eu compus da   philosaphia
         the books that I   wrote of.the philosophy

(173)   de <u>hũa Licença</u> que do   dito   senhor pera ello tenho
         of a   license   that from.the mentioned man   for that have.1SG

Adopting the system of focus and prosody interaction presented in §1.3.3.2, I assume
that in earlier stages of Portuguese, just like in CEP, the emphatic/contrastive
focus in the rightmost position (see (172)) is assigned by the Nuclear Stress Rule
(Zubizarreta 1998).

As for the non-final position of the second split part (see (173)), I take earlier
stages of Portuguese to be like CEP in that the emphatic/contrastive focus can be
marked syntactically through focus movement to a designated focus position in the
left periphery of dependent and non-dependent clauses (see §1.3.3.1). Concretely,
taking as point of departure the Rizzi's (1997) left peripheral template in (174)
(repeated from (9) in Ch. 1), I assume, in line with Bianchi (1999), that the
complementizer introducing remnant-internal relatives (*que* 'that') is spelled out in
Force and that there is a Focus projection (FocP) below Force that hosts interrogative
and focalized phrases in its specifier.

(174)   [ForceP [TopP* [FocP [TopP* [FinP [IP]]]]]]

Evidence for the focus movement of the second split part comes from the syntactic
tests provided by Costa and Martins (2011) to distinguish contrastive focus fronting
from topicalization (see §1.3.3.1). Under this proposal, a sentence like (175) (partially
repeated from (156)) involves contrastive focus fronting because it displays: (1) a

cleft-like interpretation, which is made visible in the paraphrase in (176); (2) subject-verb inversion. Note, additionally, that *deles* 'them' in (175) surfaces to the left of the proclitic *lhe* 'him', which possibly indicates that the emphatic/contrastive focus surfaces in a IP-above position.

(175) Por a   senificança que deles   lhe   dissera o   bom homem da
       for the meaning   that of.them him.CL tell.PPRF the good man   of.the
       barca
       boat

(176) It was the meaning of the three sticks that the good man of the boat had told
       him (and not the meaning of anything else).

Summing up, I submit that earlier stages of Portuguese pattern with CEP in that an emphatic/contrastive focus in non-corrective contexts must either move to a dedicated left peripheral focus position (see (173), (175)) or be clause-final (see (172)), just like narrow information focus. I elaborate on this proposal in §2.4.2.2A.

2.3.4 Competing analyses

In §1.3.2.4 I outline the contrast between the two main analyses put forward in the literature to account for RRCs: the *adjunction analysis* (Ross 1967; Chomsky 1977; Jackendoff 1977) and the *raising analysis* (Schachter 1973; Vergnaud 1974, 1985; Kayne 1994). The basic difference between these analyses is that the head noun is generated in the matrix clause in the adjunction analysis (see (177a)), but it is raised from within the relative clause in the raising analysis (see (177b)).[12]

(177) a. The book [ø$_i$ I read t$_i$] (*adjunction analysis*)
       b. The [book$_i$ I read t$_i$] (*raising analysis*)

Moreover, in §2.2.3, I offer an overview for the two main analyses that have been proposed in the literature to account for noun phrase discontinuity: the *movement analysis* and the *base-generation analysis*.

Assuming that remnant-internal relativization involves both an RRC and a discontinuous noun phrase, there are four logically possible ways to combine the competing analyses. In §§2.3.4.1–4 I examine the four hypotheses and show that the combination of the *raising analysis of RRCs* and *the movement analysis of discontinuous noun phrases* best captures the properties of remnant-internal relativization in earlier stages of Portuguese.

---

[12] I refer the reader to §1.3.2.4 for a detailed presentation of the adjunction and raising analyses.

2.3.4.1 Adjunction analysis of restrictives + movement analysis of discontinuous noun phrases   Under the adjunction analysis, the antecedent is base-generated in a relative clause external position. In order to combine the adjunction analysis with the movement analysis of discontinuous noun phrases, it is necessary to postulate that the head noun and its modifier/complement are base-generated in a relative clause-external position and that the discontinuous noun phrase is derived via the rightward movement of the modifier/complement (which ends up right-adjoined to the DP node), as in (178).

(178)   [$_{DP}$ [$_{NP}$ [$_{NP}$ head t$_{modifier/complement}$] [$_{CP}$ RRC]] modifier/complement]

A concrete example is given in (179), where the PP *da philosaphia* 'of philosophy' is taken to undergo rightward movement to a position right-adjoined to the DP.

(179)   [$_{DP}$ os [$_{NP}$ [$_{NP}$ livros t$_k$] [$_{CP}$ Op$_j$ [$_{C'}$ que [$_{IP}$ eu$_l$ [$_{I'}$ compus$_i$[$_{VP}$ t$_l$[$_{V'}$ t$_i$ t$_j$]]]]]]]]
             the   books   that   I   wrote
         [$_{PP}$ da   philosaphia]$_k$]
         of.the   philosophy

Although the combination of the adjunction analysis of RRCs and the movement analysis of discontinuous noun phrases accounts for the sentences with the modifier/complement in the rightmost position, it fails to account for the contexts involving a non-final modifier/argument, as in (180) (repeated from (159)).

(180)   e   <u>qualquer</u> que de nos primeiro morer
         and any   that of us first   die.FUT.SBJV
         'and whoever of us first die' (13th c., Martins 2001: 344)

The pattern in (180) could be interpreted as resulting from rightward movement of the PP *de nos* 'of us', placing it between the relativizer *que* 'that' and the adverb *primeiro* 'first'. Apart from several problems that this derivation raises, the strongest objection is that it would involve lowering to a non-c-commanding position (Fiengo 1977) and hence should be rejected in view of such requirements as the Proper Binding Condition or the Empty Category Principle.

2.3.4.2 Adjunction analysis of restrictives + base-generation analysis of discontinuous noun phrases   Under this scenario the head noun and its modifier/complement are generated separately in two different syntactic positions: the head noun is merged CP-externally, whereas the modifier/complement is merged CP-internally.

The basic assumption underlying this proposal is that adjuncts/arguments may not have their source inside the noun phrase with which they are associated (Baker 2003; Koster 1987; among others).

Baker (2003) argues that adjectives can be generated in any syntactic position (such as VP) as long as that position permits free adjunction. Koster (1987: 197) claims that PPs introduced by *of* do not necessarily have their source inside a noun phrase. According to the author, if this were always the case, (181a) would have an ungrammatical source, as shown in (181b).

(181)   a. *Of the students in the class*ⱼ I like [Mary *t*ⱼ] better than anyone else.

        b. *I like [Mary of the students in the class] better than anyone else. (both Koster 1987: 197)

There are at least three objections that can be raised against analyzing remnant-internal relativization along these lines. First, in contrast to Koster's example (see (181)), when remnant-internal relativization is involved, the head and the PP could have a grammatical source, as shown in (182b) (repeated from (154)).

(182)   a. <u>os livros</u> que eu compus <u>da   philosaphia</u>
        the books that I   wrote   of.the philosophy
        'the books of philosophy that I wrote' (15th c., from Martins 2004: 503)

        b. os livros da   philosaphia que eu compus
        the books of.the philosophy that I   wrote

Second, the idea that the second split parts function as event modifiers (being adjoined to the VP) rather than noun modifiers is not plausible. Although some modifiers can be related to entities and events, not all have this ability. For instance, in (182), if the book of philosophy was written by me, it is the book that is of philosophy and not the event of writing. Thus, the modifier is clearly interpreted in relation to the noun (and not in relation to the event).

Finally, it seems reasonable to assume that the semantic dependency between the head and its modifier/complement requires these elements to be in a structural relation at some point at the derivation. This cannot be achieved, however, under the combination of the adjunction analysis of RRCs and the base-generation analysis of discontinuous noun phrases, because a modifier/complement merged in a relative clause internal position cannot be structurally related to a head in a relative clause external position.

2.3.4.3 Raising analysis of RRCs + movement analysis of discontinuous noun phrases
This combination offers a natural explanation of why the head noun and the modifier/complement can split. In a nutshell, the head and its modifier/complement

are merged in a position internal to the relative clause and head movement may optionally involve pied-piping.[13] If so, the head and its modifier/complement appear consecutively (see (183a)); if it does not, the modifier/complement is stranded and the noun phrase splits into two parts (see (183b)).

(183) a. [$_{DP}$ os [$_{CP}$ [livros da   philosaphia]$_k$ [$_{C'}$ que [$_{IP}$ eu$_j$ [$_{I'}$ compus$_i$
           the   books of.the philosophy   that   I   wrote
           [$_{VP}$ t$_j$ [$_{V'}$ t$_i$ t$_k$]]]]]]]

       b. [$_{DP}$ os [$_{CP}$ livros$_k$ [$_{C'}$ que [$_{IP}$ eu$_j$ [$_{I'}$ compus$_i$ [$_{VP}$ t$_j$ [$_{V'}$ t$_i$ [t$_k$ da
           the   books   that   I   wrote   of.the
           philosaphia]]]]]]]]
           philosophy

Although this simple story needs to be qualified, it offers us a good starting point for a more elaborate analysis of remnant-internal relativization.

2.3.4.4 Raising analysis of RRCs + base-generation analysis of discontinuous noun phrases   The base-generation approaches assume that the members of the discontinuous phrase do not map onto a phrasal constituent at any point of the derivation. There are four logical ways of deriving remnant-internal relativization along these lines:[14] (1) the two parts of the discontinuous phrase are merged in the Spell Out position; (2) the two parts of the split are not merged in the Spell Out position; (3) only the first part of the split is merged in the Spell Out position; or (4) only the second part of the split is merged in the Spell Out position.

Hypotheses (1) and (3) are incompatible with the raising analysis of RRCs. While the raising analysis of RRCs requires the head to be base-generated in the relativization site, the base-generation analyses of discontinuous noun phrases in (1) and (3) require the head to be generated in [Spec, CP].

Hypotheses (2) and (4) are at first sight compatible with the raising analysis of RRCs as they assume that the Spell Out position of the head differs from its base position. There are, however, good reasons to doubt that these hypotheses are on the right track. As already discussed in §2.3.4.2, in order to be interpreted in relation to the head, the modifier/complement has to be in a structural relation with the head at

---

[13] The notion of pied-piping was first introduced by Ross (1967). The term refers to a phenomenon whereby a particular movement operation, designated to displace an element X, in fact displaces a larger phrase in which X is embedded. This is the case of (183a), where the movement operation designated to displace the head *livros* 'books', in fact displaces the larger constituent *livros da philosaphia* 'books of philosophy.'

[14] The discussion is confined to bipartite remnant-internal relativization, which is the only type attested in the data inspected from earlier stages of Portuguese.

some point of the derivation, and this requirement cannot be fulfilled if the head and the modifier/complement are not merged together.

2.3.5 Remaining problems

On the basis of this brief sketch, I conclude that the combination of the raising analysis of RRCs and the movement analysis of discontinuous noun phrases is much better equipped to handle remnant-internal relativization in general than the other theories are.

However, as already mentioned, the simple movement approach to remnant-internal relativization needs to be improved because, as it stands, it cannot derive some of the properties of remnant-internal relativization.

First, the simple movement approach cannot derive some "complex" first split parts. As already mentioned in §2.3.1, the head in the first split part may contain just the head or be associated with other elements, such as an adjectival modifier (see (184), partially repeated from (158)).

(184)   per príuelegio antigo que tẽem   do   papa
        by privilege   old   that have.3PL from.the pope

This property is not surprising at all. In Latin and in earlier stages of Portuguese, simple discontinuous noun phrases also allow for it. Take, for instance, (185)–(187) (partially repeated from (116b), (124), and (125)); here the first split part involves a head combined with other elements, such as a quantifier (185), an adjective (186), and a determiner (187).

(185)   Caesar duas legiones in   citeriore Gallia novas conscripsit
        Caesar two legions into Hither   Gaul   new   enrolled

(186)   que ma bocado a   deus de comer dele
        that bad piece have god to eat.INF of.him

(187)   Outros   fauores   se   lhe   tem feito estraordinarios.
        other.M.PL favors.M.PL SE.CL him.CL has done extraordinary.M.PL

These complex first split parts are problematic for simple movement approaches because they seem to involve non-constituent movement. Consider, for instance, the sentence in (184). Assuming that the PP originates within the DP in a structure like [DP D [NP N PP]] and that the adjectival modifier also originates within the DP as a specifier of a functional projection (Cinque 1994, among others), the problem that arises is that there is no constituent that includes the head and the adjective but excludes the PP and that can undergo leftward movement, displaying remnant-internal relativization.

Secondly, the simple movement analysis is not able to derive the non-final position of the modifier/complement in sentences like (188) (partially repeated from (162)).

(188)   de hũa Licença que do   dito   senhor pera ello tenho
         of a   license that from.the mentioned man   for   that have.1SG

In (188) the PP *do dito senhor* 'from the aforementioned man' does not appear in the final sentential position, but instead in the embedded clause initial position, after the relativizer. If remnant-internal relativization is taken to involve head movement to [Spec, CP] and the stranding of the modifier/complement, it remains a mystery why, in sentences like (188), the PP is not placed in the rightmost clausal position.

2.4 Analysis of remnant-internal relativization

Building on Fanselow and Ćavar's (2002) proposal for discontinuous phrases (see §2.2.3.1D), I show that the drawbacks of the simple movement analyses can be circumvented if remnant-internal relativization is taken as an effect of phonological deletion. Moreover, I claim that this hypothesis gains strength when considered in the light of the insights of Bošković and Nunes (2007) on the copy theory of movement.

Before focusing on remnant-internal relativization, §2.4.1 presents the basics of the copy theory of movement (in the PF side). With this background in mind, §2.4.2 provides a step-by-step analysis of remnant-internal relativization in earlier stages of Portuguese.

2.4.1 *On the copy theory of movement in the Phonological Form side*

This section presents the basics of the copy theory of movement (in the PF side) proposed by Bošković and Nunes (2007), which is based on previous work by Bošković (2001, 2002, 2004a,b) and Nunes (1999, 2004). It also summarizes a concrete analysis developed within this framework, namely Stjepanović's (2007) analysis of post-verbal subjects in Serbo-Croatian. In presenting these approaches, particular attention is given to the theoretical devices used to account for the syntax-phonology interaction.

2.4.1.1 *Bošković and Nunes (2007)*   Following Chomsky's (1995) approach to movement, where the raising of elements leaves copies behind that are subsequently deleted, Bošković and Nunes (2007) (based on previous work by Bošković 2001,

2002, 2004a,b, and Nunes 1999, 2004) argue that *traces* (i.e. copies that are structurally lower in the syntactic representation) may be phonetically realized.

The basic idea is that PF has a preference for pronouncing the highest copy of a chain, but a lower copy may be pronounced to avoid a PF violation. Technically, this statement requires further clarification.

The first point in need of clarification concerns the preference for deleting lower copies. The explanation Nunes (1999, 2004) provides for this fact is based on an economy principle that prefers fewer applications of deletion in later computations of the phonological component. As J. Nunes (2004: 33) puts it:[15]

Exploring the null hypothesis regarding the copy theory of movement, the above proposal thus takes the position that both heads of chains and traces should in principle be subject to phonetic realization. According to the logic of the proposal, there is nothing intrinsic to lower copies that prevents them from being pronounced. If Chain Reduction proceeds in such a way that only a trace survives, the derivation may eventually converge at PF. The fact that in most cases such a derivation yields unacceptable sentences is taken to follow from *economy* considerations, rather than convergence at PF. Since the highest chain link is engaged in more checking relations, it will require fewer applications of F[ormal]F[eature]-Elimination than lower chain links, thereby being the optimal candidate to survive Chain Reduction and be phonetically realized, all things being equal.

A second point needing clarification is why the deletion of a lower copy in PF is just a preference and not the only option. The reason is clear: a lower copy can be produced to avoid a PF violation. Some of the PF factors that have been considered to induce the pronunciation of lower copies are stress assignment processes, intonational requirements, and morphological restrictions on identical elements.

However, PF constraints may also block full copy deletion. In this case, a last-resort mechanism is admitted on the PF side: the so-called *scattered deletion*. It consists of the deletion of different pieces of different copies, as represented in (189).

(189) $[X\ \cancel{Y}]^i ... [\cancel{X}\ Y]^i$

Scattered deletion has been successfully applied to a range of languages and phenomena, namely to cliticization in Bulgarian and Macedonian (Bošković 2001), participle–auxiliary order in Bulgarian (Lambova 2004), and split phrases (Fanselow and Ćavar 2002).

---

[15] In the excerpt transcribed, *Chain Reduction* is a term that refers to the deletion of constituents of a non-trivial chain.

2.4.1.2 Stjepanović (2007)   Stjepanović shows that the copy theory of movement proposed by Bošković and Nunes (2007) provides a principled account of several patterns of word order in Serbo-Croatian, including the postverbal subject position.

Serbo-Croatian is characterized by great freedom of word order. Depending on the information structure involved, sentences containing a new information focus can exhibit the following word orders: SVO, SOV, OSV, and OVS. For the sake of illustration, consider the OVS word order in (190b), which can be produced as an answer to the question in (190a).

(190) a. [Who is catching the mouse?]

     b. Miša   hvata   mačka
       mouse   catches   cat
       'A cat is catching a mouse.' (both Stjepanović 2007: 235)

Stjepanović (2007) shows that in sentences with the neutral intonation pattern, the constituent bearing new information focus (such as *mačka* 'cat' in (190b)) follows elements that represent old information. In order to explain the final sentential position of focalized elements, she proposes that: (1) the subject moves in overt syntax even in the cases where it surfaces post-verbally; (2) the subject surfaces post-verbally because a lower copy of the chain is pronounced in PF.

The factor that Stjepanović takes to induce the pronunciation of the lower copy is sentential stress assignment. This implies that in the output of syntax sentences have a focus structure whereby each element is associated with an [F]-feature. For example, (190b) would have the syntactic output in (191) (from Stjepanović 2007: 236).

(191) [$_{AgrSP}$ miša [$_{AgrSP}$ mačka [$_{TP}$ mačka hvata [$_{AgrOP}$ miša hvata [$_{V1}$ mačka
        –F   +F   +F   –F   –F   –F   +F
       hvata [$_{V2}$ hvata miša]]]]]]
       –F   –F   –F

Stjepanović additionally assumes that in Serbo-Croatian the NSR[16] applies just after Spell Out, assigning prominence to the rightmost/lowest sentential constituent (Zubizarreta 1998, 1999). If the element that receives the nuclear stress has an [+F]-feature, no problem arises. On the contrary, if the rightmost element is [–F], a conflict situation emerges between the NSR and the FPR (see n. 16). To resolve this

---

[16] I refer the reader to §1.3.3.1 for the presentation of Zubizarreta's (1998, 1999) view of the relationship between prosodic prominence and focus; it is in this context that the Nuclear Stress Rule (NSR) and the Focus Prominence Rule (FPR) should be understood.

conflict, Serbo-Croatian renders defocalized [–F] elements extrametrical for the application of the NSR.

In summary, post-verbal subjects in Serbo-Croatian (as in (190b)) are a result of lower copy pronunciation. This is due to the requirements on sentential stress assignment, which force the copy associated with the nuclear stress to be pronounced. If this PF requirement is not satisfied, the derivation does not converge.

2.4.2 *The derivation of remnant-internal relativization*

I propose an analysis of remnant-internal relativization based on three central claims: (1) remnant-internal relativization constructions and regular relative constructions are derived from a continuous noun phrase; (2) remnant-internal relativization has the function of focus-marking the second split part (with emphatic/contrastive focus); and (3) non-adjacency between the head and its modifier/complement is determined by conditions of the phonological component (and not of syntactic movement per se).

On the basis of the modifier/complement position, it is possible to identify three distributional patterns that need to be derived from the present analysis.[17]

Pattern I corresponds to RRCs where the head and its modifier/complement are adjacent, as in (192).

(192) os livros da   philosaphia que eu compus
       the books of.the philosophy that I wrote

Pattern II comprises instances of remnant-internal relativization with a modifier/complement in the rightmost sentential position, as in (193).

(193) os livros que eu compus da   philosaphia
       the books that I wrote of.the philosophy

Pattern III corresponds to instances of remnant-internal relativization with a modifier/complement in a non-final position, following the relativizer, as in (194).

(194) os livros que da   philosaphia eu compus
       the books that of.the philosophy I wrote

The derivation of each pattern is presented in §§2.4.2.1–3.

---

[17] As already mentioned, only the example (193) is attested in earlier stages of Portuguese. Patterns I and II are well attested in the diachrony of Portuguese, but not with the exact words that parallel (193).

2.4.2.1 Pattern I   In order to derive Pattern I, I take the head and its modifier/
complement to be merged together in the relativization site. The noun phrase is then
copied and merged in [Spec, CP] (or [Spec, Force]), checking the wh-feature on C (or
Force) (see (195)).[18]

(195) [os [livros da   philosaphia]^i [que eu compus [livros da   philosaphia]^i]]
         the books of.the philosophy   that I wrote   books of.the philosophy

In line with Nunes (2004 and subsequent work), I consider that the syntactic object in
(195) cannot be linearized because it is not in accordance with Kayne's (1994) LCA
(see §1.3.1.3). The LCA dictates that at PF, an element cannot asymmetrically
c-command and be asymmetrically c-commanded by the same element in a structure.
Because the two instances of *os livros da philosaphia* 'the books of philosophy' are non-
distinct, the verb *compus* 'wrote' is required to precede and be preceded by the same
element. This induces a violation of asymmetry, canceling the derivation.

As shown in (196), the deletion of copies may yield outputs with different
applications of deletion: one application of deletion in (196a–b); two in (196c–f);
and three in (196g–h).

(196) a. [os [livros da philosaphia]^i [que eu compus [~~livros da philosaphia~~]^i]]
       b. [os [~~livros da philosaphia~~]^i [que eu compus [livros da philosaphia]^i]]
       c. [os [livros ~~da philosaphia~~]^i [que eu compus [~~livros~~ da philosaphia]^i]]
       d. [os [~~livros~~ da philosaphia]^i [que eu compus [livros ~~da philosaphia~~]^i]]
       e. [os [~~livros da~~ philosaphia]^i [que eu compus [livros da ~~philosaphia~~]^i]]
       f. [os [livros da ~~philosaphia~~]^i [que eu compus [~~livros da~~ philosaphia]^i]]
       g. [os [livros ~~da~~ philosaphia]^i [que eu compus [~~livros~~ da ~~philosaphia~~]^i]]
       h. [os [~~livros~~ da ~~philosaphia~~]^i [que eu compus [livros ~~da~~ philosaphia]^i]]

If there are no convergence problems resulting from these reductions, the derivations
are eligible for economy comparison, and the derivations yielding (196c,d) are
excluded for employing more operations of deletion than necessary. That is, economy principles ensure that deletion applies as few times as possible.

An economy-based explanation is also available to cancel the derivation in
(196b). The formal features associated with the higher copy have already been
rendered invisible for PF upon checking; hence the deletion of the lower copy
employs fewer applications of deletion in later computations of the phonological
component. Therefore, all else being equal, (196a) is the most economical way of
deriving (195).

---

[18] In this case, the C (or Force) also carries an EPP-feature. However, I postpone the implementation of
the EPP until §2.4.2.2B.

Under these conditions alone, remnant-internal relativization would never be derived. The most economical derivation in (196a) would always be preferred and, as a result, Pattern I would be the only option.

2.4.2.2 *Pattern II*   However, as in any economy approach, if the most economical option does not lead to convergence, a less economical option may be chosen, as is the case of Pattern II. According to the mainstream version of the copy theory of movement adopted here, lower copies can be pronounced if there is an independent well-formedness PF requirement that precludes the pronunciation of a higher copy. The same line of reasoning applies to scattered deletion: if full deletion does not satisfy PF requirements, deletion may apply within different chain links.

In the light of these assumptions, the derivation yielding the Pattern II can also be a legitimate outcome. In this case, the phonological system resorts to scattered deletion, with part of the noun phrase pronounced in the higher copy and part in the lower one, as in (197).

(197) [os [livros ~~da~~   ~~philosaphia~~]^i [que eu compus [~~livros~~ da   philosaphia]^i]]
       the books of.the philosophy   that I wrote   books of.the philosophy

I submit that this is the method to which the computational system resorts in order to accommodate the PF requirements in (198) and (199) (to be detailed in turn).

(198) *PF requirement I*
       In non-corrective contexts, emphatic stress must be rightmost.

(199) *PF requirement II*
       The EPP-feature on C (or Force) dictates that the relative head must be pronounced in the higher copy.

A. PF requirement I

Sticking to the principle that synchrony can inform historical analyses, I presume that earlier stages of Portuguese are like CEP in that (narrow) information focus always appears in the rightmost position of the sentence[19] (J. Costa 1998 for CEP, and Martins 2002 for earlier stages of Portuguese).

Moreover, I assume that earlier stages of Portuguese pattern with CEP in that an emphatic/contrastive focus in non-corrective contexts (see §1.3.3.2, n. 41) must either move to a dedicated left peripheral focus position (see (194)) or be clause-final (just

---

[19] Recall from §1.3.3.2 that this is due to the fact that the (narrow) information-focused constituent bears a nuclear neutral stress assigned via the NSR (Zubizarreta 1998, 1999).

like narrow information focus); its location in a non-final position leads to ungrammaticality (see (200b)–(201b)).[20]

(200) a. Comi   prego no   prato raspado.
          ate.1SG steak in.the dish scraped
          'I ate scraped steak in the dish.'

       b. *Comi   prego RASPADO no   prato.
          ate.1SG steak scraped   in.the dish

(201) a. Paguei de multa cem   euros.
          paid.1SG of fine   one.hundred euros
          'I paid a fine of one hundred euros.'

       b. *Paguei CEM   EUROS de multa.[21]
          paid.1SG one.hundred euros of fine

The contrast between examples a and b is not surprising under the system developed thus far. As already mentioned, if emphatic/contrastive focus is assigned by prosodic prominence alone, it is freely assigned in corrective contexts but not in non-corrective ones.[22] In the latter case, which corresponds to examples (200a)–(201a), the nuclear stress always targets the rightmost constituent (being assigned by the NSR).

Then the question arises as to how the ambiguity between (narrow) information focus and emphatic/contrastive focus in the rightmost sentential position is resolved in CEP. Following Frota (1998, 2002, and much related work), I propose that this ambiguity is eliminated by differences in peak alignment (or choice of pitch accent) (see Hualde 2002 for a brief overview). As Frota demonstrates, declarative sentences with emphatic/contrastive focus in the last word are systematically distinguished from neutral declaratives. If the last word carries a neutral prosodic/information focus, it is

---

[20] Examples (200) and (201) are adapted from Martins (2004). Making use of the notational conventions in Zubizarreta (1999), the emphatic/contrastive focus identified by the E/CSR rule is indicated by small caps, whereas the (rightmost) emphatic/contrastive focus identified by the NSR is underlined.

[21] The example (201b) would be possible in CEP if *de multa* 'of fine' were understood as a kind of afterthought, involving a prosodic contour with a pause between *cem euros* 'one hundred euros' and *de multa* 'of fine'.

[22] Remarkably, the idea that emphatic stress assignment may be constrained by construction-specific conditions is not new. Culicover and Winkler (2008) propose a solution along these lines to account for the comparative inversion structure (CI) in (ia). They show that CI is a focus construction that prosodically marks its subject, places it at the right edge of the intonational phrase and requires a contrastive focus reading. To account for these properties, they argue that the subject is in [Spec, IP] in (ib) but not in (ia). This difference follows from the markedness constraint in (ii), which applies mandatorily in CI.

(i)   a. Sandy is much smarter than is the professor.
      b. Sandy is much smarter than the professor is. (both Culicover and Winkler 2008: 1)

(ii) *Right Edge Alignment Constraint of Contrastive Focus in CI*
      Each contrastively focused constituent is right-aligned in ip [intonational phrase]. (Culicover and
      Winkler 2008: 22)

pronounced with a falling contour through the last stressed syllable from a preceding peak (H+L*). In contrast, if an emphatic/contrastive focus is intended, the last word is pronounced with a circumflex contour (rise followed by fall), with a peak over the stressed syllable. Frota (1998) illustrates this difference with the one-word utterance *casaram* 'they got married'. As depicted in (202),[23] neutral and emphatic contrastive foci are distinguished by different intonational contours.

(202) a. Neutral focus   b. Emphatic/contrastive focus

The PF facts just discussed nicely illuminate our general understanding of remnant-internal relativization, providing us with the tools to handle the Pattern II in (197) (repeated here as (203)).

(203) [os [livros ~~da~~ ~~philosaphia~~]^i [que eu compus [~~livros~~ da
      the books of.the philosophy   that I wrote   books of.the
      philosaphia]^i]]
      philosophy

First, recall from §2.3.2 that remnant-internal relativization emerges in non-corrective contexts where the second split part is assigned emphatic/contrastive focus. In this case, emphatic/contrastive focus is marked prosodically via the NSR (the neutral focus and the emphatic/contrastive focus being distinguished by different intonational contours).

    Adopting Stjepanović's (2007) view of the relation between PF deletion and stress assignment, the deletion of the higher copy of *da philosaphia* 'of philosophy' in (203) can be explained by assuming that the output of syntax (see (195)) has the focus structure in (204).

(204) [os [livros da philosaphia]^i [que eu compus
      –F   –F   –F –F   –F   –F   –F
      [livros da philosaphia]^i]]
      –F   +F +F

In earlier stages of Portuguese, just like in CEP, the NSR applies just after Spell Out, assigning prominence to the rightmost/lowest sentential constituent (i.e. to *philosaphia* in (204)). Since the element that receives the nuclear stress has an [+F]-feature, the FPR does not conflict with the NSR. As a result, the higher copy of *da philosaphia*

---

[23] For ease of reproduction, the contour presented in (202) is from Hualde (2002: 4).

is deleted, and the lower one is pronounced. Recall that a lower copy must be pronounced if it carries the nuclear stress. If this PF requirement is not satisfied, the derivation does not converge.

Remarkably, the present approach also explains why the modifier/complement in Pattern I cannot be pronounced in the lower copy (see (205), repeated from (203)).

(205) [os [livros da   philosaphia]^i [que eu compus [~~livros da~~
       the books of.the philosophy   that I wrote   books of.the
       ~~philosaphia~~]^i]]
       philosophy

Assuming that in the output of syntax in (195) has the focus structure in (206) and that in earlier stages of Portuguese (just like in CEP) the NSR applies just after Spell Out, assigning prominence to the rightmost/lowest sentential constituent, it is clear that a conflict situation arises between the NSR and the FPR because the rightmost element is [–F].

(206) [os [livros da philosaphia]^i [que eu compus
       –F   –F   –F –F   –F   –F +F
       [livros da philosaphia]^i]]
       –F   –F –F

To resolve this conflict, CEP renders defocalized [–F] elements extrametrical for the application of the NSR, and *compus* 'wrote' is assigned the neutral nuclear stress.[24] Because there is no PF requirement precluding the pronunciation of the higher copy of *da philosaphia* 'of philosophy', the most economical option in (205) is derived (with deletion of the lower copy).

B. PF requirement II

The question that remains to be answered now is why the head noun is not pronounced in the lower copy as well; in other words, why the more economical option of full copy deletion is not allowed and the last-resort mechanism of scattered deletion is used instead.

---

[24] According to Zubizarreta (1998), languages vary in the way they resolve the conflict between the FPR and the NSR. As already mentioned in §1.3.3.2, in languages such as English and French defocalized [–F] elements are treated as extrametrical in the sense that they are skipped by the NSR. Other languages (such as Spanish, Italian, and CEP) employ prosodically motivated movement (p-movement), which moves the post-focal [–F] elements out of the rightmost clausal position. If the hypothesis put forth in this analysis proves correct, it means that these two mechanisms are not necessarily incompatible; instead, they may coexist in the same language as different ways of resolving the conflict between the FPR and the NSR. Under this view, CEP differs from French and English in two aspects: (1) allowing p-movement of defocalized [–F] constituents and (2) requiring extrametrical material to be deleted in PF.

Adopting as my point of departure Chomsky's (2000) view on EPP, I assume that core functional categories, such as v, T, and C, can have an EPP-feature requiring that their specifier position be filled. This is the case of the relative C (or Force) in CEP and in earlier stages of Portuguese. In this language, there are no head-internal relative clauses, a fact that clearly indicates that the relative C (or Force) must have its specifier position filled.

However, I depart from Chomsky's (2000) syntactic view on EPP. I rather adopt a phonological approach to the EPP, in the line of what has been expressed one way or another by Holmberg (2000), Ndayiragije (2000), Bobaljik (2002), Bošković and Nunes (2007), and Landau (2007), among others.

Following Landau (2007), I assume that the EPP-feature (therefore [P]) can be characterized according to two main properties. First, [P] is a selectional feature that governs PF configurations, imposing the PF requirement in (207).

(207)   A [P]-bearing head needs to have its specifier filled with phonological material.

Importantly, the [P]-feature does not "care" about the phonological material that is used to satisfy it; it only requires that some phonological visible element be found in the specifier of a [P]-bearing head. If this requirement is not satisfied, there is a PF (selectional) violation, causing the derivation to crash.

Secondly, the [P]-feature does not trigger movement on its own, being always parasitic on some other feature (e.g. Case or [wh]) that is independently checked. Under this view, the PF interface works as a filter, eliminating representations that do not satisfy PF requirements.

The approach to EPP just outlined constitutes a good basis for explaining why the head is pronounced in the higher copy in Pattern II (see (208), repeated from (203)). Because the relative C (or Force) has a [P]-feature, failure to pronounce the head noun in [Spec, CP] (or [Spec, ForceP]) would represent a PF violation.

(208)   [os [livros ~~da   philosaphia~~]^i [que eu compus [~~livros~~ da
        the books of.the philosophy   that I wrote   books of.the
        philosaphia]^i]]
        philosophy

2.4.2.3 Pattern III   To account for remnant-internal relativization with the second split part in a non-final position (as in (209), repeated from (194)), I propose a remnant movement approach interpreted in terms of the copy theory of movement (Bošković and Nunes 2007: 65).

(209) os livros que da   philosaphia eu compus
       the books that of.the philosophy I   wrote

Under this view, two main steps are involved in the derivation: (1) the (emphatic/contrastive) focused constituent *da philosaphia* 'of philosophy' in (209) is copied and merged in [Spec, FocP], checking the [+FOC] feature on Foc;[25] (2) the noun phrase (containing a copy of the moved modifier/complement) is copied and merged in [Spec, ForceP], checking the wh-feature on Force, as depicted in (210).[26]

(210) [os [livros da philosaphia]^i [que [da philosaphia]^j eu compus [livros [da philosaphia]^j]^i]]

The particular configuration dictated by remnant movement requires PF deletion to apply to two different chains: the PP chain formed by the movement of *da philosaphia* 'of philosophy' and the noun phrase chain formed by the movement of *livros da philosaphia* 'books of philosophy'. Note that if the lower copy of these two chains were deleted (see (211)), the resulting structure would not be linearized due to the presence of more than one copy of *da philosaphia* 'of philosophy'.

(211) [os [livros da philosaphia]^i [que [da philosaphia]^j eu compus [~~livros [da philosaphia]~~^{j}]^i]]

Adopting the *representational* hypothesis proposed in Nunes (2004), I assume that Spell Out sends the whole structure in (210) to the phonological component. Chain Reduction inspects the PP chain and instructs the phonological component to delete the occurrence of *da philosaphia* 'of philosophy' that is a sister of *livro* 'book'. As there are two elements that satisfy this instruction, Chain Reduction[27] ends up deleting the two copies that satisfy this instruction, as represented in (212) (Bošković and Nunes 2007 for more technical details).

(212) [os [livros ~~da philosaphia~~]^i [que [da philosaphia]^j eu compus [livros [~~da philosaphia~~]^j]^i]]

As for the noun phrase chain formed by the movement of *livros da philosaphia* 'books of philosophy', I take the relative C (or Force) to be equipped with a wh-feature and a [P]-feature. The wh-feature must be checked before Spell Out, whereas

---

[25] From a typological point of view, the internal movement of head-related elements is not surprising. Basilico (1996) shows that in some languages internally headed relative clauses display movement of the head to a sentence-internal position.

[26] For simplicity, I am abstracting away other syntactic movements involved in this sentence.

[27] See n. 15 for a clarification of the term *Chain Reduction*.

the [P]-feature must be satisfied in PF. Given that the wh-feature can be checked in the lower copy of the chain through Agree, it is the [P]-feature that requires the higher pronunciation of the head noun.

(213) [os [livros ~~da philosaphia~~]^i [que [da philosaphia]^j eu compus [~~livros~~ [~~da philosaphia~~]^j]^i]]

2.5 Diachronic path of remnant-internal relativization

In the discussion of remnant-internal relativization in earlier stages of Portuguese, the reader might have wondered whether remnant-internal relativization is still possible in CEP and, if so, whether there is any contrast with the patterns found in the diachrony of Portuguese.

In fact, remnant-internal relativization with the modifier/complement in the rightmost position is possible in CEP (see examples a in (214)–(217)). However, the occurrence of the modifier/complement in the left periphery of the relative clause leads to ungrammaticality, as illustrated in examples b in (214)–(217).

(214) a. uma   filha   que eu tenho pequena
           a.F.SG daughter.F.SG that I   have young.F.SG
           lit. 'a young daughter that I have' (Martins 2004: 502)

       b. *uma filha   que pequena eu tenho
           a   daughter that young   I   have

(215) a. uns   touros   que aqui tinha   agrestes
           some.M.PL bulls.M.PL that here had.1SG wild.PL
           lit. 'some wild bulls that I had here' (from the TV-show *Liga dos Últimos*)

       b. *uns   touros que agrestes aqui tinha
           some bulls that wild   here had.1SG

(216) a. uma casa   que eu comprei de cinco assoalhadas
           a   house that I   bought of five   rooms
           lit. 'a house with five rooms that I bought'

       b. *uma casa   que de cinco assoalhadas eu comprei
           a   house that of five   rooms   I bought

(217) a. um rapaz que eu conheço de   Leiria
           a   boy   that I   know   from L.
           lit. 'a boy from Leiria that I know'

       b. *um rapaz que de Leiria eu conheço
           a   boy   that of L.   I   know

At least two hypotheses are worth pursuing to explain the empirical contrasts observed in the history of Portuguese: (1) the reduction of the left-peripheral space of embedded clauses constrained the patterns of discontinuity in remnant-internal relativization; (2) the restrictions on movement inside the DP blocked the extraction of the complement/modifier to the left periphery of the relative clause.

The first hypothesis is tentatively proposed by Cardoso (2010) to account for the data in (214)–(217). Under this view, the diachronic contrast could be explained in terms of a grammatical change involving the loss of a left-peripheral position dedicated to contrastive focus in relative clauses and possibly other types of subordinate clauses. However, recent findings on the syntax of focus in Romance languages and the inspection of a wider range of empirical data from Portuguese suggest that this hypothesis may not be on the right track.

In fact, it has been claimed in the literature that there is a contraction of the left-peripheral clausal space in some Old Romance languages (Cruschina 2011; Poletto 2014; Batllori and Hernanz 2015; Martins, Pereira, and Pinto forthcoming). Assuming that the CP-domain can host two different kinds of foci (the lower dedicated to fronted-unmarked/information focus and the higher specialized for fronted-contrastive focus, see Benincà 2004), it is argued that the position dedicated to fronted-unmarked/information focus ceases to be available in the history of some Romance languages, namely Portuguese (from 13th to 14th c., see Martins, Pereira, and Pinto forthcoming), Italian (from Old to Modern Italian, see Poletto 2014), and Catalan (from Old to Modern Catalan, see Batllori and Hernanz 2015). Note, however, that in these languages the position that is lost is the one dedicated to fronted-information focus, it being assumed that the position dedicated to fronted-contrastive focus (which is targeted by the modifier/complement in remnant-internal relativization—Pattern III) remains active through the history of these languages.[28]

Moreover, recent research on focus-movement in CEP (Costa and Martins 2011) shows that the left-peripheral position dedicated to emphatic/contrastive focus is still active, both in main and embedded clauses (see §1.3.3.1). Although further in-depth research is required in this domain, namely regarding the different meaning facets of emphatic/contrastive fronted focus in CEP, the evidence available favors the idea that the diachronic contrast observed in the syntax of remnant-internal relativization should be explained by some other means.

The second hypothesis that is worth exploring relies on the assumption that a change took place within the DP layer that affected word order patterns in the history of Portuguese and, concomitantly, the patterns of discontinuity available.

---

[28] Note additionally that instances of remnant-internal relativization (Pattern III) are attested beyond the 13th c., as shown in examples provided in §2.3.1, which clearly indicates that Pattern III does not involve movement to the left-peripheral position dedicated to information-focus (Martins, Pereira, and Pinto forthcoming).

Concretely, I suggest, in the line of Poletto's (2014) analysis for Italian, that in earlier stages of Portuguese modifiers/complements belonging to the DP-internal structure could target the highest specifier position inside the DP,[29] an operation that seems to parallel other fronting phenomena found within the clausal domain.[30]

Evidence for this movement comes from contexts, already described in A. Costa (2004), where the modifier/complement precedes all other DP-internal elements: a noun in (218); a numeral and a noun in (219); and a definite determiner, a noun, and a modifier in (220). Note that the fronting operation to the highest specifier position within the DP is further confirmed by examples of incomplete PP-fronting, as (221), where the PP *dazeite* (lit. 'of.olive.oil') is fronted, leaving behind a relative clause that takes the noun (*azeite* 'olive.oil') as antecedent.

(218)　E　elle ouve <u>delle</u>　doo　　como devia
　　　　and he had of.him sorrow as　　should.3SG
　　　　'And he felt sorrow for him, as he should have.' (13th c. [transmitted by a 15th-c. MS], Martins, Pereira, and Cardoso 2014–15)

(219)　hũũa leíra　　　que leua　<u>de semeadura de triguo</u> dous alqueires
　　　　a　　piece.of.land that takes of sowing　　of wheat two　bushels
　　　　'a piece of land that takes two bushels of wheat sowing' (16th c., Martins 2001: 294)

(220)　e　dedes　<u>de cantos béés</u> deus j　　der.　　a　meyadade do
　　　　and give.2PL of all　　goods god there give.FUT.SBJV the half　　of.the
　　　　ffeyto e　do　que aj　por ffazer
　　　　done　and of.the that has to　do.INF
　　　　'and you give us the half of all the goods that god there gives considering what has been done and what remains to be done' (13th c., Martins 2001: 373)

(221)　Renderom os oljuaaes　<u>dazeijte</u>　vijnte e　quatro quantaros que
　　　　yielded　the olive.groves of.olive.oil twenty and four　q.　　　that
　　　　uall　a　　saseëta Reaes o　cantaro
　　　　is.worth A.PREP sixty　r.　the c.
　　　　'The olive groves yielded twenty four *quantaros* [metric unit for liquids] of olive oil that is worth sixty *reaes* [currency] per *cantaro* [metric unit for liquids].' (15th c., from J. Costa 2004b: 415)

---

[29] I am assuming the DP hypothesis (Abney 1987) and the idea that between the DP and the NP there are functional projections (e.g. for agreement checking). Given that the concrete details of the implementation are not relevant for the discussion, I adopt simple structures like (i)–(ii) to represent a PP and an AdjP in the highest specifier position in the DP:

(i)　[DP [PP] [D]...N ~~PP~~]
(ii)　[DP [AdjP] [D]...~~AdjP~~ N]

[30] A hypothesis that is worth exploring in future research is that the fronting operations within the DP parallel the middle scrambling attested in earlier stages of Portuguese, which involve multiple specifier positions within the IP layer (Martins 2002).

Following Ledgeway (forthcoming) and Poletto (2014), a prediction arises: if an element targets the left edge of the DP, it can move further on outside the DP. This prediction is correct for earlier stages of Portuguese: as shown in examples (222) (repeated from (218)) and (223), the PP object *dele* (lit. 'of.him'), which is the complement of the noun *doo* ('sorrow') can occur in the highest specifier position within the DP (see (222)), but it can also target the left periphery of the clause (see (223)). Further examples of PP-fronting to the clausal left periphery are displayed in (224)–(226).[31]

(222)   E   elle ouve <u>delle</u>   <u>doo</u>   como devia.
        and he   had of.him sorrow as   should.3SG
        'And he felt sorrow for him, as he should have.' (13th c. [transmitted by a
        15th-c. MS], Martins, Pereira, and Cardoso 2014–15)

(223)   tal mal   treyto que nom ha homem que o   visse   que <u>dele</u>
        so badly treated that not has man   that him.CL see.SBJV that of.him
        nom   tivesse   <u>doo</u>
        not   have.SBJV   sorrow
        '(he was) so badly treated that every man who saw him would feel sorrow for him'
        (13th c. [transmitted by a 16th-c. MS], Martins, Pereira, and Cardoso 2013–15)

(224)   per quallquer Respeito que seja   posto   que <u>disto</u> facam
        by any   obligation that be.SBJV imposed that of.this make
        expressa <u>memção</u>
        express mention
        'by any imposed obligation that makes express mention of this' (16th c.,
        Martins 2001: 562)

(225)   <u>Destas   tres   cousas</u> uos   direy   eu as   signjficanças.
        of.these three   things you.CL tell.FUT I   the   meanings
        'I will tell you the meaning of these three things' (13th c. [transmitted by a
        15th-c. MS], Martins, Pereira, and Cardoso 2014–15)

(226)   Galvam, que <u>desto</u> ouve <u>gram pesar</u>, [...] disse aa   donzella
        G.   who of.this had great grief   told to.the damsel
        'Galvam, who had great grief over this, told to the damsel' (13th c. [trans-
        mitted by a 15th-c. MS], Martins, Pereira, and Cardoso 2014–15)

Importantly, the empirical data inspected thus far also suggest that adjectives (and the degree/quantificational markers associated to them) can also be fronted within the DP, as in (227)–(229). In this case, the fronting operation within the DP is

---

[31] As noted by Poletto (2014), the idea of having a preliminary internal movement that feeds the subsequent movement into the clausal left-periphery is already adopted for cases of extraction found in the Germanic languages (Corver 1990, among others).

confirmed in (229) by the non-adjacency between the adjective *ledo* 'happy' and its complement (*de ledices e prazeres e de dons conhecedores*),[32] which indicates that the adjective and the degree/quantificational marker have undergone leftward movement, leaving the complement of the adjective behind.

(227) E   depois fez   ante   eles   <u>muito fermoso</u> <u>milagro</u>
       and then   made.3SG before them very   beautiful   miracle
       'and then he performed a very beautiful miracle before them' (13th c.
       [transmitted by a 16th-c. MS], Martins, Pereira, and Cardoso 2013–15)

(228) e   fez   fazer   <u>muj rrico</u> <u>moymento</u> ao   caualleiro
       and made make.INF very rich   tomb   to.the knight
       'and had a very rich tomb built to the knight' (13th c. [transmitted by a 15th-
       c. MS], Martins, Pereira, and Cardoso 2014–15)

(229) no   mundo nom auja <u>mais ledo</u>   caualeyro <u>de lediçes e   de</u>
       in.the world   not   had more pleased knight   of joys   and of
       <u>prazeres e   dons sabedores</u>
       pleasures and gifts wise
       'in the world there was no knight more pleased with joys, pleasures, and wise gifts'
       (13th c. [transmitted by a 15th-c. MS], Martins, Pereira, and Cardoso 2014–15)

Crucially, if the adjective and the degree/quantificational marker can target the highest position within the DP, these elements (or one of them) should be able to move further on outside the DP. This prediction is correct: example (230) shows that *muito* 'very' undergoes leftward movement to the clausal domain. According to Poletto (2014), this movement is allowed because first the adjectival expression *mujto gran* 'very big' targets the highest position within the DP and, from this position, *muito* 'very' moves further on and targets the left periphery of the clause.[33]

(230) E   el cavalgou e   foi-se   mui ledo para a   oste ca   <u>muito</u>
       and he rode   and went-SE.CL very joyful to   the army because very
       <u>ouvera</u>   <u>gram</u> pavor de morte
       had.PPRF.3SG great fear of death
       'and he rode to the army because he had very great fear of death' (13th c.
       [transmitted by a 15th-c. MS], Martins, Pereira, and Cardoso 2014–15)

---

[32] In earlier stages of Portuguese the adjective *ledo* 'happy' selects a complement introduced by the preposition *de* 'of'. This can also be observed in the example below.
eu som mui ledo de   vossa vinda
I   am very joyful.DE.PREP your arrival
'I am very joyful at your arrival' (13th c. [transmitted by a 15th-c. MS], Martins, Pereira, and Cardoso 2014–15)

[33] In example (231) the marker *muito* 'very' probably undergoes movement through the specifier position of the PP.

(231) Estor caeo em terra [...] ca   mujto era de gram força   o
       E.   fell in ground, because very was of great strength the
       caualeiro que o   ferio.
       knight   that him.CL wounded
       'Estor fell to the ground because the knight that wounded him had very great
       strength.' (13th c. [transmitted by a 15th-c. MS], Martins, Pereira, and Cardoso
       2014–15)

Interpreted in this manner, the configuration of remnant-internal relativization with
the modifier/complement in the left periphery of the relative clause (Pattern III)
ceases to be available in the history of Portuguese possibly because the first step
movement of the complement/modifier to the highest specifier position within the
DP is blocked. In the absence of raising to the highest specifier position within
the DP, the other potential higher movements become illicit.

Future research will have to develop the technical details of the analysis. Nevertheless, some ideas have been put forward in the literature to derive similar diachronic
contrasts: (1) the highest specifier position within the DP ceases to be available because
this position starts to be targeted by other DP-internal elements, namely the lexical
head (Poletto 2014); (2) the concept of antilocality, according to which movement
must result in raising outside the immediate minimal domain or phrase, thereby
crossing at least one phrasal XP boundary, is parameterized across languages (Ledgeway forthcoming) and within the same language.

2.6 Conclusion

The term *remnant-internal relativization* is proposed in this chapter to describe
RRCs where the head noun and some modifier/complement related to it appear
discontinuously.

On the basis of empirical data from earlier stages of Portuguese, two distributional
patterns of remnant-internal relativization are identified: (i) remnant-internal relativization (with a modifier/complement in the rightmost clausal position), as in
(232); (ii) remnant-internal relativization (with a modifier/complement in the left
periphery of the RRC), as in (233).

(232) os livros que eu compus da   philosaphia
       the books that I   wrote of.the philosophy

(233) os livros que da   philosaphia eu compus
       the books that of.the philosophy I   wrote

From a theoretical point of view, I show that the phenomenon of remnant-internal
relativization provides important new evidence for the raising analysis of RRCs. In
particular, I demonstrate that the adjunction analysis of RRCs cannot account for the

properties of remnant-internal relativization, considering two main arguments. First, if the head and its modifier/complement were base-generated together in a relative clause external position, the pattern in (233) could not be derived, as it would require lowering of the modifier/complement to a non-c-commanding position. Secondly, if the head and its modifier/complement were generated separately (the head being CP-external and the modifier/complement being CP-internal), the semantic dependency between the head and its modifier/complement, which requires that these elements be in a structural relation at some point of the derivation, would not be satisfied.

My proposal is that remnant-internal relativization is derived by the combination of the raising analysis of RRCs with a movement analysis of discontinuous noun phrases. Concretely, I analyze remnant-internal relativization in terms of the copy theory of movement on the PF side, deriving the contrast between regular and remnant-internal relativization from the deletion operations that take place in the PF side of the grammar.

Abstracting away from particular derivations, the global picture that emerges is that earlier stages of Portuguese (and CEP, in a more restricted way) had at their disposal constituent discontinuity as a way of syntactically marking emphatic/contrastive focus. Just like clefts, remnant-internal relativization (and, more generally, phrasal discontinuities) appears to constitute a syntactic environment capable of codifying emphatic/contrastive focus. Under this view, it is not surprising that emphatic/contrastive focus in remnant-internal relativization can be additionally marked by prosodic prominence (see (232)) or syntactic movement (see (233)). This squares up nicely with the observation that different focus-marking devices may conspire to encode emphatic/contrastive focus.

From a diachronic perspective, I hypothesize that the loss of remnant-internal relativization with the modifier/complement in the left periphery of the RRCs is due to restrictions on movement that emerge inside the DP, which block the extraction of the modifier/complement to the left periphery of the RRC.

3

Extraposition of restrictive relative clauses

3.1 Introduction

The term *extraposition* is used ambiguously in the literature on syntactic theory. It is used in a pre-theoretical sense to refer to the non-adjacency between two parts of a constituent and in a theoretical sense to refer to a specific type of movement (typically rightward movement). It is usually conceived as a very general phenomenon that affects both relative clauses and a wide range of constituents (e.g. conjuncts, result clauses, appositions, comparative clauses, prepositional phrases, and complement clauses) (see De Vries 2002: 236–7 for an overview).

This chapter focuses on the extraposition of RRCs. In this context, the term *extraposition* is used in a pre-theoretical sense to refer to an RRC that does not appear adjacent to the antecedent, instead being separated from it by material that belongs to the matrix clause, as depicted in (234).

(234) [...[antecedent]...RRC]

An example of this construction is given in (235). Example a, which exhibits adjacency between the antecedent and the RRC, displays the regular word order. Example b, which exhibits non-adjacency between the antecedent and the RRC, demonstrates an extraposed RRC. In the contexts of extraposition, there are elements that intervene between the antecedent and the relative clause (e.g. the verb, the preposition, and the adverb in (235b)). These elements are henceforth referred to as *intervening material* and are underlined for ease of reading.

(235) a. A man [$_{RRC}$ that I met last year] came in yesterday.
    b. A man <u>came in yesterday</u> [$_{RRC}$ that I met last year]. (adapted from Givón 2001: 208)

In the traditional account of RRC-extraposition, the RRC is analyzed as involving rightward movement of the relative clause to a right-adjoined position (Reinhart 1980; Baltin 1984; among others). However, within more recent developments in

Portuguese Relative Clauses in Synchrony and Diachrony. First Edition. Adriana Cardoso.
© Adriana Cardoso 2017. First published in 2017 by Oxford University Press.

generative grammar, rightward movement is excluded altogether (Kayne 1994) or at least from core syntax (Chomsky 1995, 2000).

These developments in generative grammar have obviously energized the debate on the syntax of RRC-extraposition. The challenge is not an easy one, especially for the proponents of Kayne's antisymmetric framework; it is necessary to determine a syntactic analysis of extraposition that excludes not only rightward movement but also rightward adjunction.

In this context, various solutions are put forward in the literature. For instance, Kayne (1994) proposes that extraposition involves leftward movement of the antecedent and stranding of the relative clause, and De Vries (1999, 2002) proposes an analysis of extraposition in terms of coordination. Notably, these two analyses have the advantage of being compatible with the head raising analysis of RRCs.

At the same time, other solutions are offered in the literature, which cannot be accommodated in the traditional Y/T-model of grammar. This is the case for the analysis suggested by Fox and Nissenbaum (1999) and Fox (2002). Eliminating the distinction between covert and overt operations, they claim that RRC-extraposition should be analyzed as involving covert quantifier raising (QR) of the antecedent, followed by late merging of the RRC.

Despite the wide range of analyses already available in the literature, extraposition is still a rather poorly understood phenomenon. However, this is not to say that little has been written about it. In contrast, over the last years, several studies have gradually added details to the picture, but most of these studies primarily focus on Germanic languages, especially English, German, and Dutch. Unfortunately, little has been said about RRC-extraposition in Romance languages, and as a consequence, the theoretical impact of cross-linguistic variation remains largely unexplored.

The major goal of the present chapter is to contribute to a better understanding of the syntax of RRC-extraposition by discussing new empirical evidence from earlier stages of Portuguese and CEP, as well as data from other languages.[1] Specifically, the chapter aims to: (1) establish clear properties that distinguish RRC-extraposition in CEP and earlier stages of Portuguese; (2) correlate the variation documented in the diachronic dimension with that found in the cross-linguistic dimension; and (3) demonstrate that the variation found in RRC-extraposition is not compatible with a uniform account of the phenomenon.

This chapter is structured as follows. Section 3.2 presents the most relevant competing analyses of RRC-extraposition and introduces the distinction between unitary and non-unitary approaches to the phenomenon. Section 3.3 is a state-of-the-art survey of what is known about RRC-extraposition in CEP. In §3.4, a comparative approach is adopted, showing that different languages and different

---

[1] The data and the analysis presented in this chapter are partially discussed in Cardoso (2012).

stages of the same language may contrast with respect to the properties of RRC-extraposition. This leads to the postulation of two different strategies of RRC-extraposition: the specifying coordination (plus ellipsis) (De Vries 2002) and the VP-internal stranding (Kayne 1994) strategies. Sections 3.5 and 3.6 demonstrate how the contrastive properties of RRC-extraposition in CEP and earlier stages of Portuguese are derived from the dual approach advocated here. Then §3.7 focuses on the contrasts found in the diachronic and cross-linguistic dimension, and §3.8 concludes the chapter.

3.2 Competing analyses

Generally speaking, the existing approaches to RRC-extraposition can be divided into three different groups (see De Vries 2002, for an overview): extraposition as right-hand adjunction (Culicover and Rochemont 1990); extraposition as VP-internal stranding (Kayne 1994); and extraposition as specifying coordination (Koster 2000; De Vries 2002).

3.2.1 *Rightward adjunction analyses*

The basis of the rightward adjunction analysis is that the extraposed RRC is right-adjoined to some maximal projection. Within this approach, some variants can be identified, according to the exact point of the derivation where the rightward adjunction takes place.

The rightward movement analyses (see Reinhart 1980; Baltin 1984; among others) assume that the RRC is base-generated next to the antecedent. Then, the RRC undergoes rightward movement and right-adjoins to some maximal projection, as schematically represented in (236).

(236)

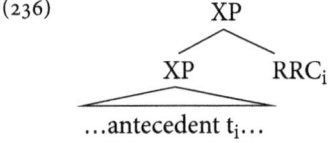

The rightward adjunction analyses (see Culicover and Rochemont 1990, among others) propose that there is no syntactic link between the antecedent and the extraposed RRC. The latter is base-generated in some right-adjoined position, as shown in (237).

(237)

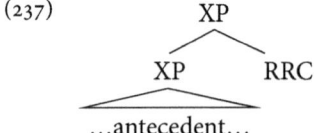

The rightward adjunction (after covert movement) analyses (see Fox and Nissenbaum 1999, Fox 2002) advance a radical alternative to the standard assumptions of overt/covert movement, suggesting that covert operations such as QR can precede overt operations. First, the antecedent undergoes covert movement QR to a rightward position (see (238a)). Then, the RRC is right-adjoined to the antecedent in the post-QR position (see (238b)). Phonology will determine that the antecedent is pronounced in its pre-QR position.

(238)   a. QR (covert)   b. RRC merger (overt)

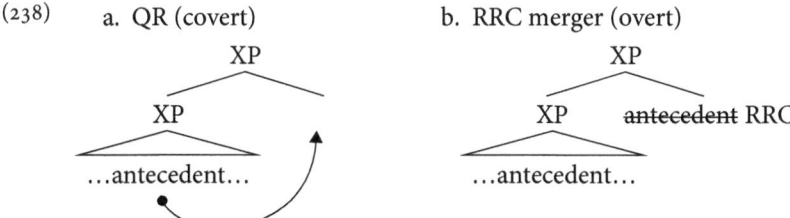

3.2.2 Stranding analyses

The rightward adjunction analyses are challenged by theoretical developments of generative grammar, such as Kayne's (1994) antisymmetric framework. Under this approach, all syntactic representations are asymmetrical in nature, and the linear order is determined by hierarchical relations (this is formulated as the LCA; see §1.3.1.3). As a result, rightward adjunction (and rightward movement) is excluded from the theory of grammar.

As has happened with other phenomena traditionally analyzed as involving rightward positioning (e.g. rightward adjuncts, heavy NP shift, and post-verbal subjects), new proposals of RRC-extraposition compatible with Kayne's theory emerged in the literature.

One of the possibilities explored is that RRC-extraposition involves leftward movement and stranding (Kayne 1994). In this paradigm, the antecedent and the RRCs are generated together. Then, the antecedent undergoes leftward movement, stranding the RRC in its base position, as represented in (239).

(239)

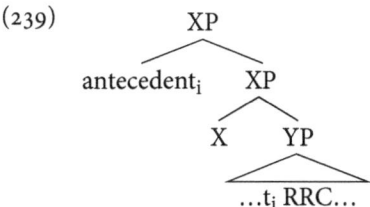

Another possibility is the leftward movement (plus deletion) analysis (Wilder 1995), in which the entire noun phrase containing the RRC undergoes leftward movement, leaving a copy behind. Then, there is a deletion of the RRC in the higher copy and a deletion of the antecedent in the lower one (i.e. scattered deletion), as shown in (240).

(240)

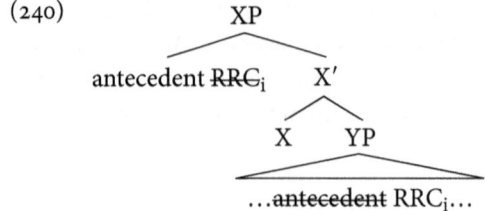

3.2.3 Coordination analyses

Coordination analyses (see Koster 2000, De Vries 2002) crucially rely on the assumption that extraposition involves the same structure as coordination. Assuming the structure of coordination in Munn (1993) and Kayne (1994) (see also Johannessen 1998), these analyses propose that the antecedent is merged within the specifier of an abstract head, whereas the extraposed RRC is merged in the complement position of the head, as schematically represented in (241).[2]

(241)

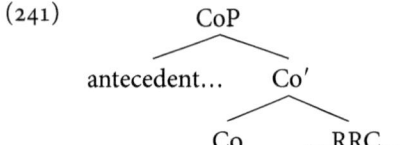

In (241), the second conjunct specifies (i.e. adds information about) the anchor, hence the term *specifying coordination*.

At least two variants of this approach can be identified. According to Koster (2000), the second conjunct contains only the RRC, which is attached at the relevant line of projection, as sketched in (242).

(242)

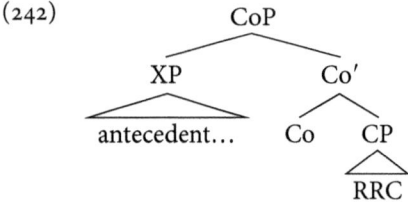

---

[2] The structure in (241) involves a semantically specialized abstract head; it constitutes an asymmetric relationship of specification between the two conjuncts. Koster (2000) symbolically represents this relator by a colon; De Vries (2002) employs an ampersand plus a colon (&:). In this book, I simply use the more general notation *Co* for coordinating head (see Ch. 1 n. 24). Additionally, note that the use of the parentheses with ellipsis in the complement position of the structure in (241) aims to capture the possible presence of additional material in some specific analyses.

According to De Vries (2002), the second conjunct has the same categorial status as the first conjunct. It repeats the material contained in the first conjunct, adding the extraposed RRC in its canonical position. Then, the repeated material is phonologically deleted, as shown in (243).

(243)

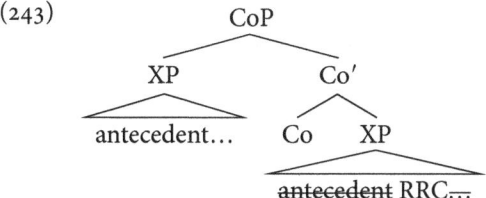

In summary, although this overview of the analyses of extraposition is extremely brief and incomplete, it shows that the emergence of different analyses of extraposition is, at least to some extent, motivated by theory-internal concerns. I return to the stranding and coordination analyses of RRC-extraposition in greater detail in §§3.5.1 and 3.6.1 respectively.

3.2.4 *Unitary vs. non-unitary approaches*

There are additional sources of variation in the approaches to extraposition available in the literature. Aside from the variation regarding the specific syntactic structure adopted, analyses may also contrast with respect to their general applicability. In this respect, two different lines of research can be identified: unitary and non-unitary approaches.

Unitary approaches claim that a single syntactic structure can cover a wide range of construction types involving extraposition (within a language and/or across languages). This is, for instance, the case of the coordination analysis proposed by Koster (2000) and De Vries (1999, 2002). These authors claim that extraposition is not a sub-strategy of relative clauses but is instead a very general phenomenon that applies to a wide range of constructions. Specifically, De Vries (2002) proposes that every construction that may be divided into a first and a second part (*duplex constructions*) allows for the extraposition of the second part (e.g. conjuncts, relative clauses, result clauses, appositions, comparative clauses, PP complements of N, complement clauses of N, and PP complements of A). The same is true of simplex phrases, such as complement clauses of V and heavy NPs. De Vries (2002) proposes that all of these construction types may involve extraposition and that in all these cases, extraposition can be dealt with in terms of specifying coordination.

By contrast, non-unitary approaches claim that more than one syntactic type is necessary to account for the extraposition involved in the different construction types. There are many variants of non-unitary approaches in the literature. Some approaches emphasize the contrast between adjunct and complement extraposition. This is, for instance, the case of the analysis put forth by Fox and Nissenbaum (1999) and Fox (2002), who propose that complement extraposition involves the rightward movement of the complement, whereas relative clause extraposition involves post-QR merging of the relative clause.

Other analyses claim that extraposition is not a unitary phenomenon, even if only relative clauses are considered. This is the case of Smits (1988), who highlights the cross-linguistic variation found in this domain:

The ways in which extraposition seems conditioned is certainly surprising. For, intuitively at least, it is hardly probable for a specific rule of the grammar [...] to be subject to some condition in one language, with that same condition having no relevance whatsoever in another, otherwise closely related language, and vice versa, without any apparent reason. The incoherence of the sprawling array of conditions [...] alone suggests, perhaps, that extraposition of RCs is only apparently a monolithic phenomenon. That is to say, it suggests that only some proportion of cases we find is the result of the rule of extraposition [...] which moves clauses from their NPs to the right end of the clause.   (Smits 1988: 183)

To account for the different properties of relative clause extraposition, Smits (1988) proposes a non-uniform approach to the phenomenon, in which extraposed RRCs are derived from rightward movement (being nevertheless subject to specific conditions in different languages), whereas ARCs are detached from the antecedent and base-generated in a rightward position.

Perhaps more surprisingly, non-uniform approaches have also been proposed to account for even more specific constructions, such as RRC-extraposition. On the basis of comparative evidence from German and English, Inaba (2005) claims that, in spite of superficial similarities, RRC-extraposition in these languages exhibits a remarkable contrast that has been ignored in previous research; RRC-extraposition is a syntactic operation in English, whereas it involves phonological movement in German.

In short, two opposing views dominate the analysis and discussion on the syntax of extraposition. On the one hand, unitary approaches claim that the concept of extraposition corresponds to an explanatory pattern in the sense that it can be accounted for by a single syntactic structure. In contrast, non-unitary approaches claim that the concept of extraposition may have descriptive adequacy (in unifying apparently related constructions) but lacks explanatory force because it does not correspond to a single construction type. It was also shown that non-unitary approaches may differ with respect to: (1) the range of syntactic construction types covered; and (2) their universal or language-specific scope.

3.3 Portuguese: Previous scholarship

Examples of RRC-extraposition have been reported in a number of languages: English (Ziv and Cole 1974; Quirk, Greenbaum, Leech, and Svartvik 1985; Givón 2001); Dutch (Koster 2000; De Vries 2002); German (Haider 1996, 1997; Kiss 2005); Italian (Cardinaletti 1987); and Spanish (Brucart 1999). See also Smits (1988) for an overview.

However, as far as CEP is concerned, only sparse allusions to RRC-extraposition are found in the literature (Brito and Duarte 2003; Barbosa, Duarte, and Kato 2005; Barbosa 2009; Smits 1988).

On the basis of the contrast in (244), Brito and Duarte (2003: 661) claim that "RRCs cannot be easily extraposed in CEP." However, they do not specify what they mean by the use of the adverb *easily*, nor do they provide any example of RRC-extraposition in CEP, presenting only the ungrammaticality of (244c).

(244)   a. Uma pessoa que tu   conheces telefonou.
        a   person that you know   phoned
        'A person that you know phoned.'

      b. Telefonou uma pessoa que tu   conheces.
        phoned   a   person that you know

      c. *Uma pessoa telefonou que tu   conheces.
        a   person phoned   that you know (all Brito and Duarte 2003: 661)

Furthermore, while discussing the position of the subject in CEP, Barbosa, Duarte, and Kato (2005) and Barbosa (2009) allude to RRC-extraposition, showing the impossibility of RRC-extraposition from an indefinite subject in a pre-verbal position, as in (245).

(245)   *Um homem apareceu   que deseja falar   contigo.
        a   man   showed.up that wants talk.INF with.you
        'A man showed up that wants to talk to you.' (Barbosa 2009: 47)

This restriction is claimed to correlate with the Null Subject Parameter. The authors contend that Null Subject Languages such as CEP do not allow extraposition from pre-verbal indefinite subjects, whereas non-Null Subject Languages such as English and French allow it. Barbosa, Duarte, and Kato (2005) and Barbosa (2009) take this contrast to result from the different positions occupied by the subject in Null Subject Languages and in non-Null Subject Languages. In the former, the subjects are left-dislocated, whereas in the latter, they are in [Spec, IP]. I return to this analysis in §3.4.2, where I show that the correlation between the possibility of extraposition from pre-verbal subjects and the Null Subject Parameter simply does not hold. Indeed, in earlier stages of its history, Portuguese was a Null Subject Language and allowed for the extraposition of indefinite subjects from pre-verbal positions.

In his overview of relative clauses in Germanic and Romance languages, Smits (1988: 407) also refers to some properties of RRC-extraposition in CEP. Considering RRC-extraposition and ARC-extraposition together, he proposes the descriptive principles in (246).

(246)   Principles of relative clause extraposition in CEP
   (i)   Extraposition of relative clauses belonging to the subject is impossible both for restrictives and appositives.
   (ii)   Extraposition of relative clauses belonging to objects is possible for restrictives only.
   (iii) Definiteness properties of the restrictive antecedent do not influence the possibilities of extraposition. (all Smits 1988: 407)

As will become clear in §3.4.1, these principles are simply not correct and must be revised.

Finally, other references can be found in the literature, but they only concern extraposition of ARCs (Brito 2004; Peres and Móia 1995). This issue is addressed, though in a slightly different context, in §§4.4.2 and 4.5.2).

As for earlier stages of Portuguese, the RRC-extraposition is almost totally neglected in the grammars and studies on the history of Portuguese. However, there are a few exceptions (see Dias 1933/1970; Mattos e Silva 1989; A. Costa 2004).

Dias (1933/1970: 329) mentions that an RRC can be separated from its antecedent if no ambiguity arises. He illustrates this possibility with the examples in (247)–(249).

(247)   aquelle se   chamará bom   prelado que tiver   letras, reputação,
        that   SE.CL call.FUT good prelate that have.FUT.SBJV letters, reputation
        e   virtudes
        and virtues
        'People will identify a good prelate as the one who has education, a good reputation, and virtues.' (16th c., from Dias 1933/1970: 329)

(248)   que naquelle coração não ha   vestigio de justiça, onde a   avareza
        that in.that heart   not has trace   of justice where the meanness
        tem feyto sua morada
        has done its home
        '[In a sermon, Pope St Leo says] that there is no trace of justice in the heart where the meanness is deeply rooted.' (16th c., from Dias 1933/1970: 329)

(249) Esse, é meu amigo, que moe no   meu moinho.
       that is my friend that mills in.the my mill
       'The one who mills (something) in my mill is my friend.' (old saying, from
       Dias 1933/1970: 329)

Mattos e Silva (1989) also reports the possibility of RRC-extraposition in sentences
such as (250)–(251).

(250) en aquela hora morrera   en que el vira   estando longe
       in that   hour die.PPRF.3SG in that he see.PPRF be.GER away
       dele   que lhi   saira   a alma do   corpo.
       from.him that him.CL fall.out.PPRF the soul of.the body
       '[and the father realized that] his son had died in that hour in which he had
       seen (being away from him) that his soul had fallen out of his body' (14th c.,
       from Mattos e Silva 1989: 766)

(251) naquela hora o   seu filho ficara   sen   féver en que hi   o
       in.that hour the his son   stay.PPRF without fever in that there the
       nosso Salvador e   nosso meestre Jesu Cristo dissera   que era
       our   Savior   and our   master J.   C.   say.PPRF that was.3SG
       são
       healed
       'his son had stopped having fever at the moment that our Savior and
       Master Jesus Christ had said that he was healed' (14th c., from Mattos
       e Silva 1989: 766)

Discussing the syntactic properties of relative constructions in fourteenth- to
fifteenth-century Portuguese, A. Costa (2004) alludes to the possibility of RRC-
extraposition in sentences such as (252).

(252) E   mando   que se outra   mãda pareçer   que eu mãndasse
       and order.1SG that if another will appear.FUT.SBJV that I   order.SBJV
       fazer   ante dessta que quebre   e   nõ ualha
       make.INF before this   that be.annulled.SBJV and not be.valid.SBJV
       'And, if another will appear that I order to be made before this one, I order it
       to be annulled and not valid.'   (14th c., from A. Costa 2004: 414)

Additional references to non-adjacency phenomena, namely those concerning the
so-called *relatif de liaison* or *connecting relative*, can be found in the literature (Dias
1933/1970: 269; Said Ali 1931/1971: 107; A. Costa 2004: 418–19). However, because
these constructions clearly do not involve RRCs, their discussion is postponed until
Chapter 4 (§§4.4.2 and 4.5.2).

   In short, this survey of previous research plainly demonstrates that
much of the syntax of RRC-extraposition in Portuguese still awaits a proper

description. Section 3.4 intends to contribute to filling this gap by offering a description of RRC-extraposition in CEP and in earlier stages of Portuguese. Although much of the discussion focuses on the contrast between CEP and earlier stages of Portuguese, evidence from other languages also plays an important role in keeping with a comparative and universalist approach to the phenomenon.

3.4 Properties in contrast

In this section, I identify three main properties of RRC-extraposition and show how CEP (§3.4.1), other languages (§3.4.2), and earlier stages of Portuguese (§3.4.3) behave with respect to them.

3.4.1 Contemporary European Portuguese

In CEP, RRCs can be extraposed, as illustrated in (253)–(254).

(253)   Ainda por cima, dá-se conta de que as obras não têm licença camarária
'As if it wasn't enough, he/she realizes there is no council license for the building work.'
e   faz   diligências na   Câmara   das   Caldas da Rainha que
and makes actions   at.the Town.Hall of.the C.   d. R.   that
levam ao   seu embargo
lead to.the its embargo
'and takes some steps at Caldas da Rainha Town Hall that lead to its embargo'
(*CETEMP*)

(254)   Houve alguém   no   meio   da   noite que decidiu agarrar   uma
had   someone in.the middle of.the night that decided grab.INF a
cana que supostamente seria   do   Aranha.
pole that supposedly   be.COND of.the A.
'There was someone in the middle of the night who grabbed a pole that supposedly belonged to Aranha.' (from the website *O Sítio do Pescador*)

However, RRC-extraposition in CEP is limited by a number of restrictions, namely: (1) definiteness effect (see §3.4.1.1); (2) extraposition from pre-verbal positions (see §3.4.1.2); and (3) extraposition from PPs (see §3.4.1.3).

3.4.1.1 The definiteness effect   In CEP, RRC-extraposition exhibits a definiteness effect reminiscent of that found in existential constructions with the verb *haver*

'to have' (Duarte and Oliveira 2003: 224 n. 32). Applied to the RRC-extraposition, the definiteness effect is a restriction against the occurrence of "definite" noun phrases as antecedents of extraposed RRCs. This restriction is illustrated by the contrasts in (255)–(256), involving (respectively) a subject and a direct object as the antecedent. As these examples show, RRC-extraposition is fine with indefinite antecedents (see a examples) but impossible with definite ones (see b examples).

Subject:

(255) a. Chegou um rapaz <u>ontem</u>   que te   quer conhecer.
          arrived a   boy   yesterday that you.CL wants meet.INF
          'A boy arrived yesterday that wants to meet you.'

       b. *Chegou o   rapaz <u>ontem</u>   que te   quer conhecer.
          arrived the boy   yesterday that you.CL wants meet.INF
          'The boy arrived yesterday that wants to meet you.'

Object:

(256) a. Encontrei um rapaz <u>no</u>   cinema que perguntou por ti.
          met.1SG   a boy   at.the cinema that asked   for you
          'I met a boy at the cinema that asked for you.'

       b. *Encontrei o   rapaz <u>no</u>   cinema que perguntou por ti.
          met.1SG   the boy   at.the cinema that asked   for you
          'I met the boy at the cinema that asked for you.'

Importantly, if no extraposition is involved, both definite and indefinite antecedents are allowed in these contexts, as illustrated in (257)–(258).

(257) Chegou ontem   um/o rapaz que te   quer conhecer.
       arrived yesterday a/the boy that you.CL wants meet.INF

(258) Encontrei no   cinema um/o rapaz que perguntou por ti.
       met.1SG   at.the cinema a/the boy that asked   for you

However, RRC-extraposition is not limited to indefinites in a narrow, grammatical sense (i.e. noun phrases with an overt indefinite article). The X-position in (259) may be filled, for example, by *um livro* 'a book' or *três livros* 'three books' but not by *o livro* 'the book' or *aqueles livros* 'those books' (see (259)–(260)).

(259) Foi/foram publicado(s) X recentemente que vale a pena ler.
       was/were published   X recently   that is.worth   read.INF
       'X that is/are worth reading was/were recently published.'

(260)

$$X = \left\{ \begin{array}{l} \textit{um livro} \text{ 'a book'} \\ \textit{três livros} \text{ 'three books'} \\ \textit{alguns livros} \text{ 'some books'} \\ \textit{muitos livros} \text{ 'many books'} \\ \textit{livros} \text{ 'books'} \end{array} \right\} \quad *X = \left\{ \begin{array}{l} \textit{o livro} \text{ 'the book'} \\ \textit{aqueles livros} \text{ 'those books'} \\ \textit{todos os livros} \text{ 'all the books'} \\ \textit{cada livro} \text{ 'each book'} \end{array} \right\}$$

Notably, the noun phrases that can fill the X-position in (259) can be grouped together under the class of *weak noun phrases* (as opposed to *strong noun phrases*), in the sense of Milsark (1974).[3] Therefore, the descriptive generalization that captures the relation between RRC-extraposition and the definiteness effect can be formulated as in (261).

(261)   *The definiteness effect and RRC-extraposition*
In CEP, RRC-extraposition can only take place from weak noun phrases.

3.4.1.2 *Pre-verbal positions*

A. Pre-verbal subjects

Extraposed RRCs can take post-verbal subjects as their antecedents, as illustrated in (262a) and (263a). However, if the subject is construed pre-verbally, the sentence is ungrammatical, as shown in (262b) and (263b).

(262)   a. Ontem   explodiu uma bomba em Israel que causou 5 mortos.
            yesterday exploded a   bomb   in I.   that caused 5 deaths
            'Yesterday a bomb exploded in Israel that caused 5 deaths.'

         b. *Ontem   uma bomba explodiu em Israel que causou 5 mortos.
            Yesterday a   bomb   exploded in I.   that caused 5 deaths

(263)   a. Chegou um senhor ontem   que fez   muitas perguntas sobre ti.
            arrived a   man   yesterday that made many   questions about you
            'A man arrived yesterday who asked many questions about you.'

         b. *Um senhor chegou ontem   que fez   muitas perguntas sobre ti.
            a   man   arrived yesterday that made many   questions about you

---

[3] Milsark (1974) distinguishes between weak determiners (e.g. *a, some, many, several,* and *few*), which can occur in *there*-insertion contexts, and strong determiners (e.g. *the, every, each, most, all*), which cannot appear in these contexts (see examples (i) and (ii)). He further claims that weak determiners are not quantifiers but cardinality words, whereas strong determiners are quantificational.

   (i) There is/are a/some/many/three fly/flies in my soup.
   (ii) *There is/are the/every/all/most fly/flies in my soup.

In the context of RRC-extraposition, the verbs typically found with post-verbal subjects are unaccusatives, as in (262)–(263): *explodir* 'to explode' in (262) is an internally caused unaccusative verb; *chegar* 'to arrive' in (263) is an unaccusative verb of inherently directed motion (Duarte 2003). Other unaccusative-related constructions, such as passive sentences, are also compatible with RRC-extraposition, as illustrated in (264a). Note again that if the subject is construed pre-verbally, the sentence is ungrammatical (see (264b)):

(264) a. Foi capturado um indivíduo <u>esta noite</u> que é responsável pelo
          was captured   a   man   this night that is responsible by.the
          assalto ao   banco.
          robbery A.PREP.the bank
          'A man who is responsible for the bank robbery was captured tonight.'

       b. *Um indivíduo <u>foi capturado esta noite</u> que é responsável pelo.
          a   man   was captured this night that is responsible by.the
          assalto ao   banco.
          robbery A.PREP.the bank

However, RRC-extraposition from the subject is not limited to the spectrum of constructions related to unaccusativity. The subject of unergative verbs may also occur in this context (see (265a)–(268a)). It is nevertheless worth noting that not all unergatives can smoothly surface with an extraposed RRC without a propitious context.

(265) a. Telefonou um rapaz <u>ontem</u>   que queria informações sobre a   tua
          phoned   a   boy yesterday that wanted details   about the your
          casa.
          house
          'A boy phoned yesterday who wanted details about your house.'

       b. *Um rapaz <u>telefonou ontem</u>   que queria informações sobre a
          a   boy   phoned   yesterday that wanted details   about the
          tua casa.
          your house.

(266) a. Dormiu uma rapariga <u>ontem</u>   em minha casa   que está a
          slept a   girl   yesterday at my   house that is   A.PREP
          tirar o   mesmo curso que tu.
          do.INF the same   degree that you
          'A girl who is doing the same degree as you slept at my house yesterday.'

       b. *Uma rapariga <u>dormiu ontem</u>   em minha casa   que está a
          a   girl   slept yesterday at my   house that is   A.PREP
          tirar o   mesmo curso que tu.
          do.INF the same   degree that you

(267) a. Trabalha um senhor na   minha empresa que nunca viu o   mar.
　　　　 works   a   man in.the my   company that never saw the sea
　　　　 'A man works in my company who has never seen the sea.'

　　　 b. *Um senhor trabalha na   minha empresa que nunca viu o   mar.
　　　　　 a   man   works in.the my   company that never saw the sea

(268) a. Tossiu   um bebé na   sala de recobro que deve estar a
　　　　 coughed a   baby in.the room of recovery that must be.INF A.PREP
　　　　 precisar de ajuda.
　　　　 need.INF of help
　　　　 'A baby who must be in need of help coughed in the recovery room.'

　　　 b. *Um bebé tossiu   na   sala de recobro que deve estar a
　　　　　 a   baby coughed in.the room of recovery that must be.INF A.PREP
　　　　 precisar de ajuda.
　　　　 need.INF of help

Extraposition from the subject is also possible when verbs with oblique complements
are involved, as in (269)–(270).

(269) a. Vivem alguns portugueses   em Paris que nunca foram à
　　　　 live   some Portuguese.people in P.   that never went to.the
　　　　 Torre Eiffel.
　　　　 T.   E.
　　　　 'Some Portuguese people live in Paris who have never been to the Eiffel
　　　　 Tower.'

　　　 b. *Alguns portugueses   vivem em Paris que nunca foram à
　　　　　 some Portuguese.people live in P.   that never went to.the
　　　　 Torre Eiffel.
　　　　 T.   E.

(270) a. Entrou um homem na   sala que deve ser   o   orador
　　　　 entered a   man in.the room that might be.INF the speaker
　　　　 convidado.
　　　　 invited
　　　　 'A man who might be the invited speaker entered the room.'

　　　 b. *Um homem entrou na   sala que deve ser   o   orador.
　　　　　 a   man   entered in.the room that might be.INF the speaker
　　　　 invited
　　　　 convidado.

In contrast, RRC-extraposition from a post-verbal subject does not seem to be
allowed with non-monoargumental verbs taking a direct object as complement.

As illustrated in (271)–(272), RRC-extraposition cannot take place if a direct object intervenes between the antecedent and the RRC.[4]

(271)   *Ontem   quando entrei   no   parque de estacionamento,
        yesterday when   entered.1SG in.the parking lot
        roubavam três   rapazes um carro que são amigos do   meu filho.
        stole.3PL three boys   a   car   that are friends of.the my   son
        'Yesterday when I entered the parking lot, there were three boys that are my
        son's friends stealing a car.'

(272)   *Quando cheguei   ao   aeroporto, vendiam três   rapazes o
        when   arrived.1SG at.the airport   sold   three boys   the
        Borda D'Água que não tinham mais de   cinco anos.
        B.   D.   that not had   more DE.PREP five   years
        'When I arrived at the airport, there were three boys that were less than five
        years old selling the *Borda D'Água* [an almanac].'

B. Discourse dedicated positions in the left periphery

In CEP, extraposed RRCs can take a wh-constituent (see (273)–(274)), a preposed emphatic/evaluative phrase (in the sense of Raposo 1995 and Ambar 1999) (see (275)) and a preposed focus[5] (see (276)–(280)) as an antecedent.

---

[4] In CEP, non-monoargumental verbs only allow for the VSO order in particular syntactic or semantic environments (see Martins forthcoming). Importantly, the VSO order is available in the syntactic environment displayed in (271) and (272), where a root sentence containing the verb in the imperfect is articulated with an adverbial clause that locates the situation described by the VSO sentence in the speaker's perceptual field (Martins forthcoming). The possibility of the VSO order in this syntactic environment is illustrated in (i) and (ii).

(i)   Ontem   quando entrei   no   parque de estacionamento,
      yesterday when   entered.1SG in.the parking lot
      roubavam três   rapazes um   carro.
      stole   three   boys   a   car
      'Yesterday when I entered the parking lot, there were three boys stealing a car.'

(ii) Quando cheguei   ao   aeroporto, vendiam três   rapazes o
      when   arrived.1SG at.the airport   sold   three boys   the
      Borda   D'Água.
      B.   D.
      'When I arrived at the airport, there were three boys selling the *Borda D'Água* [an almanac].'

[5] In line with the approach to focus adopted in this book (see §1.3.3.1), the term *preposed focus* (or *fronted focus*) is used here to refer to a constituent that undergoes emphatic/contrastive focus movement to the left periphery of the sentence, as in the following example, repeated from (85).

      COM ESTAS PALAVRAS me   despeço.
      with these   words   me.CL say.goodbye.1SG
      'It is with these words that I say goodbye.'

The fact that the preposed constituent in examples (276)–(280) has an emphatic/contrastive focus status (and not, for instance, a topic status) can be confirmed by some of the syntactic and interpretational tests provided by Costa and Martins (2011): (1) the cleft-like interpretation, which is made visible in the relevant paraphrase (see (278)); (2) the proclisis configuration (see o 'him.CL' in (278)); and (3) sensitivity to

Wh-constituent:

(273)   Quantas   pessoas apareceram que não foram convidadas?
         how.many people showed.up that not were   invited
         'How many people showed up who were not invited?'

(274)   Quantas   pessoas é que tu   conheces que não viram este jogo?
         how.many people is that you know   that not saw   this game
         'How many people do you know that did not see this game?'

Emphatic/evaluative phrase:

(275)   Muito whisky o   João bebeu que estava fora do   prazo!
         a.lot.of whisky the J.   drank that was   out of.the expiry.date
         'João drank a lot of whisky that was expired!'

Preposed focus:[6]

(276)   Poucas pessoas conheço   que fazem interpolação, mas todas elas
         few   people know.1SG that make interpolation but all   they
         produzem coisas deste tipo.
         produce things of.this type
         'I know few people who produce interpolation [structures], but all of them
         produce things like this.'

(277)   Nem uma única pessoa apareceu   que estivesse interessada em
         not a   single person showed.up that be.SBJV interested in
         colaborar.
         collaborate.INF
         'Not even a single person showed up that was interested in collaborating.'

___

referential properties of fronted constituents (see the negative words in (277), (279)). Finally, a preposed focus may contain a focus operator (such as *só* 'only' in (280)), which cannot easily be associated with a topicalized constituent. For a more detailed application of the relevant tests, see §1.3.3.1.

  [6] Although the examples in (276)–(280) display RRC-extraposition in main clauses, it is worth noting that RRC-extraposition from a preposed focus is also found in dependent clauses, as in (i) and (ii).

(i)   É certo   que novos horizontes se   vão abrir   que lhe
       is certain that new   horizons SE.CL go open.INF that him.CL
       permitirão expandir o   negócio.
       allow.FUT expand.INF the business
       'It is certain that new horizons will open up to him that will allow him to expand the business.'

(ii)   Acho   que nem uma única pessoa apareceu   que estivesse
       think.1SG that not a   single person showed.up that be.SBJV
       interessada em colaborar.
       interested in collaborate.INF
       'I think that not even a single girl showed up that was interested in collaborating.'

(278)   Uma estranha doença o   atingiu que lhe   retirou toda a alegria.
       a   strange   disease him.cl hit   that him.cl took   all   the joy
       'It was a strange disease (that hit him) that deprived him of all joy.'

(279)   Nada   fiz   que pusesse em causa   a   tua   decisão.
       nothing made.1sg that put.sbjv in   question the your decision
       'I have done nothing that would call your decision into question.'

(280)   Só   um homem havia na   terra que sabia tudo.
       only a   man   had   in.the earth that knew everything
       'There was only one man in the earth that knew everything.'

However, RRC-extraposition is incompatible with topicalization;[7] see the contrasts in (281) and (282).[8]

(281)   a.   Pessoas que não tinham bilhete, apareceram às centenas!
         people that not had   ticket   showed.up by hundreds
         'People who did not have a ticket showed up by the hundreds!'

      b.   *Pessoas, apareceram às centenas que não tinham bilhete!
         people showed.up by hundreds that not had   ticket

(282)   a.   Pessoas que praticam yoga, também conheço.
         people that practice yoga also   know.1sg
         'I also know people who practice yoga.'

      b.   *Pessoas, também conheço que praticam yoga.
         people also   know.1sg that practice yoga (Ernestina Carrilho, p.c.)

3.4.1.3 Prepositional phrases   In CEP, it is not possible to extrapose an RRC from the object of a preposition in sentences such as (283)–(287).[9] In these examples, the PP containing the antecedent is either an adjunct (see (283)–(284)), a complement of

---

[7] As mentioned in §1.3.3.4, the term *topicalization* is used in this book to refer to topic-comment structures where the topic is syntactically connected with an empty category inside the comment (see Duarte 1987 and subsequent work).

[8] Based on the contrast between RRC-extraposition from preposed foci and topics (Cardoso 2010), Costa and Martins (2011) adopt relative clause extraposition as a test for distinguishing topicalization from contrastive focus fronting in CEP (see §1.3.3.1).

[9] An anonymous reviewer remarks that he/she accepts RRC-extraposition from PP complements in CEP. However, for me and the informants I consulted, the configurations of RRC-extraposition in (283)–(287) are ungrammatical. Given these contrasting judgments, it would be important to test experimentally the well-formedness of sentences involving RRC-extraposition from PPs, controlling the eventual ambiguity between the restrictive/appositive reading. This experiment is, however, left for future research.

the verb (see (285)–(286)), or a complement of the noun (see (287)).[10] As shown in the b examples, the sentences are fine with the normal (non-extraposed) order.

PP adjunct:

(283) a. *Vi   essa notícia numa revista   <u>ontem</u>   que estava em cima
           saw.1SG that news   in.a   magazine yesterday that was   in   top
           da   mesa.
           of.the table
           'Yesterday, I saw that news in a magazine that was lying on the table.'

       b. Ontem   vi   essa notícia numa revista   que estava em cima
           yesterday saw.1SG that news   in.a   magazine that was   in   top
           da   mesa.
           of.the table

(284) a. *O Pedro morreu num atentado <u>ontem</u>   que causou mais de   100
           the P.   died   in.a attack yesterday that caused more than 100
           mortos.
           deaths
           'Yesterday, Pedro died in an attack that caused more than 100 deaths.'

       b. O Pedro morreu ontem   num atentado que causou mais de   100
           the P.   died   yesterday in.a attack that caused more than 100
           mortos.
           deaths

PP complement of V:

(285) a. *Falei   com um deputado <u>ontem</u>   que subscreveu essa proposta.
           spoke.1SG with a   member yesterday that endorsed   that proposal
           'Yesterday, I spoke to a member of the Parliament that endorsed that proposal.'

       b. Falei   ontem   com um deputado que subscreveu essa proposta.
           spoke.3SG yesterday with a   member that endorsed   that proposal

---

[10] Note that (287) involves extraposition from a PP within a DP.

(286) a. *Agradeci a algumas pessoas <u>ontem</u> que foram fundamentais
thanked.1SG to some people yesterday that were crucial
para a realização deste projeto.
to the execution of.this project
'Yesterday, I thanked some people that were crucial to this project.'

b. Agradeci ontem a algumas pessoas que foram fundamentais
thanked.1SG yesterday to some people that were crucial
para a realização deste projeto.
to the execution of.this project

PP complement of N:

(287) a. *Vi as filhas de um rapaz <u>ontem</u> que joga no Benfica
saw.1SG the daughters of a guy yesterday that plays in.the B.
'Yesterday, I saw the daughters of a guy that plays for Benfica.'

b. Vi ontem as filhas de um rapaz que joga no Benfica.
saw.1SG yesterday the daughters of a guy that plays in.the B.

3.4.1.4 Summary In this section, I have shown that RRC-extraposition is subject
to specific restrictions in CEP, which are summarized in Table 3.1 (the use of a plus
(+) denotes that RRC-extraposition can occur in the relevant context; a minus (–)
indicates that it cannot).

3.4.2 Cross-linguistic evidence
Interestingly, in a brief survey of the behavior of extraposition in different languages,
it becomes clear that the restrictions that hold for RRC-extraposition in CEP do not
universally apply. Some of the relevant cross-linguistic contrasts are presented in
§§3.4.2.1–3.

TABLE 3.1 **Extraposition of restrictive relatives: Contemporary European Portuguese**

Empirical issue		CEP
A. Extraposition from strong noun phrases		–
B. Extraposition from pre-verbal positions	subjects	–
	wh-constituents	+
	emphatic/evaluative phrases	+
	preposed foci	+
	topics	–
C. Extraposition from PPs		–

3.4.2.1 The definiteness effect   Not all languages exhibit the definiteness effect found in CEP. Extraposition from strong noun phrases is not possible in Italian, French, and Spanish, but it is possible, for example, in English,[11] Dutch, and German.

Italian:

(288) *Ho   regalato quel libro <u>a Carlo</u> che mi   avevi consigliato   tu.
       have.1SG given   that book to C.   that me.CL had   recommended you
       'I gave Carlo that book that you recommended to me.' (Cardinaletti 1987: 44
       n. 4; gloss and translation mine)

French:

(289) *La   radio   <u>a   été   volée,</u> que   tu   m'as   donné.
        the   radio   has   been   stolen   that you   me.CL.have   given
        'The radio that you gave me was stolen.' (Smits 1988: 332; gloss and
        translation mine)

Spanish:

(290) *Escribió   la   columna <u>en la   prensa la   semana pasada</u> en la   que
        wrote.3SG the   column   in the press   the week   last   in the that
        se   quejaba   amargamente de su   situación.
        SE.CL complained.3SG bitterly   of his situation
        'Last week s/he wrote in the press the column in which he complained
        bitterly about his situation.' (Brucart 1999: 465; gloss and translation mine)

(291) *De repente, apareció   el   individuo <u>en la   reunión</u> que parecía
        suddenly   showed.up the man   in the meeting   that seemed
        sacado de   una película de terror.
        taken from a movie   of horror
        'Suddenly the man who seemed to be taken from a horror movie showed
        up.' (Brucart 1999: 465; gloss and translation mine)

English:

(292) The woman <u>came in yesterday</u> that I told you about. (Givón 2001: 206)

(293) Those students <u>will pass this course</u> who complete all of their assignments on
       time. (Baltin 2006: 243)

---

[11] Note, however, that, according to Diesing (1992: 144 n. 23), there is variability in speakers' grammaticality judgments of extraposed RRCs with definite noun phrases as antecedent. See also Ziv and Cole (1974: 781) and Baltin (2006: 243).

(294)   That loaf <u>was stale</u> that you sold me. (Quirk, Greenbaum, Leech, and Svartvik 1985: 1397)

(295)   She rapidly spotted the book <u>right on my desk</u> that I had been desperately searching for all the morning. (Quirk, Greenbaum, Leech, and Svartvik 1985: 1398)

Dutch:

(296)   Ik heb de man <u>gezien</u> die zijn tas verloor.
      I   have the man seen   who his bag lost
      'I have seen the man who lost his bag.' (De Vries 2002: 65)

German:

(297)   als   sie endlich selbst über die Musikt <u>erzählen darf</u>, die sie macht
      when she finally herself about the music tell   may that she makes
      'when she finally is allowed to speak herself about the music that she makes'
      (from Strunk 2007: 51)

3.4.2.2 Pre-verbal positions

A. Pre-verbal subjects

Barbosa, Duarte, and Kato (2005) and Barbosa (2009) report that RRC-extraposition from a pre-verbal subject position is possible in some languages (e.g. English and French). However, it is impossible in Spanish, Catalan, and Italian (as well as CEP) (see (298)–(299)). According to these authors, this cross-linguistic contrast correlates with the Null Subject Parameter (see §3.3).[12]

(298)   a. A man <u>arrived</u> that wants to talk to you. [English]
      b. Un homme <u>est arrivé</u> qui veut te parler. [French] (both Barbosa 2009: 43)

(299)   a. *Un hombre <u>apareció</u> que dice que quiere hablar contigo. [Spanish]
      b. *Un home <u>va venir</u> que volia parlar amb tu. [Catalan]
      c. *Un uomo <u>è arrivato</u> che vuole parlarti. [Italian] (all Barbosa 2009: 43)

Dutch and German pattern with English and French with respect to this property, as illustrated in (300)–(301).

(300)   Iemand   heft me een boek <u>gegeven</u> die ik niet Ken
      someone has me a   book given   who I not know
      'Someone gave me a book who I do not know.' (De Vries 2002: 244)

---

[12] In §3.5.2.2, I show that the correlation between the Null Subject Parameter and the possibility of RRC-extraposition is simply not correct and must be revised.

German:

(301) weil eine Frau   gehustet hat, die mit einem Porsche kam
      since a woman coughed has who with a   P.   came
      'since a woman coughed who came with a Porsche' (Meinunger 2000: 208)

B. Discourse dedicated positions in the left periphery

As with CEP, some Germanic languages allow RRC-extraposition from a
wh-constituent (see (302) from English and (303) from Dutch), an emphatic/
evaluative phrase (see (304) from English and (305) from Dutch), and a preposed
focus (see (306) from English and (307) from Dutch).

Wh-constituent:

(302) a. Who do you know that you can really trust?
      b. Which argument do you know that Sandy thought was unconvincing?
         (both Kiss 2003: 110)

(303) Hoeveel   kinderen ken jij die niet van snoepjes houden?
      how.many children know you that not of sweets like
      'How many children do you know that do not like sweets?' (Smits 1988: 195;
      gloss and translation mine)

Emphatic/evaluative phrase:

(304) People lose their eyesight when they don't take support of the STD's and
      much more things can happen that are far worse than losing your eyesight.
      (from a blog on infectious diseases)

(305) Heel veel   mensen hebben een verre reis geboekt die daar eigenlijk
      very many people have   a   far trip booked who there actually
      niet het geld   voor hebben.
      not the money for have
      'A lot of people booked a long journey who in fact didn't have enough money
      for it.' (Mark de Vries, p.c.)

Preposed focus:[13]

(306) %Not even one painting did I see which would please Laura. (Smits 1988: 195)

(307) Alleen die   bloemen kon hij benoemen, die zijn moeder hem
      only those flowers could he identify   that his mother him
      vroeger had aangewezen.
      formerly had pointed.out
      'Only those flowers could he identify, that his mother had once pointed out to
      him.' (Smits 1988: 380; gloss mine)

---

[13] Smits (1988) uses the symbol '%' to indicate that it is a highly formal and marked construction.

Beatrice Santorini (p.c.) reports to me that RRC-extraposition from emphatic/ evaluative phrases and preposed foci is also attested in the diachrony of English. By way of illustration, see (308)–(310).

Emphatic/evaluative phrase:

(308)   Many more such worthie iniunctions and honourable ordinances I obserued, which are hardly worth pen and inke the describing (17th c., *PPCEME*)

Preposed focus:

(309)   Two or three things I recollected when it was too late, that I might have told you (19th c., *PPCMBE*)

(310)   One thing I had almost forgot which the mention of the girls brought into my minde (17th c., *PPCEME*)

However, just like CEP, English does not allow RRC-extraposition from topics (see (311c)).

(311)   a. I like micro brews that are located around the Bay Area.
        b. Micro brews that are located around the Bay Area, I like.
        c. *Micro brews, I like that are located around the Bay Area. (all Kiss 2003: 110)

The same seems to be true of Dutch, as illustrated in example (312) (involving hanging topic left dislocation).[14]

(312)   *Die   meisjes, ik ken   ze   niet die   uit   Lissabon komen.
         those girls   I   know them not that from   L.   come
         lit. 'Those girls, I don't know them, that are from Lisbon.' (Mark de Vries, p.c.)

3.4.2.3 Prepositional phrases   The restriction on RRC-extraposition from PPs does not equally apply to all languages. It is reported in the literature that extraposed RRCs can take the object of a preposition as the antecedent, for example, in English, Dutch, and German.

English:

(313)   John is going to talk [to someone] tomorrow who he had a lot of faith in. (Kayne 1994: 126)

---

[14] There is a possible terminological confusion here. Recall that there is a difference between the traditional notion of topicalization and the topic position in a cartographic sense (see §1.3.3.4). Earlier claims (Smits 1988; De Vries 2002; among others) that RRC-extraposition can take place from a topic position (say, [Spec, CP]) must not be understood as extraposition from an aboutness topic. Rather, it concerns the extraposition from a constituent in first position. As shown in the main text, such constituents are always affected by focus in some way or another (e.g. wh and contrastive foci). Therefore, it may be better to speak of focalization rather than topicalization in these cases.

Dutch:

(314)   Ik heb [op een plek] gelopen waar jij   ook bent geweest.
         I have on a   spot walked where you also have been
         'I have walked on a spot where you also have been.' (De Vries 2002: 244)

German:

(315)   weil er auf eine Frau   gewartet hat, die einen Porsche fährt
         since he for a   woman waited   has who a   P.   drives
         'since he has been waiting for a woman who drives a Porsche' (Meinunger
         2000: 208)

De Vries (2002: 246) also reports that RRC-extraposition in Dutch may take place
from a PP within a DP.

Dutch:

(316)   Ik heb [de papieren van *de man*] gecontroleerd die een rode jas droeg
         I have the papers of the man checked   who a   red coat wore
         'I have checked the papers of the man who wore a red coat.'

3.4.2.4 Summary   Although this overview has several limitations in terms of cross-
linguistic coverage (because it primarily draws on data reported in the literature), it
offers important empirical evidence showing that languages do not behave uniformly
with respect to RRC-extraposition.

One important conclusion that emerges from the data reported in §§3.4.1 and 3.4.2
is that CEP contrasts sharply with some Germanic languages (e.g. English and Dutch)
as far as the properties of RRC-extraposition are concerned. An overview of
the contrasting properties is provided in Table 3.2 (the use of a plus indicates that
RRC-extraposition can occur in the relevant context; a minus indicates that it cannot).

Another interesting conclusion is that Romance languages do not behave in a
uniform manner. On the basis of the limited data that I collected from the literature,
it is possible to identify the contrasts displayed in Table 3.3.

Strikingly, French exhibits a peculiar behavior. It contrasts with other Romance
languages in allowing extraposition from a pre-verbal position (see Table 3.3), but it
also contrasts with Germanic languages in not allowing extraposition from strong
noun phrases. This seems to be a rather puzzling set of restrictions, but from this, it
emerges (at least for now) that not all Romance languages behave equally and that
there may be other factors that additionally contribute to the contrasts presented
in Table 3.3.

TABLE 3.2 **Extraposition of restrictive relatives: Cross-linguistic contrasts**

Empirical issue		CEP	English	Dutch
A. Extraposition from strong noun phrases		−	+	+
B. Extraposition from pre-verbal positions	subjects	−	+	+
	wh-constituents	+	+	+
	emphatic/evaluative phrases	+	+	+
	preposed foci	+	+	+
	topics	−	−	−
C. Extraposition from PPs		−	+	+

TABLE 3.3 **Extraposition of restrictive relatives: Romance languages**

Empirical issue	CEP	Italian	Spanish	French
A. Extraposition from strong noun phrases	−	−	−	−
B. Extraposition from pre-verbal subjects	−	−	−	+

3.4.3 *Earlier stages of Portuguese*

In this section, I show that CEP and earlier stages of Portuguese behave differently with respect to RRC-extraposition. The historical data from Portuguese that support this view are presented in §3.4.3.1–3.

3.4.3.1 The definiteness effect Earlier stages of Portuguese pattern with CEP in allowing extraposition from weak noun phrases, as illustrated in (317)–(318).

Subject:

(317) Junto das casas [...] sta hũa llata   <u>ante a porta</u> que
        near to.the houses   is a   ±grapevine before the door that
        dara.FUT hũs anos pollos outros çinquo allmudes de vinho.
        give   some years by.the others five a.   of wine
        'Near the houses there is a grapevine before the door that on average will
        give five *allmudes* [medieval agrarian measure] of wine.' (16th c., Martins
        2001: 309)

Object:

(318) e   mãdo.   huno casale ad Monasterium in quo   morat Michael de
       and leave.1SG a   hamlet to monastery in which lives   M.   d.
       souto
       S.
       'and I leave a hamlet to the monastery in which Michael de Souto lives' (13th
       c., Martins 2001: 105)

However, unlike CEP, earlier periods of Portuguese allow for extraposed RRCs with
strong noun phrases as antecedents, as illustrated in (319)–(322).[15]

Subject:

(319) As chagas erã   muytas de   que se   uertia muyta sangue
       the sores   were many from that SE.CL shed a.lot.of blood
       'There were many sores from which a lot of blood was being shed.' (14th c.,
       Brocardo 2006: 45)

(320) mas aquelle dia sem   falha aveo que forom i   todos
       but that   day without fail came that went there all
       'but the day in which everyone went there came without fail' (13th c.
       [transmitted by a 15th-c. MS], Martins, Pereira, and Cardoso 2014–15)

(321) de tal homẽ como aquel será   que esta spada ha de   trazer
       of such man as   that be.FUT that this sword has DE.PREP carry.INF
       'of such a man as the one who will carry this sword will be' (13th c.
       [transmitted by a 15th-c. MS], Martins, Pereira, and Cardoso 2014–15)

Object:

(322) «Vede   lo escudo aqui que demandades.»
       see.IMP.2PL the shield here that look.for.2PL
       'See here the shield that you are looking for.' (13th c. [transmitted by a 15th-c.
       MS], Martins, Pereira, and Cardoso 2014–15)

3.4.3.2 *Pre-verbal positions*

A. Pre-verbal subjects

Earlier stages of Portuguese and CEP behave alike in allowing RRC-extraposition
from post-verbal subjects (see e.g. (317)). However, in contrast to CEP, earlier

---

[15] Brucart (1999) reports that extraposition from strong noun phrases is also possible in earlier stages of
Spanish:

Aquel decimos ser   mejor médico, que mejor cura y   más enfermos sana.
that say.1PL be.INF better doctor that better heals and more patients cures
'We say that the better doctor is the one who heals (the diseases) better and cures more patients.' (16th c.,
from Brucart 1999: 466; gloss and translation mine)

stages of Portuguese allowed for extraposed RRCs with pre-verbal subjects as ante-cedents, as illustrated in (323)–(328) (examples (323)–(325) are repeated for ease of exposition).

(323) se Algẽ   A eles   veer   que diga   que llʃ   eu Alguna
       if someone to them come.FUT.SBJV that says.SBJV that him.CL I some
       cousa diuía
       thing owed
       'if someone who says that I owed him something comes towards them' (13th c., *DCMP*)

(324) E   mando   que se outra   mãda pareçer   que eu mãndasse
       and order.1SG that if another will   appear.FUT.SBJV that I order.SBJV
       fazer   ante   dessta que quebre   e   nõ ualha.
       make.INF before this   that break.SBJV and not be.valid.SBJV
       'And, if another will appear that I have ordered to be made before this one, I order it to be annulled and not valid.' (14th c., Martins 2001: 464)

(325) que cayam.   e   cayades   na   pea   que filhos   e
       that fall.SBJV.3PL and fall.SBJV.2PL in.the punishment that children and
       netos   deuẽ a   caer.   que contra bééço de padre
       grandchildren should A.PREP fall.INF that against blessing of father
       uéérem
       come.FUT.SBJV
       '[and I order] that they and you receive the punishment that the children and grandchildren who go against their father's blessing should receive' (13th c., *DCMP*)

(326) se alguu   for   asy de mia parte como d' estraya que a uos
       if someone be.FUT.SBJV either of my side as   of strange that to you.CL
       queyra   cõtrastar   seya   maldito
       want.SBJV go.against.INF be.SBJV damn
       'if there is someone either from my side or from a strange side that wants to go against you, (I want him) damned' (13th c., Maia 1986: 73–4)

(327) Como Galuam se   salvou e   como a   donzella disse que algũus
       how G.   SE.CL escaped and how the damsel   said that some
       a   creriam que a   nom creiam.
       her.CL believed that her.CL not believed
       'How Galuam escaped and how the damsel said that some (people) believed her that (actually) did not believe her.' (13th c. [transmitted by a 15th-c. MS], Martins, Pereira, and Cardoso 2014–15)

(328) ca   de muitos que ja   i   seerom nunca i   tal <u>foi</u> que
       because of many   that already there were   never there such was that
       i   nom fosse   morto
       there not be.SBJV killed
       'because among the many people who have been there, there was no one who
       has not been killed' (13th c. [transmitted by a 15th-c. MS], Martins, Pereira,
       and Cardoso 2014–15)

B. Discourse dedicated positions in the left periphery

Earlier stages of Portuguese pattern with CEP in allowing extraposition from a wh-
constituent (see (329)–(330)), a preposed emphatic/evaluative phrase (see (331)),
and a preposed focus (see (332)–(335)).

Wh-constituent:

(329) Que caso /<u>pod'esse ser</u>   em que tanto   sopesais?
       what case can.that be.INF in that so.much think.2PL
       'What case can that be that you think so much about?' (16th c., Camões 1999)

(330) Já   sei   que [...] me   perguntará qual Mestre <u>conheço eu</u>
       already know.1SG that   me.CL ask.FUT   which master know   I
       que tenha   toda esta erudição.
       that have.SBJV all this erudition
       'I already know that you will ask me which master I know that has all this
       erudition.' (18th c., *TYC*)

Emphatic/evaluative phrase:

(331) Muitos letrados <u>sei   eu</u> (disse Solino) que não são moços
       many   lettered know I   said S.   that not are young
       'I know many lettered men (said Solino) who are not young.' (17th c., *TYC*)

Preposed focus:

(332) El-rey$_i$ jurou [...] que ja   cousa <u>lhe$_i$ nom pederia</u>
       the.king swore   that from.that.on thing him.CL not ask.COND.3SG
       que ele$_i$ podesse haver   que lha   nom desse
       that he   can.SBJV have.INF that him.CL.it.CL not give.SBJV
       'The king swore that he would give anything in his power that he [Hipocras]
       asked for' (13th c. [transmitted by a 16th-c. MS], Martins, Pereira, and
       Cardoso 2013–15)

(333)   nẽhũua arte nem multidoem de covas <u>lhe   prestar   podia</u> que
        no   art nor lot   of lairs him.CL be.useful.INF could that
        logo   nom fossem tomadas
        immediately not be.SBJV taken
        'there was no art or lairs useful to him that were not immediately taken' (15th
        c., Macchi 1975: 5)

(334)   nada   <u>nos acontece</u> que não tenha   já   acontecido
        nothing us.CL happen   that not have.SBJV already happened
        'nothing happens to us that has not already happened' (17th c., *TYC*)

(335)   Todos falam da   economia, e   pouca gente <u>tenho   visto</u> que
        all   speak of.the economy   and few   people have.1SG seen   that
        tenha   uma idéia distinta desta   ciência
        have.SBJV a   idea clear   of.this science
        'Everyone talks about the economy, but I have seen few people who have a
        clear idea about this science.' (18th c., *TYC*)

By contrast, if a topic is involved, RRC-extraposition does not seem to be possible in
earlier stages of Portuguese, at least in the corpus inspected thus far.[16]

C. Scrambled objects

Aside from the contexts demonstrated thus far, there is another important source of
RRC-extraposition in the history of Portuguese that is not available in CEP: IP-
scrambling.[17]

IP-scrambling is an optional syntactic process whereby a constituent scrambles
past the verb. This is illustrated in the contrast provided in (336). In (336a), the OV
order involves a scrambled object (marked in boldface), whereas in (336b), the VO
order involves a non-scrambled object surfacing in its base position.

(336)   a. sse pela   uẽtujra uos   alguẽ   **a dita**   vỹa   enbargar
           if by.the chance you.CL someone the mentioned vineyard block.FUT.SBJV
           'and if by chance someone blocks the vineyard from you'

---

[16] I found only one example that could be taken as involving RRC-extraposition from topic:

Esta barca <u>onde vai agora / que</u> assim   está apercebida?
this boat   where goes now   QUE this.way is   equipped (16th c., Camões 1999)

Note, however, that this example may instead involve a coordinate clause, introduced by the coordinating
conjunction *que*, meaning 'since, as'; in this case it would correspond to the paraphrase: 'Where does this boat
go, as it is so well equipped?' In this respect, it is also worth pointing out that Martins (2002) suggests that
topicalization (as opposed to focalization) may not be a grammatical option in earlier stages of Portuguese.

[17] Following common practice, I distinguish two types of scrambling in this study: *short scrambling* (i.e.
scrambling to VP) and *middle scrambling* (i.e. scrambling to IP). There is another type of scrambling (*long
distance scrambling*, involving movement across a CP boundary), which is not addressed here (see Takano
1998 and references therein).

b. sse pela uẽtujra uos alguẽ enbargar a dita vỹa
   if by.the chance you.CL someone block.FUT.SBJV the mentioned vineyard
   (13th c., both from Martins 2002: 234)

According to Martins (2002), IP-scrambling consists of the movement of various types of constituent to multiple specifier positions available in the IP domain. This movement has a prosodic/discourse motivation; it allows the scrambled constituent to escape the default focus stress (and the information focus interpretation). Martins (2002) claims that the prosodic/discourse approach to scrambling explains why it imposes no restrictions on the categorial status of the scrambled constituent. By way of illustration, consider examples (337)–(339), where the scrambled constituent is (respectively) a PP, an adjectival phrase, and a past participle. The scrambled element is highlighted in bold for ease of reading.

(337) de quẽ lhe **ssobre elle** embargo poser
       from whoever him.CL over it obstruction put.FUT.SBJV
       '[protecting him] from whoever tries to block it [the land] from him' (16th c., from Martins 2002: 244)

(338) todollos adubyos que lhes **conpridoiros e neçesareos** forem
       all.the fertilizers that them.CL due and necessary be.SBJV
       'all sorts of fertilizers that the land may need' (15th c., from Martins 2002: 245)

(339) com os lauradores que as **ssemeadas** teuerẽ
       with the farmers that them.CL cultivated have.FUT.SBJV.3PL
       'with the farmers who have the lands cultivated' (15th c., from Martins 2002: 245)

Crucially, IP-scrambling in earlier stages of Portuguese can generate RRC-extraposition, as illustrated in (340)–(341).

(340) que llʃ eu **Alguna cousa** diuía que nõ seia escripto en Esta
       that him.CL I some thing owed that not be.SBJV written in this
       mãda
       will
       '(And if there arrives someone who says) that I owed him something which is not written in this will...' (13th c., *DCMP*)

(341) E pera **todalas cousas** e cada hũa delas ffaser que
       and to all.the things and each one of.them make.INF that
       uerdadeyro e líjdemo procurador pode e deue ffaser
       real and legitimate proxy can and should make.INF
       'And to make all the things and each one of them that a real and legitimate proxy can and should make...' (14th c., Martins 2001: 406)

The scrambling of *Alguna cousa* lit. 'something' in (340) is confirmed by the relative position of this constituent with respect to the verb and the clitic. According to

Martins (2002), clitics in clauses with interpolation set the border between left-dislocated/focused constituents and scrambled constituents. Hence, in (340), because *Alguna cousa* 'something' is interpolated (i.e. occurs between the proclitic and the verb), it is necessarily a scrambled constituent.

3.4.3.3 Prepositional phrases   Unlike CEP, earlier stages of Portuguese allow for RRC-extraposition from the object of a preposition, as illustrated in (342)–(347) (examples (345)–(346) are repeated from (250)–(251), respectively).

(342)   e   logo   lhj   abríu   [de todo]   <u>mão</u> que sseu era
        and   immediately   him.CL   opened   of everything   hand that his was
        'and immediately he gave him (= lit. opened hand of) everything that he had'
        (14th c., from Martins 2001: 198)

(343)   E   filhoua   [de   hũa camara]   <u>per força</u> hu   jazia com grande
        and   took.her.CL   from a   room   by   force   where   was   with large
        companha de donas e   de donzellas.
        group   of ladies and of damsels
        'And he took her by force from a room where she was with a large group of
        ladies and damsels.' (13th c. [transmitted by a 15th-c. MS], Martins, Pereira,
        and Cardoso 2014–15)

(344)   e   deitousse   [sob   hũũ carualho] <u>por folgar</u>   que staua
        and   lay.down.3SG.SE.CL   under a   oak   to   rest.INF that was
        ante   a   porta da   ermida.
        in.front.of the door of.the chapel
        'and he lay down under an oak that was in front of the chapel door' (13th c.
        [transmitted by a 15th-c. MS], Martins, Pereira, and Cardoso 2014–15)

(345)   que [en aquela hora] <u>morrera</u>   en que el vira   estando longe
        that in that   hour die.PPRF.3SG   in that he see.PPRF   be.GER   away
        dele   que lhi   saira   a   alma do   corpo
        from.him   that him.CL fall.out.PPRF.3SG the soul of.the body
        '[and he realized that] he had died in the hour in which he had seen (being
        away from him) that his soul had fallen out of his body' (14th c., from
        Mattos e Silva 1989: 766)

(346)   [naquela hora] <u>o   seu filho ficara   sen   féver</u> en que hi   o   nosso
        in.that hour   the his son stay.PPRF without fever in that there the our
        Salvador e   nosso meestre Jesu Cristo dissera   que era   são
        Savior   and our   master J.   C.   say.PPRF that was.3SG healed
        'his son had stopped having fever in that hour that our Savior and Master
        Jesus Christ had said that he was healed' (14th c., from Mattos e Silva
        1989: 766)

(347) que [de mui poucos] <u>sabemos</u> que bebessem   vinho
      that of very few   know.1PL that drink.SBJV.3PL wine
      '[the sobriety and moderation of our kings is so praised] that we know of very
      few who drink wine' (17th c., *TYC*)

3.4.3.4 Summary   In this section, I have shown that earlier stages of Portuguese are
less restrictive than CEP with respect to RRC-extraposition. Table 3.4 summarizes
the relevant contrasting properties.

On the basis of a cross-linguistic comparison, another relevant conclusion that can
be drawn from this study is that earlier stages of Portuguese are (to a large extent)
Germanic-like, unlike CEP, as shown in Table 3.5.

TABLE 3.4 Extraposition of restrictive relatives: Different stages of Portuguese

Empirical issue		CEP	Earlier stages of Portuguese
A. Extraposition from strong noun phrases		−	+
B. Extraposition from pre-verbal positions	subjects	−	+
	wh-constituents	+	+
	emphatic/evaluative phrases	+	+
	preposed foci	+	+
	topics	−	−
C. Extraposition from PPs		−	+

TABLE 3.5 Extraposition of restrictive relatives: Cross-linguistic overview

Empirical issue		CEP	Earlier stages of Portuguese	English	Dutch
A. Extraposition from strong noun phrases		−	+	+	+
B. Extraposition from pre-verbal positions	subjects	−	+	+	+
	wh-constituents	+	+	+	+
	emphatic/evaluative phrases	+	+	+	+
	preposed foci	+	+	+	+
	topics	−	−	−	−
C. Extraposition from PPs		−	+	+	+

The contrasts outlined in Table 3.5 are not accidental and clearly call for an explanation. In Section 3.4.2.2A, the hypothesis is raised that some of these contrasts may correlate with the Null Subject Parameter. However, such a hypothesis must be discarded in the face of the data discussed in §3.4.3. The reasoning goes as follows: Portuguese has always been a Null Subject Language over the course of its history; hence, the fact that earlier periods of Portuguese (unlike CEP) allowed for extraposition out of pre-verbal subjects shows that the contrasting properties cannot be explained via the Null Subject Parameter. I return to this issue in §3.5.2.2.

Alternatively, in §§3.5–6 I suggest that the cross-linguistic contrasts outlined in Table 3.5 can be straightforwardly explained by a dual approach to RRC-extraposition. In particular, I contend that the diachronic (and cross-linguistic) data considered thus far provide strong empirical evidence in favor of the hypothesis that different stages of the same language (and languages in general) may resort to different strategies of RRC-extraposition.

3.5 A proposal for contemporary European Portuguese

In this section, I propose that the properties of RRC-extraposition in CEP can be accounted for in terms of the stranding analysis proposed by Kayne (1994). Section 3.5.1 establishes the basic tenets of the stranding analysis of extraposition. It also introduces the key to the present proposal: RRC-extraposition in CEP always involves leftward movement of the antecedent, either via movement to the left periphery (see §3.5.1.1) or via short scrambling (see §3.5.1.2). A closer inspection of the constituents that appear in the intervening position is provided in §3.5.1.3. Section 3.5.2 demonstrates how this theoretical apparatus accounts for the contrasting properties of RRC-extraposition outlined in §3.4.1. In §3.5.3, I examine nine arguments that have been adduced in the literature against the stranding analysis, showing that they do not offer any insurmountable obstacle to the approach proposed here. Finally, §3.5.4 presents concluding remarks.

3.5.1 The stranding analysis

Following Kayne (1994) and Bianchi (1999), I assume that RRCs are generated by the *raising analysis*, as depicted in (348) (for more details on the raising analysis see §1.3.2.4B).

(348)   a. $[_{DP} [_{D} \text{ the}] [_{CP} \text{ book}_i [_{C'} \text{ that } [I \text{ read } t_i]]]]$ (*that-relatives*)
        b. $[_{DP} [_{D} \text{ the}] [_{CP} \text{ book}_i [\text{which } t_i]]_j [_{C'} C [I \text{ read } t_j]]]$ (*wh-relatives*)

Moreover, I adopt Kayne's (1994) view that RRC-extraposition is the result of VP-internal stranding. Under this approach, the antecedent is base-generated inside the

RRC and undergoes leftward movement, stranding the RRC in situ, as schematically represented in (349).

(349) Chegou [um rapaz]$_i$ <u>ontem</u>   [t$_i$ que eu gostaria de   conhecer t$_i$].
       arrived a   boy   yesterday   that I like.COND DE.PREP meet.INF
       'A boy arrived yesterday that I would like to meet.'

The key assumption of this proposal is the following: extraposed RRCs in CEP always involve the A′-movement of the antecedent, either via movement to the left periphery (when the antecedent is in a pre-verbal position) or via short scrambling[18] (when the antecedent is in a post-verbal position).

   I examine these two possibilities in greater detail in §§3.5.1.1 and 3.5.1.2 respectively. As the reader will notice, the first section requires more detail (and space) than the latter. This is because the idea that the antecedent of an extraposed RRC undergoes movement to the left periphery is quite uncontroversial. By contrast, the claim that it undergoes short scrambling deserves a closer inspection and requires more complex explanatory devices. The question concerning the constituency of the dislocated constituent is reserved until §3.5.2.1.

3.5.1.1 Extraposition derived by movement to the left periphery In §3.4.1.2B, I demonstrated that extraposed RRCs can take a wh-constituent, a preposed emphatic/evaluative phrase and a preposed focus as an antecedent. I repeat an example of each case here to illustrate the pattern.

Wh-constituent:

(350) Quantas   pessoas <u>apareceram</u> que não foram convidadas?
       how.many people showed.up   that not were invited
       'How many people showed up who were not invited?'

Emphatic/evaluative phrase:

(351) Muito whisky o João <u>bebeu</u> que estava fora do   prazo!
       a.lot.of whisky the J. drank that was   out of.the expiry.date
       'João drank a lot of whisky that was expired!'

Preposed focus:

(352) Poucas pessoas <u>conheço</u>   que fazem interpolação, mas todas elas
       few   people know.1SG that make interpolation but all   they
       produzem coisas deste   tipo.
       produce   things of.this type
       'I know few people who produce interpolation [structures], but all of them produce things like this.'

---

[18] In this book, the term *short scrambling* refers to the scrambling to VP. See n. 17 for additional details.

In the literature on CEP, wh-constituents, emphatic/evaluative phrases and preposed foci have been argued to undergo leftward movement.

Wh-constituents are argued to move to the left periphery of the sentence, for instance, in Ambar (1992); Ambar, Obenauer, Pereira, Tapazdi, and Veloso (1998); Ambar and Veloso (2001). Assuming a split CP system, Ambar and Veloso (2001) propose that there is a projection in the left periphery of the sentence, which has strong N and V features. The raising of the wh-constituent is triggered by the need to check the N features, whereas the raising of the verb is triggered by the need to check the V features. Under this approach, a sentence like (350) (excluding the extraposed RRC) would be as in (353).

(353)   (TOP) [$_{WhP}$ quantas   pessoas$_i$ [$_{Wh'}$ apareceram$_j$ [$_{FP}$ [$_{F'}$ t$_V$ [$_{IP}$ t$_i$ t$_j$]]]]]
               how.many people   showed.up

Emphatic/evaluative phrases are also taken to undergo leftward movement (Ambar 1999; Raposo 1995; among others). In the syntactic representation of the sentence, Ambar (1999) proposes that there is a projection called *EvaluativeP* sitting above IP but below CP, where Evaluative-like elements are licensed (see (354)).

(354)   [$_{CP}$ ··· [$_{EvaluativeP}$ ··· [$_{TopicFocusP}$ ··· [$_{IP}$ ···]]]]

Under this approach, the features of EvaluativeP must be checked against evaluative features of lexical items. This explains why emphatic/evaluative phrases like *muito whisky* 'a lot of whisky' in (351) raise to [Spec, EvaluativeP].

Finally, Martins (forthcoming) argues, in line with Hernanz and Brucart (1987), Rizzi (1997), Cinque (1999), and related cartographic work, that preposed foci derive from movement. Under this analysis, *poucas pessoas* 'few people' in (352) is base-generated in a VP-internal position (as the complement of V) and undergoes movement to the left periphery. It is worth noting that the exact landing site of the preposed constituents is not crucial here. The stranding approach to RRC-extraposition is equally compatible with the existence of a functional projection in the CP domain dedicated to preposed foci or with analyses advocating a non-split CP domain.

For current purposes, what is crucial is that wh-constituents, emphatic/evaluative phrases and preposed foci are base-generated not in the left periphery but instead in a VP-internal position. In other words, the relevant conclusion is that these constituents undergo leftward movement.

Turning now to the contexts of RRC-extraposition, I submit that the RRC and its antecedent (in this case, a wh-constituent, an emphatic/evaluative phrase or a preposed focus) are base-generated within the RRC along the lines of the raising analysis. Then, these constituents undergo leftward movement, stranding the RRC in situ, as sketched in (355).

(355) a. ... wh-constituents$_i$ [t$_i$ RRC]
       b. ... emphatic/evaluative phrases$_i$ ... [t$_i$ RRC]
       c. ... preposed foci$_i$ ... [t$_i$ RRC]

I provide further details of the analysis in §3.5.2.2. For now, I will show how RRC-extraposition from post-verbal positions can be accounted for under the stranding approach to extraposition.

3.5.1.2 Extraposition derived from short scrambling   This section aims to demonstrate that RRC-extraposition from post-verbal positions can be accounted for in terms of short scrambling. I begin by arguing that subjects in [Spec, VP], just like objects and subjects of unaccusative verbs, can scramble in CEP. I provide three arguments in favor of this hypothesis: (1) adverb positioning; (2) semantic effects; and (3) the trigger for scrambling (see §3.5.1.2A). Then, on the basis of the first two arguments, I show that RRC-extraposition also involves short scrambling (§3.5.1.2B). The trigger for scrambling in sentences involving RRC-extraposition is discussed in §3.5.1.2B(c). Finally, §3.5.1.3 demonstrates how to derive the occurrence of different constituents in the intervening position.

A. Excursus on subject and object scrambling

J. Costa (1998, 2004a) reports that CEP has a scrambling rule that allows objects to move from their base position and adjoin to the VP. He also claims that the position of the scrambled object is indicated by its position relative to monosyllabic adverbs, such as *bem* 'well', which mark the left edge of the VP. The idea is that objects to the right of monosyllabic adverbs are in their base position, whereas objects to the left of these adverbs are scrambled, as sketched in (356).[19]

(356) a. [$_{IP}$ V [$_{VP}$ Adv [$_{VP}$ t$_V$ O]]] (*non-scrambled object*)
       b. [$_{IP}$ V [$_{VP}$ O [$_{VP}$ Adv [$_{VP}$ t$_V$ t$_O$]]]] (*scrambled object*)

This is illustrated in (357), from J. Costa (2004a: 40). In (357a), the adverb–object order indicates that the object is not scrambled, whereas in (357b), the object–adverb order indicates that the object is scrambled.

---

[19] In the present analysis, I assume (in line with J. Costa 1996, 1998, 2004a) that verbs move out of VP in CEP. Costa rejects Pollock's (1989, 1994) analysis for French, according to which verbs may either stay inside VP or move up to Agr, depending on the occurrence of morphologically ambiguous forms (between a nominal and verbal interpretation). Such ambiguity simply does not arise with verbal forms, such as *falou* 'spoke' in (358), which is unambiguously a verbal form in the third person singular.

(357) a. O   Paulo fala   **bem** francês. (*non-scrambled object*)
         the P.   speaks well French
         'Paulo speaks French well.'

       b. O   Paulo fala   francês **bem**. (*scrambled object*)
         the P.   speaks French well

Costa also shows that objects are not the only constituents that may undergo scrambling. Indeed, subjects of unaccusatives can also scramble, as illustrated in (358), from J. Costa (2004a: 64). Here the adverb *depressa* 'fast' marks the left edge of the VP.

(358) a. Chegou **depressa** o   Paulo. (*non-scrambled subject*)
         arrived fast   the P.
         'Paulo arrived fast.'

       b. Chegou o   Paulo **depressa**. (*scrambled subject*)
         arrived the P.   fast

My claim is that the possibility of scrambling can be extended to subjects in [Spec, VP]. To my knowledge, this issue has not been previously addressed in the literature on CEP, but similar proposals have been discussed for other languages (e.g. Dutch/German and English).[20] Hence, before proceeding with the analysis, I examine three arguments that support this view.

(a) **Distribution of adverbs**

A base-generated subject in [Spec, VP] may surface in a post-verbal position, to the left of the monosyllabic adverb *bem* 'well', as illustrated in (359b). Considering that (1) the monosyllabic adverb *bem* 'well' marks the left-edge of VP and (2) the post-verbal subject is VP-internal (J. Costa 1998, 2004a), then it follows that the subjects of unergative verbs can also scramble.

(359) A: a. Ninguém jogou   nada.
            nobody   played nothing
            'No one played anything.'

       B: b. Jogou o   Sporting **bem** até   aos últimos dez minutos.
            played the S.   well until the last   ten minutes
            'Sporting played well until the last ten minutes. (Then Benfica reacted and scored two goals.)'

(b) **Semantic effects**

When indefinite noun phrases are involved, the scrambled and non-scrambled orders can be semantically distinguished. More precisely, unscrambled indefinite

---

[20] Concretely, I refer to Broekhuis (2007) and Takano (1998). Broekhuis (2007) proposes that scrambling of objects and NP-movement of the subject in Dutch/German essentially involve the same operation, which he terms *subject/object shift*. Takano (1998) claims that English displays the short scrambling of accusative and nominative phrases.

objects may have a cardinal reading, whereas scrambled objects necessarily have a presuppositional reading (in the sense of Diesing 1992). Consider, for instance, the contrast in (360). The unscrambled object in (360a) preferably has a cardinal, non-presuppositional reading. Under this interpretation, João can actually speak only one language. This contrasts with the scrambled order in (360b). Here, the indefinite object can only have a presuppositional reading, being paraphrased as a partitive ('one of the languages').

(360) a. O   João fala   **bem** uma língua.
          the J.   speaks well one language
          'João speaks one language well.'

       b. O   João fala   uma língua   **bem**.
          the J.   speaks one language well
          'João speaks one language well (the other languages he speaks very badly).'

Turning now to the subject of unaccusative and unergative verbs, examples (361)–(362) show that the subject may either precede or follow the adverb *bem* 'well'. However, just as in the case of object scrambling, different semantic effects arise. In (361a) the unscrambled subject preferably has a cardinal reading. Under this interpretation, only two more palm trees grew. This contrasts with the scrambled order in (361b), which necessarily involves a presuppositional reading. Under this interpretation, more than two palm trees were growing. The same reasoning applies to (362). Note that this is a welcome result; if scrambling is involved in (360b)–(362b), the same semantic effects are expected to arise.[21]

Unaccusative verb:

(361) a. Cresceram **bem** mais duas palmeiras.
          grew   well more two   palm.trees
          'Two more palm trees grew well.'

       b. Cresceram mais duas palmeiras **bem**.
          grew   more two   palm.trees well
          'Two more palm trees grew well (the others didn't grow well).'

Unergative verb:

(362) a. Correram **bem** oito atletas.
          ran   well eight athletes
          'Eight athletes ran well.'

       b. Correram oito atletas **bem**.
          ran   eight athletes well
          'Eight athletes ran well (the other athletes did not run that well).'

---

[21] For similar semantic effects in object/subject shifts in German/Dutch, see Broekhuis (2007).

(c) Discourse and prosody

It has been proposed in the literature that scrambling is movement to [Spec, AgrOP] driven by the requirement of accusative feature-checking (De Hoop 1992; among others). Under this assumption, subject scrambling would be unexpected because the noun phrase in [Spec, VP] does not have an accusative feature to be checked by the complex V-AgrO. Fortunately, this problem does not arise; J. Costa (1998, 2004a) shows that scrambling in CEP is not a case-driven movement.[22] One of the arguments he provides in favor of this idea is precisely the possibility of subject scrambling (involving the subject of unaccusatives, as in (358)).

Alternatively, J. Costa (1998, 2004a) argues in favor of a prosodically/discourse-driven approach to scrambling, according to which scrambling is used to create appropriate (information) focus configurations. The basic idea is that the assignment of narrow information focus drives the constituent expressing new information to the rightmost position of the sentence, where it receives the sentence nuclear stress.[23] Scrambling is then used to create appropriate focus configurations by allowing some constituents to escape the position where sentence nuclear stress is assigned (see Reinhart 1995).

This approach accounts for the word order contrasts observed in (363)–(364). In (363) the adverb *bem* 'well' is expected to occur in the rightmost position because it is the new information requested in the question. Hence, the scrambled order in (363b) is derived: the object undergoes scrambling, being defocused, and the adverb *bem* 'well' receives the default stress.

(363)   A: a.   Como é que o   Paulo fala   francês?
                  how   is that the P.   speaks French
                  'How does Paulo speak French?'

        B: b.   O   Paulo fala   francês **bem**. [scrambled object]
                  the P.   speaks French well
                  'Paulo speaks French well.'

             c.   #O   Paulo fala   **bem** francês. [non-scrambled object]
                  the P.   speaks well French (all J. Costa 2004a: 68)

By contrast, if the object is questioned (as in (364a)), it must stay in the rightmost position and get the default stress. Therefore, the non-scrambled order in (364c) is derived.

(364)   A: a.   O   que é que o   Paulo fala   bem?
                  the what is that the P.   speaks well
                  'What does Paulo speak well?'

---

[22] Also, Broekhuis (2007) does not assume Case as the trigger for scrambling in Dutch/German (contra De Hoop 1992).

[23] The Nuclear Stress Rule assigns prominence to the rightmost/lowest constituent of the sentence, as proposed in Zubizarreta (1998, 1999). See §1.3.3.2 for additional details.

B: b. #O   Paulo fala   francês **bem.** [scrambled object]
      the P.   speaks French well

   c. O   Paulo fala   **bem** francês. [non-scrambled object]
      the P.   speaks well French (all J. Costa 2004a: 68)

Similar word order contrasts are found with the subject of unaccusative and unergative verbs. In (365), it is expected that the subject of the unergative verb *dançar*
'to dance' be the focus of the sentence because it is the new information requested in
the question; hence, the felicitous answer is (365b), where the subject occurs in the
rightmost sentential position.

Unergative verb:

(365) A: a. Quem é   que dançou bem?
        who   is that danced well
        'Who danced well?'

     B: b. Dançaram **bem** dois concorrentes.
        Danced   well two   contestants
        'Two contestants danced well (but I cannot remember their names).'

       c. #Dançaram dois concorrentes **bem.**
        danced   two contestants   well

In contrast, in (366) the adverb is the new information requested in the question.
Hence, the felicitous answer is (366c), where the subject undergoes scrambling and
the adverb surfaces in the rightmost position.

(366) A: a. Como é   que dançaram os   concorrentes?
        how   is that danced   the contestants
        'How did the contestants dance?'

     B: b. #Dançaram **bem** dois concorrentes.
        danced   well two   contestants
        'Two contestants danced well.'

       c. Dançaram dois concorrentes **bem.**
        danced   two   contestants   well
        'Two contestants danced well (the others danced very badly).'

The same word order contrasts are found with the subject of the unaccusative verb
chegar 'to arrive' in (367)–(368).

Unaccusative:

(367) A: a. Que avião aterrou bem?
        what plane landed well
        'What plane landed well?'

B: b. Aterrou **bem** o   Boeing 767.
     landed   well the B.
     'The Boeing 767 landed well.'

    c. #Aterrou o   Boeing 767 **bem**.
     landed   the B.   well

(368) A: a. Como aterraram os   aviões?
         how landed   the planes
         'How did the planes land?'

B: b. #Aterrou **bem** o   Boeing 767.
     landed   well the B.
     'The Boeing 767 landed well.'

    c. Aterrou o   Boeing 767 **bem**.
     landed   the B.   well
     'The Boeing 767 landed well (the other planes did not land that well).'

Remarkably, in the examples (366c) and (368c) two constituents are assigned narrow information focus: the adverb (which is the new information requested in the question) and the scrambled subject (which appears to the left of the adverb).[24]

At first sight, the idea that a constituent interpreted as focus may undergo scrambling is surprising, under the assumption that scrambling serves to remove unfocused material from the focus domain. However, this hypothesis receives some typological support from the so-called *focus-scrambling* in Dutch, which involves contrastive focus on a scrambled constituent (J. Costa 2004a: 69).[25]

Moreover, in CEP the configuration under scrutiny is found in other discourse contexts, such as broad information focus sentences (see (369)).

(369) Context: Maria was expected to have a risky childbirth because she was going to have triplets.
A: a. Como correu o   parto da   Maria?
       how went   the labor of.the M.
       'How did the childbirth go?'

---

[24] Following J. Costa (2004a: 86), I assume that in a sentence with more than one focus, the leftmost focused constituent bears heavy stress. Then, all constituents following the heavy stress are interpreted as focus. Applying this rule to (366c) and (368c), I assume that the post-verbal subject bears heavy stress and the adverb to its right is interpreted as focus.

[25] As an illustration of focus-scrambling in Dutch, consider the following example, taken from J. Costa (2004a: 69).

Jan zei dat ik DE KRANT gisteren las, (en het boek vandaag)
J. said that I the newspaper yesterday read, and the book today
'Jan said that it was the newspapers that I read yesterday (and not the books today).'

B: b. Mais ou menos. Nasceram dois bebés **bem**.
      more or less   were.born two babies well
      'Well and not so well. The birth of the first two babies went well (it was
      the birth of the third baby that was more complicated).'

    c. #Mais ou menos. Nasceram **bem** dois bebés.
      more or less   were.born well two babies
      'Well and not so well. The birth of the two babies went well.'

Despite the fact that the focus extends to the entire sentence in (369b) (*Nasceram dois bebés bem*), the constituent *dois bebés* 'two babies' is scrambled, as can be confirmed by its occurrence to the left of the adverb *bem* 'well'.

The question then arises of why a constituent undergoes scrambling within a focus domain. I would like to submit that in the context of double-focus or broad information focus, the constituent in the rightmost position receives more discourse prominence than the other constituents. Thus, scrambling can be used to create specific discourse effects (namely, to place the most prominent constituent in the rightmost position within the clause-internal space).

Let us examine exactly how this works in a sentence like (369b). The constituent *dois bebés* 'two babies' is contained in a sentence with broad information focus. Nevertheless, *dois bebés* 'two babies' conveys less prominent information than *bem* 'well'. There are two reasons for why this occurs. First, it is expected that during childbirth a baby is born. Second, *bem* 'well' is a direct response to *como* 'how' in (369a). Being less prominent, *dois bebés* 'two babies' undergoes short scrambling, leaving the adverb *bem* 'well' in the rightmost position.

In contrast, (369c) does not constitute an appropriate answer to the question. This can be explained by assuming that a constituent in the rightmost position tends to convey non-discourse-dependent (or non-presuppositional) information. Such a requirement is not fulfilled in (369c) because a less prominent constituent, expressing the fact that two babies were born, appears in the rightmost sentential position.[26]

B. Deriving relative clause extraposition from short scrambling

In (a)–(c), I provide three arguments that support the view that RRC-extraposition from post-verbal positions involves short scrambling.

(a) Distribution of adverbs

The antecedent of an extraposed RRC may appear to the left of the monosyllabic adverb *bem* 'well', as illustrated in (370b). Under the assumption that the monosyllabic

---

[26] It should be noted that the constituent *dois bebés* 'two babies' in (369c) could only be interpreted as referring not to Maria's babies but to other babies (out of many that were born, for instance, on the same day in the hospital). This is because the constituent in the rightmost position tends to convey non-discourse-dependent (or non-presuppositional) information.

adverb *bem* 'well' marks the left edge of the VP, the position of *uma candidatura* 'one application' indicates that this constituent has undergone short scrambling.

(370) A: a. Não analisaste com atenção nenhuma candidatura.
         'You did not analyze any of the applications carefully.'

    B: b. Analisei   uma candidatura **bem** que foi proposta pela
         analyzed.1SG one application well that was submitted by.the
         Universidade de Lisboa.
         University   of L.
         'I analyzed one application that was submitted by the University of Lisbon well (= thoroughly) (the others I actually did not analyze very carefully).'

(b) Semantic effects

When the antecedent of a non-extraposed RRC is indefinite, it may have a cardinal reading. However, when extraposition is involved, the antecedent necessarily has a presuppositional reading. This is illustrated in (371). The non-extraposed version in (371a) is compatible with the reading that there is only one homeless person in my neighborhood, whereas the extraposed version in (371b) necessarily presupposes that there is more than one homeless person in my neighborhood. The same reasoning applies to (372). The similar behavior of the antecedent of RRCs and scrambled indefinite constituents (see §3.5.1.2A(b)) suggests that in both cases, the indefinite noun phrase is scrambled.

(371) a. Há no   meu bairro   um sem-abrigo que não pede dinheiro.
      has in.the my   neighborhood one homeless   that not asks money
      'There is one homeless person in my neighborhood that does not ask for money.'

    b. Há um sem-abrigo <u>no   meu bairro</u>   que não pede dinheiro.
      has a   homeless in.the my   neighborhood that not asks money
      √ *Reading 1:* (presuppositional) *There is more than one homeless person in my neighborhood (but only one does not ask for money).*
      *Reading 2: (cardinal) *There is only one homeless person in my neighborhood (and he does not ask for money).*

(372) a. Apareceu no   meu gabinete um aluno   que precisava de   ajuda.
      showed.up in.the my office   a   student that needed DE.PREP help
      'One student showed up in my office that needed help.'

    b. Apareceu um aluno <u>no   meu gabinete</u> que precisava de
      showed.up a   student in.the my   office   that needed DE.PREP
      ajuda.
      help
      √ *Reading 1:* (presuppositional) *More than one student showed up in my office (but only one needed help).*
      * *Reading 2:* (cardinal) *Only one student showed up in my office (and he needed help).*

(c) Discourse and prosody

In CEP, RRC-extraposition from post-verbal positions arises in two different discourse contexts: (1) sentences displaying narrow information focus; and (2) sentences displaying broad information focus.

The first possibility is illustrated in (373). The extraposed RRC conveys the new information requested in the question; thus the antecedent of the RRC is scrambled (surfacing to the left of the monosyllabic adverb *bem* 'well') and the RRC stays in the rightmost sentential position.

(373) A: a. Que exercícios é que o   João faz   bem?
                what exercises is that the J.   does well
               'What exercises does João do well?'

       B: b. O   João faz   um exercício **bem** que envolve raciocínio
                the J.   does a   exercise well that involves reasoning
                matemático.
                mathematical
                'João does an exercise well that involves mathematical reasoning (but
                I can't recall how he does the other exercises).'

If the antecedent is not scrambled, there is adjacency between the antecedent and the RRC. An appropriate discourse context is given in (374b), where the object (i.e. the antecedent and the RRC) provides the new information requested in the question. As the adverb *bem* 'well' is repeated from the question, it surfaces to the left of the object. In contrast, (374c) is not a felicitous answer to the question because the antecedent, being part of the new information requested in the question, must appear to the right of the adverb *bem* 'well'.

(374) A: a. O   que é que o   João faz   bem?
                the that is that the J.   does well
               'What does João do well?'

       B: b. O   João faz   **bem** um exercício que envolve raciocínio
                the J.   does well a   exercise that involves reasoning
                matemático.
                mathematical
                'João does an exercise that involves mathematical reasoning well.'

           c. #O   João faz   um exercício **bem** que envolve raciocínio
                the J.   does a   exercise well that involves reasoning
                matemático.
                mathematical
                'João does an exercise well that involves mathematical reasoning (but
                I can't recall how he does the other exercises).'

The discourse effects described for RRC-extraposition from the object smoothly accommodate the contexts in which extraposition takes place from subjects of both unaccusative (see (375)) and unergative verbs (see (376)).

(375)   A: a. Neste jardim, que   árvores é que crescem depressa?
         in.this garden   what   trees   is that grow   fast
         'In this garden, what trees grow fast?'

      B: b. Cresce uma árvore **depressa** que é um híbrido de duas espécies
          grows   a   tree   fast   that is a   hybrid of two   species
          da   paulónia.
          of.the   Paulownia
          'A tree that is a hybrid of two species of Paulownia grows fast (the other trees grow slowly).'

(376)   A: a. Que atletas   é que nadam bem?
         what athletes is that swim   well
         'What athletes swim well?'

      B: b. Nadam três   atletas   **bem** que pertencem ao Benfica
          swim   three   atheletes well   that belong   to B.
          'Three athletes that belong to Benfica swim well (the other athletes do not swim well).'

RRC-extraposition may also appear in broad information focus sentences, such as (377c). Here the focus extends to the entire sentence, but the antecedent of the RRC is scrambled, as can be confirmed by its occurrence to the left of the adverb *bem* 'well'. As is clear from the discussion in §3.5.1.2A(c), I assume that there is no conflict between focus and scrambling; scrambling of the antecedent occurs in the focus domain to assign discourse prominence to the RRC in the rightmost sentential position.

(377)   A: a. O   que   é que aconteceu?
         the what is that happened
         'What happened?'

      B: b. Estou   muito feliz.
         am.1SG very   happy
         'I am very happy.'

        c. O   João fez um exercício **bem** que vale   50% da   nota final.
          the J.   did a   exercise well that is.worth 50% of.the grade final
          'João did an exercise that is worth 50% of the final grade well.'

From the considerations thus far, it follows that RRC-extraposition cannot be defined as a purely syntactic phenomenon. The discourse-based approach proposed here suggests that RRC-extraposition from post-verbal positions arises when the antecedent and the RRC have different discourse status.

3.5.1.3 Deriving the intervening material   Thus far, I have provided evidence for the idea that RRC-extraposition in CEP may take a scrambled constituent as an antecedent (see §1.3.1.3). In this section, I submit that such a syntactic configuration is derived as follows: (1) the antecedent is generated together with the RRC; then (2) the antecedent undergoes short scrambling and adjoins to the VP after raising, stranding the RRC in situ. This is sketched in (378); in example a, the antecedent and the RRC are generated together in the subject position ([Spec, VP]),[27] and in example b, these elements are generated in the complement position of V.

(378)   a. $[_{IP}$ V $[_{VP}$ S $[_{VP}$ *intervening material* $[_{VP}$ t$_S$ RRC t$_V$]]]]
         b. $[_{IP}$ V $[_{VP}$ DO $[_{VP}$ *intervening material* $[_{VP}$ t$_V$ t$_{DO}$ RRC]]]]

(378a) schematically represents an extraposed RRC with the subject of an unergative verb as an antecedent (corresponding to a sentence as (376b)). Example (378b) represents an extraposed RRC with a direct object (or the subject of an unaccusative verb) as an antecedent (corresponding, respectively, to a sentence as (373b) or (375b)).

Now, I must identify the elements that can (and cannot) occur as intervening material and demonstrate how the analysis proposed here can accommodate the various possibilities.

A. Deriving the occurrence of adverbs and PPs in the intervening position

When short scrambling is involved, only adverbs and PPs can intervene between the antecedent and the extraposed RRC. This is illustrated in (379)–(382).[28]

Subject:

(379)   Chegou um rapaz <u>ontem</u>   que te   quer   conhecer.
         arrived a   boy   yesterday that you.CL wants meet.INF
         'A boy arrived yesterday that wants to meet you.'

(380)   Ontem   explodiu uma bomba <u>em Israel</u> que causou 5 mortos.
         yesterday exploded a   bomb in I.   that caused 5 deaths
         'Yesterday a bomb exploded in Israel that caused 5 deaths.'

Object:

(381)   Encontrei uma rapariga <u>ontem</u>   que perguntou por ti.
         met.1SG   a   girl   yesterday that asked   for you
         'I met a girl yesterday that asked for you.'

---

[27] In this portion of the discussion I abstract away from the assumption that there are two verb phrases in the clause, a vP and a VP (Larson 1988, 1990), and for ease of exposition, I represent the double VP-shell as a single VP-shell. The double VP-shell is introduced only while discussing the syntax of double complement constructions.

[28] Note that more than one adjunct may co-occur as intervening material, as in (266a).

(382)   Comprei   uma boneca na   feira de artesanato que é feita de pasta
        bought.1SG a   doll   at.the fair of craft   that is made of paste
        de papel.
        of paper
        'I bought a doll at the craft fair that is made of paper paste.'

These intervening elements can either be modifiers (as in (379)–(382)) or arguments
of the verb (as in (383)–(384)).

Indirect object:

(383)   Dei   um livro à   Maria que foi escrito por mim.
        gave.1SG a   book to.the M.   that was written by me
        'I gave Maria a book that was written by me.'

Prepositional argument:

(384)   Deixei um recado em cima da   mesa que é para a   Rita.
        left.1SG a message on top of.the table that is for the R.
        'I left a message on the top of the table that is for Rita.'

The derivation of contexts involving modifiers and arguments as intervening material is treated separately in (a) and (b).

(a) Modifiers in the intervening position

Let me begin by examining the occurrence of adverbs in the intervening position.
Currently, there is no consensus in the literature regarding the syntactic representation of adverbs. Broadly speaking, two major lines of research can be
identified: the adjunction analyses and the functional specifier analyses. The
adjunction analyses claim that adverbs are adjoined to some projection (VP,
TP, . . .) (Ernst 2002; J. Costa 1998, 2004a, 2004b; among others). The functional
specifier analyses assume that adverbs occupy non-argumental specifier positions
and are licensed in a Spec-head configuration with respect to a head containing
semantic features related to, for example, mood, tense, and aspect (see Cinque
1999; Alexiadou 1997). Partially related to this issue, the analyses available in
the literature may also manifest divergence with respect to the distribution of
adverbs. Some linguists claim that adverbs are freely distributed within a sentence
(see Emonds 1976, among others), whereas others point out that the distribution
of adverbs is very restricted (see Cinque 1999, among others).

For reasons of overall coherence (namely, with respect to J. Costa's 1998, 2004a
approach to short scrambling and to the tests used here to identify scrambled
constituents), I assume a left-adjunction analysis of the adverbs that surface in the
intervening position. Nevertheless, I leave the hypothesis open that the approach
developed here may also be compatible with a functional specifier analysis of
adverbs.

Turning now to the analysis proper, consider (385), which shows that an adverb in CEP may either precede or follow a verb.

(385)   a. O João **ontem**   leu o   livro.
           the J.   yesterday read the book
           'João read the book yesterday.'

        b. O João leu **ontem**   o   livro.
           the J.   read yesterday the book (both J. Costa 2004a: 6)

Following J. Costa (2004a), I maintain the assumption that the adverb *ontem* 'yesterday' in (385) is left-adjoined to different projections. In (385a), the adverb is left-adjoined to TP (see (386a)), and in (385b), it is left-adjoined to VP (see (386b)).[29]

(386)   a. [$_{AgrSP}$ O João [$_{TP}$ ontem [$_{TP}$ leu [$_{VP}$ t$_V$ o livro]]]]
        b. [$_{AgrSP}$ O João [$_{TP}$ leu [$_{VP}$ ontem [$_{VP}$ t$_V$ o livro]]]] (both J. Costa 2004a: 7)

I also assume, along with J. Costa 2004b, that adverbs only adjoin to the left. With this background in mind, I submit that if RRC-extraposition involves an adverb in the intervening position, the adverb is left-adjoined to VP, as in (386b). Then, the object/subject scrambles over the adverb, deriving the antecedent–adverb–RRC order represented in (387).

(387)   a. [$_{IP}$ V [$_{VP}$ DO [$_{VP}$ <u>adverb</u> [$_{VP}$ t$_V$ t$_{DO}$ RRC]]]]
        b. [$_{IP}$ V [$_{VP}$ S [$_{VP}$ <u>adverb</u> [$_{VP}$ t$_S$ RRC t$_V$]]]]

In more concrete terms, what this means is that the source structure of an extraposed RRC taking an object as antecedent is as depicted in (388a). Then, if the antecedent of the RRC undergoes short scrambling (stranding the RRC in situ), the extraposed order in (388b) is derived.

(388)   a. O João comprou ontem   um portátil que custou 1000€.
           the J.   bought   yesterday a laptop   that cost   €1,000
           'Yesterday, João bought a laptop that cost €1,000.'

        b. O João comprou um portátil <u>ontem</u>   que custou 1000€.
           the J.   bought   a laptop   yesterday that cost   €1,000

Let me consider now the occurrence of modifying PPs in the intervening position. There is an ongoing debate in the literature about the way in which modifying PPs integrate into the structure of the clause. Broadly speaking, the syntactic analyses of

---

[29] Recall that CEP displays V-to-I movement, which derives the order Verb–Adverb/Object in (386b) (see also §3.5.1.2A, n. 19).

modifying PPs can be divided in three major groups: adjunction analyses, Larsonian analyses, and specifier analyses.

Adjunction analyses assume that modifying PPs are adjoined to VP. Two variants of this approach can be identified: modifying PPs can be taken to involve right-hand adjunction (Chomsky 1981) or left-hand adjunction (Barbiers 1995). Larsonian analyses neutralize the structural distinction between arguments and modifiers, claiming that modifying PPs are base-generated below the arguments of the verb as complements of V (Larson 1988, 1990; Chomsky 1995: 333). Specifier analyses claim that modifying PPs (and arguments) are all merged in specifier positions in a strict order, with the verb in the innermost position; a different order of constituents may be derived by successively moving larger and larger constituents containing the VP into higher Specs (Cinque 2006).

The analyses proposed in the literature may also differ in the way that they account for the complements/modifying PPs order. Some approaches claim that there is a unique (and universal) order of merge between these constituents (Cinque 2006), whereas others claim that these constituents do not enter the derivation in a strict order (Jackendoff 1990).

In this study, I assume (in line with Barbiers 1995) that modifying PPs that surface in the intervening position are left-adjoined to the VP (just like intervening adverbs). Therefore, the derivation proceeds in the same way as described for adverbs: the antecedent raises leftward past the intervening PP and adjoins to VP, stranding the RRC in situ. This is presented in (389a,b), where the extraposed RRCs have, respectively, an object and a subject as an antecedent.

(389) a. [$_{IP}$ V [$_{VP}$ DO [$_{VP}$ modifying PP [$_{VP}$ t$_V$ t$_{DO}$ RRC]]]]
       b. [$_{IP}$ V [$_{VP}$ S [$_{VP}$ modifying PP [$_{VP}$ t$_S$ RRC t$_V$]]]]

Therefore, the source structure of an extraposed RRC with a subject as an antecedent corresponds to a sentence like (390a), where the modifying PP is left-adjoined to VP, and the subject is in its base position. Then, if the antecedent of the RRC undergoes short scrambling, stranding the RRC in situ, the extraposed order in (390b) is derived.

(390) a. Ontem   explodiu em Israel uma bomba que causou 5 mortos.
          yesterday exploded in I.   a   bomb that caused 5 deaths
          'Yesterday a bomb exploded in Israel that caused 5 deaths.'

       b. Ontem   explodiu uma bomba em Israel que causou 5 mortos.
          yesterday exploded a   bomb in I.   that caused 5 deaths

(b) Complements in the intervening position

In double complement constructions, the PP may appear in the intervening position, as illustrated in (391) (repeated from (383)).

(391) Dei   um livro à   Maria que foi escrito por mim.
      gave.1SG a   book to.the M.   that was written by me
      'I gave Maria a book that was written by me.'

Although double complement constructions have received much attention in the generative literature, their exact status remains controversial (see Kayne 1984; Larson 1988; Pesetsky 1995; Philips 1996; among others). Indeed, one point of disagreement concerns the choice between the shell structure represented in (392a) and the layered structure represented in (392b).

(392)   a. shell structure   b. layered structure

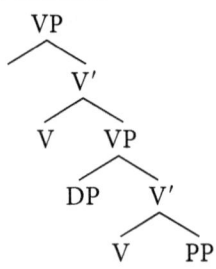   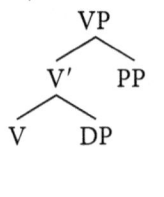

As noted in Philips (1996) and J. Costa (2004a), part of the debate results from the fact that the tests applied to these constructions yield contradictory results. For instance, (393) provides evidence for an analysis as in (392a) under the assumption that Licensing of Polarity Items requires c-command. In turn, (394c) provides evidence for a layered structure as in (392b), because *give candy* is a constituent in (392b) but not in (392a).

(393)   a. John gave nothing to any of the children on his birthday.
         b. *John gave anything to none of the children on his birthday. (both J. Costa
            2004a: 144)

(394)   John intended to give candy to children on his birthday.
         a. ... and [give candy to children on his birthday] he did
         b. ... and [give candy to children] he did on his birthday
         c. ... and [give candy] he did to children on his birthday (all J. Costa 2004a: 144)

J. Costa (2004a) additionally shows that binding facts suggest that the PP–DP order cannot be derived from the base DP–PP order through scrambling of the PP to the left of the DP. This is due to the fact that the PP can bind an anaphor contained in the DP (see (395)), which suggests that it occupies an A-position.

(395)   A: a. A quem é que deste   os livros?
               to whom is that gave.2SG the books
               'To whom did you give the books?'

B: b. Dei   [$_F$ A   CADA   AUTOR]   o   seu   livro.
       gave.1SG   to   each   author   the   his   book
       'I gave his book to each author.' (both J. Costa 2004a: 143)

Based in part on the facts mentioned above, J. Costa (2004a) (in line with Philips 1996) suggests that both the DP–PP and PP–DP orders can be base-generated in CEP. To keep the discussion simple, I will abstract away from the technical implementation of the analysis (see J. Costa 2004a for additional details), and I will simply refer to the two final structures;[30] see (396a)–(396b).

(396)   a. DP–PP order   b. PP–DP order

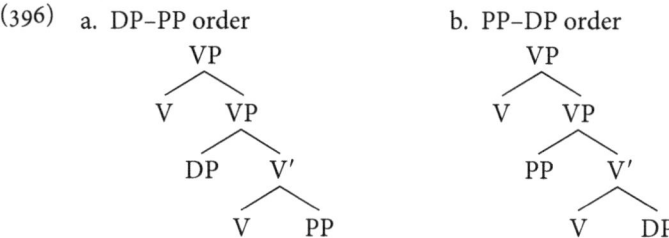

Crucially, Costa argues that the fact that both word orders are base-generated does not entail that they should be optional. According to his proposal, the structure in (396b) is only generated if necessary for satisfying binding requirements or any other constraint forcing the PP–DP order, such as heaviness.[31]

    As its point of departure, the analysis that I propose here adopts J. Costa's (2004a) claim that the PP–DP order can be base-generated in CEP.[32] It also takes from J. Costa (2004a) the idea that heaviness factors may legitimize this configuration. With these assumptions in mind, let me briefly consider how a sentence like (397) (containing an extraposed RRC and a PP-complement in the intervening position) can be derived.

(397)   Dei   um livro à   Maria que foi escrito por mim.
       gave.1SG a   book to.the M.   that was written by   me
       'I gave Maria a book that was written by me.'

---

[30] Importantly, the structures in (396a) and (396b) are apparently similar to the VP-shell structure represented in (392). However, (396a) and (396b) are derived by building a right-branching phrase marker from left to right (Philips 1996).

[31] Without going into further detail, please note that under this approach, the constituency problem in (394c) is derived by the possibility of targeting a step of the V–DP–PP derivation in which V and DP form a VP, an option that is available under the right-branching structures (see J. Costa 2004a: 148).

[32] Note that the present approach is also compatible with an analysis that postulates the DP–PP base-order. In this case, the PP–DP order would be derived from scrambling of the PP to the left of the DP, followed by scrambling of the antecedent to the left of the PP.

First, I assume that (397) is derived from the PP–DP base-order (as in (398)). This is due to heaviness effects: the DP *um livro que foi escrito por mim* 'a book that was written by me' is heavier/longer than the PP *à Maria* 'to Maria' and therefore surfaces in the rightmost sentential position.[33]

(398) Dei   à   Maria um livro que foi escrito por mim.
       gave.1SG to.the M.   a   book that was written by   me
       'I gave Maria a book that was written by me.'

Then, *um livro* 'a book' can be adjacent to the RRC (as in (398)) or may undergo short scrambling, assigning discourse prominence to the RRC that is stranded in the rightmost sentential position. In the later case, *um livro* 'a book' moves leftward past the position of the intervening PP and adjoins to VP, stranding the RRC in situ. This derives the pattern of RRC-extraposition displayed in (397).

   The idea that there are two verb phrases in a clause (the so-called double VP-shell approach proposed by Larson 1988, 1990) provides two possible landing sites for the scrambled object: left-hand adjunction to the higher vP or to the lower VP, as sketched in (399a) and (399b), respectively.

(399) a.   b.

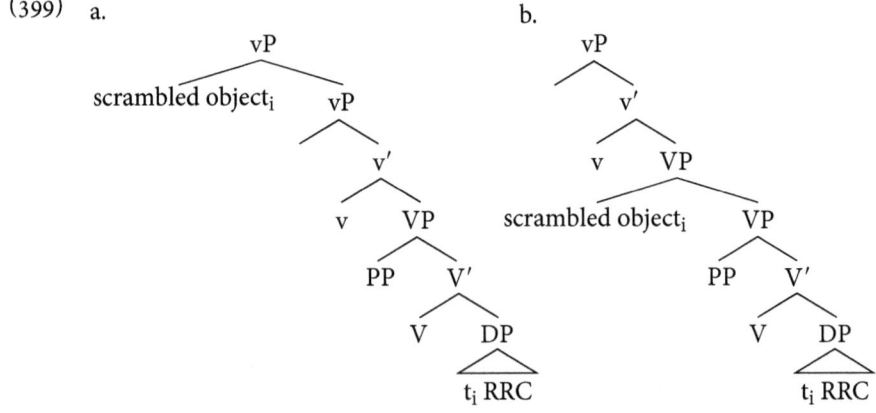

One possible way to identify the exact landing site of the scrambled object could be to examine its relative position with respect to a post-verbal subject in [Spec, vP]. However, as I discuss in §3.5.1.3B, in sentences involving RRC-extraposition, the subject and the object cannot independently co-occur in a post-verbal position. Therefore, this test must be discarded for present purposes.

---

[33] Also note that, as already mentioned, there are different constraints that may lead to the PP–DP base-generation order. In (397) it results from heaviness, whereas in (395) it results from binding requirements.

Another possibility is to assume that adverb placement can be used to identify the exact position of a constituent within a double VP-shell. Unfortunately, because J. Costa (1998, 2004a, 2004b) assumes a single VP-shell in his studies of adverbs in CEP, adverbs cannot be used as a reliable test for this specific purpose, at least until more research is developed in this domain.

Finally, let me consider the validity of another test: the so-called *Fronting/ Preposing* (J. Costa 2004a: 49, 147) or *VP-topicalization* (see Kato and Raposo 2007; Bastos 2001). This construction involves two instances of the same verb in a single sentence: an infinitival form in the preposed constituent and a finite form in the normal position of the verb in CEP (see (400)).[34]

(400) Visitar os amigos, a   Maria visita todos os anos.
       visit.INF the friends the M.   visits every the years
       'Visit her friends, Maria does it every year.' (Kato and Raposo 2007: 211)

An extraposed RRC involving a double complement construction can surface in the preposed constituent, as illustrated in (401).

(401) Eu queria dar   um presente à   Maria que tivesse   um
       I   wanted give.INF a   present to.the M.   that have.SBJV a
       significado especial e [dar   um presente à   Maria que
       meaning   special and give.INF a   present to.the M.   that
       tivesse   um significado especial] eu dei.
       have.SBJV a   meaning   special   I gave
       'I wanted to give a present that had a special meaning to Maria and give a present that had a special meaning to Maria I did.'

Let me assume, along the lines of Kato and Raposo (2007), that this construction: (1) involves VP-topicalization and that (2) the topicalized constituent contains a copy of the V (which moves to I) that is spelled out in its default infinitive form.[35] Under these assumptions, the order of constituents within the topicalized constituent in

---

[34] It is worth noting that there is no consensus in the literature as to the analysis of the construction in (400). Matos (1992: 195–6) claims that the preposed constituent is merged in situ, whereas Kato and Raposo (2007) suggest that it undergoes movement to the left periphery. Moreover, Matos claims that the preposed constituent is a clausal constituent adjoined to the matrix clause, whereas Kato and Raposo claim that it is a topicalized VP. For a non-uniform approach to the phenomenon of VP-topicalization, see also Bastos (2001).

[35] Kato and Raposo (2007) assume that the verb form that appears in the numeration is the infinitive, which after the addition of the inflection loses the final r. Therefore, when the verb is spelled out inside the VP, it surfaces in the default infinitive form, as no inflection was added to it at this point of the derivation. In contrast, when the verb is spelled out in I, it surfaces in a finite form because the addition of the inflection has already taken place.

(401) (i.e. the *verb-scrambled object* order) can only be derived by assuming that:
(1) the verb is spelled in the light *v*; and (2) the antecedent of the relative clause is
left-adjoined to the lower VP, as sketched in (402). As can be easily concluded, if
the antecedent of the RRC were adjoined to the higher vP, it would precede the verb
dar 'give'.

(402)

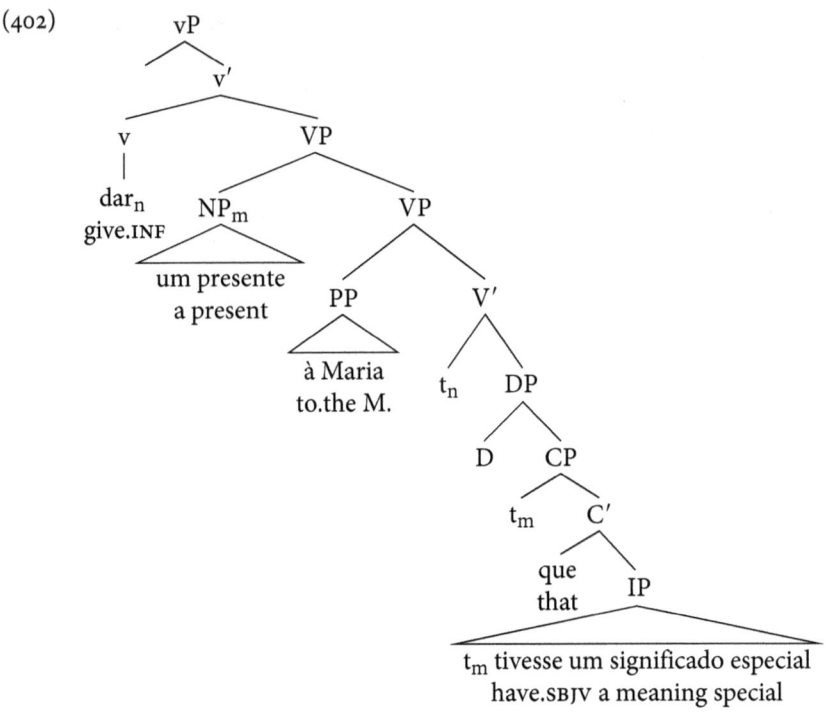

Note that the same line of reasoning applies to the instances of VP-topicalization that
involve the monosyllabic adverb *bem* 'well' and a scrambled object, as in (403).

(403) a. Falar   francês bem, o João fala.   [scrambled object]
           speak.INF French well the J.   speaks
           'Speak French well, João does it.'

       b. Falar   bem francês, o João fala.   [non-scrambled object]
           speak.INF well French the J.   speaks

The V–O–Adv order in (403a) and the V–Adv–O order in (403b) emerge from a
configuration in which the verb is spelled out in the light *v*, and the scrambled object
and/or the monosyllabic adverb *bem* 'well' are left-adjoined to the lower VP, as
sketched in (404a–b). Note that if the adverb (and the scrambled object) were left-
adjoined to vP, they would precede the verb *falar* 'speak'.

(404)

a. V–DO–Adv order

b. V–Adv–DO order

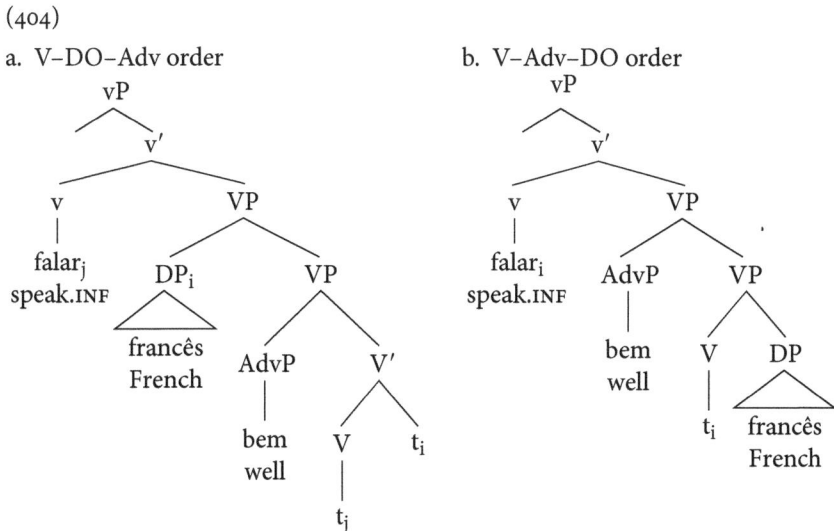

In summary, VP-topicalization suggests that scrambled constituents in CEP may be left-adjoined to the lower VP. However, note that other contexts independently reveal scrambled objects to be left-adjoined to the higher vP. This is the case of the sentences displaying the VOS order, as in (405). Under the assumption that the post-verbal subjects are in [Spec, vP] (J. Costa 1998, 2004a), it is clear that the scrambled object in (405) is left-adjoined to the higher vP.

(405) Comeu a sopa o Paulo.
       ate   the soup the P.
       'Paulo ate the soup.'

The same is true of the cases of RRC-extraposition involving the subject of an unergative verb as an antecedent, as in (406), repeated from (265). In this case, the adverb *ontem* 'yesterday' is left-adjoined to the higher vP, and the subject in [Spec, vP] undergoes scrambling to a vP-adjoined position.

(406) Telefonou um rapaz <u>ontem</u>   que queria informações sobre a tua
       phoned   a boy yesterday that wanted details   about the your
       casa.
       house
       'A boy phoned yesterday who wanted details about your house.'

Cumulatively, I conclude that scrambled constituents in CEP may be adjoined to the higher vP, for example in VOS contexts and in the contexts involving scrambling of the subject of unergative verbs. However, they can also be left-adjoined to the lower VP, as is the case for scrambled objects in double object constructions.

Therefore, I propose that the (simplified) structure of an extraposed RRC with a PP complement as intervening material is as in (407).

(407)

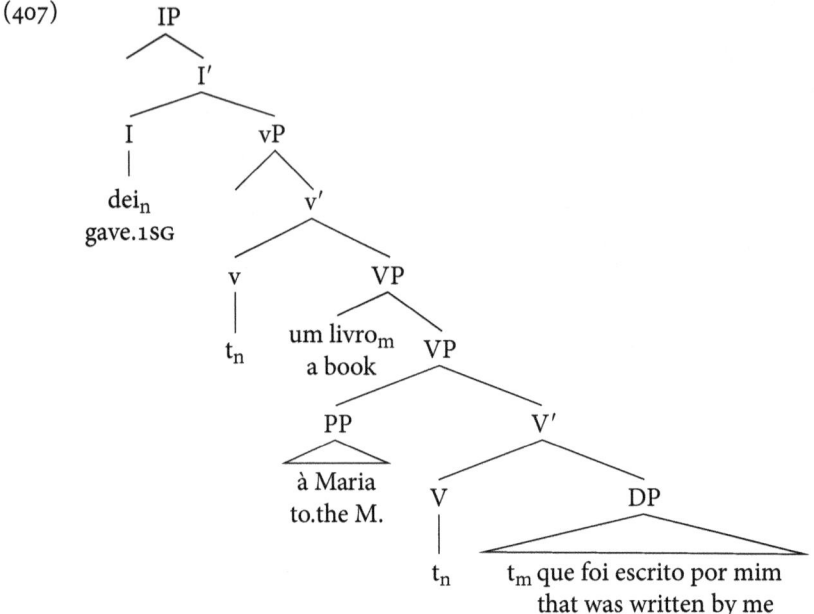

B. Blocking other constituents in the intervening position

This section is devoted to explaining why the subject and the direct object cannot surface in the intervening position in CEP. Given that facts regarding the word order have an important bearing on the syntax of RRC-extraposition, I first make a few remarks about the word order in CEP (in particular, with respect to subject inversion) and then demonstrate how the syntactic constraints that independently hold for CEP can explain the impossibility of the subject and the direct object surfacing in the intervening position.

In CEP, sentences with broad information focus exhibit a restriction on subject inversion that is related to the type of verb involved (see Martins forthcoming). Although subject inversion is possible with unaccusative, unergative, and indirect transitive verbs (see (408b–d), it is impossible with direct transitive and ditransitive verbs (see (408e–f)).[36]

---

[36] A similar pattern has been observed in other constructions cross-linguistically (see Alexiadou and Anagnostopoulou 2001 for an overview). It is found, for instance, in expletive constructions in French and English, which are well formed with intransitive verbs but not with direct transitive verbs (see (i) and (ii), respectively), and in stylistic inversion in French, which is also well formed with intransitive verbs but not with transitives (see (iii)). Examples (i)–(iii) are from Alexiadou and Anagnostopoulou (2001: 195–6).

(i)   a. Il   est arrivé   un homme.
         EXPL is arrived a   man
         'There has arrived a man.'

(408) [A]: a. O que aconteceu?
the what happened
'What happened?'

[B]: b. Chegou uma carta anónima. (*unaccusative verb*)
arrived a letter anonymous
'An anonymous letter arrived.'

c. Telefonou a Maria. (*unergative verb*)
phoned the M.
'Maria phoned.'

d. Apareceram dois polícias em nossa casa. (*indirect transitive verb*)
showed.up two cops at our home
'Two cops showed up at our home.'

e. *Comprou o João uma casa. (*direct transitive verb*)
bought the J. a house
'João bought a house.'

f. *Ofereceu o João um anel de noivado à
offered the J. a ring of engagement to.the
Ana. (*ditransitive verb*)
A.
'João offered an engagement ring to Ana.'

Under J. Costa's (2004a) analysis of CEP, post-verbal subjects in simple declarative affirmative sentences arise in the following way: the verb moves up to T and stops there. The subject does not precede it because it has never moved from its base position.

On the basis of Costa's analysis, the contrasts found in the paradigm (408) can be captured by the generalization in (409).[37]

b. *Il a lu un élève le livre.
EXPL has read a student the book
'There has read a student the book.'

(ii) a. There arrived a man.
b. *There finished somebody the assignment.

(iii) a. Je me demande quand partira Marie.
I myself.CL ask when leave.FUT M.
'I wonder when Marie will leave.'

b. *Je me demande quand achèteront les consommateurs les pommes.
I myself.CL ask when buy.FUT the consumers the apples
'I wonder when the consumers will buy the apples.'

[37] An explanation for this restriction is beyond the scope of the book. Nevertheless, it is worth mentioning that an analysis such as Alexiadou and Anagnostopoulou's (2001) may explain the restrictions under scrutiny. According to these authors, there is a general ban against having the subject and the direct object in a VP-internal position. This is explained by postulating that a head cannot have more than one unchecked Case feature in LF. Without going into the details of their analysis, the derivation of the

(409)   Restriction on subject inversion in CEP (I)
        The subject and the direct object cannot stay in a VP-internal position; one of
        them must vacate the VP.

However, the restriction in (409) does not hold for all syntactic and discourse
contexts. Abstracting away from the sentences that involve V-to-C movement,[38]
the subject and the direct object may co-occur inside the VP in sentences displaying
narrow information focus. Two possible word orders may be found: (1) the VOS
word order is found when the subject is assigned narrow focus (as in (410c)); and (2)
the VSO word order arises when both the subject and the direct object are assigned
narrow information focus (as in (411b)).

(410)   Subject is focused.[39]
        [A]: a. Quem é que partiu a   janela?
                who is that broke the window
                'Who broke the window?'

        [B]: b. #Partiu o   Paulo a   janela.
                broke the P.   the window
                'Paulo broke the window.'

             c. Partiu (a janela) o   Paulo
                broke the window the P.   (all J. Costa 2004a: 80)

(411)   Subject and direct object are focused:
        [A]: a. Ninguém partiu nada.
                nobody   broke nothing
                'Nobody broke anything.'

        [B]: b. Partiu o   Paulo a   janela.
                broke the P.   the window
                'Paulo broke the window.'

---

ungrammatical V [$_{VP}$ S O] generically proceeds as follows: (1) V raises overtly to T; (2) after Spell Out, v
raises to T forming a complex head (T^{max}); and (3) T^{max} inherits the Case features of T (traditionally the
nominative Case) and the Case features of v (traditionally the accusative Case), and as a consequence, the
derivation crashes.

[38] According to Martins (forthcoming), there are some factors that may contribute to making the VSO
order available in broad information focus sentences, e.g. paratactic factual concessive constructions, which
express the speaker's disapproval of (or disappointment with) the unpredictability of an event or situation
(see example). However, as Martins notes, these constructions seem to involve V-to-C movement.

   Convidei eu a   Maria para jantar e   ela não apareceu.
   invited I the M.   for dinner and she not appeared
   'I invited Mary for dinner but she didn't come./Although I invited Mary for dinner, she didn't come.'

[39] According to my judgment, sentence (410c) cannot occur with the direct object to the right of the
verb, and only the subject is possible as an answer to (410a). Nevertheless, assuming that other speakers
may share J. Costa's (2004a) judgments, I will pursue the argument as though the VOS order in CEP were
possible in the context given in (410), leaving the investigation of this issue open for future research.

c. #Partiu a janela o Paulo
broke the window the P. (all J. Costa 2004a: 80)

Assuming (along with J. Costa 2004a) that in narrow information focus sentences, the post-verbal subject stays in its base position,[40] the restriction in (409) can be reformulated as in (412).

(412) Restriction on subject inversion in CEP (II)
In sentences with broad information focus, the subject and the direct object cannot remain in a VP-internal position; one of them must vacate the VP.

With this in mind, let me return now to the syntax of RRC-extraposition. The facts about CEP word order in inversion contexts predict the availability of RRC-extraposition in sentences displaying narrow information focus, with the subject or the direct object as intervening material, as in (413).

(413) a. [VDO $\underline{S}$ t_{DO} RRC]
b. [V S $\underline{DO}$ t_S RRC]

In subsections (a) and (b), I will show why this prediction is not borne out.

(a) Subject in the intervening position

The analysis developed thus far predicts the occurrence of the subject in the intervening position in sentences displaying narrow information focus, when an extraposed RRC takes a direct object as an antecedent, as sketched in (414).

(414) [$_{IP}$ V [$_{VP}$ DO [$_{VP}$ $\underline{S}$ [$_{VP}$ t_V t_{DO} RRC]]]]

However, sentences involving the structure in (414) are ungrammatical in CEP, as illustrated in (415).

(415) *Trouxe um bolo a Rita que tinha compota de morango.
brought a cake the R. that had jam of strawberry
'Rita brought a cake that had strawberry jam.'

Recall from the discussion above (around (412)) that the VOS order in CEP arises in narrow information focus sentences, where only the subject is focused. The object is not interpreted as information focus because it is previously referred to in the discourse. Therefore, (415) is not a possible configuration in CEP because the focused subject must surface in the rightmost sentential position in order to receive the default stress.

---

[40] According to J. Costa (2004a), the VOS order (in (410c)) is derived by short scrambling the object past the subject, whereas in the VSO order (in (411b)), the subject and the object remain in their base position inside the VP.

(b) Direct object in the intervening position

In CEP, sentences with narrow information focus can display VSO order (see e.g. (411b)). However, an extraposed RRC taking a subject as an antecedent cannot surface with a direct object in the intervening position, according to the scheme in (416).

(416)　*[V S DO t$_S$ RRC]

The impossibility of (416) is straightforwardly derived from the stranding analysis of RRC-extraposition proposed here. Under a single VP-shell, the subject is base-generated in [Spec, VP] and the direct object in the complement position of V. Then, an RRC stranded in the subject position can never follow a direct object in the complement position of V.

3.5.2 Deriving the relevant properties

Having taken this excursus into the derivation of RRC-extraposition (via movement to the left periphery or short scrambling), I will now return to the properties of RRC-extraposition in CEP outlined in §3.4.1: (1) definiteness effect; (2) restriction on extraposition from pre-verbal positions; and (3) restriction on extraposition from PPs. In §§3.5.2.1–3, I show how the theoretical apparatus presented in §3.5.1 derives these properties.

3.5.2.1 The definiteness effect　As already mentioned in §3.4.1.1, extraposed RRCs in CEP can take weak noun phrases as their antecedent but not strong noun phrases. This property can be explained by considering Bowers' (1987) proposal that strong and weak noun phrases differ in their structure. Strong determiners are of category D, whereas weak determiners are adjectives and attach within NP, as illustrated in (417).

(417)　a.　[$_{DP}$ each [$_{NP}$ picture of manatees]]
　　　　b.　[$_{NP}$ [$_{AP}$ many] [$_{N'}$ pictures of manatees]]

This proposal is based on the contrasting behavior of strong and weak noun phrases in extraction configurations. For instance, in (418) extraction can take place from a PP embedded in a weak noun phrase (see (418a)) but not from a PP within a strong noun phrase (see (418b)). According to Bowers (1987), the presence of an additional layer (i.e. a DP layer) in the strong noun phrase in (418b) blocks the extraction out of the PP.

(418)　a.　Who did you buy a/three/many picture(s) of?
　　　　b.　*Who did you buy the/those/each/every/those picture(s) of? (both Bowers 1987: 49)

Extending Bowers' proposal to the raising analysis of relative clauses, I assume (in line with Kayne 1994 and Lee 2007) that strong determiners are located in the external determiner, whereas weak determiners are within NP. This explains in a straightforward manner why extraposed RRCs can take only weak noun phrases as antecedents. Weak noun phrases can be moved leftward as a constituent, whereas strong noun phrases cannot because there is no constituent that includes the strong determiner and the noun phrase but excludes the RRC, as shown in (419).

(419)

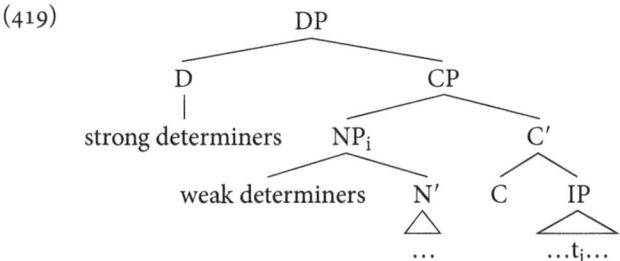

The view that strong and weak determiners occupy different structural positions is supported by two additional arguments: (1) indefiniteness effect of the relative trace; and (2) licensing of the strong determiner (Bianchi 1999).

A. Indefiniteness effect of the relative trace

In the raising analysis, the relative clause is the complement of a determiner generated outside the relative CP. Assuming that strong determiners are of D category, the grammaticality of (420) can be explained by the fact that the weak noun phrase inside the relative CP (*três baloiços* 'three swings') satisfies the indefiniteness effect of the existential construction (see Browning 1987 and Bianchi 1999, among others). Hence, the strong determiner *o* 'the' cannot be generated within the raising head, as can be confirmed by the contrast in (421).

(420)   Os três   baloiços que havia em tua   casa   eram muito confortáveis
        the three swings   that were in   your house were   very   comfortable
        'The three swings that there were in your house were very comfortable.'

(421)   a. Havia três   baloiços em tua   casa.
           were   three swings   in   your house
           'There were three swings in your house.'

        b. *Havia os   três   baloiços em tua   casa.
           were   the three swings   in   your house

B. Licensing of the strong determiner

There are some contexts in which the definite determiner *o(s)/a(s)* 'the.M(PL)/the. F(PL)' seems to be licensed by the presence of an RRC (see (422)).[41]

---

[41] The example in (422a) is constructed from Bianchi (1994: 40), whereas (422b–d) are built from Schmitt (2000: 311–12).

(422) a. A   Lisboa *(que eu conheço)
           the L.   that I   know
           'The Lisbon that I know.'

       b. A   Maria comprou uma casa   com as janelas   *(que queria)
           the M.   bought   a   house with the windows   that wanted
           'Maria bought the house with the windows that she wanted.'

       c. A   Maria pesa   os 50 quilos *(que a   Rita gostaria de   pesar).
           the M.   weighs the 50 kilos   that the R.   love.COND DE.PREP weigh.INF
           'Maria weighs the 50 kilos that Rita would love to weigh.'

       d. Comprei   o   tipo de pão   *(que tu   preferes)
           bought.1SG the type of bread   that you prefer
           'I bought the type of bread that you prefer.'

The close connection between the RRC and the definite determiner in (422) has been
used by the proponents of the raising analysis to support the claim that the determiner selects the relative CP (in the configuration [$_{DP}$ D CP]) (Vergnaud 1974,
among others).[42] The fact that such a relation typically holds between the strong
determiner and the RRC might suggest that a weak determiner does not select the
relative CP. Thus, it is not merged in a position external to the relative CP but within
the internal NP.

3.5.2.2 *Pre-verbal positions*   In CEP , extraposed RRCs can take post-verbal subjects
as antecedents but not pre-verbal subjects. Additionally, extraposed RRCs can take
wh-constituents, emphatic/evaluative phrases, and preposed foci as antecedents but
not topics. Barbosa (2009) provides an explanation for this contrast in terms of a
prosodic account of extraposition. First, I discuss Barbosa's (2009) proposal, showing
that it is incompatible with the analysis adopted here. Then I offer an alternative
explanation for the phenomenon that rests upon the semantic interpretation of the
antecedent.

As mentioned in Chapter 1 n. 46, there are currently two competing proposals
for the syntactic analysis of pre-verbal subjects in CEP. J. Costa (2001, 2004a) and
Costa and Duarte (2002) claim that pre-verbal subjects A-move to [Spec, IP],
whereas Barbosa (1995, 2000, 2009) claims that subjects are base-generated in a

---

[42] Obviously, the ability to license a determiner is not limited to relative clauses (e.g. *a Lisboa dos anos
60* 'the Lisbon of the 60s') (see Jackendoff 1977). Note, however, that Kayne's approach to relative clauses
also extends to other restrictive modifiers (Bianchi 1999: 280 n. 17).

left-dislocated position (as adjuncts to CP/IP). The two hypotheses are sketched in (423a–b), respectively.

(423)   a. [$_{IP}$ S V [$_{VP}$ t$_S$ t$_V$]]
        b. [$_{IP/CP}$ S [$_{IP/CP}$ V [$_{VP}$ *pro* t$_V$]]]

One of Barbosa's arguments in favor of the left-dislocated position of subjects in CEP (and in Romance Null Subject Languages in general) is precisely the impossibility of extraposition from pre-verbal indefinite subjects. Assuming Truckenbrodt's (1995) prosodic approach to extraposition, Barbosa claims that relative clause extraposition is sensitive to Intonational Phrase (IntP) boundaries. More precisely, for extraposition to be possible, no IntP boundary may intervene between the antecedent and the rest of the clause. Because dislocated elements are (at least initially) mapped onto an IntP domain that is separated from the IntP domain onto which the rest of the clause is mapped, the impossibility of relative clause extraposition in CEP is straightforwardly derived (see (424), from Barbosa 2009: 44).

(424)   a. Syntax:
           [um homem que quer falar   contigo]$_k$ [$_{IP}$ *pro*$_k$ apareceu]
            a   man   that wants talk.INF with.you   showed.up
           'A man showed up that wants to talk to you.'
        b. Prosodic Structure:
           [um homem que quer falar   contigo]IntP apareceu]IntP
            a   man   that wants talk.INF with.you   showed.up

In contrast, because the pre-verbal subject is in [Spec, IP] in Romance non-Null Subject Languages (and English), no IntP boundary intervenes between the pre-verbal subject and the rest of the clause. Consequently, extraposition is allowed.

As for the cases in which non-referential QPs and focalized DPs appear in a pre-verbal position in CEP, Barbosa claims that these constituents are not left-dislocated but rather fronted by A[prime] movement. In this case, no IntP boundary intervenes between the fronted constituent and the rest of the clause, and extraposition is allowed.

As can be easily concluded, Barbosa's account of RRC-extraposition is not compatible with the stranding analysis of RRC-extraposition proposed here because the subject is base-generated in a left-dislocated position. To be compatible with the analysis presented here, this account must be "massaged" to provide for the base-generation of the subject in a VP-internal position.

Additionally, note that Barbosa's analysis makes the wrong prediction with respect to the availability of RRC-extraposition in Null Subject Languages. Barbosa claims that there is a correlation between the possibility of extraposition from pre-verbal subject positions and the Null Subject Parameter. Specifically, she claims that Null

Subject Languages do not allow extraposition from pre-verbal subjects, whereas non-Null Subject Languages allow for it. Again, this is simply not correct. Over the course of its history, Portuguese has always been a Null Subject Language, but in earlier periods of its history it allowed extraposition from pre-verbal subjects, as illustrated in (425) (repeated from (323)).[43]

(425) se Algẽ   A eles   veer   que diga   que llj   eu
       if someone to them come.FUT.SBJV that says.SBJV that him.CL I
       Alguna cousa diuía
       some   thing owed
       'if someone who says that I owed him something comes towards them' (13th c.,
       DCMP)

Alternatively, I would like to suggest that the explanation for the restriction on extraposition from pre-verbal subjects rests upon the semantic interpretation of the antecedent. More precisely, I claim that RRC-extraposition in CEP obeys the *Interpretative Principle* given in (426).

(426) Interpretative Principle
       The antecedent of an extraposed RRC must occur in a position non-ambiguously
       interpreted as non-topic (in Kuroda's 2005 sense).[44]

The fact that the restriction on extraposition from pre-verbal positions is semantically motivated should not come as a surprise because several authors have already observed that word order in CEP reflects both information structure and the contrast

---

[43] Interestingly, Fiéis and Lobo (2010) show that earlier stages of Portuguese are also problematic for Barbosa's hypothesis concerning the position of the subject in absolute gerund clauses. Barbosa claims that Null Subject Languages and non-Null Subject Languages contrast with respect to the possibility of having pre-verbal subjects in absolute gerund clauses: non-Null Subject Languages are subject initial (*Your brother having called...*), whereas Null Subject Languages are V/Aux initial (*Aparecendo a Maria...* lit. 'showing up Maria...'). Fiéis and Lobo (2010) demonstrate that this correlation is simply not correct. In earlier stages of its history, Portuguese is a Null Subject Language and allows for pre-verbal subjects in absolute gerund clauses, as illustrated in the following example, from Fiéis and Lobo (2010: 422).

Joham Rodriguez estando no   logar, veo sobr'elle o   concelho de Ledesma
J.   R.   be.GER in.the place came over.him the ±group of L.
'Joham Rodriguez being in the place, the group of Ledesma attacked him.'

One hypothesis that is worth exploring in future research is that the Null Subject Parameter does not necessarily correlate with specific subject positions. I tentatively hypothesize that Null Subject Languages might display different positions for pre-verbal subjects and that this may be subject to cross-linguistic and diachronic variation. Hence, I conjecture that earlier stages of Portuguese and CEP may differ in the structural position occupied by pre-verbal subjects. However, further research is necessary in this domain to warrant the validity of these suggestions.

[44] In this context, the term *topic* is not used as a syntactic concept (i.e. as referring to a constituent that is placed at the sentential left periphery) nor as a discourse-theoretical concept (i.e. as referring to a constituent that expresses old information in the organization of the discourse) but as a semantic concept. In this sense, it is understood as a constituent that expresses an *aboutness relation* (Kuroda 2005). For more details, I refer the reader to §1.3.3.3.

between categorical and thetic judgments (in the sense of Kuroda 1965, 1972, 2005).[45]

Let me now explore in detail how the Interpretative Principle in (426) explains the restriction on extraposition from pre-verbal subjects and topics.

A. Pre-verbal subjects

Assuming the distinction between categorical and thetic judgments originally proposed by Kuroda (1965), Martins (forthcoming) provides evidence for the idea that [Spec, IP] is an ambiguous position in CEP. It can be filled by topic elements (i.e. the subject of predication in sentences expressing categorical judgments), but it can also be filled by non-topic elements (i.e. the subject of a sentence expressing thetic/descriptive judgments). For details and examples, see §1.3.3.3.

This explains why extraposed RRCs cannot take a pre-verbal subject as an antecedent. According to the Interpretative Principle in (426), the antecedent of an extraposed RRC must occur in a position non-ambiguously interpreted as non-topic. Given that [Spec, IP] does not satisfy this requirement, a constituent occurring in this position cannot be the antecedent of an extraposed RRC.

In contrast, as already shown in §1.3.3.3, post-verbal subjects occupy positions non-ambiguously interpreted as non-topic. Hence, a scrambled subject left-adjoined to VP satisfies the Interpretative Principle in (426) and, therefore, can be taken as the antecedent of an extraposed RRC.

B. Discourse dedicated positions in the left periphery

The Interpretative Principle in (426) can also explain why RRC-extraposition cannot take place from topics. Assuming a split-CP approach (Rizzi 1997), according to which there are different functional projections especially dedicated to single discourse functions (e.g. TopP and FocP; see §1.3.1.4), the position occupied by a topic constituent is non-ambiguously interpreted as topic. Therefore, RRC-extraposition is ruled out by the Interpretative Principle in (426).

Conversely, the position occupied by wh-constituents, emphatic/evaluative phrases and preposed foci is non-ambiguously interpreted as non-topic. Therefore, the possibility for extraposition from these constituents is straightforwardly derived.

3.5.2.3 Prepositional phrases   In CEP, RRC-extraposition is not permitted if the antecedent is the object of a preposition. This restriction is straightforwardly derived

---

[45] Based on the Brentano–Marty theory of judgments, Kuroda distinguishes two types of judgment: categorical/predicational vs. thetic/descriptive. A categorical/predicational judgment is a cognitive act of attributing a predicate to a subject, whereas a thetic/descriptive judgment is grounded, in its basic form, on perception. For further details see §1.3.3.3.

under the standard assumption that movement only applies to constituents. As sketched in (427), the preposition, the determiner, and the noun phrase in [Spec, CP] do not form a constituent (excluding the RRC). As a result, they cannot undergo leftward movement, stranding the RRC in situ.

(427)

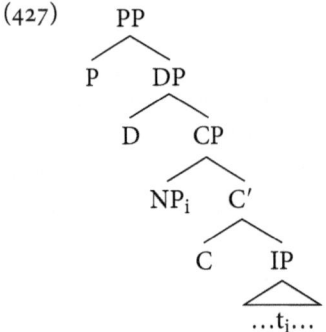

3.5.2.4 *Summary*   The results of Section 3.5.2 are summarized in Table 3.6. A plus indicates that the stranding analysis can straightforwardly derive the restriction or derive it with reference to independent principles; a minus would indicate that it cannot.

I conclude that the stranding analysis accounts for the restrictions on RRC-extraposition in CEP. However, it is worth noting that this analysis has received much criticism in the literature (Büring and Hartmann 1997; Koster 2000; De Vries 2002; among others). In §3.5.3, I review some of the arguments that have been put forth in the literature against the stranding analysis and show that they do not offer any insurmountable obstacle to the approach proposed here because they do not apply to CEP.

TABLE 3.6 Contemporary European Portuguese: Evaluation of the stranding analysis

Empirical issue		Stranding analysis
A. No extraposition from strong noun phrases		+
B. Extraposition from pre-verbal positions	no pre-verbal subjects	+
	wh-constituents	+
	emphatic/evaluative phrases	+
	preposed foci	+
	no topics	+
C. No extraposition from PPs		+

3.5.3 Problems

A number of arguments have been adduced in the literature against the stranding analysis of RRC-extraposition, namely: (1) extraposition from strong noun phrases; (2) extraposition from PPs; (3) ungrammaticality of the source structure; (4) constraints on the surface position of extraposed RRCs; (5) extraposition from subjects; (6) emptiness of the VP; (7) mirror effects; (8) VP-topicalization; (9) extraposition from split antecedents. These arguments are listed in A–I and are discussed in turn.

A. Extraposition from strong noun phrases

One of the most frequently adduced arguments against the stranding analysis is that it cannot derive extraposed RRCs taking a definite article+head as an antecedent. For instance, Koster (2000) shows that an extraposed RRC can take a definite article +head as an antecedent in Dutch, as illustrated in (428) (see also (296)).

(428)   Hij heeft [de vrouw]$_i$ <u>gezien</u> t$_i$ die   het boek geschreven heeft.
         he has   the woman seen   who the book written   has
         'He has seen the woman who has written the book.' (Koster 2000: 5)

Koster argues that sentences like (428) undermine the stranding analysis: *de* and *vrouw* do not form a constituent to the exclusion of the RRC and, as a result, cannot undergo leftward movement, stranding the RRC in situ. However, note that this does not constitute a problem for the analysis adopted here. CEP, unlike Dutch, does not allow for extraposed RRCs with a definite article+head as an antecedent, as shown in §3.4.1.1. In actual fact, the unavailability of sentences like (428) in CEP supports an analysis of RRC-extraposition in CEP in terms of stranding.

B. Extraposition from prepositional phrases

A similar obstacle for the stranding analysis regards extraposition from PPs. Koster (2000) points out that extraposition from NPs within PPs is entirely grammatical in Dutch. See (429); also (314) and (316).

(429)   Hij heeft [met een vrouw] <u>gesproken</u> die   alles   wist
         he has   with a   woman talked   who everything knew
         'He has talked with a woman who knew everything.'   (Koster 2000: 23)

Koster (2000) and De Vries (2002) claim that the stranding analysis cannot derive (429); *met een vrouw* 'with a woman' is not a constituent and consequently cannot be moved leftwards. Alternatively, assuming that the PP and the head can be generated separately, the movement of *een vrouw* 'a woman' to a position inside the PP would involve movement to a non c-commanding position. Again, this problem does not arise in CEP because RRC-extraposition cannot take place from prepositional phrases positions, as shown in §3.4.1.3.

C. Ungrammaticality of the source structure

Another obstacle to the stranding analysis concerns the ungrammaticality of the source structure in languages like Dutch. Recall that under the stranding analysis, the antecedent and the RRC are base-generated together. According to Koster (2000), such an analysis does not even have initial plausibility because the presumed source structure in (430), displaying the SVO order, is ungrammatical in Dutch.

(430)   *Hij heeft gezien de vrouw   die het boek geschreven heeft.
         he has   seen   the woman who the book written   has
         'He has seen the woman who has written the book.' (Koster 2000: 7)

Sentence (430) is ungrammatical because in an SOV language like Dutch, NP objects do not generally follow the verb. Note that in the extraposed version, the forbidden sequence *V-NP would still be involved, as illustrated in (431).

(431)   Hij heeft [NP de   vrouw]ᵢ gezien [NP [NP tᵢ] [CP die   het boek
         he has   the woman   seen   who the book
         geschreven heeft]]
         written   has (Koster 2000: 7)

Of course, this problem does not arise in an SVO language like CEP, where NP objects usually follow the verb. Therefore, sentences where the head plus its RRC are construed post-verbally are entirely grammatical, as illustrated in (432a). Given that the sequence V-NP is not forbidden, an RRC is likely to be stranded in a post-verbal position, as illustrated in (432b).

(432) a. Encontrei ontem   uma rapariga que perguntou por ti.
          met.1SG   yesterday a   girl   that asked   for you
          'Yesterday I met a girl that asked for you.'

       b. Encontrei uma rapariga ᵢ ontem   tᵢ que perguntou por ti.
          met.1SG   a   girl   yesterday   that asked   for you

D. Constraints on the surface position of extraposed RRCs

Another problem concerns the clause-final position of extraposed RRCs. It has been argued in the literature that if the RRC-extraposition is derived from stranding, it becomes a mystery why an extraposed RRC cannot surface in an intermediate position. Koster (2000) and De Vries (2002) demonstrate that if the antecedent is preposed in Dutch, the relative clause cannot be left behind at the normal object position; see (433), adapted from De Vries (2002: 254).

(433)   *Een man heb ik die   een rode koffer   draagt gesignaleerd.
          a   man have I   who a   red suitcase carries noticed
          'I have noticed a man who carries a red suitcase.'

De Vries (2002) argues that if extraposition were stranding, nothing should exclude the schematic derivation of (433) given in (434).

(434)   a. V [NP RC] →
        b. [NP RC]$_i$ V t$_i$ →
        c. NP Aux S [t$_{NP}$ RC]$_i$ V t$_i$ (all De Vries 2002: 255)

Although it can be a problem for Dutch, such an objection is not applicable to CEP. In this language, if the antecedent is focalized, the extraposed RRC can be left behind at the normal object position, as illustrated in (435).

(435)   Nada   mais   disse   que valesse a pena   até   ao   final da
        nothing more   said.3SG that be.worthwhile.SBJV until to.the end of.the
        conferência.
        conference
        'He did not say anything else that was worthwhile until the end of the conference.'

The same is true of contexts involving a wh-constituent as the antecedent of an RRC. As shown in (436), an extraposed RRC can be left behind at a non-final position.

(436)   Quantas   pessoas apareceram que não foram convidadas naquela
        how.many people showed.up that not were   invited   in.that
        festa   horrível que organizámos   em   minha casa!
        party   horrible that organized.1PL at   my   house
        'How many people showed up that were not invited to that horrible party that we organized at my house!'

In sentences (435)–(436), there is a clear pause between the extraposed RRC and the constituent in the clause-final position. This pause, which appears to be crucial to the acceptability of these sentences, seems to suggest that an extraposed RRC may surface in a non-final position if the constituent following the RRC is mapped into an independent intonational phrase. This guarantees that the extraposed RRC receives prosodic stress and is interpreted with prosodic and discourse prominence.

   Although various aspects of the interaction between extraposition and prosody remain open for future research, it is clear that the (prosodic) constraints on the surface position of extraposed RRC do not undermine the syntactic analysis of RRC-extraposition in CEP in terms of stranding.

E. Extraposition from subjects

Another problematic aspect discussed by Koster (2000) is the possibility of having extraposition from subjects in Dutch, as illustrated in (437).

(437)   Een vrouw   heeft het boek geschreven die   alles   wist.
        a   woman has   the book written   who   everything   knew
        'A woman who knew everything has written the book.' (Koster 2000: 8)

It is generally assumed that Dutch verbs are spelled out in V (apart from V_2 position of the finite verb in main clauses). Therefore, under the stranding analysis, the source structure of (437) would have the head plus its RRC to the right of the VP as a subject, which is not a legitimate base position for the subject in any language.

However, this problem does not arise in CEP. Suppose that subjects are base-generated VP-internally, as suggested by Koopman and Sportiche (1991). Furthermore, consider that CEP displays V-to-I movement. Under these two assumptions, it is clear that an extraposed RRC taking a subject as an antecedent can be stranded in its base position. As depicted in (438), the RRC can be stranded in [Spec, VP] (under a single VP-shell), preceding the trace of V (which moved to I).

(438) $[_{IP}$ V $[_{VP}$ S $[_{VP}$ adverb $[_{VP}$ t_S RRC $[_{V'}$ $t_V]]]]]$

F. Emptiness of the VP

De Vries (2002) argues that the stranding analysis is implausible because it requires that all the material must vacate the VP or an even higher projection. Focusing on extraposition from non-objects, he claims that everything would be generated within the VP, and the VP would always be emptied, as represented, for instance, in (439).[46]

(439) S Aux…O V AdvP $[_{VP}$ $[t_S$ RRC$]$ t_V t_O $]$

However, the emptiness of the VP does not constitute a problem for RRC-extraposition in CEP given that most of the operations are independently motivated. First, there is independent V-to-I movement. Therefore, the main verb and, concomitantly, pre-verbal subjects always vacate the VP. Moreover, there is a restriction against having both the subject and the object in a VP-internal position; one of them must vacate the VP (see (412)).

G. Mirror effects

De Vries (2002) shows that if two RRCs are extraposed in Dutch, a mirror effect emerges: an RRC extraposed from the object must precede an RRC extraposed from the subject. This is illustrated in (440), from De Vries (2002: 248).

(440) a. Een zekere misdadiger heeft de   kluis gekraakt die   tweehonderd
           a   certain criminal   has the safe cracked that two.hundred
           diamanten bevatte,   die ook meneer X heeft vermoord.
           diamonds   contained, who also mister X has   killed
           lit. 'A certain criminal has cracked the safe that contained two hundred
           diamonds, who also has killed Mister X.'

---

[46] Additionally note that the derivation in (439) would still be a problem because it leads to the wrong word order in Dutch.

b. *Een zekere misdadiger heeft de kluis gekraakt die ook
　　a　certain criminal　has　the safe　cracked　that also
　　meneer X heeft vermoord, die tweehonderd diamanten bevatte.
　　mister X has　killed　　that two.hundred diamonds contained

He argues that this is a problem for the raising analysis because crossing dependencies are expected (see (441)), contrary to fact.

(441)　S...O...[t$_S$ RRC]...[t$_O$ RRC]

Unfortunately, this test does not yield conclusive results in CEP. A sentence that could virtually instantiate the mirror effect under discussion could be one involving an RRC extraposed from a wh-constituent and an RRC extraposed from the object. However, such sentences are excluded, independently of the relative order of the two extraposed RRCs, as shown in (442).

(442)　a. *[Quantas　　pessoas]$_i$ requisitaram [livros]$_j$ ontem　　t$_j$ que são
　　　　　　how.many people　checked.out　books　yesterday　that are
　　　　　recomendados pelo　Ministério t$_i$ que são sócias　da　biblioteca?
　　　　　recommended　by.the ministry　　that are members of.the library
　　　　　'How many people checked out books yesterday that are recommended by the ministry that are library members?'

　　　b. *[Quantas　　pessoas]$_i$ requisitaram [livros]$_j$ ontem　　t$_j$ que são sócias
　　　　　　how.many people　checked.out　books　yesterday　that are members
　　　　　biblioteca t$_j$ que são recomendados pelo　Ministério?
　　　　　library　　that are recommended by.the ministry

Another possible candidate for such a test would be a sentence involving an RRC extraposed from a preposed focus and an RRC extraposed from the object. Again, the two possible orders excluded:

(443)　a. *[Poucas pessoas]$_i$ conseguiram comprar [casas]$_j$ no　leilão　de
　　　　　　few　　people　managed　buy.INF　houses at.the auction of
　　　　　ontem　　t$_j$ que fossem baratas t$_i$ que ficassem satisfeitas.
　　　　　yesterday　that be.SBJV cheap　　that be.SBJV satisfied
　　　　　lit. 'Few people managed to buy houses at the auction yesterday that are cheap that are happy.'

　　　b. *[Poucas pessoas]$_i$ conseguiram comprar [casas]$_j$ no　leilão　de
　　　　　　few　　people　managed　buy.INF　houses at.the auction of
　　　　　ontem　　t$_i$ que ficassem satisfeitas t$_j$ que fossem baratas.
　　　　　yesterday　that be.SBJV satisfied　　that be.SBJV cheap

Importantly, sentences (442)–(443) become grammatical if one of the extraposed RRCs is removed. The explanation behind the ungrammaticality of (442)–(443) may rely on two independent factors. First, it may be due to the effect of processing factors; as De Vries (2002: 248) notes, sentences with two extraposed RRCs are extremely hard to comprehend. Second, it may be explained by the same restriction that prevents the occurrence of the subject and the object in a post-verbal position in sentences displaying broad information focus (see (412)). Note that in (442)–(443), after the extraction of the antecedents, the subject and the object positions are still filled with an RRC. Therefore, it is likely that the restriction against the occurrence of a subject and an object in a post-verbal position becomes active in these contexts as well.

H. VP-topicalization

Koster (2000) and De Vries (2002) claim that if an extraposed RRC is stranded within the VP, the verb should be allowed to topicalize along with the extraposed RRC. However, VP-topicalization along these lines is simply not allowed in Dutch, as is illustrated in (444).

(444) *[gezien die een rode jas draagt] heb ik de man
        seen   who a   red coat wears have I the man
        'I have seen the man who wears a red coat.' (De Vries 2002: 256)

In CEP, a post-verbal antecedent and its RRC are within the VP. Therefore, both elements are expected to surface in the topicalized constituent in a construction like (445) (repeated from (400)).[47] This prediction is borne out, as illustrated in (446).

(445) Visitar os amigos, a   Maria visita todos os   anos.
        visit.INF the friends the M.   visits every the years
        'Visit her friends, Maria does it every year.'

(446) Encontrar uma pessoa na_____escola que esteja   interessada em ir
        find.INF a   person in.the school that be.SBJV interested in go.INF
        para Angola, não acredito   que encontres.
        to   A.   not believe.1SG that find.2SG
        'Find a person in the school that is interested in going to Angola, I do not
        believe you will do it.'

As for sentences involving extraposition from a pre-verbal constituent, there are three options in CEP: the antecedent may be a preposed focus, an emphatic/evaluative phrase, or a wh-constituent (see §3.4.1.2). However, when these elements are extracted from the VP, VP-topicalization is simply not allowed, as shown in (447)–(449).

---

[47] I assume, along the lines of Kato and Raposo (2007), that the structure in (445) involves VP-topicalization (see §3.5.1.3A(b)).

(447) a. Nada   de jeito   ele viu na   sua recente ida   a   Paris.
       nothing worthwhile he saw in.the his recent visit to P.
       'He did not see anything worthwhile in his recent visit to Paris.' (Raposo
       1995: 456)

       b. *Ver   na   sua recente ida a   Paris, nada   de jeito   ele viu.
       see.INF in.the his recent visit to P.   nothing worthwhile he saw

(448) a. Muito whisky bebi   ontem   à   noite!
       a.lot.of whisky drank.1SG yesterday at.the night
       'I drank a lot of whisky last night!'

       b. Beber   ontem   à   noite, muito whisky bebi!
       drink.INF yesterday at.the night a.lot.of whisky drank.1SG

(449) a. Quantas   pessoas conheceste em Inglaterra?
       how.many people met.2SG   in England
       'How many people did you meet in England?'

       b. *Conhecer em Inglaterra, quantas   pessoas conheceste?
       meet.INF in England   how.many people met.2SG

Consequently, it comes as no surprise that extraposed RRCs taking a preposed focus,
an emphatic/evaluative phrase, or a wh-constituent as an antecedent are not allowed
in a topicalized VP; see (450)–(452).

(450) a. Poucas pessoas conheço   que vão ao   ginásio.
       few   people know.1SG that go to.the gym
       'I know few people who go to the gym.'

       b. *Conhecer que vão ao   ginásio, poucas pessoas conheço.
       know.INF that go to.the gym   few   people know.1SG

(451) a. Muito whisky bebi   ontem   que estava fora do   prazo!
       a.lot.of whisky drank.1SG yesterday that was   out of.the expiry.date
       'I drank a lot of whisky yesterday that was expired!'

       b. *Beber   ontem   que estava fora do   prazo,   muito
       drink.INF yesterday that was   out of.the expiry.date a.lot.of
       whisky   bebi!
       whisky   drank

(452) a. Quantas   pessoas conheces que vão ao   ginásio?
       how.many people know.2SG that go to.the gym
       'How many people do you know that go to the gym?'

       b. *Conhecer que vão ao   ginásio, quantas   pessoas conheces?
       know.INF that go to.the gym   how.many people know.2SG

It seems fair to conclude that the impossibility of having an extraposed RRC within a topicalized constituent (see (450b)–(452b)) does not undermine the stranding analysis; examples (447)–(449) independently show that VP-topicalization is incompatible with the extraction of a preposed focus, an emphatic/evaluative phrase, or a wh-constituent.

I. Extraposition from split antecedents

De Vries (2002) claims that English and Dutch allow for split antecedents, as illustrated in (453). In this example, the relative pronoun triggers plural agreement on the verb in the relative clause (which shows that (453) is not simply a Right Node Raising construction).

(453)   Ik heb   een vrouw$_i$ gezien en   ji$_j$ hebt een man$_j$ bespied
       I   have   a   woman seen   and you have a   man   spied.on
       die$_{i+j}$ beide een rode jas   droegen.
       who both   a   red coat wore.PL
       'I saw a woman and you have spied on a man who wore a red coat.' (De Vries
       2002: 264)

According to De Vries (2002), the stranding analysis cannot derive sentences like (453) because the head and its relative clause are always generated together. Hence, the plural relative pronoun and verb in (453) cannot be derived.

Fortunately, this problem does not even arise in CEP because RRCs with a split antecedent are completely excluded:

(454)   *Eu comprei um computador ontem   e   o   meu marido
       I   bought a   computer   yesterday and the my   husband
       ofereceu-me   uma impressora hoje   que estavam em promoção no
       offered-me.CL a   printer   today that were   at   discount at.the
       centro comercial.
       center shopping
       'I bought a computer yesterday and my husband offered me a printer today;
       both the computer and the printer were at a discount at the shopping center.'

3.5.3.1 Summary   In this section, I examined nine problems that have been adduced in the literature against the stranding analysis. Because most of the problems were identified in the literature on Dutch (especially by Koster 2000 and De Vries 2002), it was possible to systematically compare the behavior of Dutch and CEP with respect to the same phenomena. The results are summarized in Table 3.7. Here, the stranding theory is evaluated in the following way: a plus indicates that the stranding analysis can derive the property straightforwardly or with reference to independent

TABLE 3.7 Dutch and contemporary European Portuguese: Global evaluation of the stranding analysis

	Dutch	CEP
A. Extraposition from strong noun phrases	−	*
B. Extraposition from PPs	−	*
C. Ungrammaticality of the source structure	−	*
D. Constraints on the surface position of extraposed RRCs	−	+
E. Extraposition from subjects	−	+
F. Emptiness of the VP	−	+
G. Mirror effect	−	*
H. VP-topicalization	−	+
I. Extraposition from split antecedents	−	*

principles, a minus indicates that it cannot, and an asterisk indicates that the property does not hold for a specific language.

I conclude that the stranding analysis can account for the properties of RRC–extraposition in CEP but not in Dutch. The differences in RRC-extraposition exhibited in both languages reinforce the conclusion that I drew on the basis of the empirical data discussed in §3.4.2, that is, that RRC-extraposition is not a uniform phenomenon, being subject to cross-linguistic variation.

3.5.4 Conclusion

This section focused on the syntactic nature of RRC-extraposition in CEP. I showed that an analysis in terms of stranding can account for the properties of RRC-extraposition in CEP. Specifically, I proposed that RRC-extraposition in CEP involves A′-movement of the antecedent, either via short scrambling (when the antecedent is in a post-verbal position) or via movement to the left periphery (when the antecedent is in a pre-verbal position).

I attempted to keep the technical details of the analysis to a minimum. However, because the theory proposed here has an important impact on different domains of the clause structure (e.g. on the VP and the CP domains), its implementation required some technical discussion, especially with regard to short scrambling. The fact that word order in CEP is constrained by discourse/semantic/prosodic effects also added somewhat complex explanatory devices to the picture.

Nevertheless, it is worth noting that the analysis behind this theoretical apparatus actually amounts to a simple idea: RRC-extraposition in CEP results from leftward movement of the antecedent and stranding of the RRC. Note further that the complex restrictions/principles that seem to interfere with this phenomenon have been independently proposed in the literature to account for other phenomena (e.g. the different word-order patterns found in CEP).

3.6 A proposal for earlier stages of Portuguese

In this section, I submit that RRC-extraposition in earlier stages of Portuguese involves the same syntactic structure as coordination. Section 3.6.1 establishes the basic tenets of this analysis, introducing Koster's (2000) and De Vries' (2002) approaches to extraposition. Section 3.6.2 depicts how the *specifying coordination plus ellipsis* analysis proposed by De Vries (2002) can account for the properties of RRC-extraposition in earlier stages of Portuguese outlined in §3.4.3. Finally, in §3.6.3, I address some problems of this analysis, providing solutions capable of overcoming some of its drawbacks.

3.6.1 *The specifying coordination analysis*

3.6.1.1 *Koster (2000)*   Koster proposes that in general, phrase structure takes two forms: primary phrase structure and parallel structure. Syntactically, both forms display the same configuration, consisting of a specifier, a head, and a complement. However, they are licensed in different ways. As Koster puts it:

Primary phrase structure has a functional part and a lexical part embedded in it. All lexical elements must be licensed in some functional position to their left, a consequence of universal head-initial structure (Kayne 1994). The elements of parallel structure are not directly licensed in this way, but at the most indirectly, by linking them to elements of the primary phrase structure.   (Koster 2000: 16)

Coordination has been seen as a form of parallel structure. However, Koster claims that parallel structure should be conceived as a broader phenomenon, encompassing coordination, extraposition, specifications found in equatives, and possibly other phenomena such as appositions and right dislocations.

Assuming Munn's (1993) and Kayne's (1994) analysis of coordination (see also Johannessen 1998), Koster claims that parallel structure is syntactically represented as in (455). The primary phrase structure element is in the specifier position, and the parallel conjunct is in the complement position of a Boolean head.

(455)   [XP$_1$ [Boolean head XP$_2$]]

Although the parallel construal has the uniform syntactic configuration in (455), it encompasses structures with different semantics, depending on the nature of the Boolean head involved. In standard coordination, the Boolean head corresponds to coordinators such as *and* and *or*. In extraposition (and in equatives), the parallel construction involves an empty head (as in the asyndetic coordination in the traditional grammar). Koster (2000) represents this empty head as a colon head (':') and claims that it functions as an abstract Boolean operator, leading to the addition of properties, that is, to the introduction of a specifying addition.

To support the idea that standard coordination and extraposition involve a similar syntactic representation, Koster (2000) demonstrates that they behave alike with respect to a number of properties.

First, in standard coordination two conjuncts may be non-adjacent in Dutch, as illustrated in (456a).

(456) a. Zij heeft Marie <u>gezien</u> en mij.
          she has   M.   seen   and me
          'She saw Mary and me.'

       b. Zij heeft Marie en mij gezien
          she has   M.   and me seen (both Koster 2000: 16)

Example (456a) cannot be derived from (456b) through rightward movement because it would constitute a violation of Ross's Coordinate Structure Constraint. Alternatively, Koster proposes that both sentences involve a parallel construal and that the difference between them may be attributed to the properties of pied-piping.[48] In this view, the coordinated phrases in (456) involve the abstract representation given in (457). According to Koster, the first XP checks the features of *and* (or [*and* XP]). This mechanism expresses the fact that an XP of a given type in the complement position typically requires an XP of the same type in the specifier position.

(457) [XP [and XP]]

If the specifier position is filled by the checking phrase only, the adjacency between the two conjuncts is derived, as in (456b). In this example, both conjuncts are noun phrases, and the noun phrase in the specifier position (*Jan*) checks the features of *en* (or [*en Marie*]); see (458).

(458) Hij heeft [[_{NP} Jan] [en [_{NP} Marie]]] gezien.
       he has   J.   and   M.   seen
       'He saw John and Mary.' (Koster 2000: 18)

However, as in the cases of standard pied-piping, the checking phrase can be contained in a larger constituent (e.g. a VP or AgrOP). This happens in sentences involving non-adjacency of conjuncts, as in (456a). In this case, the checking phrase

---

[48] Note that Koster (2000) proposes an extension of the concept of pied-piping that is not standardly assumed in the literature on the topic, given that this phenomenon is traditionally associated with movement.

(*Jan*) and the elements to be checked (*en* or *en Marie*) are the same. The difference is that in (456a), the specifier position is filled both by the checking phrase and by a larger constituent containing it, as depicted in (459).

(459) Hij heeft [$_{AgrOP}$ [$_{AgrOP}$ [$_{NP}$ *Jan*] [AgrO [$_{VP}$ gezien]]] [en
       he has   J.   seen   and
       [$_{NP}$ *Marie*]]]
       M. (Koster 2000: 18)

As in the standard cases of pied-piping, the extension of the checking phrase has a limit: it cannot go beyond clausal boundaries. This explains the Right Roof Constraint on this construction. As illustrated by the ungrammaticality of (460), the checking phrase (*Jan*) cannot be contained in a subject clause CP that does not contain the elements to be checked (*en Marie*).

(460) *[$_{CP}$ dat hij Jan gezien heeft] is duidelijk en   Marie
              that he   J.   seen   has   is clear   and M.
       'It is clear that he saw Jan and Marie.' (Koster 2000: 18)

Koster also demonstrates that all forms of parallel construal have the properties of Ross's Coordinate Structure Constraint. Among other things, this entails that the first conjunct cannot be moved without the second, as is illustrated in (461).

(461) *Jan heb ik$_i$ [t$_i$ en   Marie] gezien.
        J. have I   and M.   seen
       'I saw Jan and Marie.' (Koster 2000: 19)

In light of these facts,[49] Koster proposes that extraposition does not have the properties of movement, but those of parallel construal. Let me examine in detail how this approach works in the case of RRC-extraposition.

According to Koster, relative clauses are analyzed in terms of parallel construal. This structure is schematically represented in (462), where the relative clause is taken to provide a further specification of the head placed in the specifier of the colon.[50]

(462) [$_{NP}$ [$_{NP}$ een vrouw] [: [$_{CP}$ die alles   wist]]]
              a   woman   who everything knew
       'a woman who knew everything' (Koster 2000: 22)

The extraposition of relative clauses is then derived from the property of pied-piping. If only the head occurs in the specifier position, there is adjacency between the head

---

[49] Koster (2000) also discusses evidence from specifications found in equatives, which I do not address here.

[50] As for the contrast between RRCs and ARCs, Koster (2000) claims that the colon indicates set interaction in the case of RRCs and set union in the case of ARCs. He also suggests that RRCs and ARCs can be distinguished by the level of attachment of the specifying conjunct (NP or DP).

and the relative clause (see (463a)). If the specifier is filled by a larger constituent containing the head, the extraposed order is derived (see (463b)).

(463) a. Ik heb [$_{NP}$ [$_{NP}$ een vrouw] [: [$_{CP}$ die   alles   wist]]] gezien.
            I   have   a   woman   who everything knew   seen
            'I saw a woman who knew everything.'

        b. Ik heb [[$_{AgrOP}$ [$_{NP}$ een vrouw]] gezien] [: [$_{CP}$ die   alles   wist]]
            I   have   a   woman seen   who everything knew
            (both Koster 2000: 23)

In (463b), the checking head (*een vrouw* 'a woman') is included in AgrOP, but more inclusive phrases can occupy the specifier position of a parallel construal. For instance, if the antecedent of an extraposed RRC is in [Spec, IP], the entire IP surfaces in the specifier position, but if the antecedent is a topic, the minimal CP surfaces in this position, as illustrated in (464).

(464) a. [$_{IP}$ [$_{IP}$ [Een vrouw] heeft hem gezien] [: [die   alles   wist]]]
            a   woman has   him seen   who everything knew
            'He saw a woman who knew everything.'

        b. [$_{TopP}$ [$_{TopP}$ [Een vrouw] heeft hij t gezien] [: [die   alles   wist]]]
            a   woman has   he   seen   who everything knew
            (both Koster 2000: 23)

As in the cases of standard coordination, the extension of the checking phrase has a limit: it cannot go beyond the minimal CP containing the relative clause (see (460)). This explains the ungrammaticality of (465).

(465) *[$_{CP}$ Dat hij een vrouw   gezien heeft] is duidelijk die   alles   wist
            that he a   woman seen   has   is clear   who everything knew
            'It is clear that he saw a woman who knew everything.' (Koster 2000: 23)

Moreover, the Coordinate Structure Constraint also applies to relative clause-extraposition, which is confirmed by the impossibility of having the first part of the construction moved away from the relative clause in sentences like (466).

(466) *Een vrouw$_i$ heeft hij [t$_i$ die   alles   wist] gezien
            a   woman has   he   who everything knew seen
            'He saw a woman who knew everything.' (Koster 2000: 23)

Koster's (2000) account is conceptually attractive because it unifies a variety of apparently unrelated constructions under the label of *parallel construal*. However, it faces substantial empirical and theoretical difficulties, which I briefly comment on.

From an empirical point of view, the biggest problem is that Koster's approach overgenerates in a number of ways. If the constituent that surfaces in the specifier position may belong to any category (within the minimal CP domain), extraposition should take place from any constituent, and this is simply not true. As discussed in §3.4, in some languages, there are important restrictions on RRC-extraposition. For instance, in CEP, RRC-extraposition cannot take place from strong noun phrases or from the object of prepositions. As can be easily concluded, Koster's (2000) analysis leaves these restrictions unexplained.

Second, the syntactic structure proposed by Koster allows the specifier and the complement positions of a parallel construal to be filled by unequal categories. For example, an extraposed RRC taking an object as an antecedent would have an AgrOP in the specifier position and an RRC in the complement position. As De Vries (2002, 2009) notes, the problem is that in this case, the constituents are neither of the same category nor functionally equivalent, which is not allowed in standard coordination (e.g. *He looks great and at me).

Another empirical problem with Koster's analysis concerns the assumption that the categorial status of the constituent in the specifier position depends on the structural position of the antecedent. Such assumption works in a language like Dutch, where it is generally assumed that the verb is spelled out in V (apart from the V_2 position of the finite verb main clauses) but raises some problems for languages displaying V-to-I movement.

Consider, for instance, a sentence containing an RRC extraposed from an object, as in (467) (repeated from (381)) from CEP.

(467)   Encontrei uma rapariga <u>ontem</u>   que perguntou por ti.
        met.1SG   a   girl   yesterday that asked   for you
        'I met a girl yesterday that asked for you.'

Under the assumption that the checking phrase in the first conjunct extends until the structural position occupied by the antecedent, the specifier position in (467) would be filled by the VP, and the complement position would be filled by the RRC, as depicted in (468).[51]

(468)   [$_{IP}$ encontrei$_i$ [[$_{VP}$ uma rapariga$_j$ [$_{VP}$ ontem t$_i$ t$_j$]] [: que perguntou
        met.1SG   a   girl   yesterday   that asked
        por ti]]]
        for you

This structure is problematic because V-to-I movement violates the Coordinate Structure Constraint, which prevents movement from one conjunct in a coordinate

---

[51] In accordance with the analysis proposed in §3.5.1.2, I assume that in the structural representation given in (468), the direct object is scrambled (i.e. left-adjoined to VP). Note, however, that this is not crucial here: the same line of reasoning would hold if the object were in its base position.

structure unless movement also occurs from the other conjunct (Ross 1967). There-fore, if RRC-extraposition were derived by the parallel structure proposed by Koster, a sentence like (467) would be ungrammatical, contrary to fact.[52]

From a theoretical point of view, Koster's proposal is also problematic for not being compatible with the raising analysis of relative clauses (because it assumes that the head and the RRC are generated separately). Therefore, among other things, it cannot account for the reconstruction effects discussed in Chapter 1 (see §1.3.2.4B), which suggest that the head of the RRC is generated in an RRC-internal position, as witnessed in (469).

(469)   Bill liked the [stories about himself$_i$] which John$_i$ told.

Capitalizing on Koster's (2000) proposal, De Vries (2002) proposes a different account of extraposition, which overcomes some of the drawbacks of Koster's proposal. Section 3.6.1.2 is devoted to the presentation and discussion of De Vries' (2002) analysis.

3.6.1.2 De Vries (2002)   Building on ideas from Koster (2000), De Vries (2002) proposes the *specifying coordination plus ellipsis analysis* of extraposition. There are at least three major differences between the two proposals.

First, De Vries (2002) explicitly analyzes extraposition as coordination. Whereas Koster (2000) resorts to the concept of parallel construal and claims that coordin-ation and extraposition are particular subcases of parallel construal, De Vries (2002) assumes the concept of coordination as the encompassing notion. The conceptual divergence between the two proposals is depicted in (470a–b).

(470)

a. Koster (2000)   b. De Vries (2002)

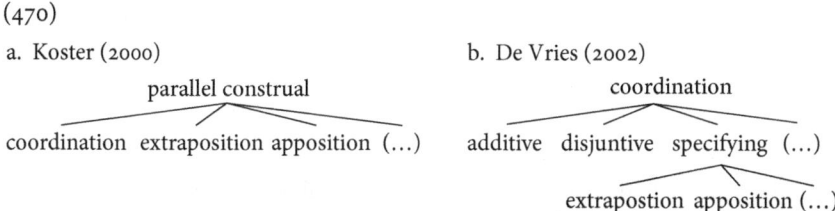

De Vries (2002) claims that coordination is a syntactic construction with varying semantics. Aside from the traditional types of coordination (such as additive and disjunctive), there is another type called *specifying coordination* that is involved, for instance, in extraposition, apposition, and other constructions (such as parenthesis and left- and right-dislocation; see De Vries 2009 for a general overview). In all these

---

[52] Here, I abstract away from the movement of the subject to [Spec, IP], which would also violate the Coordinate Structure Constraint. See De Vries (2002, 2009) for similar problems in Dutch.

constructions, the second conjunct provides an alternative description, an example, or a property of the first conjunct.

The second difference between the two proposals concerns the categorial status of the constituents that occupy the specifier and the complement positions. Like Koster, De Vries assumes that RRC-extraposition is obtained according to the scheme in (471): the antecedent is generated within the specifier position, and the extraposed RRC is generated within the complement position of an abstract head.[53]

(471)   [CoP [...antecedent...] [Co [...RRC...]]]

However, unlike Koster, De Vries proposes that the constituents that occupy the specifier and the complement positions are of the same category. In his framework, the first conjunct may range from VP to CP, depending on the position of the antecedent. The second conjunct has the same categorial status as the first conjunct; it repeats the material contained in the first conjunct, adding the extraposed RRC in its canonical position. Then, the repeated material is phonologically deleted. Take, for instance, the example (472), where the antecedent of the extraposed RRC is a direct object. Here, both conjuncts are represented as involving the AgrOP-level of projection (under the assumption that in Dutch the object moves to [Spec, AgrOP], for reasons of case).

(472)   [CP Ik heb   ... [CoP [AgrOP-1 de   man gezien]
            I   have   the man seen
                          [Co [AgrOP-2 [DP de man die   zijn tas verloor] gezien]]]]
                                         the man who his bag lost   seen
                                                              (De Vries 2002: 241)

De Vries (2002, 2009) proposes that the deletion used in the specifying coordination plus ellipsis analysis has three important characteristics: (1) the deletion may involve non-constituents and discontinuous material; (2) the deletion of all material that is repeated is obligatory; and (3) the deletion is directed forward (i.e. left-to-right).

These characteristics can be observed in the structural representation in (472). The fact that the deletion may involve non-constituents is illustrated by the deletion of *de* 'the' and *man* 'man', which do not form a constituent. The requirement that all repeated material must be deleted is confirmed by the deletion of *de* 'the', *man* 'man', and *gezian* 'seen', which are the elements repeated from the first conjunct. Finally, the demand on forward deletion can be demonstrated by the fact that deletion targets

---

[53] The structure in (471) involves an abstract coordinator that is semantically specialized: it constitutes an asymmetric relationship of specification between the two conjuncts. Koster (2000) symbolically represents this relator using a colon; De Vries (2002) employs an ampersand plus a colon, '&:'. Here, I simply use the more general denotation *Co* for the coordinating head.

only constituents in the second conjunct. For more details see De Vries (2002, 2009) and G. de Vries (1992).

The third difference between the two proposals concerns the (non)-autonomous syntactic status of extraposition. According to Koster, extraposed and non-extraposed orders involve the same grammatical configuration. As already shown in §3.6.1.1, standard coordination and relative clauses involving adjacency (between conjuncts and between the head and the relative clause, respectively) are analyzed in terms of parallel construal, consisting of a specifier-head-complement configuration. In this view, extraposition does not involve a different grammatical structure, being simply derived from the property of pied-piping (i.e. the possibility of having a larger constituent in the specifier position containing the checking phrase). In contrast, under the specifying coordination plus ellipsis account, the extraposed and the non-extraposed configurations involve a different derivational story. In this case, the specifying coordination configuration is present in sentences involving extraposition but not in sentences involving the normal (i.e. non-extraposed) order.

Now, after this brief comparison between the two proposals, let me determine if De Vries' approach is capable of overcoming the drawbacks of Koster's analysis. First, consider the violation of the Coordinate Structure Constraint caused by V-to-I movement. Under the specifying coordination plus ellipsis analysis, the violation of the Coordinate Structure Constraint does not arise because there is a representation of the verb inside the second conjunct as well. Therefore, the verb is moved in an across-the-board fashion,[54] as shown in the schematic representation in (473).

(473) [$_{IP}$ V [$_{CoP}$ [$_{VP}$ O [$_{VP}$ adverb t_V t_O]] [Co [$_{VP}$ Θ RRC [$_{VP}$ ~~adverb~~ t_V t_O]]]]]

Another advantage of De Vries' approach is that it eliminates unbalanced coordination. Recall that under Koster's approach, the specifier and the complement positions of the parallel construal can be filled by unequal categories. Under De Vries' analysis, this problem does not arise because both conjuncts are of the same category (e.g. a VP, as in (473)).

Finally, from a theoretical point of view, De Vries' analysis has the advantage of being compatible with the raising analysis of RRCs because the head is syntactically present in the second conjunct.

However, there is one non-trivial problem that remains unsolved in De Vries' proposal. As in Koster's analysis, the specifying coordination plus ellipsis analysis overgenerates in a number of ways: it predicts that RRC-extraposition from any

---

[54] As is well known, across-the-board extraction is not subject to the Coordinate Structure Constraint. Rules apply in an across-the-board fashion if they affect all conjuncts in a coordinate structure at the same time. This is what happens in (473): V-to-I movement extracts the V out of both conjuncts.

constituent should be allowed. However, though this may be true of languages like Dutch, it is simply not correct for languages like CEP, where RRC-extraposition cannot take place, for instance, from strong noun phrases and objects of prepositions (see §3.4.1).

The non-uniform view on RRC offers a straightforward explanation for the fact that different stages of the same language (and different languages) may differ on the properties of RRC-extraposition. More precisely, the fact that the specifying coordination plus ellipsis analysis cannot explain the restrictions on RRC-extraposition found in CEP is a welcome result. It corroborates the hypothesis that RRC-extraposition in CEP is derived from stranding, whereas RRC-extraposition in earlier stages of Portuguese is derived from specifying coordination plus ellipsis.

To provide further support for this claim, I show in §3.6.2 how the specifying coordination plus ellipsis analysis can account for the properties of RRC-extraposition in earlier stages of Portuguese.

3.6.2 *Deriving the relevant properties*

Section 3.4 shows that CEP and earlier stages of Portuguese behave differently with respect to the following properties: (1) the definiteness effect; (2) restriction on extraposition from pre-verbal positions; and (3) restriction on extraposition from PPs.

My claim is that the different restrictions to RRC-extraposition found in the diachronic (and cross-linguistic) dimension can be explained under a dual approach to the phenomenon. The rationale behind this proposal is that RRC-extraposition is not a unitary phenomenon; it may involve stranding or specifying coordination plus ellipsis. Languages and different stages of the same language differ with respect to the type of extraposition they display. Considering in particular the case of Portuguese, the hypothesis is that RRC-extraposition is generated by stranding in CEP and by specifying coordination plus ellipsis in earlier stages of Portuguese.

In §3.5, I demonstrated that the properties of RRC-extraposition in CEP can be accounted for in terms of stranding. Now I show how the contrasting properties of RRC-extraposition in earlier stages of Portuguese can be derived from the specifying coordination plus ellipsis analysis.

3.6.2.1 *The definiteness effect* In earlier stages of Portuguese, extraposed RRCs can take strong noun phrases as their antecedent. This property can be straightforwardly derived under the specifying coordination plus ellipsis analysis because there is no movement relationship between the visible antecedent and the extraposed RRC. As illustrated in (474), the strong noun phrase *aquelle dia* 'that day' in the first conjunct is a constituent: it is detached from the relative clause and base-generated in the first conjunct of the coordinate structure. In contrast, the strong noun phrase *aquelle dia* 'that day' in the second conjunct is not a constituent (because there is no constituent

that includes the determiner and the noun and excludes the RRC). However, this is not a problem because it is the DP (containing the antecedent and the RRC) that undergoes leftward movement. Given that deletion may target non-constituents, the repeated material in the second conjunct is deleted, and RRC-extraposition is derived.

(474) [$_{CoP}$ [$_{IP}$ [$_{DP}$ aquelle dia]$_i$ sem   falha aveo t$_i$]
                 that   day without fail   came
      [Co [$_{IP}$ [$_{DP}$ ~~aquelle~dia~~ que forom i   todos]$_i$ ~~sem~~   ~~falha~~ ~~aveo~~ t$_i$]]]
                 that   day that went there all   without   fail   came
      'the day everyone went there came without fail'

3.6.2.2 *Pre-verbal positions*

A. Pre-verbal subjects

In earlier stages of Portuguese, extraposed RRCs may take pre-verbal subjects as an antecedent. This can be derived by resorting to IP-level coordination; see (475).

(475)   [$_{CoP}$ [$_{IP}$ S V DO] Co [$_{IP}$ S RRC ~~V DO~~]]

From a comparative perspective, the fact that CEP does not allow RRC-extraposition from pre-verbal subjects is surprising. As shown in §3.5.2.2, the explanation for the pattern of ungrammaticality in CEP depends upon the Interpretative Principle in (476) (repeated from (426)). RRC-extraposition from [Spec, IP] is not allowed because such a position is ambiguously filled by topic and non-topic elements.

(476)   Interpretative Principle
      The antecedent of an extraposed RRC must occur in a position non-ambiguously interpreted as non-topic (in Kuroda's 2005 sense).

Apparently, nothing prevents RRC-extraposition in earlier stages of Portuguese from being subject to the same semantic restrictions as CEP. However, as shown in §3.4.3, there is strong empirical evidence suggesting that earlier stages of Portuguese (and other languages) allow for it.

    Somewhat tentatively, I would like to suggest that CEP and earlier stages of Portuguese may resort to different strategies to resolve the ambiguity referred to in (476). Whereas in CEP the ambiguity associated with [Spec, IP] is resolved syntactically and prosodically (through subject inversion), in earlier stages of Portuguese, it may be resolved only prosodically. In this case, a constituent in [Spec, IP] can be unambiguously interpreted as non-topic if it is prosodically marked by a pitch accent.[55]

---

[55] I assume that the kind of prosodic prominence that serves to mark focused constituents is the pitch accent (see Avesani and Vayra 2003, among others).

This hypothesis may suggest that there is a language split as far as the codification of semantic information is concerned. Some languages codify the topic/non-topic status of the subject prosodically and syntactically (as may be the case of CEP), whereas other languages (and different stages of the same language) may codify it only prosodically (as seems to be the case for earlier stages of Portuguese).

B. Discourse dedicated positions in the left periphery

The behavior of RRC-extraposition from other pre-verbal positions is summarized in Table 3.8.

Extraposed RRCs taking a wh-constituent, an emphatic/evaluative phrase, or a preposed focus as an antecedent can be derived without further ado by resorting to coordination of a CP-level projection (see (477)). For ease of representation, the functional projections dedicated to the discourse values previously mentioned (e.g. FocP, EvaluativeP) are represented by FP.

(477) $[_{\text{CoP}}$ $[_{\text{FP}}$ *wh-constituent/emphatic phrase/preposed focus* S V]
        Co $[_{\text{FP}}$ ~~*wh-constituent/emphatic phrase/preposed focus*~~ RRC ~~S V~~]]

Comparing (477) and (475), it becomes clear that in (477) the coordinate structure involves a higher level of projection than in the case of RRC-extraposition from the subject.

The impossibility of extraposition from topics follows from the Interpretative Principle in (476). Although extraposition generated by specifying coordination plus ellipsis is not syntactically constrained (because the second conjunct can be freely attached at any structure level, within the minimal CP domain), the semantic principle in (476) prevents extraposed RRCs from taking topics as an antecedent. Notice that under a split-CP approach, the position occupied by topicalized constituents is non-ambiguously interpreted as topic.

C. Scrambled objects

In earlier stages of Portuguese, RRC-extraposition can occur from scrambled constituents in [Spec, IP] (see §3.4.3.2C). This can be accounted for by resorting to coordination at the IP level, as schematically represented in (478).

(478) $[_{\text{CoP}}$ $[_{\text{IP}}$ *scrambled constituent* S V] [Co $[_{\text{IP}}$ ~~*scrambled constituent*~~ RRC ~~S V~~]]]

TABLE 3.8 **Extraposition from the left periphery in earlier stages of Portuguese**

Empirical issue		Earlier stages of Portuguese
Extraposition from left periphery	wh-constituents	+
	emphatic/evaluative phrases	+
	preposed foci	+
	topics	−

The reason why RRC-extraposition from scrambled constituents in [Spec, IP] is not available any more in CEP is independently explained by the loss of IP-scrambling in the history of Portuguese. According to Martins (2002), the loss of IP-scrambling is a result of a change in the properties of the AgrS functional head. AgrS ceased to allow multiple specifiers, that is, it lost the option for being associated with an Attract-all-F EPP-feature. Therefore IP-scrambling disappeared because a structural position for scrambled elements ceased to be available in the IP space. In this view, it is easy to see why RRC-extraposition cannot be derived from IP-scrambling in CEP; a structural position for scrambled constituents is not available anymore in the IP space.

3.6.2.3 Prepositional phrases   In earlier stages of Portuguese, extraposed RRCs can take the object of a preposition as their antecedent. As illustrated in (479), the PP *de mui poucos* 'of very few' in the first conjunct is a constituent because it is detached from the relative clause and base-generated in the first conjunct of the coordinate structure. In contrast, *de mui poucos* 'of very few' in the second conjunct is not a constituent. However, this is not a problem because it is the PP (containing the RRC) that undergoes leftward movement. Then, the repeated material in the second conjunct is deleted, leading to RRC-extraposition.

(479) $[_{CP}$ que $[_{CoP}$ $[_{IP}$ $[_{PP}$ de mui poucos$]_i$ sabemos $t_i]$
         that   of very few   know.1PL
        $[_{Co}$ $[_{IP}$ $[_{PP}$ ~~de   mui   poucos~~ que bebessem   vinho$]_i$ ~~sabemos~~ $t_i]]]]$
               of   very   few   that drink.SBJV wine   know.1PL

3.6.2.4 Summary   Section 3.6.2 shows how the properties of RRC-extraposition in earlier stages of Portuguese can be derived from the specifying coordination plus ellipsis analysis proposed by De Vries (2002). The results are summarized in Table 3.9. The specifying coordination plus ellipsis analysis is evaluated thus: a plus indicates that the analysis can derive the property straightforwardly or with reference to independent principles; a minus indicates that it cannot.

On the basis of these results, I conclude that the specifying coordination plus ellipsis analysis accounts for the properties of RRC-extraposition identified in §3.4.3. It goes without saying that if RRC-extraposition in earlier stages of Portuguese was generated by stranding, not all these properties would be derived.

Despite the success of the specifying coordination plus ellipsis analysis in deriving the properties of RRC-extraposition in earlier stages of Portuguese, it is worth noting that such an approach also uncovers some problems, for instance, with respect to scope relations. In §3.6.3, I discuss one scope relation that can be documented in historical Portuguese: the licensing of subjunctive mood in extraposed RRCs.

TABLE 3.9 **Earlier stages of Portuguese: Evaluation of the specifying coordination plus ellipsis analysis**

Empirical issue		Specifying coordination plus ellipsis
A. Extraposition from strong noun phrases		+
B. Extraposition from pre-verbal positions	pre-verbal subjects	+
	wh-constituents	+
	emphatic/evaluative phrases	+
	preposed foci	+
	no topics	+
C. Extraposition from PPs		+

3.6.3 Problems

The specifying coordination plus ellipsis analysis faces some problems in explaining the scope relations that can be established between the matrix and the extraposed RRC. Given the limitations of historical inquiry, I confine the discussion to one scope relation that is documented in the written sources: the licensing of subjective mood in extraposed RRCs.[56]

The choice of mood in RRCs is not determined lexically as in the case of verbal complementation. Subjunctive RRCs are typically licensed in a set of intensional environments created, for example, by strong intensional predicates, negation, future tense, interrogatives, conditionals, or imperatives (Quer 1998). Moreover, it is standardly assumed that some of these contexts, such as intensional predicates or negation, only license subjunctive RRCs in their complement or c-command domain (Quer 1998). Therefore, it can be assumed that in an RRC like (480), the subjunctive mood is licensed by the c-commanding negative marker *não* 'not'.

(480) Não abro   anexos   que possam   ter   vírus.
       not   open.1SG attachments that might.SBJV have.INF virus
       'I do not open attachments that might have a virus.'

Crucially, subjunctive mood is also licensed in extraposed RRCs. See (481), from CEP.

---

[56] I thank Jairo Nunes (p.c.) for drawing my attention to these facts.

(481)   Não apareceu   uma única pessoa <u>ontem</u>   que tivesse   o
       not showed.up a   single person yesterday that had.SBJV the
       perfil   adequado.
       profile appropriate
       'Not even a single person showed up yesterday that had the appropriate profile.'

The subjunctive mood can be easily accounted for under the assumption that extraposed RRCs in CEP are derived from stranding. In this case, a subjunctive RRC is licensed because an RRC stranded in a VP-internal position is in the c-command domain of the negation. However, the situation is not as straightforward in the case of extraposed subjunctive RRCs derived from specifying coordination plus ellipsis, as in (482).

(482)   ca   nom ha cousa <u>no   mundo</u> que tanto   deseje
       because not has thing in.the world   that as.much want.SBJV.1SG
       como honra de cavallaria
       as   honor of cavalry
       'because there is nothing in the word that I want so much as the honor of cavalry' (13th c. [transmitted by a 15th-c. MS], Martins, Pereira, and Cardoso 2014–15)

However, it is not uncontroversial that in (482) the extraposed RRC in the second conjunct is in the scope of the negation. Recall that, according to De Vries (2002), the categorial status of conjuncts depends on the position of the antecedent. Under this assumption, a sentence like (482) involves coordination at the VP-level of projection, as depicted in the simplified structure given in (483).

(483)   [CP ca   nom ha   [CoP [VP cousa no   mundo]
       because not   has   thing in.the world
       [Co [VP ~~cousa~~ que tanto   deseje   como a   honra
               thing that as.much want.SBJV.1SG as   the honor
       de cavallaria ~~no mundo~~]]]]
       of cavalry   in.the   world

Assuming that second conjuncts are *invisible* for the higher context in terms of c-command (see De Vries 2005, 2007), the subjunctive extraposed RRC is not in the c-command domain of the negative marker *nom* 'not'.[57] As a result, sentences such as (482) should not be allowed, contrary to fact.

---

[57] A similar problem arises in (483) for the interpretation of the word *cousa* 'thing'. *Cousa* is a contextually negative word, i.e. a word that receives a negative meaning from a negative word in the relevant context (see Martins 2008). Again, it is not clear how the negative meaning of *cousa* arises in the coordinate structure in (483).

There are at least two possible ways to circumvent the problem. The first one is to assume that when RRC-extraposition is involved, conjuncts are always CP-level projections (or IP, if CP is not projected).[58] In this case, the negation is contained within the second conjunct, and the RRC is in its c-command domain, as sketched in (484).

(484) [$_{CoP}$ [$_{CP}$ca   nom ha cousa no   mundo] [Co [$_{CP}$ ca̶────── ̶n̶o̶m̶ ̶h̶a̶
                because not has thing in.the world   because not has
       ̶c̶o̶u̶s̶a̶que tanto   deseje   como a   honra de cavallaria ̶n̶o̶ ̶m̶u̶n̶d̶o̶]]]
       thing that as.much want.SBJV.1SG as   the honor of cavalry in.the world

Another hypothesis that is worth pursuing builds on the competing-grammars hypothesis put forward by Kroch (1989, 1994). As I will show in §3.7.1, it might be assumed that earlier stages of Portuguese have two variants in competition to generate RRC-extraposition: the specifying coordination plus ellipsis structure and the stranding structure. Abstracting away from other scenarios (to be addressed in §3.7.1.2), I argue that the stranding structure might take over in the cases that cannot be derived from the specifying coordination structure, as is the case of the c-command-based relations established between a licensor (higher than CoP in a corresponding specifying coordination structure) and an extraposed RRC. If this hypothesis is correct, then the subjunctive mood of the extraposed RRC in (482) would be licensed by the negative marker in a stranding configuration.

3.6.4 Summary

Section 3.6 discusses the syntactic nature of RRC-extraposition in earlier stages of Portuguese. Based on De Vries (2002), I claim that RRC-extraposition in earlier stages of Portuguese involves a special type of coordination, called *specifying coordination*. Under this approach, a constituent containing the visible antecedent is related by coordination to a constituent containing the extraposed RRC. Repeated material is phonologically deleted, as schematically represented in (485).

(485) [$_{CoP}$ [$_{XP_1}$ antecedent YP] [Co [$_{XP_2}$ [̶a̶n̶t̶e̶c̶e̶d̶e̶n̶t̶ RRC] ̶Y̶P̶]]]

RRC-extraposition generated by (485) is an extremely flexible operation, which allows, among other things, extraposition from any constituent. Concretely, the

---

[58] The idea that conjuncts are generally root CPs is proposed by Wilder (1994) for normal coordination. Under this approach, the apparent coordination of small conjuncts is derived by ellipsis (i.e. by the deletion of PF material). Wilder rejects the idea that coordination can be applied at any level of the syntactic structure and claims that this is simply an effect of ellipsis in non-initial conjuncts.

structure in (485) explains why earlier stages of Portuguese, as opposed to CEP, allow extraposition from strong noun phrases, pre-verbal subjects, and PPs. As mentioned in §3.5.2, the constrained nature of RRC-extraposition in CEP can be partially derived from the restrictions on movement inherent to the stranding analysis.

As a final point, let me mention that the study of RRC-extraposition in earlier stages of Portuguese faces obvious difficulties, given the limited nature of the written sources and the impossibility of manipulating data. This fact is particularly evident in the impossibility of testing different scope relations between the matrix and the extraposed RRC. For this reason, the cross-linguistic comparison developed in §3.4.2 is crucial in showing that earlier stages of Portuguese pattern like Germanic languages in the properties of RRC-extraposition. Therefore, comparative research can provide an interesting and fruitful method to overcome the limitations of historical data. In particular, studying the behavior of RRC-extraposition in contemporary Germanic languages provides the means to understand better the syntax of RRC-extraposition in earlier stages of Portuguese.

3.7 Comparative perspective

The present section is devoted to comparative remarks on the syntax of RRC-extraposition. Section 3.7.1 is dedicated to the diachronic path of RRC-extraposition in the history of Portuguese. Section 3.7.2 demonstrates how this approach can contribute to the understanding of cross-linguistic variation.

3.7.1 Diachronic path

In this section I show that the dual approach to the syntax of extraposition provides an important tool to explain the contrasting behavior of RRC-extraposition in CEP and earlier stages of Portuguese. The analysis is developed mainly within the model proposed by Lightfoot (see Lightfoot 1991, 1999, and subsequent work), but it also benefits from insights of the synchronic grammatical competition approach proposed by Kroch (1989, 1994, 2001) (see §1.3.4).

3.7.1.1 Hypothesis I The basic idea underlying Lightfoot's model of language change is that syntactic change involves reanalysis: a language learner, on the basis of primary linguistic data, abduces a grammar that differs in one or more respects from that of the previous generation (Lightfoot 1979, 1991). The change is driven by a gradual shift in usage frequencies. If frequencies of some crucial forms drop below a certain threshold of learnability, grammar changes.

Adopting this model as background, I hypothesize that the diachronic path of RRC-extraposition involves the steps described in Table 3.10, which are discussed in turn.

(a) Step 0

In earlier stages of Portuguese, RRC-extraposition is derived from the specifying coordination plus ellipsis structure (De Vries 2002). Under this approach, the visible antecedent occurs in the first conjunct of a coordinate structure. The second conjunct repeats the material contained in the first conjunct, adding an RRC generated by head raising (Kayne 1994) in its canonical position. Then the repeated material is phonologically deleted (see (486)).

(486)   [$_{\text{CoP}}$ [$_{\text{XP}_1}$ antecedent YP] [Co [$_{\text{XP}_2}$ [~~antecedent~~ RRC] ~~YP~~]]]

Under the structure in (486), extraposed RRCs can take any constituent as their antecedent (including noun phrases within PPs and strong noun phrases) because no movement chain is established between the visible antecedent and the RRC-internal position (see §3.6.2).

(b) Step 1

After the sixteenth century there is a change in the diachrony of Portuguese that has major repercussions on the clausal architecture: the loss of middle scrambling (or IP-scrambling). Martins (2002) reports that earlier stages of Portuguese display middle scrambling, which consists of the movement of various types of constituents (e.g. DPs, PPs, APs, and AdvPs) to multiple specifier positions selected by the functional head I (AgrS in her terms). After the sixteenth century, I ceases to allow multiple specifiers, that is, it loses the option of being associated to an Attract-all-F EPP-feature (see Martins 2002). As a consequence, a structural position for scrambled elements is no longer available in the IP space.

This change has an important impact on the syntax of RRC-extraposition because the configuration involving a scrambled antecedent in [Spec, IP] ceases to be an option. For the sake of illustration, such a configuration is repeated here in examples (487) and (488); the structural representation of (488) is provided in (489).

(487)   E   pera todalas cousas e   cada hũa delas   ffaser   que
        and to   all.the things and each one of.them make.INF that
        uerdadeyroe   lijdemo   procurador pode e   deue   ffaser
        real   and legitimate proxy   can and should make.INF
        'And to make all the things and each one of them that a real and legitimate proxy can and should make...' (14th c., Martins 2001: 406)

TABLE 3.10 **Extraposition of restrictive relatives: Diachronic path**

Steps	Description	Result	Date (ca.)
0.	RRC-extraposition derived from the specifying coordination (plus ellipsis) structure		until 16th c.
1.	Loss of IP-scrambling (and PP-scrambling)	Decrease in frequency of the cue for the specifying coordination structure: [XP1 antecedent] YP [XP2 RRC]: XP1= embedded noun phrase OR strong noun phrase	after 16th c.
2.	a. Reanalysis of RRC-extraposition from the specifying coordination plus ellipsis structure to the stranding structure: $[_{CoP} [_{XP1} [_{DP}$ antecedent$]_i$ YP $t_i]$ Co $[_{XP2}$ $[_{DP}$ antecedent RRC$]_i$ YP $t_i]] \rightarrow [_{XP}$ antecedent$]_i$ YP $[_{DP} t_i$ RRC$]]$ b. Reanalysis of PP-extraposition from the specifying coordination plus ellipsis structure to the stranding structure	Decrease in frequency of configurations derived from the specifying coordination plus ellipsis structure	
3.	Loss of conjunct extraposition	Decrease in frequency of configurations derived from the specifying coordination plus ellipsis structure	

Note: The gray-shade indicates that the line contains a description of an independent change that took place in the history of Portuguese.

(488) que llʃ   eu Alguna cousa diuía que nõ seia   escripto
       that him.CL I   some   thing owed that not be.SBJV written
       en Esta mãda
       in this will
       '(And if there arrives someone who says) that I owed him something which is
       not written in this will' (13th c., *DCMP*)

(489)

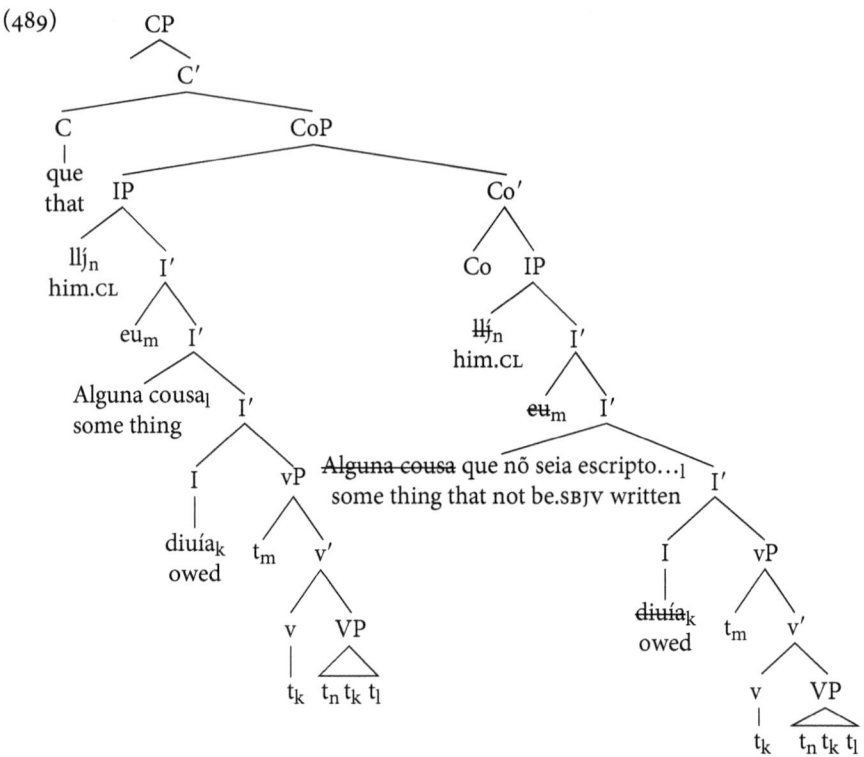

With the loss of IP-scrambling, there is a decrease in frequency of extraposition
contexts in general. As a result, Portuguese began displaying short scrambling only,
which consisted of the movement of noun phrases (either subjects or direct objects)
to a VP-adjoined position (see §3.5.1.2). In this environment, the linear distance
between the antecedent and the extraposed RRC decreases, and more importantly,
PPs cease to occur in a scrambled position.[59]

---

[59] This hypothesis is independently supported by Martins (2002, 2011), who shows that PPs are
scrambled in earlier stages of Portuguese. J. Costa (2004a), in turn, suggests that short scrambling does
not target PPs in CEP. Evidence for this comes from the fact that PPs cannot surface to the left of
monosyllabic adverb *bem* 'well', which marks the left edge of the VP (see following example).

(c) Step 2a

Given the loss of an important trigger of the specifying coordination plus ellipsis structure, children converge on a new grammar that derives RRC-extraposition from a stranding structure (see Kayne 1994).

Under Lightfoot's (1991, 1999) insights, the scenario just sketched entails that positive evidence triggering the acquisition of a specifying coordination plus ellipsis structure ceased to be available to learners. Concretely, I hypothesize that such evidence was found in the contexts in which extraposed RRCs take a strong noun phrase or the object of a preposition as antecedent (see §3.6.2). The cue for grammars with the specifying coordination plus ellipsis analysis might then be an abstract structure such as (490), with a strong noun phrase or the object of a preposition in the antecedent position.

(490)　[*strong noun phrase/object of a preposition*] $\underline{XP}$ [RRC]

In earlier stages of Portuguese, children knew that the (visible) antecedent was generated in a position external to the relative clause because no movement chain could be established between the visible antecedent and a position inside the extraposed RRC.

If this hypothesis is correct, then the scenario that emerges is that in earlier stages of Portuguese the cue (490) occurred robustly in the primary linguistic data. Then, with the loss of IP-scrambling (and PP-scrambling) the expression of the cue decreased. Given that language learners heard contexts of extraposition less frequently than required, they reanalyzed RRC-extraposition from a specifying coordination plus ellipsis structure to a stranding structure. A tentative schematic representation of this process is given in (491).

(491)　a.　$[_{CoP} [_{XP_1} [_{DP} \text{antecedent}]_i \text{YP } t_i]$ Co $[_{XP_2} [_{DP} \text{~~antecedent~~ RRC}]_i \text{~~YP~~ } t_i]] \rightarrow$
　　　　b.　$[_{XP} [\text{antecedent}]_i \text{YP } [_{DP} t_i \text{ RRC}]]$

The two conjoined XPs (see XP_1 and XP_2 in (491a)) are reanalyzed as a single XP (see (491b)). In this structure, the visible antecedent is taken to originate in an RRC-internal position and no deletion mechanism applies.

---

a.　O　Paulo olha　bem para aqueles quadros.
　　the P.　　looks well　at　those　pictures
　　'Paulo looks well at those pictures.'

b.　*O　Paulo olha　para aqueles quadros bem
　　　the P.　　looks at　those　pictures well (both J. Costa 2004a: 40)

In addition, J. Costa (2004a: 142–53) pursues the argument in favor of the base-generation of both the V-DO-IO and V-IO-DO orders in CEP. On the basis of binding effects of ditransitives, he assumes that the IO is in an A-position in both word order patterns (see §3.5.1.3A(b)). Hence I will assume that this hypothesis is correct, though I have no explanation for why PP-scrambling ceased to be an option in CEP.

Given that the RRC is derived from raising (and has a spelled-out head noun), RRC-extraposition can straightforwardly be derived from a stranding structure: the head noun undergoes leftward movement (in this case out of the external DP) stranding the RRC in its base position.

For the sake of illustration, consider the example (492) and the representations in (493a–b), which display the same extraposed RRC in step 0 and step 2 respectively. Importantly, in both structures the antecedent (plus the RRC in (493a)) undergoes short scrambling, but it is only in (493b) that short scrambling directly originates RRC-extraposition.

(492) ca   vos   ganhastes ũu cavallo <u>por i</u> que vos   nom
       because you.2PL won   a horse   by that that you.2PL not
       avíades
       had
       'because of that you won a horse that you did not have'

(493)

a.

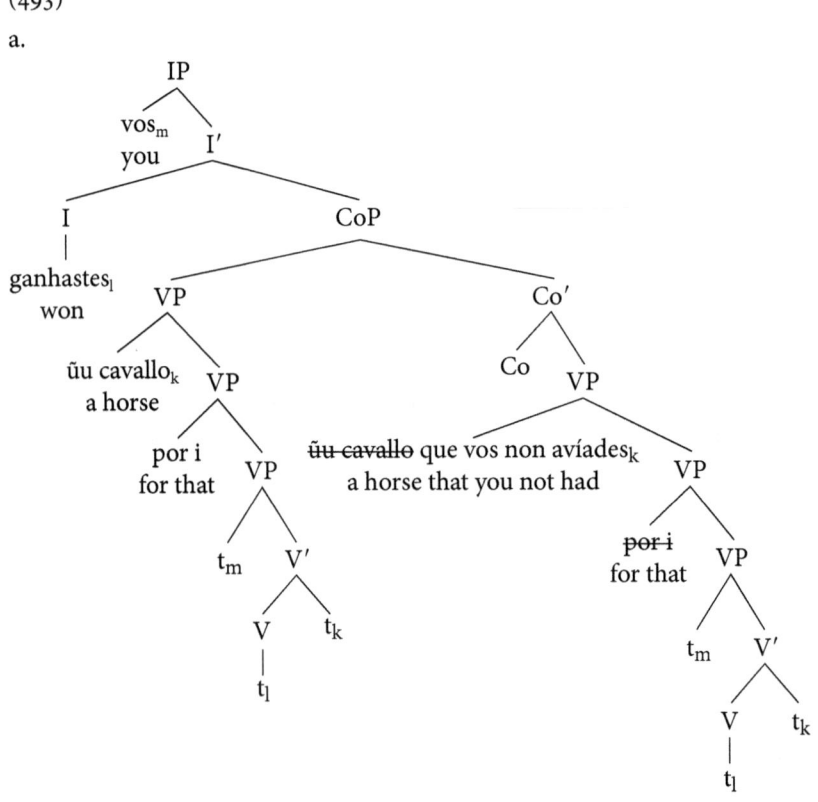

b.

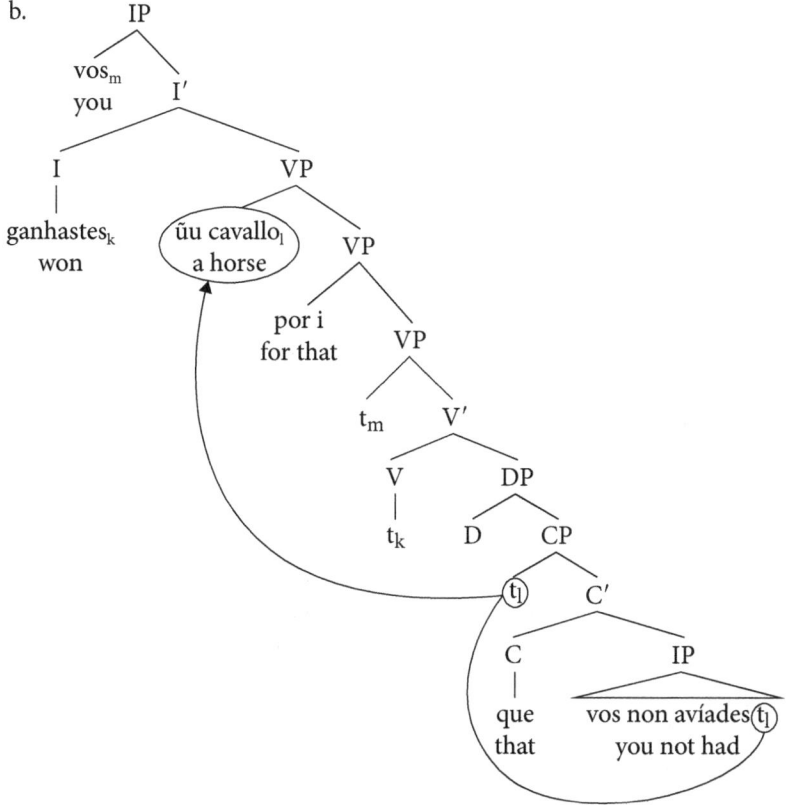

(d) Step 2b

If RRC-extraposition is reanalyzed from a specifying coordination plus ellipsis structure to a stranding structure, extraposition of other constituents should also have been
affected by this change. At least for the extraposition of PPs, this prediction might be
correct. (Additional evidence from *o qual*-ARCs is discussed in Ch. 4.)

There is no systematic study on PP-extraposition in CEP. For this reason, I restrict
the discussion to the extraposition of PP complements of the noun. According to
Brito's (2003: 337) analysis of noun phrases in CEP, the noun cannot undergo leftward
movement leaving its PP-complement behind, as shown in (494)–(495).[60]

---

[60] Martins (2004) shows that when a contrastive reading is obtained, noun phrase discontinuity may
comprise an extraposed PP as in the following example (overleaf), from CEP. Note, however, that the PP
here is not a complement of the noun. For this reason it will not be addressed in the present discussion.

20 contos paguei eu de multa por conduzir sem   cinto
20 c.   paid I of fine for drive.INF without belt
'I paid a fine of 20 contos [the currency] for driving without wearing seat belt.' (Martins 2004: 502)

(494) *Várias fugas, <u>vimos</u> de refugiados.
       several escapes saw.1PL of refugees
       'We saw several escapes of refugees.' (Brito 2003: 337)

(495) *Muitas destruições <u>tem havido</u> de cidades.[61]
       many destructions has been of cities
       'There have been many destructions of cities.' (Brito 2003: 337)

In earlier stages of Portuguese, the situation seems to be radically different. PP-extraposition is freer, being allowed in a wide range of syntactic environments. Take, for instance, the examples in (496)–(497), which display non-adjacency between the noun and its PP-complement. In (496) the post-verbal subject *Joseph* (in [Spec, VP]) breaks the adjacency between the noun *doo* 'sorrow' and its PP-complement *da morte de Jesu Cristo* 'of the death of Jesus Christ',[62] whereas in (497), repeated from (121), both the verb and the subject intervene between the noun *noticia* 'notitia' and its PP-complement *de fiadores* 'of guarantors'.

(496) Muito houve gram doo <u>Joseph</u> da   morte de Jesu Cristo.
       very had deep sorrow J.   of.the death of J.   C.
       'Joseph had deep mourning over the death of Jesus Christ.' (13th c. [trans-
       mitted by a 16th-c. MS], Martins, Pereira, and Cardoso 2013–14)

(497) Noticia <u>fecit pelagio romeu</u> de fiadores
       notitia made P.   R.   of guarantors
       'Pelagio Romeu made a *notitia* of guarantors.' (12th c., from Martins 2004: 501)

Although more research is necessary to explain the restrictions on PP-extraposition in CEP, the contrast between (494)–(495) and (496)–(497) suggest that PP-extraposition is less restrictive in earlier stages of Portuguese. Therefore, it may well be the case that the restrictions found in CEP result from the fact that PP-extraposition is also reanalyzed from a specifying coordination structure to a stranding structure.

(e) Step 3

The change affecting the syntax of extraposition might also explain the loss of conjunct extraposition in the history of Portuguese.

Conjunct extraposition refers to coordinate structures in which the last conjunct (plus the coordinator) is not adjacent to the previous conjunct(s). As in Dutch (see

---

[61] The sentence is grammatical only with an exclamative intonation and a very marked pause before *de cidades* 'of cities'.

[62] Note that (496) involves three split parts because *muito* 'very' undergoes additional leftward movement to the CP domain, but I will set this step aside because it is not crucial for the argument.

(498))[63] and Latin (see (499)–(500)), earlier stages of Portuguese allow for extraposition of the second conjunct of a coordinate phrase, as shown in (501)–(506).

Dutch:

(498) Zij heeft Marie gezien en   mij.
       she has   M.   seen   and me
       'She saw Mary and me.' (Koster 2000: 16)

Latin:

(499) quae frigus defendant et   solem
       which cold   keep.off   and sun
       'to keep off the cold and the sun' (2nd c. BC, from Devine and Stephens
       2006: 586; gloss mine)

(500) Aqua restabat et   terra.
       water remained and   earth
       'There remained water and earth.' (1st c. BC, from Devine and Stephens
       2006: 589; gloss mine)

Earlier stages of Portuguese:

(501) e   sse os #iij   anos o   dyto   canpo nõ chantardes   ou
       and if the three years the mentioned land not plant.FUT.SBJV.2PL   or
       a   dyta   ujnha
       the mentioned vineyard
       'and if you do not plant the aforementioned land or the aforementioned
       vineyard during the three years...' (13th c., Martins 2001: 373)

(502) E   por séér   mays firme esta carta seelamos dos   nossos séélos
       and to be.INF more firm this letter stamp.1PL of.the our   stamps
       e   outra tal.
       and other such
       'And, to be irrevocable, we stamp this letter and a duplicate of it.' (13th c.,
       Martins 2001: 350)

(503) que he setuada na   egreia de sã Johane da praça ẽ que
       that is located in.the church of S. J.   d. P.   in that
       o   dicto   diego afomso Jaz ẽterrado e   seus filhos
       the mentioned D.   A.   lies buried and his sons
       'that is located in the church of S. Johane da Praça, in which the aforementioned Diego Afomso and his sons lie buried' (15th c., from A. Costa 2004: 415)

---

[63] The example (498) is repeated from (456a) for ease of exposition.

(504) E   estes bées   E   quinhom acõteçeo aa dita   lionor
      and these belongings and part   went   to mentioned L.
      uaasquez madrre da   dicta   viollante em seu derecto e
      V.   mother of.the mentioned V.   in her right   and
      meatade da   dita   terça
      half   of.the mentioned third
      'And these belongings, part, and half of the aforementioned third part went
      to the aforementioned Lionor Vaasquez, mother of the aforementioned
      Viollante, by her own right...' (15th c., from A. Costa 2003: 10)

(505) E   quando el vio Lançarot ir   e   a   donzella
      and when   he saw L.   go.INF and the damsel
      'And when he saw Lançarot and the damsel coming...' (13th c. [transmitted
      by a 15th-c. MS], Martins, Pereira, and Cardoso 2014–15)

(506) Tamanho o   ódio foi   e   a   má   vontade
      such   the hate was and the bad will
      'Such was the hate and the malice' (16th c., Pimpão 1972/2000: 19)

In contrast, extraposition of the last conjunct of a coordinate phrase (plus the
coordinator) is ungrammatical in CEP, as illustrated in (507b)–(509b).

(507) a. O Pedro e   a   Maria chegaram.
         the P.   and the M.   arrived
         'Pedro and Maria arrived.'

      b. *O Pedro chegou e   a   Maria.
         the P.   arrived and the M.   (both Colaço 2006: 79)

(508) a. O medo e   a   ansiedade espalharam-se.
         the fear and the anxiety   spread-SE.CL
         'The fear and the anxiety spread.'

      b. *O medo espalhou-se e   a   ansiedade.
         the fear spread-SE.CL and the anxiety

(509) a. Eu vi o   João e   a   Maria no   cinema.
         I saw the J.   and the M.   at.the cinema
         'I saw João and Maria at the cinema.'

      b. *Eu vi o   João no   cinema e   a   Maria.
         I saw the J.   at.the cinema and the M.

Assuming that conjunct extraposition in Dutch and earlier stages of Portuguese is
derived from specifying coordination plus ellipsis (see the schematic representation
in (510)), the loss of conjunct extraposition in the diachrony of Portuguese might be

explained by the impossibility of deriving conjunct extraposition from stranding because it would require moving only one of the conjuncts, as in (511). Such extraction would violate the Coordinate Structure Constraint[64] and, more precisely, the Conjunct Constraint (see Grosu 1973), which bars the movement of whole conjuncts of coordinate structures.[65]

(510) quando el vio [$_{CoP}$ [$_{VP}$ [$_{DP}$ Lançarot] ir]]
      when he saw   L.   come.INF
      Co [$_{VP}$ [$_{CoP}$ [$_{DP1}$ ~~Lançarot~~] Co [$_{DP2}$ a donzella]] ~~ir~~]
                       L.   the damsel come.INF
      'when he saw Lançarot and the damsel coming'

(511) *[$_{XP1}$]$_i$ YP [$_{CoP}$ t$_i$ Co [$_{XP2}$]]

3.7.1.2 Hypothesis II The second hypothesis that I would like to formulate here is an attempt to articulate the diachronic path sketched in §3.7.1.1 with the theory of competing grammars originally proposed by Kroch (1989, 1994). I will not provide an exhaustive explanation of the change under this new scenario, but I will simply outline how the diachronic path of RRC-extraposition can be generically thought of in terms of the competing grammars theory.

Under this view, the starting point would involve two variants in competition to generate RRC-extraposition in earlier stages of Portuguese: the specifying coordination plus ellipsis structure and the stranding structure.

The stranding structure would be available for: (1) the cases in which it leads to the same overt results as the specifying coordination plus ellipsis structure; and (2) the cases that cannot be derived from the specifying coordination structure. As I mentioned in §3.6.3, type (2) can be illustrated by configurations involving c-command-based relations between a licensor (higher than CoP in a corresponding specifying coordination structure) and an extraposed RRC. Consider, for instance, the sentence in (512) (repeated from (482)), which has an extraposed subjunctive clause licensed by the negative marker *nom* 'not'.

(512) ca   nom ha cousa no mundo que tanto deseje
      because not has thing in.the world that as.much want.SBJV.1SG
      como honra de cavallaria
      as   honor of cavalry
      'because there is nothing in the world that I want so much as the honor of cavalry' (13th c. [transmitted by a 15th-c. MS], Martins, Pereira, and Cardoso 2014–15)

---

[64] For an alternative analysis of conjunct extraposition, see De Vries (2002: 279).
[65] For a different interpretation of the Coordinate Structure Constraint, see Zhang (2007).

Under De Vries' (2002) approach, the extraposition in (512) involves the coordination at the VP-level of projection, as represented in (513) (repeated from (483)).
However, under this configuration, the negative marker *nom* 'not' does not
c-command subjunctive RRC. Assuming that second conjuncts are invisible for the
higher context (De Vries 2005), the subjunctive mood is not licensed, and therefore
sentences like (482) should not be allowed, contrary to fact.

(513) [CP ca   nom ha [CoP [VP cousa no   mundo]
           because not has   thing in.the world
       [Co [VP ~~cousa~~ que tanto   deseje   como a   honra
               thing that as.much want.SBJV.1SG as   the honor
       de cavallaria ~~no   mundo~~]]]]
       of cavalry   in.the   world

The problem can be circumvented by assuming that the stranding structure takes
over in the cases that cannot be derived from the specifying coordination structure, as
in (512). In that case the subjunctive RRC could be licensed in a stranding structure
because an RRC stranded in a VP-internal position is in the c-command domain of
the negation. Note further that the CEP counterpart of (512) is grammatical, as
predicted by the analysis of CEP extraposition is terms of stranding.

Conversely, the specifying coordination plus ellipsis structure would be used in the
cases that cannot be derived from stranding. As shown in §3.6.2, such configurations
involve extraposed RRCs taking a strong noun phrase or a noun phrase embedded
within a PP as their antecedent. These cases cannot be derived from stranding
because movement only applies to constituents. For more details about the derivation, see §§3.6.2.1 and 3.6.2.3, respectively.

With the loss of IP-scrambling (and PP-scrambling), the frequency of extraposition derived from the specifying coordination plus ellipsis structure declines. As a
result, the stranding structure gains advantage over the specifying coordination
structure and ends up winning the competition.

Under this view, the change affecting RRC-extraposition in the diachrony of
Portuguese can be thought of in terms of the loss of RRC-extraposition derived
from specifying coordination plus ellipsis. No reanalysis is required because the
stranding structure is already available in the grammar.

3.7.1.3 Hypothesis III   There is another line of research that I will not pursue in this
book, but that might be worth exploring in the future: the ellipsis types available in
the diachrony of Portuguese. A possible conjecture would be that earlier stages of
Portuguese and CEP differ with respect to the types and properties of ellipsis they
allow: whereas earlier stages of Portuguese allow for a broad range of ellipsis types
(including the ones that derive extraposition under the specifying coordination plus

ellipsis structure), in CEP ellipsis is severely constrained. Further research on ellipsis phenomena in earlier stages of Portuguese is, however, necessary to test the validity of this hypothesis.

3.7.2 *Cross-linguistic contrasts*

Throughout this chapter, I have provided cross-linguistic evidence showing that languages vary in respect of the properties of RRC-extraposition they exhibit. Although the overview offered in §3.4.2 has several limitations in terms of cross-linguistic coverage, it provides sufficient evidence to conclude that CEP contrasts with other languages (e.g. English and Dutch) with respect to the properties of RRC-extraposition. The main findings are summarized in Table 3.11 (repeated from Table 3.2 for ease of exposition).

To account for these contrasts, I propose that RRC-extraposition can be derived from two different structures: specifying coordination plus ellipsis and stranding. Building on the diachronic path proposed for extraposition in the diachrony of Portuguese (see §3.7.1) and the insights of the competing grammars theory (see §3.7.1.2), I submit that the two structures generating (RRC-)extraposition are not instantiated in all languages, it being possible to identify two types of language (see (514)).

(514)   Type I.   Languages that do not allow for extraposition derived from specifying coordination plus ellipsis (e.g. CEP and possibly Italian, Spanish, and French).

Type II. Languages that allow for extraposition derived from specifying coordination plus ellipsis (e.g. English and Dutch).

Type-I languages do not have extraposition derived from specifying coordination plus ellipsis and generate RRC-extraposition by stranding, whereas Type-II languages allow for extraposition derived from specifying coordination plus ellipsis.

TABLE 3.11 **Extraposition of restrictive relatives: Cross-linguistic contrasts**

Empirical issue		CEP	English	Dutch
A. Extraposition from strong noun phrases		−	+	+
B. Extraposition from pre-verbal positions	subjects	−	+	+
	wh-constituents	+	+	+
	emphatic/evaluative phrases	+	+	+
	preposed foci	+	+	+
	topics	−	−	−
C. Extraposition from PPs		−	+	+

This explains why (RRC-)extraposition is much less constrained in Type-II languages than in Type-I.

Interestingly, the formulation in (514) leaves open the possibility of Type-II languages also making use of the stranding structure to derive RRC-extraposition. This is an interesting result because it reveals a close connection between cross-linguistic variation and diachronic change. Under the synchronic grammatical competition hypothesis outlined in §3.7.1.2, the starting point involves precisely two different structures in competition to generate (RRC-)extraposition in earlier stages of Portuguese: the specifying coordination plus ellipsis structure and the stranding structure. This corresponds to the scenario proposed for Type-II languages (e.g. Dutch and English). Moreover, similarly to historical Portuguese (after the sixteenth century), which ceases to have extraposition derived from specifying coordination plus ellipsis, contemporary Type-I languages lack this coordinate-style configuration.

For the sake of illustration, let me show how this hypothetical scenario could be implemented in a Type-II language such as Dutch. Koster (2000) and De Vries (2002), among others, criticize the stranding approach to (RRC-)extraposition (see Kayne 1994) showing that it cannot derive the properties of extraposition in Dutch. But an analysis in terms of specifying coordination, as suggested by these authors, also faces some problems. For instance, how does one block head noun extraction via movement operations that are independently available in the grammar? If Dutch noun phrases can be scrambled and fronted in Dutch, why is the antecedent of an RRC an exception?

The dual approach to the syntax of RRC-extraposition posited in this chapter actually suggests that specifying coordination plus ellipsis and stranding might both be involved in Dutch (RRC-)extraposition. The stranding structure could be available for those cases where it leads to the same overt results as the specifying coordination plus ellipsis structure, whereas the specifying coordination plus ellipsis structure would take over in the cases that cannot be derived from stranding (e.g. RRC-extraposition from a strong noun phrase or an object of a preposition).

This hypothesis has the advantage of deriving from stranding the contexts of (RRC-)extraposition that involve movement. Consider, for instance, the examples in (515), from Dutch. The head plus the RRC can occur together in the middle field (515a) but these elements may also surface in a discontinuous manner (515b–c). Under the hypothesis that Dutch is head-initial, sentences such as (515b–c) can be derived from stranding by assuming that the head undergoes leftward movement, stranding the RRC in the object's base position (see Zwart 2011).

(515) a. Tasman heeft verschillende eilanden die   niet bewoond
          T.   has   different   islands which not inhabited
          waren ontdekt.
          were discovered
          'Tasman discovered several islands that were inhabited.'

b. Tasman heeft verschillende eilanden <u>ontdekt</u>　die　niet
　T.　　has　different　　islands　discovered which not
　bewoond　waren.
　Inhabited were

c. Verschillende eilanden <u>heeft Tasman ontdekt</u>　die　niet
　different　　islands　has　T.　　discovered which not
　bewoond　waren.
　inhabited were　　(all Zwart 2011: 271–2)

An argument that has been used against the stranding analysis is that extraction of the head noun ceases to be possible after movement of the head noun plus the RRC to the middle field. See, for instance, (516a), where the extraction of the head *verschillende eilanden* 'different islands' yields ungrammaticality. Only the entire noun phrase can be fronted, as shown in (516b).

(516)　a. *Verschillende eilanden <u>heeft</u> <u>Tasman</u> die　niet
　　　　　different　　islands　has　T.　　which not
　　　　　bewoond　waren ontdekt.
　　　　　inhabited were　discovered

　　　b. Verschillende eilanden die　niet bewoond　waren
　　　　　different　　islands　which not inhabited were
　　　　　heeft Tasman ontdekt.
　　　　　has　T.　　discovered (both Zwart 2011: 271–2)

However, the ungrammaticality of (516a) does not necessarily entail that stranding cannot be involved in (RRC-)extraposition. It might simply mean that there are independent principles and operations available in the grammar that block the extraction of the head noun from the middle field. A similar line of reasoning holds for CEP. The fact that an extraposed RRC cannot take a pre-verbal subject in [Spec, IP] as its antecedent does not entail that stranding cannot derive (RRC-) extraposition in CEP. It simply reveals that an independent principle available in the grammar blocks this configuration.

Another interesting conclusion drawn in §3.4.2 is that Romance languages do not behave in a uniform way with respect to RRC-extraposition. The main findings of this comparison are summarized in Table 3.12, repeated from Table 3.3 for ease of exposition.

French exhibits a peculiar behavior: it contrasts with other Romance languages in allowing extraposition from a pre-verbal position, but it also contrasts with some Germanic languages (like English and Dutch) in not allowing extraposition from strong noun phrases. I propose that these facts can be accounted for by assuming that languages may differ in the way they resolve the ambiguity of a constituent in [Spec, IP], expressed in (517) (repeated from (426)).

TABLE 3.12 **Extraposition of restrictive relatives: Romance languages**

Empirical issue	CEP	Italian	Spanish	French
A. Extraposition from strong noun phrases	−	−	−	−
B. Extraposition from pre-verbal subjects	−	−	−	+

(517)   Interpretative Principle
The antecedent of an extraposed RRC must occur in a position non-ambiguously interpreted as non-topic (in Kuroda's 2005 sense).

Whereas in CEP (and possibly in Spanish and Italian), the ambiguity associated with [Spec, IP] is resolved syntactically and prosodically (through subject inversion), in French and in earlier stages of Portuguese, it may be resolved only prosodically. In this case, a constituent in [Spec, IP] can be unambiguously interpreted as non-topic if it is prosodically marked by pitch accent. Ultimately, this amounts to saying that the cross-linguistic variation in RRC-extraposition from pre-verbal subjects is determined by how the different languages mark the topic/non-topic status of the subject.

Of course, further comparison between languages in this domain is necessary to understand if these hypotheses are correct.

3.8 Conclusion

As I announced in §3.1, the main goal of this chapter is to contribute to a better understanding of the syntax of RRC-extraposition. This is achieved by discussing new empirical evidence from CEP and earlier stages of Portuguese, which is systematically compared to data from other languages.

From a descriptive point of view, I identify three contrasting properties of RRC-extraposition: (1) the definiteness effect; (2) extraposition from pre-verbal positions; and (3) extraposition from PPs. Additionally, I provide empirical evidence suggesting that languages may be subject to diachronic and cross-linguistic variation in respect of the type of RRC-extraposition that they display. More precisely, I have shown that: (1) earlier stages of Portuguese contrast sharply with CEP with respect to the properties of RRC-extraposition; (2) RRC-extraposition in earlier stages of Portuguese is, to a large extent, Germanic-like, unlike CEP.

Exploring the theoretical impact of these findings, I submit that the variation found in the syntax of RRC-extraposition is not compatible with a uniform approach to the phenomenon. Therefore, I argue for a dual approach to RRC-extraposition, whereby

RRC-extraposition may involve two different structures: (1) specifying coordination plus ellipsis (De Vries 2002); and (2) VP-internal stranding (Kayne 1994).

In order to explain the variation found across languages and different stages of the same language, I argue that grammars may diverge in respect to the possibility of deriving extraposition from specifying coordination plus ellipsis.

Diachronically, I submit that earlier stages of Portuguese have RRC-extraposition derived from specifying coordination plus ellipsis (and possibly stranding as well). The loss of IP-scrambling and PP-scrambling gives rise to differences in the relative frequency of the two competing structures, which ultimately resulted in the loss of extraposition derived from specifying coordination plus ellipsis.

Cross-linguistically, I suggest that there are at two types of language: Type-I languages that do not allow for extraposition derived from specifying coordination plus ellipsis, as CEP (and possibly Italian, Spanish, and French), and Type-II languages that allow for it, as do English and Dutch. I additionally hypothesize that Type-II languages also make use of the stranding structure to derive RRC-extraposition.

Ultimately, the approach advocated in this chapter reveals that competing theoretical analyses need not be either true or false universally, but can help to explain the variation found among languages that are separated over space and time.

4

Appositive relativization

4.1 Introduction

In the literature on the syntax of ARCs, considerable attention has been given to the idea that ARCs do not constitute a unified type of construction (Cinque 1982, 2008 and Smits 1988, among others). These analyses contrast with the traditional view, according to which the different ARCs found in all languages can be derived from the same syntactic structure.

In this chapter, I go against the traditional view and claim that there is no unified account of ARCs across languages. This claim is supported by the comparative study of ARCs introduced by the complex relative pronoun *o qual* 'the which' (henceforth *o qual*-ARCs) in CEP and earlier stages of Portuguese, considering also evidence from other languages. The investigation of this micro-variation leads to the conclusion that the syntactic properties of *o qual*-ARCs have changed over time and that this fact can only be explained by a non-unified approach to the phenomenon.

That this conclusion can be reached in the diachronic dimension is particularly telling in view of the highly constrained nature of this variation. In fact, it is found within the same language (Portuguese), in the same construction (ARC), introduced by the same relativizer (*o qual*), which makes it possible to control important variables that may interfere with the results obtained in other studies (involving, for instance, the comparison of languages quite distant historically and typologically).

With this background in mind, the present chapter has descriptive and explanatory goals. From a descriptive point of view, it aims to: (1) establish clear syntactic properties to distinguish *o qual*-ARCs in CEP from *o qual*-ARCs in earlier stages of Portuguese; and (2) correlate the variation documented in the diachronic dimension with the one found in the cross-linguistic dimension.

From an explanatory (or theoretical) point of view, it aims both to argue for a dual approach to *o qual*-ARCs, according to which *o qual*-ARCs in CEP involve the head raising analysis (see Kayne 1994; Bianchi 1999), whereas *o qual*-ARCs in earlier stages of Portuguese involve the specifying coordination analysis (see De Vries 2006b), and to demonstrate that the dual approach to ARCs provides a good basis

Portuguese Relative Clauses in Synchrony and Diachrony. First Edition. Adriana Cardoso.
© Adriana Cardoso 2017. First published in 2017 by Oxford University Press.

for understanding the variation found within a language and across languages, both in the synchronic and diachronic dimensions.

The chapter is organized as follows. Section 4.2 provides background information on unitary and non-unitary approaches to ARCs. Section 4.3 gives an overview of the properties of *o qual*-ARCs similar in CEP and in earlier stages of Portuguese, while §4.4 sets out the syntactic properties that differentiate the two constructions. In order to explain the contrasting properties identified, §4.5 outlines the dual approach proposed for *o qual*-ARCs, and §§4.5.1–9 demonstrate how this proposal accounts for the contrasts found between CEP and earlier stages of Portuguese. Finally, §4.6 offers some comparative remarks on the diachronic and synchronic variation found in the syntax of *o qual*-ARCs. Section 4.7 summarizes.

4.2 Unitary analyses vs. non-unitary analyses

ARCs are traditionally regarded as a unitary type of construction.[1] Under this view, the properties of ARCs found in all languages can be derived from the same syntactic structure. There are, however, early indications in the literature that one universal analysis of appositives across and within languages is untenable. In §§4.2.1–4, I summarize the most relevant aspects of the non-unitary approaches put forward by Cinque (1982, 2008), Smits (1988), and Bianchi (1999), focusing on the evidence provided for a non-unitary approach to ARCs.

4.2.1 Cinque (1982)

Cinque claims that a single syntactic structure cannot account for the properties of ARCs found in Italian. In particular, he is concerned with the contrast between ARCs introduced by *che/cui* (lit. 'that/who') and by *il quale* (lit. 'the which'). According to Cinque, these two types exhibit contrasting properties, and, consequently, must involve two different structures. Among the syntactic properties that differentiate them, Cinque (1982) highlights the contrasts on the relativized positions and pied-piping.

As for the relativized positions, Cinque shows that when either a subject or an object is relativized, a wh-pronoun appears in *il quale*-ARCs but not in *che/cui*-ARCs. In the latter, only the form *che* is found, which is identical to the ordinary complementizer of subordinate clauses. Examples (518)–(519) illustrate this restriction: the a examples involve subject relivization, whereas the b examples involve direct-object relivization.

---

[1] For an overview of existing analyses of ARCs see §1.3.2.5.

(518) a. Giorgio, che/*cui ti   vuole, è là.
          G.   that/who you.CL wants is there
          'Giorgio, who wants you, is there.'

       b. Giorgio, che/*cui stimi,   l'ha   fatto.
          G.   that/who respect.2SG it.CL.has done
          'Giorgio, who(m) you respect, has done it.' (both Cinque 1982: 249;
          glosses and translation in example b mine)

(519) a. Giorgio, il   quale ti   vuole, è là.
          G.   the which you.CL wants is there
          'Giorgio, who wants you, is there.'

       b. Giorgio, ?il quale} stimi,   l'ha   fatto.
          G.   the which respect.2SG it.CL.has done
          'Giorgio, who(m) you respect, has done it.' (both Cinque 1982: 249;
          glosses and translation in example b mine)

As for pied-piping, Cinque notes that in *che/cui*-ARCs, no pied-piping is allowed
except for that of PPs, whereas in *il quale*-ARCs, pied-piping of different phrasal
categories is available. Examples (520)–(521) illustrate the relevant contrast: a
examples display pied-piping of DP; b examples display pied-piping of complex
PP; and c examples involve pied-piping of an infinitival clause.

(520) a. *Giorgio, la figlia   di cui   fuma,   è contrario.
          G.   the daughter of whom smokes is against
          'Giorgio, whose daughter smokes, is against it.'

       b. *Giorgio, alla figlia   di cui   hai   scritto, è in collera.
          G.   to.the daughter of whom have.2SG written is in anger
          'Giorgio, to whose daughter you have written, is angry.'

       c. *Giorgio, fuggire da cui   non osava, è morto.
          G.   flee.INF from.whom not   dared is dead
          'Giorgio, from whom he did not dare to flee, has died.' (all Cinque 1982:
          248–9; glosses and translation in example c mine)

(521) a. Giorgio, la figlia del qual fuma, è contrario.
       b. Giorgio, alla figlia del quale hai scritto, è in collera.
       c. Giorgio, fuggire dal quale non osava, è morto. (all Cinque 1982: 249)

On the basis of these empirical contrasts, Cinque hypothesizes that in Italian, there are
two separate paradigms of ARCs, one belonging to the "core" grammar of Italian and
other being peripheral to it. Under Cinque's proposal, the core grammar of Italian
employs the structure [$_{NP}$ NP S̄] for RRCs and ARCs introduced by *che/cui*. In addition,
a more peripheral option is available for *il quale*-appositives, in which the relative is a

juxtaposed clause (with the structure NP..., $\bar{S}$,...).[2] Because *il quale*-ARCs are felt to be slightly more formal in style than *che/cui*-ARCs, Cinque (1982) argues that stylistic markedness can be interpreted as a manifestation of the use of a more peripheral structure allowed by the grammar.

In this view, Cinque explains the restrictions on the relativized positions using principle of "obligatory deletion of (relative) wh-phrases in COMP up to recoverability" (1982: 251). In formal terms, a wh-phrase can be deleted (1) if it is non-distinct from the head and (2) if it is c-commanded by the head.

In subject or object *che/cui*-ARCs, the wh-phrase is deleted (and the complementizer is expanded to *che*) because the wh-phrase (1) is non-distinct from the head and (2) is c-commanded by the head (in the configuration $[_{NP}\,NP\,\bar{S}]$). In contrast, in subject and object *il quale*-ARCs the wh-phrase is not deleted because it is not c-commanded by the head; recall that the relative clause is juxtaposed (in the configuration NP..., $\bar{S}$,...) and, consequently, is syntactically invisible for c-command relations.

In turn, the restrictions on pied-piping follow from the (non)-anaphoric nature of the wh-pronoun. On the basis of an ambiguous lexical characterization of some wh-pronouns, Cinque claims that all relative pronouns belong to the inventory of lexical (bound) anaphors of language, but only a few can be further used as non-anaphoric elements. This is the case for *il quale* but, crucially, is not the case for *cui*.

Anaphoric pronouns can enter the structure $[_{NP}\,NP\,\bar{S}]$ because in this configuration, they are c-commanded by the head (as required by Principle A of the Binding Theory). They cannot, however, enter the juxtaposed structure (NP... $\bar{S}$,...) because in this case, the c-command requirement is not satisfied. Non-anaphoric pronouns behave differently in this respect: they can enter the juxtaposed structure simply because they are not limited by Principle A of the Binding Theory.

Assuming that S and NP are the only governing categories, the restrictions found in *che/cui*-ARCs can be represented as in (522) (the minimal governing categories of *che/cui* are boxed for emphasis).

(522)

a. ...$[_{\boxed{NP}}\,NP_i\,[_{\bar{S}}\,[_{COMP}\,[_{PP}\,P\,[_{NPi}\,wh]]\,-WH]\,S]]...$ (*pied-piping of PP*)

b. ...$[_{NP}\,NP_i\,[_{\bar{S}}\,[_{COMP}\,[_{\boxed{NP}}\,\bar{N}\,[_{PP}\,P\,[_{NPi}\,wh]]]\,-WH]\,S]]...$ (*pied-piping of an NP*)

c. ...$[_{NP}\,NP_i\,[_{\bar{S}}\,[_{COMP}\,[_{\boxed{S}}\,...[_{NPi}\,wh]]\,-WH]\,S]]...$ (*pied-piping of a clause*)

(all Cinque 1982: 255)

---

[2] Note that, under the terms proposed in §1.3.2.5A, the structures $[_{NP}\,NP\,\bar{S}]$ and NP..., $\bar{S}$..., qualify, respectively, as a constituency analysis and an orphanage analysis.

Pied-piping of PPs is allowed because the wh-anaphor is bound within its minimal governing category (the emphasized NP in (522)). In turn, pied-piping of NPs and clauses is not allowed because the wh-anaphor is free in its minimal governing category (the emphasized NP in (522b) and S in (522c)), in violation of Principle A of the Binding Theory.

The unconstrained availability of pied-piping observed in *il quale*-ARCs is explained by the non-anaphoric nature of *il quale*-pronouns. Unlimited by Principle A of the Binding Theory, *il quale*-pronouns can refer back to their antecedent independently of the category of the pied-piped constituent. The relation between non-anaphoric *il quale*-pronouns and the antecedent can be analogized to the relation between a demonstrative pronoun and its antecedent, the nature of the relation being one of discourse grammar rather than one of sentence grammar.

From a cross-linguistic perspective, Cinque suggests that the non-unitary approach proposed for Italian does not universally hold. For instance, whereas French and Italian display two structures for ARCs, English only displays the juxtaposed structure (NP... S̄,...) This explains some of the differences between English and Italian/French ARCs, namely, that only wh-pronouns are allowed to introduce ARCs in English (*Mary, who/*that/ *Ø you met yesterday*) and the possibility of generalized pied-piping.

The topic of cross-linguistic variation resumes in the section dedicated to Cinque's (2008) paper (see also §1.3.2.5B(d)).

4.2.2 Smits (1988)

Smits claims that a single syntactic analysis cannot account for the heterogeneous types of ARC found within a language and across languages. Alternatively, two different analyses are proposed: a constituency analysis (more precisely, an adjunction analysis) and an orphanage analysis, in which the antecedent and the ARC are two completely independent parts of the sentence containing them (see (523)).

(523)   [$_{XP}$ *antecedent*]...[*ARC*]

Two arguments are provided for the existence of the structure in (523). One is that ARCs may have split antecedents,[3] as illustrated in (524).

(524)   A man entered the room and a woman went out, who were quite similar.
         (Demirdache 1991: 166)

---

[3] The term *split antecedent* is used for an antecedent that consists of more than one non-conjoined noun phrases as in *John suggested to Mary that they should leave*; here, *they* takes as an antecedent the split antecedent *John* and *Mary*.

A constituency analysis is untenable because it would require the derivation of (524) to start with ARCs adjoined to each noun phrase, with one of the appositives deleted later. The problem is that such an analysis would not explain the presence of a plural verb form (*were*) found in the alleged visible ARC. An orphanage analysis, in contrast, can successfully derive ARCs with split antecedents. In this case, there is no direct structural link between the antecedent and the relative clause; therefore, nothing prevents the appositive from taking non-conjoined noun phrases as antecedent.

A second argument in favor of an orphanage approach concerns the existence of *pseudo-relatives* (see (525), from French) and *apparent extraposed ARCs* (see (526), from Dutch).

(525)   Marie est là,   qui pleure comme une Madeleine.
        M.   is there who cries   like   a   M.
        'Marie is there, and she is crying her heart out.' (Smits 1988: 181; gloss mine)

(526)   Ik wilde   mijn zuster opzoeken, die echter   niet thuis   was.
        I wanted my   sister visit   who however not at.home was
        'I wanted to visit my sister, who wasn't at home, however.' (Smits 1988: 185; gloss mine)

Pseudo-relative clauses look like extraposed relatives; however, they are interpretationally different because they express an event in progress (whereby the apparent antecedent—*Marie* in (525)—participates). Apparent extraposed ARCs also look like extraposed relatives, but they have a specific type of meaning (such as continuative, resultative, or contrastive). Therefore, instead of referring to a noun phrase, they modify the whole state of affairs that is expressed in the preceding clause. For instance, the apparent extraposed ARC in (526) expresses the result of the action described in the main clause with the meaning "but the action described in the predicate was in vain" (Smits 1988: 186).

Given the interpretation associated with pseudo-relatives and apparently extraposed ARCs, Smits considers that they are closer to adverbial clauses than to true relative clauses, and, consequently, should be analyzed as involving the orphanage structure in (523). Note that, under this hypothesis, neither of the structures is limited by locality constraints and may freely occur in the rightmost position of the sentence.

4.2.3 Bianchi (1999)

The limitations of unitary approaches are also addressed in Bianchi (1999: 151 ff.), at least to some extent, by suggesting that not all types of ARC can be derived from the same syntactic structure (in this case, the raising analysis).

One serious problem Bianchi faces concerns the analysis of ARCs with non-nominal antecedents, as in (527). The raising analysis cannot derive such examples because the antecedent has to be selected by the relative determiner D_{rel} within the relative clause; thus, it has to be a nominal projection.

(527) a. Mary is courageous, which I will never be.
       b. John is in the garden, which is where I should be.
       c. Mary has resigned, which John hasn't.
       d. John was late, which was unfortunate. (all Bianchi 1999: 151)

Another property Bianchi identifies as problematic for the raising analysis of appositives concerns the so-called *relatif de liaison* or *connecting relative*. These terms refer to relative pronouns that apparently introduce a main clause. Such an impression is given by the fact that they are separated from the antecedent by a full stop or other heavy punctuation (e.g. a colon or a semicolon), as in (528), from Latin.

(528) id oppidum Lentulus Spinther X   cohortibus tenebat; qui
       this town   L.   S.   with.ten cohorts   held   who
       Caesaris adventu cognito profugit ex   oppido
       of.Caesar arrival known   fled   from   town
       'Lentulus Spinther held this town with ten cohorts; who, when he was
       informed of the arrival of Caesar, left the town.' (1st c. BC, from Ramat
       2005: 123)

According to Bianchi (1999: 152), this construction cannot be derived from the raising analysis because the head would be separated from the relative clause by a sentence boundary.

Even while recognizing these problems, Bianchi (1999) holds to a unitary approach to ARCs. To solve this paradox, she argues that sentences such as (527) and (528) may not be relative constructions at all; the relative pronoun can be taken as an anaphoric pronoun and the purported appositive may be either coordinated to the main clause or parenthetical.

4.2.4 Cinque (2008)

Cinque again takes up the non-unitary approach put forth in his 1982 paper, adding more empirical evidence and proposing a theoretical apparatus that reflects the recent developments in syntactic theory.

Assuming a cross-linguistic perspective, Cinque (2008) claims that there are two different types of ARC: the *integrated* and the *non-integrated* constructions (which roughly correspond to a constituency analysis and an orphanage analysis, respectively). Some languages display both constructions (e.g. Italian and

TABLE 4.1 Properties distinguishing *che/cui*-appositives from *il quale*-appositives

	che/cui-ARCs	*il quale*-ARCs
Subjects and objects represented by a wh-pronoun	−	+
Generalized pied-piping	−	+
Non-declarative illocutionary force	−	+
Non-adjacency	−	+
Split antecedents	−	+
Retention of the "internal" head	−	+
Non-identity of the "external" and "internal" heads	−	+
Non-nominal antecedents	−	+
Relative clause preposing	−	+
Parasitic gaps	+	−
Temporal DPs as antecedent	+	−
wh-pronoun coordinated with another DP	−	+

French), while others display only one. In the latter case, two options are available: some languages have only the integrated type (e.g. northern Italian dialects and, possibly, Chinese), whereas others have exclusively the non-integrated type (e.g. English and Romanian).[4]

In Italian, *il quale*-ARCs belong to the non-integrated type, whereas *che/cui*-ARCs belong to the integrated type.[5] Evidence for this distinction comes from a number of syntactic properties that differentiate *che/cui*-ARCs from *il quale*-ARCs.[6] These properties are summarized in Table 4.1; here a plus means 'possible' and a minus means 'impossible'.[7]

From a cross-linguistic perspective, Cinque (2008) demonstrates that the behavior of ARCs with respect to the properties listed in Table 4.1 follows from the type of ARCs available in each language. Consider, for instance, the case of English, a language that displays only the non-integrated type. ARCs

---

[4] Additionally there are some languages that apparently lack ARCs. As Cinque (2007) notes, these languages have to resort to coordination (e.g. Gungbe and Bunun) or to the apposition of generic nouns (such as *person*) followed by an RRC (e.g. Mixtecan).

[5] In Cinque (1982 and 2008), it is assumed that there are two different types of ARC. However, Cinque (2008) does not retain the idea (suggested in Cinque 1982) that the two constructions have different "statuses" in the grammar of Italian, one belonging to the core grammar and the other being peripheral to it. In Cinque (2008) it is simply assumed that these constructions may coexist in the same language.

[6] Some of these properties are discussed in Cinque (1982), but in less detail.

[7] There is, however, one exception. In the first property listed in Table 4.1 (subjects and objects represented by a wh-pronoun), a minus means 'no' and a plus means 'yes'.

in English pattern with Italian *il quale*-ARCs in that they: (1) obligatorily retain wh-pronouns when the subject or the object is relativized (*Mary, who/*that/ *Ø you met yesterday*); (2) allow pied-piping of phrases other than PPs (*Mary, to hire whom would be a great opportunity*); (3) may have non-declarative illocutionary force (*Your father, by whom will we ever be forgiven for what we have done?, would never have behaved like that*); (4) may have an additional internal head (*John was almost at the end of his financial resources, which fact led him to look for a cheaper house*).

Conversely, in northern Italian dialects, which only display the integrated type, appositive relatives pattern with Italian *che/cui*-ARCs; as a result, they behave like Italian *che/cui*-ARCs as far as the properties in Table 4.1 are concerned.

As for the syntax of ARCs, Cinque (2008) argues that the integrated type involves a syntactic structure similar to RRCs. Following the ideas put forth in his recent work (2003, 2009), Cinque claims that relative clauses are generally merged in a pre-nominal position and that the post-nominal order found in languages such as English and Portuguese is ultimately derived from the leftward movement of the head past the relative clause,[8] as represented in (529).

(529) a. $[IP_{rel}$ $[_{DP}$ Dem [Num [A NP]]]] (*merge of C_0 and attraction of IP*) →

 b. IP_{relj} C_0 $[t_j$ $[_{DP}$ Dem [Num [A NP]]]]
   (*merge of C_1 and attraction of the wh-pronoun/'internal Head'*) →

 c. wh_i- $[C_1$ $[_{IPrel}$ $t_i]_j$ C_0 $[t_j$ $[_{DP}$ Dem [Num [A NP]]]]]
   (*merge of C_2 and attraction of the 'external Head'*) →

 d. $[_{DP}$ Dem [Num [A NP]]]$_k$ C_2 wh_i- $[C_1$ $[_{IPrel}$ $t_i]_j$ C_0 t_j $[t_k]]$
     quei dieci bei gattini   che io amo
   'those ten nice kittens, which I love' (all Cinque 2008: 116–17)

Note that, first, the relative IP is merged above the determiner/demonstrative;[9] this yields the order in (529a), with the relative clause in a pre-nominal position. The

---

[8] Cinque (2003, 2009) aims to derive the different types of relative clause found in the languages of the world (post-nominal, pre-nominal, internally headed, headless, correlative) from the same structure. Specifically, he proposes that pre-nominal relatives (found in "rigid" OV languages) reflect the structure of Merge, and that post-nominal (and the other types of) relative are derived from this basic structure.

[9] RRCs differ from ARCs in this respect: in RRCs the relative IP is merged in the specifier above the specifiers that host attributive adjectives and numerals and below the projection that hosts determiners and demonstratives; in ARCs, the relative IP is merged in the specifier of a nominal projection dominating DP (to be outside of the scope of the determiner or demonstrative).

procedure for deriving the post-nominal order is complex, as it involves a *matching* and a *raising* variant. The basic idea is that after IP raising to a higher licensing position, the complementizer C_1 is merged and attracts the wh-pronoun/internal head. Then, there are two possible ways for the derivation to proceed. Under the matching variant, the complementizer C_2 is merged, which attracts the external head, and the internal head is deleted. Under the raising variant, the external head is not raised but rather deleted in situ under identity with the raised internal head.

As for the non-integrated type, Cinque (2008) proposes a more tentative approach. Extending Kayne's LCA to discourse grammar, the author derives linear precedence in a discourse from asymmetric c-command. Technically, a linearly preceding main sentence occupies the specifier of an (empty) head, which, in turn, takes the following main sentence as its complement, as in (530).

(530)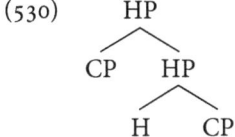

However, discourse fragments do not always involve concatenation at the CP level. A DP may precede a CP, as in: *A pink shirt? I will never wear any such thing in my life!* (Cinque 2008: 118). Hence, a representation like (531) is also available.

(531)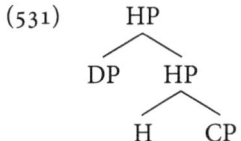

According to Cinque, similar structures are involved in non-integrated ARCs. In this case, the complement position hosts the relative clause and the specifier hosts the relevant discourse unit containing the antecedent. If non-integrated ARCs take an antecedent across the discourse, the specifier hosts the preceding sentence (or discourse fragment), as in (530). If there is adjacency between a nominal antecedent and the relative clause, the specifier position hosts a DP, as in (531).

4.3 Properties of *o qual*-appositive relatives

In this section, I provide background information on the relative pronoun *o qual* (§4.3.1) and offer an overview of the properties of *o qual*-ARCs in CEP (§4.3.2) and earlier stages of Portuguese (§4.3.3).

4.3.1 *The relative pronoun* o qual

The relative pronoun *o qual* (and its counterparts in other Romance languages: Italian *il quale*, Engadine *il quêl*, French *lequel*, Catalan *el qual*, Spanish *el cual*, Romanian *care*) is etymologically derived from the Latin form QUĀLIS (Posner 1996: 306, among others).

In Latin, *quālis* was used as a wh-element in interrogative clauses (see (532)) and exclamatives (see (533)). It could also occur in correlative structures of the type *quālis . . . talis* (see (534)).

(532)   qualis ista philosophia est?
        what   this philosophy is
        'What kind of philosophy is this?' (1st c. BC, from Ernout and Thomas 1972: 156; gloss and translation mine)

(533)   hei mihi, qualis erat!
        oh my   what was.3SG
        'Oh my! How sad he looked!' (1st c. BC, from Ernout and Thomas 1972: 156; gloss and translation mine)

(534)   qualis pater, talis filius
        like   father like son
        'Like father, like son.' (Stone 2005: 198)

However, there is no evidence for the use of *quālis* as a relative pronoun in Classical Latin, nor in Vulgar Latin (Middleton 2000: 121–2). For this reason, there is a debate in the literature regarding the emergence of this relative pronoun. The basic question is whether it is a Romance innovation, or the result of a process that started in Latin. For further details about this debate, see Kunstmann (1991), Middleton (2000), and Ramat (2005).

4.3.2 *Contemporary European Portuguese*

In CEP, the form *qual*, derived from *quālis*, can still be used in interrogatives (535), exclamatives (536),[10] comparatives (537), and as a member of correlative connectives (538).

(535)   a. Quais livros compraste?
          what books bought.2SG
          'What books did you buy?' (Brito, Duarte, and Matos 2003: 464)

---

[10] The sentence in (536) expresses metalinguistic negation, a phenomenon that occurs in English sentences such as *Like hell Al and Hilary are married; Al and Hilary are married my eye* (Drozd 2001: 55).

b. Quais compraste?
what bought.2SG
'Which ones did you buy?' (Brito, Duarte, and Matos 2003: 464)

c. Qual deles tinha coragem para começar?
which of.them had courage to start.INF
'Which of them had the courage to start?' (Cunha and Cintra 1984/1997: 355)

(536) Quais feitios, qual vida!
what tempers what life
'Tempers life, my eye!' (Cunha and Cintra 1984/1997: 356)

(537) Nadava qual peixe.
swam.3SG like fish
'He swam like a fish.' (Cuesta and Luz 1971/1980: 507)

(538) Este chapéu é tal qual o meu.
this hat is just like the mine
'This hat is just like mine.' (Cuesta and Luz 1971/1980: 507)

Crucially, in these contexts, *qual* cannot be preceded by a definite article. In contrast, when introducing relative clauses, *qual* is always preceded by the definite article; see (539).[11]

(539) Este governo atacou os direitos dos professores, *(os) quais
this government attacked the rights of.the teachers the which
ficaram bastante prejudicados com as medidas tomadas.
became very affected with the measures taken
'This government limited the rights of the teachers, who were very affected by the measures implemented.'

In this case, the definite article is incorporated in the relative pronoun because no element can break the adjacency between the definite article and the wh-element (*o preposition/adverb/noun/adjective qual*). Within the complex pronoun,[12] the definite article is inflected for gender and number, whereas *qual* is inflected only for number (*o qual* 'the.M.SG which.SG'; *os quais* 'the.M.PL which.PL'; *a qual* 'the.F.SG which.SG', and *as quais* 'the.F.PL which.PL').

---

[11] The same is true of other Romance languages: the counterparts of the relative *o qual* also incorporate a definite article. The only exception is the Romanian *care*, which cannot be preceded by the article. It could have an article, however, in the 19th century: masculine *care-le*, feminine *care-a* (Ramat 2005).

[12] The internal complexity of *o qual* explains why it is sometimes dubbed a *complex pronoun* (Inada 2007).

As for the syntactic and semantic properties of *o qual*-ARCs in CEP, two proper-ties are worth describing (Brito 1991; Brito and Duarte 2003). First, *o qual*-ARCs can relativize the subject (see (540)), the direct object (see (541)), and the object of a preposition (see (542) and (543)).[13]

(540) Já   entreguei o processo ao   meu advogado, o qual
       already gave.1SG the process to.the my lawyer   the which
       dispõe de   um mês   para contestar a   decisão.
       has   DE.PREP one month to   contest.INF the decision
       'I have already referred the matter to my lawyer, who has one month to
       contest the decision.'

(541) Recebemos   algumas candidaturas incompletas, as quais excluímos
       received.1PL some   applications incomplete   the which excluded.1PL
       de   imediato.
       DE.PREP immediate
       'We received some incomplete applications, which we excluded
       immediately.'

(542) O ministro foi alvo   de   muitas críticas, às   quais
       the minister was subject DE.PREP many critiques to.the which
       respondeu   com agressividade.
       answered.3SG with aggressiveness
       'The minister was subject to severe criticism, to which he replied in an
       aggressive manner.'

(543) No   passado dia 2 realizou-se   a   5.ª edição do   *Portugal*
       in.the last   day 2 took.place-SE.CL the 5th edition of.the P.
       Fashion, na   qual participaram dez estilistas   portugueses.
       F.   in.the which participated ten fashion.designers Portuguese
       'On the 2nd of this month, the 5th edition of *Portugal Fashion* took
       place, in which ten Portuguese fashion designers participated.'

---

[13] In CEP, *o qual* may also introduce RRCs. However, in such a syntactic environment, it cannot relativize the subject and the object. By way of illustration, see examples (i) and (ii), from Brito (1991: 156).

(i) *O homem o qual   escreveu é meu amigo.
      the man   thewhich wrote   ismy friend
      'The man who wrote (it) is a friend of mine.'

(ii) *O homem o qual   eu vi ontem   é meu amigo.
      the man   the which I saw yesterday is my friend
      'The man whom I saw yesterday is a friend of mine.'

Secondly, the pronoun *o qual* is compatible with human and non-human antecedents (see e.g. the contrast between (540) and (541)).

Finally, a word is in order regarding the use of *o qual*-ARCs in CEP. In general, relative clauses introduced by *o qual* are perceived by speakers as a formal and 'prestige' construction. Its use is regarded as somewhat artificial and less natural than, for instance, the use of relative clauses introduced by *que* 'that' (the same form as the complementizer).

Closely related to speakers' perception of these relatives is the higher frequency of *o qual* relatives in written than in spoken texts. To confirm this tendency, I performed a corpus-based analysis of spoken and written Portuguese. Two corpora of roughly the same size were selected: *C-ORAL-ROM* (containing 320,452 words, in the Portuguese section), for spoken Portuguese, and a subcorpus of *CRPC* (jornal_anotado_RL), containing texts from some Portuguese newspapers (with 336,151 words). The results clearly show the tendency of *o qual* to occur in written texts; the spoken corpus yields 56 tokens of *o qual*, whereas the written corpus contains 207 tokens.[14]

The same tendency is observed for other contemporary Romance languages. Corominas and Pascual (1980: 257ff.), for instance, mention that contemporary spoken Spanish has totally abandoned *el cual*, and Fiorentino (1999: 92–3) notes the rarity of *il quale* in a spoken corpus of contemporary Italian (see Ramat 2005, and references therein).

4.3.3 *Earlier stages of Portuguese*

Earlier stages of Portuguese pattern with CEP with respect to the properties of *o qual*-ARCs mentioned in §4.3.2.

Regarding the internal structure of *o qual*, the same pattern is found: in the corpus edited by Martins (2001), the wh-element is always combined with the definite article, and no element can disrupt the article+wh-element sequence. The wh-element may occur without the definite article, but not in ARCs.[15] Its occurrence is limited to RRCs (see (544)) and free relative clauses, with or without an additional internal head (see (545) and (546), respectively).[16]

---

[14] Note that these tokens include both *o qual*-ARCs and *o qual*-RRCs.

[15] For the occurrence of *qual* without article, see also Maia (1986: 696) and Mattos e Silva (1989: 752 n. 17). The examples cited in these studies seem to corroborate the idea that *o qual* without an article introducing a headed relative clause preferentially has a restrictive interpretation.

[16] In the corpus edited by Martins (2001), *qual* (without the definite article) can also occur as a member of the correlative pair *tal ... qual* 'such ... as' (see (i)) and as an element introducing a nominal constituent (see (ii)).

(i) e   quaéés dereituras sēpre deu   táées dares   tu
     and which rents   always gave.3SG such give.INF.2SG you
     'and you must pay the same rent that he paid' (13th c., Martins 2001: 117)

(544) que faça   ou façã   ende strom̃eto ou strom̃etos
that make.SBJV.3SG or make.SBJV.3PL of.it deed   or deeds
quaes les   o   dito   Steuã perez mãdar   fazer
which them.CL the mentioned S.   P.   order.FUT.SBJV make.INF
'(and I order that) he make or they make the deed or deeds that the aforementioned Steuã Perez ordered them to make' (13th c., Martins 2001: 132)

(545) quays fforom pressentes.
which were   present
'who were present: [list]' (13th c., Martins 2001: 363)

(546) e   pera fazer   ende carta [...] per qual   Tabelĺion que a esta
and to   make.INF of.it letter   by which notary   that to this
cousa for   demandado
thing be.FUT.SBJV summoned
'and to compose a letter by whichever notary that be summoned to this thing'
(13th c., Martins 2001: 355)

Likewise, earlier stages of Portuguese allow *o qual*-ARCs to take human and non-
human antecedents, as shown in (547)–(548).

(547) todollos herdam̃etos e   Cassaes que nos Auemos [...] ẽno   Couto
all.the lands   and hamlets that we have   in.the ±property
de negrelhos que este Alen   doyro o   qual   ha nos   fficou de   parte
of N.   that is   beyond D.   the which to us.CL stayed from part
de nosso padre
of our   father
'all the lands and hamlets that we have in the property of Negrelhos, which is
beyond Doyro, which was left to us by our father' (14th c., *DCMP*)

(548) e   leixo   a dita   mha tesstam̃eteira por affom que auera
and leave.1SG to mentioned my   executor   by work that have.FUT.3SG
dez libras aA   qual   dou   e   outorgo comprido poder
ten l.   to.the which give.1SG and grant.1SG full   power
'and I leave ten *libras* [currency] to my executor for the work that she will
have; and I give and grant her full power (to distribute my money and
property)' (14th c., Martins 2001: 464)

(ii) damos [...] a uos Afonso rodriguiz nosso irm̃aão qual filho de nosso
give.1PL to you A.   R.   our   brother as   son of our
padre quantos herdamentos nos auemos
father all.that lands   we have
'we give you Afonso Rodriguiz, our brother, as son of our father, all the lands that we have' (13th c.,
Martins 2001: 154)

Finally, *o qual*-ARCs in earlier stages of Portuguese pattern with their contemporary counterparts in the possibility of relativizing the subject (547), the object of a preposition (548), and the direct object (549).[17]

(549) per hũa procuraçõ   feyta per mááo de Domĩgos stephães Tabellion
       by   a letter.of.attorney made by hand of D.   S.   notary
       das Alcaçouas. a   qual eu Johã soarez Tabellion da   Cidade de
       of.the A.   the which I J.   S.   notary of.the city of
       Lixbõa ui, líj
       L.   saw read
       'by one letter of attorney created by Domĩgos Stephães, notary of Alcaçouas,
       which I, Johã Soarez, notary of Lisbon, saw and read.' (13th c., Martins 2001:
       354)

4.4 Contrasting properties of *o qual*-appositive relatives

Whereas §4.3 focuses on some properties with respect to which *o qual*-ARCs in CEP and in earlier stages of Portuguese behave alike, the present section offers an overview of the syntactic properties that differentiate the two constructions, namely: (1) additional internal head (§4.4.1); (2) extraposition (§4.4.2); (3) pied-piping (§4.4.3); (4) clausal antecedent (§4.4.4); (5) split antecedents (§4.4.5); (6) coordination of the wh-pronoun with another DP (§4.4.6); (7) illocutionary force (§4.4.7);

---

[17] In the case of RRCs introduced by *o qual*, there is, however, one important contrast between CEP and earlier stages of Portuguese. As mentioned in n. 14, *o qual*-RRCs in CEP can only relativize the object of a preposition (see (i)). This restriction does not hold, however, for earlier stages of Portuguese (Lucchesi 1991). See e.g. (ii) and (iii), where the direct object is relativized.

(i)   O   Millennium é o banco ao qual recorro mais vezes.
      the M.   is the bank to.the which resort.1SG more times
      'The Millennium is the bank I work with more often.'

(ii) obligo   a uos e empenhoro hũa nossa Casa. a qual nos auemos en Lixbõa.
      pawn.1SG to you and pledge.1SG a   our house the which we have   in L.
      'I pawn and pledge to you a house of ours that we have in Lisbon.' (13th c., Martins 2001: 354)

(iii) que façã   a eles entregar todalas herdades as quaes a esses Moesteiros e   a
      that make.SBJV.3PL to them return.INF all.the lands   the which to those monasteries and to
      essas Ejgreias tẽẽ   e   teuerõ filhados.
      those churches have.3PL and had.3PL seized
      '(I order) that they make them return all the lands that they have seized from those monasteries'
      (13th c., Martins 2001: 168)

and the presence of a spelled-out coordinator (§4.4.8).[18] Each section comprises three parts: evidence from CEP, cross-linguistic evidence, and evidence from earlier stages of Portuguese. As the reader will notice, there are some sections (§§4.4.1–3) that require more detail (and space) than others. This is due to the properties discussed there being robustly attested in earlier stages of Portuguese and being subject to various restrictions, which require more complex descriptive devices.

I base the discussion in this chapter on my own intuitions, supplemented by judgments obtained from other native speakers of CEP. Whenever possible, I support the introspective judgments with data taken from corpora. Divergent judgments are reported and discussed in §4.6.2.

4.4.1 Internal head

4.4.1.1 Contemporary European Portuguese　*O qual*-ARCs in CEP cannot exhibit an additional internal head. This impossibility is illustrated in (550) and (551) with a nominal and a non-nominal ARC, respectively.[19]

(550)　*Existem argumentos fortes a favor dessa análise,
　　　　there.are arguments strong in favor of.that analysis
　　　　os quais <u>argumentos</u> apresentarei de seguida.
　　　　the which arguments present.FUT.1SG DE.PREP next
　　　　'There are strong arguments in favor of that analysis, which arguments I will present next.'

(551)　*Os portugueses não gostam de música portuguesa, o
　　　　the Portuguese.people not like DE.PREP music Portuguese the
　　　　qual <u>facto</u> explica a escassa produção musical deste país.
　　　　which fact explains the sparse production musical of.this country
　　　　'The Portuguese people do not like Portuguese music, which fact explains the sparse musical production of this country.'

Two alternative constructions can be used in these contexts: (1) the ARC can be introduced by a relative pronoun (and no internal head is present) (see (552a)–(553a)); (2) the appositive construction can surface with an additional external head;[20] in this case, a noun phrase is modified by an RRC, and the

---

[18]　These properties are partially discussed in Cardoso (2008, 2011) and Cardoso and De Vries (2010).
[19]　In §4.4.1, the internal head is underlined for expository purposes.
[20]　For technical details on the implementation of the additional internal head, see §1.3.2.5B(d)).

complex (noun phrase + RRC) is in apposition to the antecedent (see (552b)–(553b)).[21]

(552) a. Existem argumentos fortes a favor dessa análise, os quais
there.are arguments   strong in favor of.that analysis the which
apresentarei   de seguida.
present.FUT.1SG next
'There are strong arguments in favor of that analysis, which I will present
next.'[22]

   b. Existem argumentos fortes a favor dessa análise, argumentos que
there.are arguments   strong in favor of.that analysis arguments   that
apresentarei   de   seguida.
present.FUT.1SG DE.PREP next
'There are strong arguments in favor of that analysis, arguments that I will
present next.'

(553) a. Os portugueses   não gostam de   música portuguesa, o   que
the Portuguese.people not like   DE.PREP music Portuguese the which
explica   a   escassa produção   musical deste país.
explains the sparse   production musical of.this country
'The Portuguese people do not like Portuguese music, which explains the
sparse musical production of this country.'

   b. Os portugueses   não gostam de   música portuguesa, facto
the Portuguese.people not like   DE.PREP music Portuguese fact
que explica   a   escassa produção   musical deste país.
that explains the sparse   production musical of.this country
'The Portuguese people do not like Portuguese music, a fact that explains
the sparse musical production of this country.'

4.4.1.2 Cross-linguistic evidence Languages do not behave uniformly regarding the
occurrence of an additional internal head. Smits (1988) shows that there is cross-
linguistic variation in this respect, as summarized in Table 4.2. Some examples of this
structure are given in (554)–(558) (from Smits 1988: 65, 306, 321, 369, 272, 288).[23]

---

[21] For more details on the constructions in (552b) and (553b), see Peres and Móia (1995: 270–1),
Brucart (1999: 423), and Brito and Duarte (2003: 674–5).

[22] Note that the English translation of the sentence (552a) is ambiguous because *which* can take as
antecedent either *analysis* or *strong arguments*. In CEP, this ambiguity does not arise because the
inflectional marks (for number and gender) of the relative pronoun *os quais* 'the.M.PL which.PL' indicate
that the antecedent is necessarily *fortes argumentos* 'strong arguments'.

[23] Smits (1988) uses the symbol '%' to indicate that it is a highly formal and marked construction.

TABLE 4.2 **Appositive relatives with an additional internal head**

Languages	Pronoun	Nominal ARCs	Non-nominal ARCs
Italian	*il quale*	+	−
Spanish	*el cual*	+	−
Catalan	*el qual*	arch.	+
French	*lequel*	+	+
Dutch	*welke*	+	+
German	*welcher*	+	+
English	*which*	+	+
Swedish	*vilken*	+	
Norwegian	*hvilken*	+	
Danish	*hvilken*	+	
Portuguese	no form		
Romanian	no form		
Icelandic	no form		

Note: The table is from Smits (1988: 65). The abbreviation arch. stands for 'archaic'.

Italian:

(554)   %Cercavo   una ragazza, con la   quale ragazza uscire   a
        looked.for.1SG a   girl   with the which girl   go.out.INF A.PREP
        cena.
        dinner
        'I was looking for a girl, with which girl to go out and dine.' (Smits 1988: 65;
        gloss mine)

Spanish:

(555)   %Los ejemplos de este fenómeno   que he   presentado, en los
        the examples of this phenomenon that have.1SG presented,   in the
        cuales ejemplos he   pensad mucho, no dejan de
        which examples have.1SG thought much   not cease DE.PREP
        confundirme.
        confuse.me.CL
        'The examples of this phenomenon that I presented, about which examples
        I have thought much, never cease to confuse me.' (Smits 1988: 306; gloss mine)

French:

(556)   Toutes les idées que j'aurais   à   développer, lesquelles idées sont
        all   the ideas that I.have.COND to develop.INF the.which ideas are
        exposées en détail dans ce   mémoire[…]
        laid.out in detail in   this report
        'All the ideas that I would have to develop, which ideas are laid out in this
        report…' (Smits 1988: 321; gloss mine)

German:

(557) Er sagte "Guten Tag," welchen Gruβ   sie freundlich erwiderte.
 he said good day which greeting she friendlily returned
 'He said "good day," which greeting she friendlily returned.' (Smits 1988:
 272)

English:

(558) My dog, which faithful <u>animal</u> has guarded me for years, died last week.
 (Smits 1988: 288)

4.4.1.3 Earlier stages of Portuguese   Variation can also be found in the diachronic dimension. Several authors have pointed out that *o qual*-ARCs in earlier stages of Portuguese can exhibit an additional internal head (Dias 1933/1970: §93; Said Ali 1931/1971: §515–16; Huber 1933/1986: §347; Barreto 1911/1980: 141; Neto 1957/1970: 509; Maia 1986: 696–7; Lucchesi 1991: 181; A. Costa 2004: 419). A case in point is given in (559).

(559) entrego e   outorgo.   ao   Mosteiro de san Saluador de
 give.1SG and concede.1SG to.the monastery of S. S.   DE.PREP
 Moreyra. hũu casal que e en Rial de   Pereyra. o qual <u>casal</u> a
 M.   a   hamlet that is in R. DE.PREP P.   the which hamlet the
 dita   dona Mayor uẽegas [...] mandou ao   dito   Mosteiro.
 mentioned D. M. V.   left   to.the mentioned monastery
 'I give and concede a hamlet that is located in Rial de Pereyra to the monastery of San Saluador de Moreyra, which hamlet the aforementioned Dona Mayor Vẽegas left to the monastery.' (13th c., Martins 2001: 143)

This possibility is also documented in Latin, as illustrated in (560). According to Ernout and Thomas (1972: 332) and Bassols de Climent (1967: 240), an additional internal head is found primarily in formal contexts, especially in legal documents. Its use can be explained as a strategy to avoid ambiguity when the relative and the antecedent are non-adjacent, as a way of conferring more precision on the utterance.

(560) erant omnino itinera duo, quibus <u>itineribus</u> domo   exire
 were in.all routes two by.which routes   from.home leave.INF
 possent
 could.SBJV.3PL
 'There were but two routes, by which routes they could leave home.' (1st c. BC, from Finch 2006: 36)

In historical Portuguese, *o qual*-ARCs with an additional internal head are attested in texts from different periods and belonging to different textual typologies. Examples (561)–(567) provide illustrations of the construction in different textual genres, namely, notarial documents (561), historiographic texts (562), dissertations (563), travel literature (564), theatre (565), letters (566), and religious texts (567). Note further that examples (559) and (561)–(567) range over different periods, from the thirteenth to the eighteenth century.

(561) E   ffica ao   dito   Gomez perez e   a ssa molher hũu
       and stays to.the mentioned G.   P.   and to his wife   a
       prazo   que cõta   que e de   Orraca perez e   de
       ±contract that mentions that is DE.PREP O.   P.   and DE.PREP
       Affonso bẽetíz pelo qual   prazo   deuyã   a dõna. Steuahỹa hũa
       A.   B.   by.the which ±contract owed.3PL to D.   S.   a
       soma   de dinheiros.
       amount of money
       'And a contract—which was made with Orraca Perez and Affonso Bẽetíz—is assigned to Gomes Perez and his wife, under which contract they owed an amount of money to Dona Steuahỹa.' (14th c., Martins 2001: 401)

(562) ao   quall foy emcomemdada outra   torre que está jumto com
       to.the which was commissioned another tower that is   close by
       ha   outra de   Fez […], a   quall torre emtão hera chamada
       the other DE.PREP F.   the which tower then   was called
       de   Madraba
       DE.PREP M.
       'who was commissioned another tower that is close by the other tower of Fez, which tower was then called Madraba' (15th c., from Brocardo 1997: 201)

(563) Esquizo são as primeiras linhas ou traços   que se   fazem com a pena,
       sketch are the first   lines or strokes that SE.CL make with a pen
       ou com o carvão, dados   com grande mestria e   depressa, os
       or with the charcoal, executed with great   perfection and rapidly   the
       quaes traços comprendem a idea e   invenção do que queremos
       which strokes contain   the idea and invention of what want.1PL
       fazer.
       make.INF
       'A sketch is the first lines or strokes that are made with a pen, or with charcoal, executed with great perfection and quickly, which strokes contain the idea and the invention of what we want to make.' (16th c., *TYC*)

(564)   a   origem   do   rio   procedia de   hum lago que se   chamaua
        the beginning of.the river came   DE.PREP a   lake that SE.CL called
        Pinator, que demoraua a   leste daquelle mar duzentas   e
        P.   that was   A.PREP east of.that   sea two.hundred and
        sessenta legoas, no   reyno   de Quitirvão, o   qual lago estaua
        sixty   leagues in.the kingdom of Q.   the which lake was
        cercado   de   grandes serranias
        encompassed DE.PREP huge   mountains
        'the river had its source in the lake known as Pinator, which was two hundred
        and sixty leagues east of the sea in the kingdom of Quitirvão, encircled by
        high mountains' (16th c., *TYC*)

(565)   imaginei   ũa festa / à   nossa Júlia modesta / nacida per mão de
        imagined.1SG a   party to.the our J.   modest   born by hand of
        Deos / a   qual   festa será   esta.
        God   the which party be.FUT this
        'I imagined a party/for our modest Júlia/born by the hand of God/which
        party will be as follows.' (16th c., Camões 1999)

(566)   os padres totalmente desconfiam de   os índios haverem   de
        the priests fully   doubt   DE.PREP the Indians have.INF.3PL DE.PREP
        descer   sem   violência a   qual   violência não é menos duvidosa
        resettle.INF without violence the which violence not is less   doubtful
        'the priests fully doubt that the Indians would resettle without
        violence, which violence is no less doubtful' (17th c., *TYC*)

(567)   esta prodigiosa demonstraçaõ, foy a   reposta que o   Senhor lhe
        this prodigious demonstration was the answer that the Lord   her.CL
        deu, da   qual veyo a   entender   hauia muyto que
        gave from.the which came A.PREP understand.INF had   much what
        cortar [...]. A qual   revelaçaõ se   veyo a   verificar.
        cut.INF   the which revelation SE.CL came A.PREP verify.INF
        'this prodigious demonstration was the answer that the Lord gave her, from
        which she realized that there was a lot to be cut. This revelation came true.'
        (18th c., *TYC*)

In earlier stages of Portuguese, *o qual*-ARCs with an additional internal head can be
characterized according to five main properties: (1) categorial nature of the internal
head; (2) semantic class of the nominal internal head; (3) relation between the
antecedent and the internal head; (4) expansion of the internal head; and (5) contexts
of occurrence. These properties are listed in §§4.4.1.3A(a)–(e).

A. Properties of the additional internal head

(a) Categorial nature of the internal head

The antecedent of an ARC with an additional internal head can be nominal or non-nominal. ARCs with nominal antecedents are given, for instance, in (561) and (562). ARCs with non-nominal antecedents are illustrated in (568)–(569). Note that in (568) the antecedent is clausal, whereas in (569), it is an adverbial phrase (modified by an RRC).

(568) os ditos   cassaaes fforõ cõprados dos   dinheiros do
       the mentioned hamlets were bought   DE.PREP.the moneys of.the
       dito   mosteiro polla quall <u>Razom</u> de   derejto perteçem
       mentioned monastery by.the which reason DE.PREP right   belong.3PL
       e   perteçyam   ao   dito   mosteiro
       and belonged.3PL to.the mentioned monastery
       'the aforementioned hamlets were bought with the money of the aforementioned monastery, for which reason they belong and belonged to the monastery by right' (15th c., Martins 2001: 262)

(569) A   sombra não se   ha de   dar   senão ali   onde não
       the shade   not SE.CL has DE.PREP apply.INF except there where not
       alcança   a lux e   claridade, o   qual <u>lugar</u> fica logo
       reach.3SG the light and brightness the which area is consequently
       inobre.
       degraded
       'Shade is not to be applied except where the light and clarity do not reach, which area is consequently degraded.' (16th c., *TYC*)

Importantly, these examples show that, regardless of the category of the antecedent, the internal head is always nominal.

(b) Semantic class of the nominal internal head

There seems to be no restriction on the semantic class of nouns that can appear as an internal head. For instance, the additional head can be a proper name (570), a count noun (571), or a non-count noun (572).[24]

---

[24] Note that in (572) the antecedent includes a non-count noun (*vinho* 'wine') associated with a unit of measurement (*tonell* 'vat').

(570) o   dito   Johã viçente disse que a   dita   vjnha
the mentioned J.   V.   said that the mentioned vineyard
trouxera   ẽ outro tempo Luzia domingujz [...] A   qual   <u>Luzía</u>
bring.PPRF in other time   L.   D.   the which L.
<u>domingujz</u> Era ffínada   deste   mondo
D.   was deceased from.this world
'the aforementioned Johã Viçente said that Luzia Domingujz once owned the aforementioned vineyard (in emphyteusis), which Luzía Domingujz was no longer in this world' (14th c., Martins 2001: 454)

(571) cõfesamos   que nos Recebemos de uos Martjn saluadorez Cjncoeẽta
confess.1PL that we   received   of you M.   S.   fifty
libras de dinheiros portugééses as   quaes   #Lta <u>libras</u> a nos erõ
l.   of currency Portuguese the which fifty l.   to us   were
Julgadas   per Sentẽca
attributed by   sentence
'we confess that we received from you Martjn Saluadorez fifty *libras* of the Portuguese currency, which fifty *libras* were assigned to us by court order' (14th c., Martins 2001: 454)

(572) que dem   e   paguem   de   foro   e   pensom da
that give.SBJV.3PL and pay.SBJV.3PL DE.PREP tenancy and rent   of.the
dicta   qujntãa en cada hũu ãno hũu tonell de vinho, puro do
mentioned farm   in each a   year one vat   of wine   pure of.the
que deus der   nas vjnhas   [...] o quall <u>vinho</u> sera   vermelho.
that god give.FUT.SBJV in.the vineyards   the which wine be.FUT red
'as for the renting of the aforementioned farm, I demand that they pay each year one vat of the pure wine that God gives in the vineyards, which wine will be red' (16th c., Martins 2001: 538)

(c) Relation between the antecedent and the internal head

There can be phonological and semantic identity between the head noun contained within the antecedent and the internal head, as shown, for instance, in (566). However, both elements can also differ. In this case, there are a number of possibilities. When the antecedent is nominal, the internal head can be a true synonym of the antecedent, as in (573). It can also express a defining property of the antecedent, as in (574), or a more specific classificatory property, as shown in (575).

(573) mostrarõ   logo   ẽ Jujzo   húú testamẽto [...] na
showed.3PL immediately in judgment a   testament   in.the
qual <u>mãda</u> fazía mẽçom Antre as outras coussas que A
which will   made mention among the other   things   that it.CL

mãdara   fazer   Sancha gíl.
order.PPRF make.INF S.   G.
'they immediately showed a testament before the judge, in which will it was
mentioned, among other things, that Sancha Gil ordered him to make it.'
(14th c., Martins 2001: 189)

(574) e   começou a   era de quatrocentos e   oito: no   quall ano, estando
       and started   the era of four.hundred and eight in.the which year be.GER
       el-rrei   dom Henrrique na   villa de   Touro, soube   [...]
       the.king D.   H.   in.the village DE.PREP T.   knew.3SG
       'and the era of four hundred and eight started, in which year, being in the
       village of Touro, the king Dom Henrrique became aware that...' (15th c.,
       Macchi 1975: 129)

(575) as   quaees leteras forõ   probicadas a   dom lourenço [...] o   qual
       the which letters were addressed to D.   L.   the which
       arçebispo   obedeçendo aas   dictas   leteras fez   sobre ello seus
       archbishop obey.GER   to.the mentioned letters made on   it   his
       processos
       processes
       'these letters were addressed to Dom Lourenço, which archbishop based his
       processes upon them' (15th c., Martins 2001: 240)

If the antecedent is clausal, the additional internal head is typically a general abstract
noun such as *Razom* 'reason' in (568). However, it can also be a more specific verbal
noun that is morphologically related to a verb introduced in the preceding context;
see (576), where the noun *pitiçon* 'request' is morphologically related to the preceding verb *pedir* 'to request'.

(576) E   como Eu dito   priol lhe   pedise   e   Mãdase
       and as   I   mentioned prior him.CL request.SBJV and order.SBJV
       pedir   A dita   palha [...] A   qual   pitiçon o   dito
       request.INF the mentioned straw   the which request the mentioned
       francisco martjnz cõtestou   dela
       F.   M.   contested of.it
       'And as I, the aforementioned prior, requested and ordered them to request
       of him the straw, which request Francisco Martjnz contested...' (14th c.,
       Martins 2001: 223)

(d) Expansion of the internal head

The internal head NP can be a conjoined phrase, as is shown in (577). In these
contexts, there is typically first conjunct agreement for phi-features between the
relative pronoun and the noun in the first conjunct (*casal* 'hamlet' in (577)).

(577) ffazemos prazo   [...] dūu Casal   que auemos en Cūpustelá e
       make.1PL ±contract   of.a hamlet that have.1PL in C.   and
       dūu meío Barco en verdugo O   qual   <u>casal   e   meío Barco</u>
       of.a half boat in V.   the.M.SG which.SG hamlet and half boat
       ora trage Maria
       now brings M.
       'we make a contract of a hamlet in Cūpustelá and half a boat in Verdugo, which
       hamlet and half boat now belong to Maria' (14th c., Martins 2001: 171)

The internal head can also be modified by different categories, such as a PP (578) or
even a relative clause (579).

(578) o quall <u>casal</u> com suas perteenças disse   que trazia ē pregā
       the which hamlet with its   belongings said.3SG that brought in cry
       'which hamlet with its belongings was being announced to be for sale' (15th
       c., Martins 2001: 513)

(579) os quaaes <u>dinheiros</u> que uos   eu assy   hey de   dar
       the which moneys   that you.CL I   this.way have DE.PREP give.INF
       e   pagar uos   aúýa de   pagar Joham
       and pay.INF you.CL had   DE.PREP pay.INF J.
       'which money that I will give and pay you Joham should pay you' (15th c.,
       Martins 2001: 492)

Furthermore, the internal head can be extended by a numeral, as in (571), or a
possessive, as in (580). Both are construed pre-nominally. The occurrence of universal quantifiers is also attested, typically in a post-nominal position (581).

(580) aos   quaes meus <u>procuradores</u> dou   cōprido poder
       to.the which my attorneys   give.1SG full   power
       'to which my attorneys I give full power' (14th c., Martins 2001: 422)

(581) das   quaées <u>coussas</u> todas o dito   Priol por ssj e pelo
       of.the which things all   the mentioned prior by him and by.the
       Conuēto de sseu Mostejro   pedeu ende A mj dito   tabaliō este
       convent of his monastery asked of.it to me mentioned notary this
       strumento
       deed
       'of which things the aforementioned prior in his name and in the name of
       the convent of the monastery asked me to make this deed' (14th c., Martins
       2001: 190)

(e) Contexts of occurrence

As previously mentioned, the presence of an internal head can sometimes be explained as a way of avoiding ambiguity. Consider, for instance, the sentence in (582); in this example, the lack of the internal head could lead to ambiguity, as it would not be clear whether the antecedent was *sua força* 'his force' or *Autorydade* 'authority'.

(582) o   dito   prioll per sua força e   Autorydade lha
       the mentioned prior by his force and authority   him.CL.it.CL
       tomara fforçãdóó   della A qual ͟f͟f͟o͟r͟ç͟a djzia   que [...]
       take.PPRF forcing.him.CL of.it the which force said.3SG that
       'the prior had taken it [the cow] and his daughter from him by force and authority, resorting to violence, which force he said (had taken place in March)' (14th c., Martins 2001: 226)

The presence of an additional internal head is also favored in contexts in which the antecedent and the ARC are not adjacent. In the corpus-based investigation presented in Cardoso (2008), I have shown that, in earlier periods of Portuguese until approximately the seventeenth century, ARCs with an additional internal head are more frequent than ordinary ARCs in contexts of extraposition, as in (583), and when the relative clause is preceded by stacked or multiple embedded relative clauses, as in (584).

(583) o   dicto   Juiz per sentença defenetiua asy   o   Julgou
       the mentioned judge by sentence definitive this.way it.CL judged
       da   quall ͟s͟e͟n͟t͟e͟n͟ç͟a o dicto   Reeo   nõ apellou
       of.the which sentence the mentioned defendant not appealed
       'the aforementioned judge passed this sentence, against which the defendant did not appeal' (15th c., Martins 2001: 484)

(584) ẽ hũa vĩnha   que chamã o   cõchouso que e A par da
       in a vineyard that call.3PL the C.   that is next DE.PREP.the
       de   Pero. caramos termho de Santarẽ A qual ͟v͟ĩ͟n͟h͟a   deziam
       DE.PREP P.   C.   environs of S.   the which vineyard said.3PL
       que Era do   Moesteyro dachellas
       that was DE.PREP.the monastery of.C.
       'in a vineyard called the Cõchouso, which is next to the vineyard of Pero Caramos in the environs of Santarẽ, which vineyard is said to belong to the Monastery of Chellas' (14th c., Martins 2001: 454)

4.4.2 Extraposition

4.4.2.1 Cross-linguistic evidence
Ziv and Cole (1974: 777–8), Emonds (1979: 234–5), and Alexiadou, Law, Meinunger, and Wilder (2000: 31) assume that ARCs cannot be extraposed in English,[25] as exemplified in (585).[26]

(585) a. *A boy was kissing Mary, whom I had never seen before.
      b. *A boy was here, whom I had never seen before.
      c. *John was here, whom I had never seen before.
      d. *My father just came in, who runs his own business. (all Ziv and Cole 1974: 777–8)

Vergnaud (1974) also asserts the non-extraposability of ARCs in French (see (586)).

(586) *Paul vient de   passer   qui portait un fedora.
      P.   comes DE.PREP pass.INF who wore   a   fedora
      'Paul just passed wearing a fedora.' (Vergnaud 1974: 181; gloss and translation mine)

However, this view has recently been challenged by various authors (De Vries 2002, 2006b; Arnold 2007; Strunk 2007). On the basis of examples such as (587) from Dutch, De Vries (2002, 2006b) refutes the traditional view, showing that it is plainly false that ARCs cannot be extraposed.

(587) Gisteren heb ik mijn zuster bezocht, die blond haar heeft
      yesterday have I my   sister visited, who blond hair has
      (zoals je   weet).
      (as   you know)
      'Yesterday I have visited my sister, who has blond hair (as you know).' (De Vries 2006b: 254)

Additional counterexamples can be found in English and German, as shown, respectively, in (588), from Arnold (2007: 306), and (589), from Strunk (2007: 41).

(588) I was also given a Jubilee mug at school, which I still have.

---

[25] According to Alexiadou, Law, Meinunger, and Wilder (2000), extraposition of ARCs appears to be marginally possible with presentative focus on the antecedent, as in b.

(i)   *John arrived, who happens to be an expert in aerodynamics.
(ii) ??John arrived, who happens to be an expert in aerodynamics. (both Alexiadou, Law, Meinunger, and Wilder 2000: 31)

[26] In §4.4.2, following the same practice as in Ch. 3, the elements that intervene between the antecedent and the relative clause are referred to as *intervening material* and are underlined for expository purposes.

(589) Allerdings habe er mit Prodi <u>gesprochen</u>, zu dem er "ein enges und
however   has he with Prodi talked   to who he a   close and
intensives Verhältnis" pflege.
intensive relationship cultivates
'However, he has spoken with Prodi, with whom he has a close and intensive
relationship.'

4.4.2.2 Contemporary European Portuguese   Based on examples such as (590), Brito
(2004) argues that extraposition of ARCs is not possible in CEP.

(590) a. Vi   o João, que é o   meu amigo preferido.
          saw.1SG the J.   that is the my friend favorite
          'I saw João, who is my favorite friend.'

       b. O João, que é o   meu amigo preferido, foi visto por mim.
          the J.   that is the my friend favorite was seen by me
          'João, who is my favorite friend, was seen by me.'

       c. *O João <u>foi visto por mim</u>, que é o   meu amigo preferido.
          the J.   was seen by me   that is the my friend favorite
          (all Brito 2004: 402)

However, and contrary to traditional belief, ARCs can be extraposed in CEP; see
(591), from a CEP newspaper corpus.[27]

(591) O leiloeiro,   para não levantar   suspeitas, utilizava ainda   um
       the auctioneer to   not arouse.INF suspicions used   additionally a
       outro indivíduo <u>nos   negócios</u>, o   qual muitas vezes aparecia
       other man   in.the negotiations the which many times showed.up
       a   arrematar os bens   em seu lugar.
       A.PREP buy.INF   the goods in his place
       'Not to arouse suspicion, the auctioneer used another man in the negoti-
       ations, who showed up frequently buying goods in his place.' (*CETEMP*)

In some discourse contexts, ARC-extraposition may even be obligatory, as illustrated
in (592). In this case, the event referred to in the ARC is subsequent to that referred
to in the main clause. Hence, the ARC must be extraposed in order to respect
the sequence of events: the crash into a lamppost occurs after the passenger is
thrown into the air. This type of ARC has been referred to in the literature as a

---

[27] Given the object of study of the present chapter, I will henceforth focus the discussion on extraposition of *o qual*-ARCs.

continuative appositive clause (see Jespersen 1949; Loock 2007; among others) or *supplementary appositive clause* (see Huddleston, Pullum, and Peterson 2002).

(592) a. O   carro despistou-se, projectando um passageiro <u>pelo</u>
the car   skidded-SE.CL throw.GER   a   passenger POR.PREP.the
<u>ar,</u> o   qual foi   embater contra um poste.
air the which went crash.INF against a   lamppost
'The car skidded, throwing a passenger into the air, who crashed into a lamppost.' (adapted from Peres and Móia 1995: 367)

   b. *O   carro despistou-se, projectando um passageiro, o   qual   foi
the car   skidded-SE.CL throw.GER   a   passenger the which went
embater contra um poste,   pelo   ar.
crash.INF against a   lamppost POR.PREP.the air

However, just as observed for RRCs (see §3.3.2), there are some constraints on the extraposition of *o qual*-ARCs in CEP, namely: (1) the definiteness effect; (2) restriction on extraposition from pre-verbal positions; and (3) restriction on extraposition from prepositional phrases. These restrictions are described in §§4.4.2.2A–C.

A. The definiteness effect

In CEP, the antecedent of an extraposed *o qual*-ARC can be a weak noun phrase but not a strong noun phrase (in the sense of Milsark 1974). The contrasts given in (593)–(594) illustrate this point: an extraposed *o qual*-ARC can be made acceptable if the antecedent is changed from a strong noun phrase to a weak noun phrase.

(593) Em França, um grupo de skinheads atirou *o/um jovem
in F.   a   group of skinheads threw   the/a young.man
marroquino <u>ao   rio   Sena,</u> o   qual   acabaria   por
Moroccan to.the river S.   the which end.up.COND POR.PREP
morrer afogado.
die.INF drowned
'In France, a group of skinheads threw the/a young Moroccan man into the river Seine, who would end up drowning.'

(594) Deverá ser   construída brevemente *a/uma ponte <u>no   Barreiro,</u>
shall.FUT be.INF built   soon   the/a bridge in.the B.
a   qual terá   mais de 5 quilómetros e   cerca de   5
the which have.FUT more than 5 kilometers and about DE.PREP 5
faixas de rodagem.
lanes of vehicle.traffic
'The/a new bridge, which will be more than 5 kilometers and have about 5 lanes, will be built soon in Barreiro.'

B. Pre-verbal positions

B1. Pre-verbal subjects

Extraposed *o qual*-ARCs can take post-verbal subjects as antecedents, as shown in (595a)–(596a). However, if the subject is construed pre-verbally, the sentence is ungrammatical, as shown in (595b)–(596b).

(595) a. Terá   lugar uma reunião <u>no   dia 21 de setembro</u>, na   qual
          have.FUT place a   meeting on.the day 21 of September in.the which
          se   discutirá   a   viabilidade do   projecto.
          SE.CL discuss.FUT the viability   of.the project
          'A meeting will take place on September 21; the viability of the project will
          be discussed there.'

       b. *Uma reunião <u>terá   lugar no   dia 21 de Setembro</u>, na   qual
          a   meeting have.FUT place on.the day 21 of September in.the which
          se   discutirá   a   viabilidade do   projecto.
          SE.CL discuss.FUT the viability   of.the project

(596) a. Será   adoptado um novo modelo de avaliação de professores
          be.FUT adopted a   new model of evaluation of teachers
          <u>no   próximo ano lectivo</u>, do   qual   todos os professores
          in.the next   year school of.the which all   the teachers
          discordam.
          disagree
          'A new evaluation model for teachers will be adopted in the next school
          year; all teachers disagree with it.'

       b. *Um novo modelo de avaliação de professores <u>será   adoptado</u>
          a   new model of evaluation of teachers   be.FUT adopted
          <u>no   próximo ano lectivo</u>, do   qual   todos os professores
          in.the next   year school of.the which all   the teachers
          discordam.
          disagree

B2. Discourse dedicated positions in the left periphery

Extraposed *o qual*-ARCs cannot take as antecedent a topicalized constituent. This impossibility is illustrated by the contrast displayed in (597).[28]

---

[28] Example (597b) is a little marked (given the heaviness of the topicalized constituent), but acceptable in general.

(597) a. *Filmes cómicos, <u>não aprecio,</u>   com os quais todos se   riem
movies comic   not appreciate.1SG with the which all   SE.CL roar
às   gargalhas.
to.the laughter
'I do not appreciate comedy movies, at which everyone roars with
laughter.'

   b. Filmes cómicos, com os quais todos se   riem às   gargalhadas,
movies comic   with the which all   SE.CL roar to.the laughter
não aprecio.
not appreciate.1SG

However, this restriction does not seem to hold for other constituents at the left
periphery. As shown in (598) and (599), extraposition is allowed when the antecedent is a wh-constituent or a preposed focus.[29]

(598) Que desporto é que tu   praticas, sem   o qual não sobreviverias?
what sport   is that you practice without the which not survive.COND.2SG
lit. 'What sport do you practice, without which you would not survive?'

(599) Outras pessoas se   manifestaram contra a   barragem, com as quais
another people SE.CL demonstrated against the dam   with the which
eu concordei inteiramente.
I agreed   fully
'Another group of people, whom I fully agreed with, demonstrated against
the dam.'

---

[29] The description of RRC-extraposition set out in Ch. 3 also takes into account sentences involving
preposed emphatic/evaluative phrases. This context is not considered here because *o qual*-ARCs
cannot take emphatic/evaluative phrases as antecedent, as shown by the non-extraposed variant in (ii).

(i)   *Muito whisky o   João bebeu, com o   qual ficou completamente
a.lot.of whisky the J.   drank with the which got   completely
embriagado!
drunk
'João drank a lot of whisky; he got completely drunk on it!'

(ii)   *Muito whisky, com o   qual ficou completamente embriagado,
a.lot.of whisky with the which got   completely   drunk
o João bebeu!
the J.   drank

C. Prepositional phrases

Extraposition of *o qual*-ARCs does not seem to be allowed when the antecedent is the object of a preposition. Examples (600)–(601) illustrate this impossibility.

(600) *Foi preso   o   mestre   de uma embarcação <u>ontem,</u>
       was arrested the.M.SG skipper.M.SG of a.F.SG boat.F.SG   yesterday
       na   qual   foram encontrados 10 quilos de cocaína.
       in.the.F.SG which.SG were   found   10 kilos of cocaine
       'The skipper of a boat was arrested yesterday; 10 kilos of cocaine were found
       in the boat.'

(601) *Discuti   com um amigo meu <u>ontem,</u> o   qual teima em dizer
       argued.1SG with a   friend mine yesterday the which insists on say.INF
       que não vai votar   nas   próximas eleições.
       that not goes vote.INF in.the next   elections
       'Yesterday I argued with a friend of mine; he insists on saying that he is not
       going to vote in the next elections.'

D. Extraposition across conjuncts

In CEP, an extraposed *o qual*-ARC cannot take the first conjunct of a multiple coordinate structure as its antecedent, as illustrated in (602).

(602) *O Pedro e   a   Maria <u>chegaram,</u> o   qual   (Pedro) disse que
       the P.   and the M.   arrived   the.M.SG which.SG (P.)   said that
       se   tinha sentido mal.
       SE.CL had felt   unwell
       'Pedro and Maria arrived. He said that he felt unwell.'

E. Extraposition across discourse

In CEP, *o qual*-ARCs cannot take an antecedent across the discourse. Take, for instance, the ungrammatical (603), in which the antecedent and the *o qual*-ARC appear in different utterances.

(603) —Quero   desejar boa sorte aos   jogadores da   seleção
       want.1SG wish.INF good luck to.the players of.the team
       portuguesa— disse o presidente.
       Portuguese   said the president
       'I want to wish good luck to the players of the Portuguese team—said the
       president.'
       *Os   quais   ficaram muito comovidos com estas palavras.
       the.M.PL which.PL were   very moved   with these words
       'The which (players) were very moved by these words.'

4.4.2.3 Earlier stages of Portuguese   Having seen the restrictions that hold for CEP, let me now turn to the properties of extraposition in earlier stages of Portuguese. For ease of comparison, the same set of properties used for CEP is inspected for these earlier stages.

A. The definiteness effect

In earlier stages of Portuguese, the extraposition of *o qual*-ARCs was not sensitive to the definiteness effect. Sentences (604)–(607) exemplify extraposed *o qual*-ARCs taking strong noun phrases as antecedents. In (604) and (607), the antecedent is introduced by a definite article (followed by an adjective), in (605) by a definite article (followed by a possessive), and in (606) by a demonstrative.

(604)   depos morte da   dicta   dona Gyralda fficou o   dicto
        after death of.the mentioned D.   G.   stayed the mentioned
        herdamento ao   dicto   Moesteyro de suso   nomeado. o   qual
        land   to.the mentioned monastery of above mentioned the which
        herdamento est assy como os   manios   Çinquaenta astíís.
        land   is such as the ±untilled.grounds fifty   a.
        'after Dona Gyralda's death, the aforementioned monastery got the afore-
        mentioned land, which land has, like the untilled grounds, fifty *astíís*
        [medieval agrarian measure]' (13th c., Martins 2001: 366)

(605)   mãdamos   dar   esta Sentemça Seelada do   nosso Seelo
        demand.1PL give.INF this sentence stamped of.the our   stamp
        ao   dicto   Conuëto no   qual screuemos nosso nome data
        to.the mentioned convent in.the which wrote.1PL our   name date
        'we demand that this sentence with our stamp, in which we wrote our name
        and date, be given to the aforementioned convent' (14th c., Martins 2001: 216)

(606)   Eu Affomso goterrez [...] que este stromento pera ho dicto   lujs
        I   A.   G.   that this deed   to   the mentioned L.
        EAnes scripuý en no   quall meu Sjgnal fjz   que tall e%.
        E.   wrote in in.the which my sign made.1SG that such is
        'I, Affomso Goterrez, who wrote this deed to the aforementioned Lujs EAnes,
        in which I made my sign, which is as follows % [sign].' (15th c., Martins 2001:
        475)

(607)   cõ outras confrontações cõ   que de dereito os ditos   bẽes
        with other limits   with that of right the mentioned properties
        deuẽ departir,; os quaees elas [...] enprazam nouamente aa
        should border.INF the which they   give   again   to.the

dicta   antonja
mentioned A.
'with other limits on which the aforementioned properties should border by
right, which [properties] they give again (in emphyteusis) to the aforementioned Antonja' (16th c., Martins 2001: 543)

B. Pre-verbal positions

B1. Pre-verbal subjects

In earlier periods of its history, Portuguese allowed for extraposed *o qual*-ARC
with a pre-verbal subject as antecedent. Sentences (608)–(610) attest to the relevant
pattern.

(608) diserom que os dictos   logares danboroes e   <u>mõte valem</u>
       said.3PL that the mentioned lands of.A.   and hill are.worth
       todo onze maravedis da   boa   moeda cõ ho dicto   monte os
       all eleven m.   of.the good coin with the mentioned hill   the
       quaes logares danboroes partem cõ   erdade darouqua
       which lands of.A.   border with land   of.A.
       'they said that the aforementioned lands of Anboroes and the hill, which
       lands are worth eleven *maravedis* [currency] of good coin, including the hill,
       which lands of Anboroes border on land of Arouqua' (15th c., Martins
       2001: 255)

(609) e   toda a   outra cidade <u>era devassa,</u> na   quall moravam muitas
       and all the other city   was opened   in.the which lived   many
       gentes avondadas de grandes rriquezas e   bẽes
       people full   of great   wealth   and belongings
       'and the rest of the city, in which many rich people lived, could be easily
       attacked' (15th c., Macchi 1975: 258)

(610) onde então o Rey dos   Batas se   estaua fazẽdo   prestes para
       where then the king of.the B. SE.CL was make.GER ready to
       yr   <u>sobre o Achẽ,</u> o qual tanto que soube do   presente &
       go.INF over the A.   the which as.soon.as knew of.the gift   and
       carta que lhe   eu leuaua do   Capitão de Malaca, me   mandou
       letter that him.CL I took   from.the captain of M.   me.CL ordered
       receber   pelo   Xabandar
       receive.INF by.the X.
       '(from the city of Panaajû,) where the king of the Battak was busy with
       preparations to attack the Achinese, who as soon as he heard about the gift
       and letter that I was taking to him, sent out Xabandar to welcome me'
       (16th c., *TYC*)

B2. Discourse dedicated positions in the left periphery

In earlier stages of Portuguese, *o qual*-ARCs may take a preposed focus as antecedent. Example (611) illustrates the point at hand.

(611)   Arato [...] fez   tirar   em publico as   outras pinturas dos
        A.   made remove.INF in public   the other paintings of.the
        tiranos, mas a   de Aristrato determinava   de   quebrar, a   qual
        tyrants but the of A.   determined.3SG DE.PREP break.INF the which
        pintura era nobre á   maravilha;
        painting was noble to.the wonder
        'Arato ordered the other paintings of the tyrants to be removed in public, but
        he was determined to break the painting of Aristrato, which was very
        impressive;' (16th c., *TYC*)

However, in the corpora inspected thus far, no clear occurrence of *o qual*-ARCs with a topic as antecedent was found.[30]

B3. Scrambled objects

Earlier stages of Portuguese had a richer clausal structure than CEP, making available more syntactic positions with specific interpretative effects. This is the case with the multiple specifier positions that were available in the IP domain, which were responsible for the IP scrambling (or middle scrambling) attested in earlier stages of the language (see §3.4.3.2C). Not surprisingly, extraposition may emerge in this context; see (612) (repeated as (614)).[31]

---

[30] There are some complex structures in which the alleged antecedent of the ARC is introduced into the universe of discourse and then referred to anaphorically by different elements, such as wh-constituent *o qual (N)*. This gives rise to complex sequences, such as the one displayed below. For ease of reading, the antecedent is marked in italic and the anaphoric links in bold.

   a   preza de Ribell tem este casall daredor **dela** [...] e   da   **dita**   **preza** tem   no
   the dam of R.   has this hamlet around of.it   and of.the mentioned dam   has.3SG in.the
   verã   dauguoa **della** hũ dia cada somana e   asy en todo Ãno a   **quall** he de
   summer of.water of.it   one day each week   and such in all year the which is of
   muyto pouca auguoa
   very little water
   'the dam of Ribell has this hamlet around it [...]; there is water in the dam one day each week during all
   the year; the dam has very little water' (16th c., Martins 2001: 331)

Note, however, that although one of the intermediate chain links is a topic in a left dislocation construction (*da dita preza* 'of the mentioned dam'), the anaphoric link that is nearer the wh-constituent *o qual* is *ella* 'she', which is not in a topic position.

[31] Note that the scrambling of *nesta carta* 'in this letter' in (612) is confirmed by the relative position of this constituent with respect to the verb and the clitic. According to Martins (2002), clitics in clauses with interpolation set the border between left-dislocated/focused constituents and scrambled constituents;

(612)   que este emprazamento valha   e   se   cumpra   como
         that this emphyteusis   be.valid.SBJV and SE.CL carry.out.SBJV as
         se   nesta carta <u>contem</u> haa   quaL dou   minha auctoridade
         SE.CL in.this letter contains to.the which give.1SG my   authority
         '(I want) this emphyteusis to be valid and to be carried out as it is written in
         this letter, to which I give my authority.' (16th c., Martins 2001: 318)

C. Prepositional phrases

In earlier periods of the history of Portuguese, an extraposed *o qual*-ARC can take as
an antecedent the object of a preposition. See examples (613)–(614), in which the PP
containing the antecedent is the indirect object and an oblique constituent,
respectively.

(613)   Joham Lourenço mandou rrecado a   sua molher <u>que sse</u>
         J.   L.   sent   message to his wife   that SE.CL
         <u>fosse   pera elle</u>: da   quall ja   tiinha   hũu filho, que chamavom
         go.SBJV to   him of.the which already had.3SG a   son   that called.3PL
         Alvoro
         A.
         'Joham Lourenço sent his wife a message saying that she should go back
         home. He already had a son by her called Alvoro' (15th c., Macchi
         1975: 199)

(614)   que este emprazamento valha   e   se   cumpra   como
         that this emphyteusis   be.valid.SBJV and SE.CL carry.out.SBJV as
         se   nesta carta <u>contem</u> haa   quaL dou   minha auctoridade
         SE.CL in.this letter contains to.the which give.1SG my   authority
         '(I want) this emphyteusis to be valid and to be carried out as it is written in
         this letter, to which I give my authority.' (16th c., Martins 2001: 318)

Note additionally that the PP may be further embedded in another constituent. See
example (615), where extraposition takes place from a PP within a DP.

(615)   os   quaes posam penhorar [...] em quaesquer bẽes   dos
         the which can   seize.INF   in any   belongings of.the
         ditos   enprazadores <u>honde quer que achados fforem</u> os   quaes
         mentioned lessees   wherever   found   were   the which

---

hence, in (612), because *nesta carta* 'in this letter' is interpolated (i.e. occurs between the proclitic and the
verb), it is necessarily a scrambled constituent. If it occurred to the left of the clitic, it would be a left-
dislocated/focused constituent.

nam terã   poder de   tolher   o   dito   penhor
not have.FUT power DE.PREP block.INF the mentioned seizure
'(so that) they can seize any properties of the aforementioned lessees, wher-
ever they are, and the lessees have no power to block the aforementioned
seizure' (15th c., Martins 2001: 292)

D. Extraposition across conjunct(s)

Earlier stages of Portuguese, contrary to CEP, allow an extraposed *o qual*-ARC to
take the first conjunct of a multiple coordinate structure as its antecedent. See (616),
which involves coordination at the DP-level of projection.[32]

(616) testemunhas que Eram presemtes llopo martjz orjuez e   alluaro
       witnesses   that were present   L.   M.   jeweller and A.
       gomcalluez barbeJro e   bento velloso ao   **quall llopo martīz** a
       G.   barber and B.   V.   to.the which L.   M.   the
       dita   catarjna periz rrogou que asynasse   por   sy   e
       mentioned C.   P.   asked that sign.SBJV.3SG POR.PREP him and
       por   ella
       POR.PREP her
       'witnesses that were present: Llopo Martjz, a jeweler, Alluaro Gomcalluez, a
       barber, and Bento Velloso, the which Llopo Martīz Catarjna Periz asked to
       sign in her place' (16th c., Martins 2001: 307)

Another possibility is that the antecedent is contained within the first conjunct and
other conjunct(s) appear in the intervening position. Consider, for instance, the
examples in (617)–(618), which display, respectively, coordination at the VP and
IP levels of projection.

(617) os Reys comarcaõs della o   mandaraõ visitar por seus
       the king neighboring of.it him.CL ordered visit.INF by their
       Embaixadores, &   darlhe   os parabẽ   da   sua
       ambassadors   and give. him.CL the congratulations for.the his
       capitania, [...] entre **os quais** veyo hum del   Rey dos   Batas
       appointment   among the which came a   of.the king of.the B.
       'the neighboring kings sent their ambassadors to visit him and congratulate
       him on his appointment (with offers to renew the peace and friendship
       treaties they had maintained with the king of Portugal). Among those who
       came was an ambassador of the king of the Battak.' (16th c., *TYC*)

(618) E   logo   os ssobreditos lançarõ ssortes das   ditas
       and immediately the mentioned drew.lots   of.the mentioned

---

[32] For expository purposes, the relative pronoun and the internal head are marked in bold.

partições E   acõteçeo A ljonor gonçaluez os oljuaaes   e
divisions and went   to L.   G.   the olive.groves and
herdades que som ẽ santarẽ [...] E   acõteçeo Ao   dito
lands   that are in S.   and went   to.the mentioned
Affonsso martĩjz e   a ssa molher A   herdade de mõte maior [...]
A.   M.   and to his wife   the land   of M.   M.
as quaes partições os ssobreditos outorgarõ.
the which divisions the mentioned granted
'And the aforementioned (people) drew lots for the aforementioned divisions. And the olive groves and the lands located in Santarẽ went to Ljonor
Gonçaluez; the land in Mõte Maior went to Affonsso Martĩjz and to his wife,
which divisions the aforementioned people granted.' (14th c., Martins 2001)

E. Extraposition across clauses

In earlier stages of Portuguese, an embedded clause can break the adjacency between
the antecedent and the *o qual*-ARC. See (619)–(620), which involve, respectively, a
nominal and an adverbial clause in the intervening position.

(619)   Joham Lourenço mandou rrecado a **sua molher** que sse   fosse
    J.   L.   sent   message to his wife   that SE.CL go.SBJV
    pera elle: da   quall ja   tiinha   hũu filho, que chamavom Alvoro.
    to   him of.the which already had.3SG a   son   that called.3PL A.
    'Joham Lourenço sent his wife a message saying that she should go back
    home. He already had a son by his wife, who was called Alvoro.' (15th c.,
    Macchi 1975: 199)

(620)   era concertada cõ   Joham goncaluez [...] de   lhe   auer
    was concerted with J.   G.   DE.PREP him.CL have.INF
    denprazar   o   dicto   pardieiro   porque asy   ho
    DE.PREP.give.INF the mentioned old.building because as.such it.CL
    aujã   por   serujço de deus e   proueito da   dicta
    had.3PL POR.PREP service of god and benefit   of.the mentioned
    dona mjcia e   do   dicto   seu moesteiro; o **quall pardieiro**
    D.   M.   and of.the mentioned her monastery the which old.building
    lhe   logo   enprazarõ
    him.CL immediately gave.3PL
    'she had a deal with Joham Goncaluez to give him (in emphyteusis) the
    aforementioned old building because they had it in the service of God and
    in benefit of the aforementioned Dona Mjcia and her monastery; which old
    building they promptly gave to Joham Goncaluez' (15th c., Martins 2001: 531)

F. Extraposition across the discourse

Surprisingly, the non-adjacency between the antecedent and the ARC can lead to a far more radical situation: the units that appear as intervening material may belong not to the sentence level but rather to the discourse level. More specifically, a textual fragment may intervene between the antecedent and the ARC. Consider, for instance (621), where a document is transcribed before the *o qual*-ARC.

(621) luis dallmeida dom prioll do   mosteiro de uillarinho e   francisco
     L.   D.   D.   prior of.the monastery of U.   and F.
     fernandez [...] me   emviaram dizer   per   sua pitição o̲
     F.   me.CL sent   say.INF through their petition the
     seguinte [...] a   **quall** petição vista per mjm mãdei   vasar
     following   the which petition seen by me   ordered.1SG make.INF
     carta de vedoria
     letter of assessment
     'Luis de Allmeida, prior of the monastery of Uillarinho, and Francisco Fernandez sent me a petition saying the following [copy of the petition], having seen which petition, I ordered a letter of assessment to be made' (16th c., Martins 2001: 327)

In (621), the extraposed ARC clearly relates to an antecedent across discourse. Another possibility is that the antecedent and the *o qual*-ARC appear in different utterances. See, for instance, examples (622) and (623), where the antecedent appears in a first-person direct speech (punctuated with an introductory dash), whereas the ARC appears in the third-person narration.

(622) —Senhor, chegou ally o allmocadẽ, e pareçe-me que diz que lhe he neçessario de vos fallar llogo amte que amanheça.
     '—Sir, the Moorish captain arrived there and it seems to me he is saying he needs to speak to you promptly, before it dawns.'
     O qual o   comde mamdou que viesse.
     the which the count ordered that come.SBJV
     'The which (Moorish captain) the count ordered to come.' (15th c., Brocardo 1997: 296)

(623) —Ora—disse o comde—nõ abasta que vos esto comteis a mỹ soo, mas quer que o digaes assy presemte todos estes fidallgos que aquy sõ.
     '—Well—said the count—I want you to tell this story not only to me, but also to all the noblemen here.'
     Os quaes forã mui comtemtes do   que lhe   as
     the which were very happy   DE.PREP.the that him.CL the

escuitas   disserão
eavesdroppers said
'The which noblemen became very happy with what the eavesdroppers
said...' (15th c., Brocardo 1997: 310)

4.4.3 *Pied-piping*

A. Contemporary European Portuguese

In CEP, there are category-specific restrictions with respect to the constituent that
can be pied-piped[33] in *o qual*-ARCs. As illustrated in (624) and (625), pied-piping is
allowed if the constituent to be raised is a PP or an AdvP.

(624)   Recomendo   este livro, [$_{PP}$ no   qual] podes   encontrar toda a
        recommend.1SG this book   in.the which can.2SG find.INF   all   the
        informação que procuras.
        information that look.for.2SG
        'I recommend this book, in which you can find all the information you are
        looking for.'

(625)   os proprietários da   garagem são os subscritores do   pedido de
        the owners   of.the garage are the subscribers of.the request of
        licenciamento que deu entrada na   autarquia,
        licensing   that gave entrance in.the council
        [$_{AdvP}$ relativamente ao   qual] a   ACIB foi   convidada a
               relatively   to.the which the A.   was invited to
        pronunciar-se.
        pronounce.INF-SE.CL
        'The owners of the garage are the subscribers of the licensing request that was
        submitted to the council, relative to which the ACIB was invited to pro-
        nounce.' (*CETEMP*)

However, pied-piping is not allowed if the constituent to be raised is a DP or an AP
(see (626) and (627), respectively).

---

[33] The term *pied-piping* refers to a phenomenon whereby a particular movement operation, designated
to displace an element X, actually displaces a larger phrase in which X is embedded. Piped-piping occurs in
various contexts (e.g. questions, wh-exclamatives, and relative clauses). When applied to relativization, it
involves the movement to the C-domain not only of the relative noun phrase but also of its surrounding
structure (e.g. a PP, in the example below). Note that in §4.4.3, the pied-piped constituents are in square
brackets, as in

the man [to whom] I gave the book

(626) *O Pedro, [_DP_ a mulher do qual] conheceste ontem, perguntou
the P. the wife of.the which met.2SG yesterday asked
por ti.
for you.
'Pedro, the wife of whom you met yesterday, asked for you.'

(627) *Vou convidar o João, [_AP_ admirador do qual] eu sempre fui.
go.1SG invite.INF the J. admirer of.the which I always was
'I will invite João, an admirer of whom I have always been.'

An apparent exception to the generalization that DPs cannot get pied-piped concerns the contexts involving partitive structures.[34] In these cases, when the relative pronoun is the complement of the preposition, the whole partitive structure can get pied-piped along with the relative pronoun. This possibility is illustrated in (628), where the pied-piped constituent is a quantificational phrase (QP) headed by a numeral.[35] Another possibility is that it involves a non-numeral quantifier (such as *algumas* 'some' in (629)).[36]

(628) Este acto terá levado o industrial a disparar três tiros,
this act have.FUT led the industrialist to fire.INF three shots
[_QP_ dois dos quais] terão atingido o filho no abdómen.
two of.the which have.FUT hit the son in.the stomach
'This act might have led the industrialist to fire three shots, two of which might have hit his son in the stomach.' (*CRPC*)

---

[34] A partitive structure typically has the following structure: expression of quantity + *of* + noun phrase. The complement of the preposition designates a set out of which certain individuals are selected. An example is

[Two of the girls] showed up.

[35] In the label associated with the pied-piped constituent, I assume that partitive structures involve a QP. See §4.5.3 for more details.

[36] Interestingly, the pied-piping of a partitive structure is also possible in appositions, where no verb occurs:

Com a sua prisão já são cinco as pessoas detidas no
with the his imprisonment already are five the people arrested in.the
âmbito do processo Lasa e Zabala, [_QP_ quatro das quais]
context of.the case L. and Z. four of.the which
comandos e militares da guarda.
commandoes and military.men of.the guard
'With his detention, there are already five people arrested in the Lasa and Zabala case, four of whom (are) commandos and men of the military guard.' (*CRPC*)

This construction may provide evidence for an analysis of appositions as involving an (implicit) clausal structure with a null copula, as proposed by Cardoso and De Vries (2010) (see §1.3.2.5B(d) for more details).

(629) Nas   últimas provas   de   natação,   foram seleccionadas
       in.the last   competitions DE.PREP swimming were   selected
       vinte crianças, [_{QP} algumas das   quais] o   Paulo tinha treinado.
       twenty children   some   of.the which the P.   had coached
       'In the last swimming competitions, there were selected twenty children,
       some of whom Paulo had coached.' (Peres and Móia 1995: 278)

An additional restriction on pied-piping concerns the contexts in which the constituent to be moved is a non-finite clause.[37] As shown in (630)–(632), infinitival,
gerundive, and participial clauses cannot get pied-piped in CEP.[38]

Infinitival clauses:

(630) *Entregaram-me   ontem   os documentos, [_{CP} para analisar   os
       delivered.3PL-me.CL yesterday the documents   to   analyze.INF the
       quais], preciso de   pelo menos um mês.
       which   need.1SG DE.PREP at least   a   month
       'They delivered me the documents yesterday, to analyze which I need at
       least a month.'

Gerundive clauses:

(631) *Convocámos os responsáveis,   [_{CP} reflectindo com os   quais]
       called.1PL   the people.in.charge   reflect.GER with the which
       chegámos a   uma conclusão.
       came.1PL to a   conclusion
       'We called the people in charge for a meeting; in a joint reflection, we came
       to a conclusion.'

---

[37] There is no consensus among scholars with respect to the analysis of sequences such as (i), from Horvath (2007), and originally reported by Nanni and Stillings (1978).

(i)   The elegant parties, [to be invited to one of which] was a privilege…(Horvath 2007: 23–46)

Some authors assume that they involve pied-piping (more precisely *heavy* or *massive* pied-piping) (Heck 2008; Cable 2007); others claim that they do not involve true instances of pied-piping, but rather topicalization (Emonds 1976, 1979; Webelhuth 1992). Truswell (2011), when analyzing sentences such as (ii), attested in 16th- to 19th-century English, claims that they do not involve pied-piping but rather base-generation of the clause in a left-adjoined position.

(ii) This seemed to be done in distrust of the privy council, as if they might stifle his evidence; [[which to prevent], he put it in safe hands]. (from Truswell 2011: 292)

Here I assume that these constructions are true instances of pied-piping. See §4.5.3 for more details.

[38] In labels associated with the pied-piped clauses, I assume, following Lobo (2003), that gerundive and participial clauses involve a CP projection. The same analysis is adopted for infinitival clauses, under the assumption that the connective introducing the infinitival clause (as *para* 'to' in (630)) occupies the C-position. These are the criteria for Portuguese examples reported here; for the examples taken from other authors, I will adopt the original bracketing and labels (where present).

TABLE 4.3 **Restrictions on pied-piping: Contemporary European Portuguese**

	DPs	APs	CPs	AdvPs	PPs	Partitives
CEP	−	−	−	+	+	+

Participial clauses:[39]

(632) *A direcção   vai apresentar os resultados, [CP conhecidos
      the management goes present.INF the results   known.PTCP
      os quais] algumas soluções estratégicas serão   discutidas.
      the which some   solutions strategic   be.FUT discussed
      'The management will present the results, which being known some of the
      strategic solutions will be discussed.'

To sum up, the restrictions reviewed up to this point are presented in Table 4.3.

Interestingly, the restrictions in Table 4.3 do not universally hold but are subject to cross-linguistic variation, as I will show in§4.4.3B.

B. Cross-linguistic evidence

Whereas some languages are very strict about the category of the pied-piped constituents, other languages seem to be much less constrained, allowing generalized

---

[39] A word is in order regarding the apparent pied-piping of participial clauses. There is a special context in which the construction seems to be possible in CEP, as shown in (i) and (ii). However, only a very restricted number of verbs can enter the construction, namely the verb *terminar* 'to expire', as in (i), or a synonym of it, such as *findar* in (ii) or *concluir*. A change of the verb seems to block its viability, as indicated in (632). This fact can be explained by assuming that the apparent pied-piping of participial clauses is not a productive syntactic structure in CEP (as opposed to the situation in earlier stages of Portuguese). Hence, the sequence *terminado/findo/concluído o qual* 'expired which' behaves as a fixed expression, involving specific lexical items and not admitting the occurrence of other verbs.

(i) Será   definido   um período, [CP terminado o qual] ninguém poderá
     be.FUT established a period   ended.PTCP the which nobody can.FUT
     reclamar.
     complain.INF
     'A period will be defined; this period ended, nobody can complain.' (Peres and Móia 1995: 279)

(ii) Os analistas estimam que estas negociações [...] se   prolonguem por um prazo entre
     the analysts estimate that these negotiations SE.CL extend.SBJV for a period between
     12 e   18 meses, [CP findo   o qual] deverá   haver   um acordo.
     12 and 18 months   ended.PTCP the which should.FUT have.INF a   deal
     'The analysts estimate that these negotiations will be extended for a period of 12 to 18 months; ended
     which period, there must be a deal.' (*CETEMP*)

pied-piping in ARCs. This is reported, for instance, by Cinque (2008), for Italian *il quale*-ARCs; see (633).

(633) a. Inviterò   anche Giorgio, [$_{PP}$ del   quale] avete   certamente
           invite.FUT.1SG also   G.   of.the which have.2PL certainly
           sentito parlare.
           heard   speak.INF
           'I will also invite Giorgio, of whom you have certainly heard.'

       b. Inviterò   anche Giorgio, [$_{DP}$ il   fratello del   quale] è uno
           invite.FUT.1SG also   G.   the brother of.the which is one
           dei   nostri più   cari amici.
           of.the our   more dear friends
           'I will also invite Giorgio, the brother of whom is one of our dearest friends.'

       c. Inviterò   anche Giorgio, [$_{AP}$ affezionato al   quale] per
           invite.FUT.1SG also   G.   fond   A.PREP.the which for
           altro non sono.
           other not am.1SG
           'I will also invite Giorgio, fond of whom nevertheless I am not.'

       d. Inviterò   anche Giorgio, [$_{CP}$ liberarmi   del   quale] non
           invite.FUT.1SG also   G.   get.rid.INF.me.CL of.the which not
           mi   è proprio possibile.
           me.CL is really possible
           'I will also invite Giorgio, to get rid of whom is really not possible for me.'

       e. Inviterò   anche Giorgio, [$_{ADVP}$ diversamente dal   quale]
           invite.FUT.1SG also   G.   differently DA.PREP.the which
           io non serbo rancore.
           I not bear   grudge
           'I will also invite Giorgio, unlike whom I bear no grudge.' (all Cinque 2008:
           101; glosses and translations in examples a, b, and e mine)

Similar possibilities of pied-piping are reported for English. Heck (2008) shows that English ARCs allow for the pied-piping of PPs, APs, DPs, and clausal constituents (see (634)). Fabb (1990) also reports the pied-piping of DPs (635a) and partitive structures (635b).

(634) a. Egbert, [$_{PP}$ to whom] you were talking only yesterday,...
       b. ?this earthquake, [$_{AP}$ affected by which] the area was,...
       c. the royal family, [$_{DP}$ pictures of whom] are permanently on sale,...
       d. Egbert, [$_{α}$ to hire whom] would be a real scoop,... (all Heck 2008: 168)

(635) a. The man, [the mother of whom] I met yesterday, is a French speaker.

        b. The men, [some of whom] I like, arrived yesterday. (both Fabb 1990: 64)

C. Earlier stages of Portuguese

Interestingly, the restrictions on pied-piping are also subject to variation in the diachronic dimension. Comparing the properties of pied-piping in CEP with the ones in earlier periods of Portuguese, the differences are remarkable. The general scenario is that earlier periods of Portuguese pattern with contemporary English and Italian in allowing generalized pied-piping.

To be more concrete, *o qual*-ARCs in earlier stages of Portuguese allow pied-piping of PPs, partitive constructions, and AdvPs, just like their contemporary counterparts. This is illustrated in (636)–(638).

(636) Reçebemos de   Giral dominguiz [...] Cem   libras de
        received.1PL DE.PREP G.   D.   one.hundred l.   of
        dinheiros portugaeses [pp polos quaes] lhj   nós vendemos [...]
        currency Portuguese   by.the which him.CL we sold
        'We received from Giral Dominguiz one hundred *libras* of the Portuguese currency, for which we sold him (two houses that we have in the aforementioned village).' (14th c., Martins 2001: 208)

(637) nos   matou   logo   seis homens, [QP hum dos   quais] foy Diogo
        us.CL killed.3SG outright six   men   one of.the which was D.
        Vaz Coutinho filho do   Capitão mòr
        V.   C.   son of.the admiral
        'it killed six of our men outright, one of whom was Diogo Vaz Coutinho, the admiral's son' (16th c., *TYC*)

(638) taes são os   importantes objectos, [AdvP relativamente aos   quaes]
        such are the important   topics   relatively   to.the which
        devem os factos ser   escolhidos, e   detalhados
        should the facts be.INF selected   and detailed
        'these are important topics, relative to which the facts that should be selected are detailed' (19th c., *CP*)

However, historical Portuguese, contrary to CEP, allows pied-piping of DPs and clausal constituents.[40] Examples (639)–(643) illustrate pied-piping of DPs; notice that in these examples the gap corresponds either to the subject (as in (639)–(641), (643)–(644)) or to the direct object position (as in (642)).

---

[40] In the corpora of historical Portuguese inspected, pied-piping of APs is not attested. For this reason, in this section I mainly focus on the pied-piping of DPs and clausal constituents.

DPs:

(639) recebj   hua procuraço   do   Abade san Joane da
       received.1SG one letter.of.attorney of.the abbot S.   J   DE.PREP.the
       pendorada e   do   Conuĕto [DP o teor da   qual] atal e
       P.   and DE.PREP.the convent   the tenor of.the which such is
       de   ueruo. a   ueruo
       DE.PREP word   A.PREP word
       'I received one letter of attorney from the abbot of San Joane of Pendorada
       and from the convent; the tenor of which is the following, word for word...'
       (13th c., Martins 2001: 132)

(640) como mais larguamente consta   dapeguação   que
       as   more extensively is.reported DE.PREP.the.possession.letter that
       aqui mandei   treladar de   verbo a   verbo
       here ordered.1SG copy.INF DE.PREP word A.PREP word
       [DP o   trelado da   quall] he o   seguinte
           the copy   of.the which is the following
       'as it is more extensively reported in the possession letter that I ordered to be
       copied here, word for word; the copy of which is as follows...' (16th c.,
       Martins 2001: 328)

(641) A   composição dos   edeficios consta de symetria,
       the composition of.the buildings consists of symmetry
       [DP a   razão da   qual] os   deligentes arquitetos hão de
           the reason of.the which the diligent   architects have DE.PREP
       entender.
       master.INF
       'The composition of buildings consists of symmetry, the principles of which
       diligent architects have to master.' (16th c., *TYC*)

(642) e   ſe os particulares devem ſer   amparados na   ſua   menor idade,
       and if the individuals should be.INF protected in.the their minor age
       quanto mais o   deve   ſer   hum Rey; [DP a   boa criaçaõ do
       let   alone it.CL should be.INF a   king   the good education of.the
       qual] ſe   dirige ao   bem de muitos, ao   ſerviço de Deos, e
       which SE.CL directs to.the good of many to.the service of God   and
       à   protecçaõ da   Religiaõ Catholica
       to.the protection of.the Religion Catholic
       'and if the common people should be protected when they are under-age, let
       alone the king, the good education of whom benefits not only the wellbeing of
       many, but also the service of God and the protection of the Catholic Religion'
       (18th c., *TYC*)

(643)   Agora falarei   nos requisitos   para a   inteligência   da
       now   talk.FUT.1SG in.the requirements for   the understanding of.the
       dita   língua, [DP a falta dos   quais]   não se   deve
       mentioned language   the lack of.the.PL which.PL not SE.CL should
       contar   entre os menores abusos;
       number.INF among the minor   abuses
       'I will now talk about the requirements for the understanding of the afore-
       mentioned language; the lack of which must not be numbered among the
       minor abuses.' (18th c., *TYC*)

Over the course of its history, Portuguese also allowed for pied-piping of non-finite
CPs. By way of illustration, see examples (644)–(658), which involve participial
clauses (see (644)–(650)), gerundive clauses (see (651)–(655)), and infinitival clauses
(see (656)–(658)).

Participial clauses:

(644)   sobre o   negado ffoy ffilhada Enqueriçõ [CP A qual   vista per mj̃]
       about the ±denial was accepted inquiry   the which seen by me
       Julgey   que o dito   prioll prouaua quanto Auõdaua
       judged.1SG that the mentioned prior proved   all.that was.sufficient
       'an inquiry about the denial was accepted, seeing which I judged that the
       aforementioned prior has proved conclusively (that he was right)' (14th c.,
       Martins 2001: 227)

(645)   Dona Thareyía martĩis dona da Chelas mostrou hũa carta de nosso senhor El
       Rey e sseelada do seu seelo pendẽte da qual o tẽhor atal he. […]
       'Dona Thareyía Martĩis, Dona of Chelas, showed a letter from the King,
       stamped with his hanging stamp; the tenor of the letter is as follows:
       [transcription of the letter]'
       [CP A qual   carta mostrada e   leuda] a dita   Thareyía
           the which letter shown   and read the mentioned T.
       martĩis comprou tres courelas de vinhas   en Barathoío per outoridade
       M.   bought three lands   of vineyards in B.   by authority
       da dita   carta
       of.the mentioned letter
       'this letter being shown and read, Thareyía Martĩis bought three vineyards in
       Barathoío under the authority of the aforementioned letter' (14th c., Martins
       2001: 405)

(646)   Eu Nicollaao de ffreitas tabaliam del Rey na dicta villa de guimarãães que esta
       procuraçom per mãdado e outorgamẽto da dicta Maria fernandez screpuj e
       aquy meu synal fiz que tal. he.
       'I, Nicollaao de Ffreitas, notary of the king in the village of Guimarãães, wrote
       this letter of attorney under Maria Fernandez's consent. I put here my sign,
       which is as follows.'

[cp A quall presentada] os dictos   procuradores do   dicto
    the which presented   the mentioned attorneys   of.the mentioned
Moesteíro disserom que antre   elles Era preito.
monastery said   that between them was legal.dispute
'Shown which, the attorneys of the aforementioned monastery said that they
were involved in a legal dispute.' (15th c., Martins 2001: 251)

(647) E   com os ingreses viinha o   alferez do   duque d'Allancastro [...],
       and with the English came the ensign of.the duke   of.A.
       que tragia   sua bandeira; [cp a quall tendida na   batalha], braadavom
       that brought his flag   the which stretched in.the battle   yelled
       os ingreses todos.
       the English all
       'And the ensign of the duke of Allancastro, carrying his flag, came along with
       the English knights; the which being raised in the battle, the English knights
       started yelling out.' (15th c., Macchi 1975: 532)

(648) O Capitão mór entendendo quão importante cousa esta era, lhe aceitou a
       promessa, & lhe concedeo de nouo as pazes,
       'The captain, fully aware of the gravity of the situation, accepted her promise
       and renewed the peace treaty,'
       [cp as quais juradas aly   logo   &   confirmadas de
           the which sworn there immediately and confirmed   DE.PREP
       ambas as partes com as cerimonias costumadas entre   aquelles
       both the parties with the ceremonies used   among those
       Gentios],   a   Raynha buscou todos os meyos possiueis para
       heathen.people the queen tried all the means possible to
       cumprir a   sua palaura
       keep.INF the her word
       'which sworn to there and then, and confirmed by both parties in accordance
       with the local ceremonies, the queen tried in every way possible to keep her
       word' (16th c., TYC)

(649) Depois de   faber   ler,   e   efcrever, ouvio El Rey
       after   DE.PREP know.INF read.INF and write.INF heard the.king
       Grammatica, [cp na   qual inftruido] paffou ao   eftudo de Authores
       grammar   in.the which instructed moved to.the study of authors
       Latinos
       Latin
       'After learning to read and write, the king learned grammar; instructed in
       which, he started studying the Latin authors...' (18th c., TYC)

(650)   e   no   anno de   699. foy   mandado   ouvir   Artes
        and in.the year   DE.PREP 699 was.3SG commanded listen.INF Arts
        no   Real Mofteiro de   Santa Maria de Ceiça, e   Theologia
        in.the Royal Monastery DE.PREP S.   M.   d. C.   and Theology
        no   noffo Collegio de   S. Bernardo de Coimbra; [CP acabados
        in.the our   College DE.PREP S. B.   d. C.   ended
        os quaes Curfos], fe   graduou   de   Doutor Theologo
        the which courses SE.CL graduated.3SG DE.PREP Doctor Theologian
        'in the year of 699, he attended Arts in the Royal Monastery of Santa Maria de
        Ceiça and Theology in our College of S. Bernardo de Coimbra, the which
        courses ended, he received his doctorate in Theology' (18th c., *TYC*)

Gerundive clauses:

(651)   enprazou a afonsso periz de lestosa e   a sua molher marja anes e
        gave.3SG to A.   P.   d. L.   and to his wife M.   A.   and
        a hũu filho ou filha   dantre anbos [CP o qual hi   nom avendo]
        to a son or daughter of   both   the which there not have.GER
        a hũa pessoa qual   ho postumeiro que deles   mais viuer
        to a   person which the last   that of.them more live.FUT.SBJV
        nomear
        appoint.FUT.SBJV
        'he gave it in emphyteusis to Afonsso Periz de Lestosa, to his wife Marja Anes,
        and to a son or daughter of them, whom not existing, to a person that the
        later of them to die will appoint' (15th c., Martins 2001: 286)

(652)   avendo   primeiro salvo-conducto de dona Johana, rrainha entom
        have.GER first   safe-conduct   of D. J.   queen then
        d'aquella provencia; [CP na   quall estando per pouco tempo], Pero
        of.that   province   in.the which be.GER by short time   P.
        Bernalldez, cossairo d'Aragom, chegou hi   com gallees armadas
        B.   corsair of.A,   arrived there with galleys armed
        'they had a safe-conduct given by Dona Johana, who was the queen of that
        province; being in which for a short time, Pero Baernalldez, a corsair from
        Aragom, arrived there with armed galleys' (15th c., Macchi 1975: 393)

(653)   estamdo hi em cabido scilicet o Reueremdo senhor lujs dalmeida prioll do
        dito mosteiro e manuell JorJe conjgo do dito mosteiro
        'The Reverend Sir Lujs dalmeida, prior of the monastery, and Manuell JorJe,
        canon of the monastery, being there gathered for the chapter'

[CP o   quall   prioll   e   conjgo estamdo no   dito   cabido
       the which   prior and   canon be.GER   in.the mentioned chapter
Jumtos per   som   de campam tamgida como tem de   seus
together through sound of bell   rung   as   has DE.PREP its
costumes] o   dito   prioll dise que [...]
costumes   the mentioned prior   said that
'which prior and the canon, being gathered in the chapter by the sound of the
bell ringing, as usual, the prior said that...' (16th c., Martins 2001: 312)

(654) a suecessaõ delRey D. Joaõ III. filho primogenito delRey D. Manoel, acabou
       em ElRey D. Sebastiaõ seu neto; e tornando aos filhos do mesmo Rey
       D. Manoel, naõ achou varaõ vivo, mais que o Cardeal D. Henrique,
       'the succession of the king D. Joaõ III, firstborn son of the king D. Manoel,
       ended at the king D. Sebastiaõ, his grandson; among king D. Manoel's
       children, there was no living son besides Cardinal D. Henrique'
       [CP o   qual   morrendo sem   successaõ, e   sem   irmaõ, ou
              the which die.GER   without succession and without brother or
       irmãa, a quem deixasse o   Reyno], necessariamente havia de
       sister to whom pass.SBJV the kingdom necessarily   had   DE.PREP
       hir   a hum de muitos sobrinhos seus
       go.INF to one of many   nephews his
       'which (Cardinal D. Henrique) dying without succession and without a sister
       or a brother to whom to leave the kingdom, had necessarily to leave the
       succession to one of his many nephews' (17th c., *TYC*)

(655) e   me   disse   como se lhe   pedissem   juramento, o
       and me.CL said.3SG that if her.CL ask.SBJV.3PL oath   it.CL
       daria   na   verdade deste cazo; [CP o   qual   relatando ao
       make.COND in.the truth   of.this case   the which tell.GER to.the
       mesmo Padre], lhe   respondeo, que [...]
       same priest her.CL replied.3SG that
       'and she told me that, if she was asked to make an oath, she would make it in
       the name of the truth of this case; telling which to the same priest, he told her
       that...' (18th c., *TYC*)

Infinitival clauses:

(656) no   Latim há três   Gerúndios, um em Di, outro em Do, outro
       in.the Latin has three gerunds   one in -di other in -do other
       em Dum, [CP para explicar   os quais] se   serve a língua
       in -dum   to   express.INF the which SE.CL uses the language

Portuguesa da   voz   do   Infinitivo com alguma preposição
Portuguese of.the voice of.the infinitive with some   preposition
'in Latin, there are three gerunds ending in *–di, –do* and *–dum,* to express which
the Portuguese language uses the infinitive with a preposition' (18th c., *TYC*)

(657)   se descobriu em mim culpas, [CP para remir   as quais] me
        if found.3SG in me   faults   to   reedem.INF the which me.CL
        marcou esta penitência, bem vê   com que resignação eu a   aceito
        gave.3SG this penance   well see.3SG with what resignation I   it.CL accept
        'if you found my faults, to cleanse me from which you gave me this penance,
        you can see with how much resignation I accept it' (19th c., *CP*)

(658)   Burlado até na   esperança de colher   às   mãos o   audaz
        deceived even in.the hope   of catch.INF A.PREP.the hands the bold
        primo do   senhor de Cresconhe, Egas, que ele supunha   em
        cousin of.the S.   d. C.   E.   that he presumed in
        Guimarães, e   [CP para achar   o   qual] tinham sido vãs as mais
        G.   and to   find.INF the which had   been vain the more
        severas pesquisas
        severe   researches
        'Deceived even in the hope of catching the bold cousin of the Senhor de
        Cresconhe, Egas, whom he presumed to be in Guimarães, and to find whom
        several attempts had been in vain...' (19th c., *CP*)

A closer inspection of the examples (644)–(658) reveals that they involve a rather
complex syntactic environment containing at least three different clauses: the clause
that contains the antecedent (antecedent clause), the embedded clause (ARC), and the
pied-piped clause contained within the ARC. See the schematic representation in (659).

(659)

                          antecedent clause
                             |
┌──┐
no   Latim há três Gerúndios, um em Di, outro em Do, outro   em   Dum,

in.the Latin has three gerunds   one in -di other in -do other   in   -dum

        pied-piped clause
             |
┌─────────────────────┐
[CP para explicar   os quais] se   serve a língua Portuguesa da   voz

    to   express.INF the which SE.CL uses   the language Portuguese of.the voice

└──┘
                             |
                            ARC

There is a lot going on in pied-piped clauses, but there are three aspects that I would like to highlight: (1) the chronology; (2) the position of the relative pronoun; and (3) the clause types involved.

(a) The chronology

In the corpora inspected in this research, the pied-piping of non-finite clausal constituents is attested in earlier periods of Portuguese. However, it is not evenly distributed across non-finite clauses but is found almost exclusively in participial and gerundive clauses. For instance, in the texts edited by Martins (2001), pied-piping of participial and gerundive clauses is attested, but pied-piping of infinitival clauses is not. I found it in other corpora, but only in later periods (see examples (656)–(658)). Further evidence from larger corpora is needed to assess whether this is real or corresponds to an accidental gap.

(b) The position of the relative pronoun

Within the pied-piped clause, the relative pronoun can occur in its base position or can undergo internal movement to the CP domain. In (650) and in (656)–(658), the relative pronoun stays in its base position within the pied-piped clause, whereas in (644)–(649) and in (651)–(655) it undergoes internal movement to the CP domain. The latter case corresponds to the so-called *internal wh-movement* or *secondary wh-movement* (see Bianchi 1999; Smits 1988; Cable 2007; Heck 2008; Truswell 2011).[41]

In the earliest texts inspected, the internal wh-movement is predominant. In the corpus edited by Martins (2001), all participial and gerundive clauses involve internal *wh*-movement. The occurrence of the wh-pronoun in its base position is attested in latter texts, as shown by the examples in (650) and in (656)–(658), involving a participial clause and infinitival clauses, respectively.

In the data inspected thus far, internal wh-movement may also display these properties: (1) pied-piping of a PP (see (649) and (652)); (2) additional internal head (see (645) and (650));[42] (3) across-the-board extraction of the relative pronoun out of coordinate pied-piped clauses (see (645) and (648), which involve participial clauses).

---

[41] Truswell (2011) reports the existence of internal wh-movement in earlier stages of English, as shown in (i) and (ii). Bianchi (1999), in turn, reports the possibility of internal wh-movement in earlier stages of Italian, as illustrated in (iii). I also refer the also to Danckaert (2012), who provides empirical evidence of this phenomenon in Latin.

(i)   a sarmon, somthing better then that in the morninge: [cp which ended, with all Ceremones], I returned to my lodginge. (16th/17th c., from Truswell 2011: 292)

(ii) Mr Hoby, my Mother, and my selfe, went to visitt some freindes [cp who, beinge not at home], we retourned (16th/17th c., from Truswell 2011: 292)

(iii) Non si meravigli dunque alcuno se lunga è la digressione della mia scusa, ma, sì come necessaria, 'hence nobody be astonished if the digression of my justification is long, but, as it is necessary, la   sua lunghezza paziente sostenga.   [cp La quale proseguendo], dico [...]
the its length   patient   tolerate.IMP   the which continue.GER   say.1SG
'tolerate its length with patience. Continuing the digression, I say...' (14th c., from Bianchi 1999: 143, gloss and translation mine)

[42] The additional internal head can be a conjoined phrase, as in (582). For more details on the internal head, see §4.4.1.

(c) The clause types involved

The clausal pied-piping is not, however, confined to non-finite clauses. Pied-piping of finite adverbial clauses is also attested in earlier stages of Portuguese, as shown in (660)–(662).[43]

(660)   E   emtom a   molher disse ao   segumdo marido   que matasse
        and then   the woman said   to.the second   husband that kill.SBJV.3SG
        o   primeiro marido   e   que ella teria   a   elle por seu
        the first   husband and that she have.COND A.PREP him as   her
        marido. [_{CP} O   quall   como   nom quisesse   fazer   tamanha traiçom],
        husband   the which   because not   want.SBJV make.INF such   betrayal
        a   dita   molher matou ao   dito   primeiro marido
        the mentioned wife   killed   A.PREP.the mentioned first   husband
        em no   çeleiro.
        in in.the barn
        'The woman told the man to kill her first husband. She promised him that if
        he did, she would become his wife. The which (man) not willing to make such
        a betrayal, the woman killed her husband in the barn.' (13th c. [transmitted
        by a 15th-c. MS], *CP*)

(661)   Admite além   disso   a   nossa língua   com grande elegância,
        admits besides DE.PREP.that the our   language with great   elegance
        e   particular graça as   metáforas, [_{CP} as quais como   se   podem
        and particular grace the metaphors   the which because SE.CL can.3PL
        aplicar   a   tantas   cousas], fica   uma mesma sentença servindo
        apply.INF to so.many things   stays a   same   sentence serve.GER
        muitos sentidos
        many   meanings
        'With great elegance and particular grace, our language also admits meta-
        phors, and because the which can apply to many things, the same sentence
        can have many meanings.' (17th c., *CP*)

---

[43] Truswell (2011) reports similar constructions for 16th- to 19th-century English (see (i)–(iii)).

(i)   receive then this Draught [[with which when thou art refresh'd], thou mayst more strongly proceed
      to other Matters which yet remain]. (17th c., from Truswell 2011: 292).

(ii) I make a square, that is G.H.K.L, [[In which square if I drawe crosse lines frome one side to the other,
      according to the diuisions of the line G.H], then will it appear plaine, that the theoreme doth
      affirme]. (16th c., from Truswell 2011: 306).

(iii) but not so easie work found Ethelfrid against another part of Britans that stood in arms, [[whom
      though at last he overthrew], yet with slaughter nigh as great to his own souldiers]. (17th c., from
      Truswell 2011: 306).

(662) nem tenham   diante dos-olhos   estas circunstancias: [cp as
       nor have.sbjv.3pl before DE.PREP.the-eyes these circumstances   the
       quais se eu nam tivese   executado], totalmente me-faltaria   aquela
       which if I not have.sbjv executed   totally   me.cl-lack.cond that
       benevolencia, que certamente me-mostram, os que examinam as
       benevolence that certainly me.cl-show the that examine   the
       minhas asoens
       my   actions
       '(Do you think there are persons who) do not consider these circumstances?
       Had I not taken the which into account, I would lack that benevolence that
       the ones who examine my actions say I have.' (18th c., *TYC*)

Note that the adjacency between the relative pronoun and the connective introducing
the adverbial finite clause and the fact that the relative pronoun does not play any
function within the main clause clearly show that the relative pronoun is not
extracted from the adverbial clause, but rather internally moved to the left
periphery.[44]

To summarize, the contrasts between CEP and earlier stages of Portuguese with
respect to pied-piping are displayed in Table 4.4.

TABLE 4.4 **Restrictions on pied-piping: Different stages of Portuguese**

	DPs	APs	CPs	AdvPs	PPs	Partitives
CEP	−	−	−	+	+	+
Earlier stages of Portuguese	+	?	+	+	+	+

[44] Peres and Móia (1995: 287) report a construction from a 16th-century Portuguese text that, in my
opinion, is similar to the ones discussed here (see example below). However, they claim that it involves
extraction of the relative pronoun out of the subordinate clause. I depart from their analysis (and
interpretation) because, as clearly shown by the translation, the relative pronoun does not play any
function in the main clause.

       Esta é a   ditosa   pátria   minha amada,
       this is the delightful homeland my   beloved
       À   qual se o céu   me   dá   que eu sem   perigo
       to.the which if the heaven me.cl gives that I without danger
       Torne   com esta empresa já   acabada
       return.sbjv with this war   already ended
       Acabe-se   esta luz ali comigo.
       end.sbjv-se.cl this light there with.me
       'This is my own beloved delightful land/to which if heaven accord me safe/return, with this war ended,/
       there may the light of life leave me.' (16th c., from Peres and Móia 1995: 287)

4.4.4   *Clausal antecedent*

A. Contemporary European Portuguese

In CEP, *o qual*-ARCs cannot take a clausal antecedent, as can be observed in the ungrammatical sequence in (663).[45]

(663)   *O João chegou a   horas, **o qual** muito   me   surprendeu.
         the J.   arrived A.PREP hours the which very.much me.CL surprised
         'João arrived on time, which surprised me very much.'

The only relativizers that can introduce clausal antecedents are *o que* lit. 'the that' and *que* lit. 'that'. This is illustrated, respectively, in the grammatical sentences provided in (664)–(665).[46]

(664)   O João chegou a   horas, **o que** muito   me   surprendeu.
        the J.   arrived A.PREP hours the that very.much me.CL surprised
        'João arrived on time, which surprised me very much.'

(665)   O   João faltou   à   reunião, **que** era o **que** eu devia
        the J.   missed A.PREP.the meeting that was the that I   should
        ter   feito.
        have.INF done
        'João missed the meeting, which was what I should have done.'

B. Earlier stages of Portuguese

Earlier stages of Portuguese behave differently in this respect. As examples (666)–(670) show, *o qual*-ARCs can take a clausal antecedent; in this case, the ARC is introduced by an invariable *o qual*.

(666)   e se obrygou de paguar os dytos duzemtos Reaes e dous fframguãos e a dyta
        galinha de fforo despoys do ffaleçimemto da dyta molher do dito alluaro
        fernandez em cada hũu Ano pelo dito dia de natall
        'and he committed himself to pay, after the death of Alluaro Fernandez's wife, the
        aforementioned two thousand *reaes* [currency], two cockerels, and one hen as
        rent; this payment must take place every year, on Christmas day'

---

[45] In §4.4.4, the relativizer *o qual* (and its internal head, if present) is highlighted in bold for ease of reading.
[46] Note that, in (665), the ARC *que era* [...] *feito* 'which was [...] done' accidentally contains a free relative clause. For further examples of ARCs with a clausal antecedent in CEP, see Brito and Duarte (2003: 674–5).

pera o **qual** loguo   obrygou   seus bẽes
for   the which immediately pawned.3SG his   belongings
'for which he pawned his belongings' (16th c., Martins 2001: 556)

(667)   e tantas lagrimas e gritos e taaes pallavras diziam, que nom havia homem que
as ouvisse que nom ouvesse d'ellas compaixom e doo;
'and the women cried so many tears, let out so many screams, and said such
words that all the men hearing them felt compassion and pity for them;'
o   **quall** tanto esforço fez   cobrar   aos   que dentro eram
the   which such   strength made gather.INF to.the that inside   were
que rrijamente aderençarom pera aquell logar em que os   mouros
that sturdily   went.3PL   to   that   place in   that the Moors
estavom
were
'which made the men that were inside the city gather so much strength that they
sturdily went to the place where the Moors were' (15th c., Macchi 1975: 66)

(668)   se assentou com este mercador por esta maneyra, que o padre lhe desse
duzentos taeis, que saõ trezentos cruzados da nossa moeda, & que auia de yr
daly da nao ate a cidade sempre cos olhos tapados porque se caso fosse que por
elle ser estrangeyro, a justiça entendesse nelle, como estaua certo que auia de
ser, & pondoo a tormento lhe dissessem que confessasse quem o aly trouxeraõ
elle o não soubesse dizer, nem conhecesse quem o aly trouxera, porque se temia
que se fosse descuberto lhe mãdassem por isso cortar a cabeça
'They agreed with this merchant as follows: the father was to give him two
hundred *taeis* [currency]—which is worth three hundred *cruzados* [currency]
in our money—to take him from where the *nao* was anchored all the way to
the city with his eyes blindfolded, so that in case—because he was a for-
eigner—the police got hold of him, as was bound to happen, and tried to
make him confess under torture who had brought him there, he would not be
able to tell them nor recognize the one who had brought him there, for fear
that if he were discovered they would have his head chopped off'
o   **qual** o   padre aceitou   com todos estes partidos
the   which the father accepted with all   these conditions
'which the father accepted with all these conditions.'
(16th c., *CP*)

(669)   E depois de feito Deos e home deitou outro pregão sobre o mesmo caso
dizendo aos discípulos: nam convém a vós outros saber o que está por vir,
porque isso pertence à omnipotência do padre.
'And after making God and the man, he made another statement on the same
case telling his disciples: it is not in your interest to know what will happen in
the future because that belongs to the Father's omnipotence.'

Polo   **qual**   mui maravilhado estou dos   letrados
POR.PREP.the which very amazed   am.1SG DE.PREP.the lettered.men
mostrarem-se tam bravos contra tam hórridos pregões.
be.INF-SE.CL   so   furious against such horrible notices
'For which, I am amazed at the lettered man being so furious with such horrible notices.' (16th c., Camões 1999)

(670)   acrescentando ele suplicante [...] que por obedecer levaria os papéis e apontamentos que tinha feito no estado em que estivessem como lhe era mandado.
'he, supplicant, added that to obey (the tribunal's order) he would bring them the papers and the notes he had made, exactly as they were, as requested'
Emcumprimento do   **qual**   foi   ele suplicante ao   Santo Ofício
in observance   of.the which went he supplicant to.the S.   O.
em 14   do   dito   mês.
on 14th of.the mentioned month
'In the observance of which he, supplicant, went to the Santo Ofício [tribunal of the Inquisition] on July 14th.' (17th c., Muhana 1995: 117)

Further examples making the same point are given in (671)–(673). These examples contrast with (666)–(670) in that an additional internal head follows the relative pronoun. Recall from §4.4.1 that, in the contexts of ARCs with a clausal antecedent, the additional internal head is typically a general abstract noun such as *cousa* 'thing' (see (671)) or *razom* 'reason' (see (672)–(673)).

(671)   E   dou   por firme e   por estauil pera todo sempre todalas cousas
and give.1SG as firm and as steady to   every always all.the things
que forem   feytas e   procuradas per este meu procurador [...] No
that be.FUT.SBJV made and represented by this my   attorney   in.the
testemoyo da   **qual cousa** roguey   Domĩgos esteueiz tabelliom
testimony of.the which thing asked.1SG D.   E.   notary
das   alcaceuas que mi fezesse   ende esta procuraçom.
of.the A.   that me make.SBJV.3SG of.it this letter.of.attorney
'I confirm whatever my attorney does. As a testimony of which I asked Domĩgos Esteueiz, notary of Alcaceuas, to make this letter of attorney.' (13th c., Martins 2001: 359)

(672)   nom declarar   que os ditos   cassaaes fforõ cõprados dos
not   declare.INF that the mentioned hamlets were bought   DE.PREP.the

dinheiros do   dito   mosteiro polla **quall Razom** de
moneys   DE.PREP.the mentioned monastery by.the which reason by
derejto perteçem   e   perteçyam   ao   dito   mosteiro
right   belong.3PL and belonged.3PL to.the mentioned monastery
'(considering that he would feel a pang of conscience at) not declaring that the
aforementioned hamlets were bought with the money of the monastery, for
which reason they belong and belonged by right to the monastery...' (15th c.,
Martins 2001: 262)

(673) Bem sabe   el-rrei   dom Henrrique, meu irmaão e   amigo, como
       well knows the-king D.   H.   my brother and friend that
       el-rrei   de Graada tem tomados navios e   averes e   gentes cativas
       the-king of G.   has taken   ships and goods and people captive
       de   minha terra, por **a   quall rrazom** eu ei   com ell guerra.
       from my   land by the which reason I   have with him war
       'The king Dom Henrrique, my brother and friend, knows very well that the
       king of Graada has my ships and goods in his possession, and keeps the
       people of my land captive, for which reason I am at war with him.' (15th c.,
       Macchi 1975: 330)

C. Cross-linguistic evidence

There are some contemporary languages that pattern with earlier stages of
Portuguese with respect to this property. Cinque (2008) reports that Italian *il
quale*-ARCs may take a clausal antecedent; see, for instance, the example in (674).
The same point can be made for English. As shown in (675), the relativizer *which* can
take a clausal antecedent, optionally followed by an internal head.

(674) Carlo lavora troppo poco. **La qual   cosa** verrà   certamente
       C.   works too   little the which thing come.FUT certainly
       notata.
       noticed
       'Carlo works too little. A thing which will certainly be noticed.' (Cinque
       2008: 106; gloss and translation mine)

(675) a. Little Joey snatched the letter away, **which** infuriated his sister.
       b. They are said to have taught a baboon to write, **which claim** has imme-
          diately been ridiculed by most scholars. (both Smits 1988: 287)

4.4.5 *Split antecedents*

A. Contemporary European Portuguese

In CEP, *o qual*-ARCs cannot have split antecedents. This impossibility is illustrated in (676).

(676) *Se o Carlos$_i$ já   não gosta da   Maria$_j$, os   quais$_{i+j}$ nunca
      if the C.   already not likes DE.PREP.the M.   the.M.PL which.PL never
      se   deram nada bem, então acho   que não vale a pena
      SE.CL went at.all well then think.1SG that not is.worth
      continuarem juntos.
      stay.INF.3PL together
      'If Carlos no longer loves Maria, who never got along with each other, then
      I think they should not stay together.'

B. Cross-linguistic evidence

Interestingly, a different pattern is reported for other languages. Cinque (2008) points out that Italian *il quale*-ARCs can take split antecedents (see (677)); Arnold (2007) reports the same behavior for English ARCs (see (678)).

(677) Se Carlo$_i$ non amava più   Anna$_j$, i   quali$_{i+j}$ d'altra   parte
      If C.   not loved more A.   the.M.PL which.PL DI.PREP.other part
      non si   erano mai   voluti veramente bene, una ragione c'era.
      not SI.CL were never loved really   well a   reason there.was
      'If Carlo was no longer in love with Anna, who had after all never really loved
      each other, there was a reason.' (Cinque 2008: 104; gloss and translation mine)

(678) Kim likes muffins$_i$, but Sandy prefers scones$_j$, which$_{i+j}$ they eat with jam.
      (Arnold 2007: 274)

C. Earlier stages of Portuguese

The same, however, is not true of earlier stages of Portuguese. As shown in (679)–(682), *o qual*-ARCs with split antecedents are documented in the history of Portuguese. In the corpora inspected in this research, two options are available: (1) the ARC may be introduced by the plural form of the relative pronoun, as shown in (679)–(680); (2) the relative pronoun may be followed by an additional internal head, which may be a conjoined noun phrase, as in (681)–(682).[47]

---

[47] Recall from §4.4.1 that if the internal head corresponds to a conjoined noun phrase, there is typically first conjunct agreement for phi-features between the relative pronoun and the noun in the first conjunct.

(679) Julgo   per sentença que este ẽprazamento valha   e   se
       judge.1SG by sentence that this emphyteusis be.valid.SBJV and SE.CL
       cũpra   como se   nesta carta_i cõtẽ,   e   no   vltimo
       fulfill.SBJV as   SE.CL in.this letter contains and in.the last
       consentimento do   dicto   prior e   convento_j faz   menção
       approval   of.the mentioned prior and convent   makes mention
       Aos   quaes_{i+j} dou   e   hey   por dada mynha autorydade.
       to.the.M.PL which.PL give.1SG and have.1SG as given my   authority
       'I order this contract to be valid and fulfilled, as stated in this letter and in the
       last approval of the aforementioned prior and convent, to which I give my
       authority.' (16th c., Martins 2001: 326)

(680) E   por séér   mays firme esta carta_i seelamos dos   nossos
       and to be.INF more firm this letter stamp.1PL DE.PREP.the our
       séélos e   outra tal_j. das   quaes_{i+j} deue téér   o
       stamps and other such DE.PREP.the.F.PL which.PL should have.INF the
       dicto   ffernã yohanes hũa e   a   dicta   dona outra.
       mentioned F.   Y.   one and the mentioned D.   other
       'And, to be irrevocable, we stamp this letter with our stamps and a duplicate
       of it, of which Ffernã Yohanes should have one and the aforementioned Dona
       another.' (13th c., Martins 2001: 350)

(681) per a   dicta   soprioresa ffuj logo   apresentada hũa carta
       by the mentioned vice-prioress was immediately shown   a   letter
       dEl   Rey_i [...] na   quall ffazya mençõ antre as outras cousas
       from.the king   in.the which made mention among the other things
       que Em Ella Era conthyudo hũa clausulla_j [...] a   quall   carta_i E
       that in it   was contained a   clause   the.F.SG which.SG letter and
       clausulla_j Em Ella conthyuda asy   amostrada
       clause   in it   contained this.way shown
       'the aforementioned vice-prioress immediately showed a letter from the king,
       in which it was mentioned, among other things, that a clause was contained
       in it; showing which letter and the clause contained in it (the aforementioned
       vice-prioress said...)' (15th c., Martins 2001: 488)

(682) E   pagam de   cada casal ou courella dezasete alqueires de
       and pay.3PL DE.PREP each hamlet or land   seventeen bushels   de
       pam_i [...] Item pagam mais em dinheiro_j [...] mjl   &
       bread   also pay.3PL more in money   one.thousand and

trezentos & trimta Reaaes. O qual pam_i & dinheiro_i
three.hundred and thirty r. the.M.SG which.SG bread and money
sam obrigados repartirem antre ssy.
are.3PL forced share.INF.3PL between them
'And they pay for each hamlet and land seventeen bushels of bread. They also pay in money one thousand three hundred and thirty *reais* [currency]. Which bread and money they are forced to share between them.' (15th/16th c., *CP*)

4.4.6 *Coordination of the wh-pronoun with another Determiner Phrase*

A. Contemporary European Portuguese

In contemporary *o qual*-ARCs, coordinating the wh-pronoun with another DP results in ungrammaticality (see (683)).[48]

(683) *O presidente elogiou o João, [o qual e a sua mulher]
the president praised the J. the.M.SG which.SG and the his wife
têm desenvolvido um óptimo trabalho naquela instituição.
have developed a great work in.that institution
'The president praised João, who, with his wife, has been developing great work in that institution.'

B. Cross-linguistic evidence

However, such coordination is possible in other contemporary languages, such as Italian and English. As reported in Cinque (2008), Italian *il quale*-ARCs and English ARCs may display coordination of the relativizer with a DP. This possibility is illustrated in (684) and (685) respectively.

(684) a. ?Gianni e Mario, [le rispettive consorti e i quali] non
G. and M. the respective wives and the.M.PL which.PL not
si erano mai potuti soffrire
SI.CL were never could endure
'Gianni and Mario, the respective wives and whom had never been able to stand each other...'

b. Gianni e Mario, [fra le rispettive consorti e
G. and M. between the respective wives and

---

[48] In §4.4.6, the fronted constituent containing the relative pronoun and the coordinated DP are in square brackets for ease of reading.

i   quali]   non c'era   mai   stato un grande affiatamento
the.M.PL which.PL not there.was never exist a   real   understanding
'Gianni and Mario, between their respective wives and whom there had
never been a real understanding...' (both Cinque 2008: 108; glosses and
translation in example b mine)

(685)   He recalled the name of the solicitor, [between whom and himself] there had
been occasional correspondence. (Jespersen 1949, from Cinque 2008: 115)

C. Earlier stages of Portuguese

O qual-ARCs displaying coordination of the wh-pronoun with a DP is found in
earlier stages of Portuguese, as illustrated in (686) and (687).

(686)   filho de hum seu filho chamado per nome dom Henrrique, o qual era lidimo
e, segundo conta a cronica, era o primeiro filho que o dito rei de Ungria ouve
'son of one of his sons called Dom Henrique, who was legitimate and,
according to the chronicle, was the first son that the king of Ungria had'
[O   qual   dom Henrrique e   hum seu tio,   irmão   de sua
the.M.SG which.SG D.   H.   and a   his uncle brother of his
madre], [...] se   vierão   a Castela aa   corte, donde o   dito
moher   SE.CL came.3PL to C.   to.the court where the mentioned
rei   dom Affonsso estava.
king D.   A.   was
'The which Dom Henrrique and his uncle, brother of his mother, came to
Castela, to the court, where the king Dom Affonsso was.' (15th c., *CP*)

(687)   [As   quais   razões e   outras muitas que o   padre.mestre Francisco
the.F.PL which.PL reasons and others many   that the father-master F.
lhe   dava], o   rei   gentio   de Bungo ouviu e   entendendo
him.CL gave   the king heathen of B.   heard and understand.GER
de   maneira que deu   em   pródigo com os pobres.
DE.PREP way   that became EM.PREP prodigal with the poor
'The heathen king of Bungo heard these and many other reasons that the
Father Master Francisco gave him; these words impacted on him in such a
way that he became prodigal, helping the poor.' (17th c., *CP*)

Similarly, *o qual* and a DP can occur as the object of prepositions within conjoined
PPs. See examples in (688) and (689).

(688)   pedindo-lhe   usasse   livremente dos   poderes que trazia
ask.GER-him.CL use.SBJV.3SG freely   DE.PREP.the powers that had
de   Sua Santidade, [com os   quais   e   com sua doutrina e
from His Holiness   with the.M.PL which.PL and with his doctrine and

exemplo] estava mui certo havia de   fazer   grandes serviços a
example was   very sure had   DE.PREP do.INF great   services to
Deus
God
'asking him to freely use the power that he was given by His Holiness; with
which and with his doctrine and example, he would certainly do great things
to serve God' (17th c., *CP*)

(689)   em que aponta   as conveniências de se   fazer   a   impressão antes
        in   that points.out the advantages   of SE.CL do.INF the printing   rather
        em Madrid que   em Lisboa, [com as   quais   e   com o   partido
        in M.   than in L.   with the.F.PL which.PL and with the advantage
        que oferece] eu me   conformei
        that proposes I   myself.CL resigned
        'in which he points out the advantages of doing the printing in Madrid rather
        than in Lisbon; with which, and with the conditions he proposed, I agreed'
        (17th c., *CP*)

Note that although there is a tendency for the occurrence of an additional internal
head in these contexts (see (686)–(688)), the internal head need not necessarily be
spelled out. This is illustrated in (689), where the wh-pronoun *as quais* lit. 'the.F.PL
which.PL' occurs per se within the first PP.

4.4.7 *Illocutionary force*

A. Contemporary European Portuguese

Contemporary *o qual*-ARCs can be declarative, even if the matrix is interrogative or
imperative. This is illustrated in (690) and (691). In both cases the ARC is declarative
and the matrix is either interrogative (see (690)) or imperative (see (691)).

(690)   Será   que o   João, com o   qual   pudemos sempre contar,
        be.FUT.3SG that the J.   with the which could.1PL always   count.INF
        estará   disponível desta   vez?
        be.FUT available   DE.PREP.this time
        'Will João, whom we have always counted on, be available this time?'

(691)   Telefona   aos   teus pais,   os   quais estarão   certamente
        phone.IMP.2SG to.the your parents the which be.FUT.3PL certainly
        disponíveis para te   ajudar!
        available   to   you.CL help.INF
        'Phone your parents, who will certainly be available to help you!'

The reverse does not hold, however. *O qual*-ARCs in CEP do not allow any clause types beyond the declarative, as shown by the unacceptability of the interrogative in (692) and the imperative in (693).

(692) *O único que te   apoiou   foi o João, ao   qual já
       the only that you.CL supported was the J.   to.the which already
       agradeceste devidamente por tudo o   que te   fez?
       thanked.2SG properly   by all the which you.CL did.3SG
       'The only person who supported you was John; have you already thanked
       him properly for everything he did for you?'

(693) *Acabou de   chegar   o João, ao   qual vai   já
       has.just DE.PREP arrive.INF the J.   to.the which go.IMP.2SG now
       oferecer uma bebida!
       offer.INF a   drink
       'João has just arrived; offer him a drink now!'

B. Cross-linguistic evidence

Unlike CEP, other contemporary languages allow the ARC to have a non-declarative illocutionary force. This is reported by Cinque (2008) for Italian *il quale*-ARCs (see (694)–(695)) and English ARCs (see (696)–(697)). In (694) and (696) the ARCs have interrogative force, whereas in (695) and (697) they have imperative force.

(694) L'unico che potrebbe è tuo padre, il quale potrà,   credi,   perdonarci
       the.only that can.COND is your father the which can.FUT think.2SG forgive.us.INF
       per   quello che abbiamo fatto?
       PER.PREP that   that have.1PL done
       'The only one who could is your father, who will be able to forgive us, do you
       think, for what we have done?' (Cinque 2008: 102; gloss and translation mine)

(695) Ci   sono poi i Rossi, per i quali, ti   prego,   cerca   di
       there are then the R.   for the which you.CL beg.1SG find.IMP DI.PREP
       trovare una sistemazione!
       find.INF a   accommodation
       'There are then the Rossis, for whom please try to find accommodation!'
       (Cinque 2008: 103; gloss and translation mine)

(696) a. There is then our father, by whom will we ever be forgiven for what we
          have done? (Cinque 2008: 111)
       b. It may clear up, in which case would you mind hanging the washing out?
          (Huddleston, Pullum, and Peterson, from Cinque 2008: 111)
       c. She may have her parents with her, in which case where am I going to
          sleep? (Huddleston, Pullum, and Peterson, from Cinque 2008: 111)

(697)   a. Please accept my check for $3.69, which find enclosed! (Martin 1972, from Cinque 2008: 112)

b. He said he'd show a few slides towards the end of his talk, at which point please remember to dim the lights! (Huddleston, Pullum, and Peterson 2002, from Cinque 2008: 112)

c. My friend, who God forbid you should ever meet,... (Werth 1974, from Cinque 2008: 112)

C. Earlier stages of Portuguese

Earlier stages of Portuguese, unlike CEP, allow *o qual*-ARCs with other clause types beyond the declarative. This is illustrated, for instance, in (698)–(700); in this case, the matrix is declarative and the ARC has imperative force.[49]

(698)   e posto que hũuas pallavras sejam contra as outras, e todas em soma contra-digam aa verdade, nós porém creemos que suas erradas rrazoões nom foi per malicia dos autores mas per inorancia da verdade
'and although some information is contradictory and clearly far from the truth, we nevertheless believe that the mistakes result not from the author's malice but rather from ignorance of the truth'
a   quall   sabee   que foi d'esta   guisa.
the which know.IMP.2PL that was DE.PREP.this way
'which know that was as follows' (15th c., Macchi 1975: 377)

(699)   ho prior do moesteiro de uilarinho do dicto arcebispado me emviou dizer que sentindo por proueito do dicto mosteiro queria enprazar como de feito enprazou a quebrada de penellas que o dicto mosteiro tem sita na frequesia de sam frausto a fernam correa escudeiro morador em a villa de guimarães e a sua molher mjcía fferrnandez
'the prior of the monastery of Uilarinho of the aforementioned archbishopric ordered me to say that, for the aforementioned monastery's benefit, he wanted to give in emphyteusis—as in fact he did—the land of Penellas, which the monastery has in the parish of Sam Frausto, to Fernam Correa, squire, inhabitant of Guimarães, and to his wife, Mjcia Fferrnandez'
Os quaees aJam   e   pessuam   a   dicta   quebrada Com
the which have.SBJV and possess.SBJV the mentioned land   with
todas suas casas   vinhas   soutos
all   its   houses vineyards thickets

---

[49] Note that in Portuguese, imperative sentences use the imperative mood for the second person. For other grammatical persons and for every negative imperative sentence, the subjunctive is used.

'The which (Fernam Correa and Mjcia Fferrnandez) have and possess the aforementioned land with all its houses, vineyards, thickets' (16th c., Martins 2001: 294)

(700)   Com o teor do qual mandei passar esta carta testemunhável ao dito Bento Henriques, à qual mando que seja dada tanta fé e autoridade, em juízo e fora dele, e onde quer que fôr apresentada, quanta por direito se lhe deve dar.
'I ordered to send this letter, with the content of the aforementioned document, to Bento Henriques; I order that this letter be given all the faith and authority recognized by law, within our jurisdiction or outside of it.'
O qual   uns   e   outros assim   cumpram   e   al   não
the which some and others as.such obey.sbjv.3pl and another not
façais.
make.sbjv.2pl
'The which all the intervening parties should obey and not make differently.'
(16th c., Pereira 1987: 44)

Furthermore, both the matrix and the ARC may have non-declarative force. See, for instance, example (701), in which the matrix and the ARC have imperative force.

(701)   E ponha ẽ corporall posissom della o dicto prioll de vilarinho. ou seu certo procurador scilicet per pedra terra telha altar ljuros calezes chaues vestimẽtas E per outros quaeesquer hornamentos e bẽes que em ella forem achados,
'And give the aforementioned prior of Vilarinho or his attorney the possession of the church, with its land, tile, altar, books, chalices, keys, vestments, and any other adornments and belongings that might be found there,'
dos   quaees lhe   seJa   fecto Enuentairo segundo Costume
of.the which him.cl be.sbjv made inventory   as   usual
'of which should be made an inventory, as usual...' (15th c., Martins 2001: 270)

4.4.8 Coordinator

A. Contemporary European Portuguese

In CEP, *o qual*-ARCs cannot be preceded by a coordinator. The example given in (702) illustrates this point: the sentence becomes ungrammatical if the ARC is preceded by the coordinator *e* 'and'.[50]

---

[50] In §4.4.8, the coordinator preceding ARCs is in bold for ease of reading.

(702) Foi detectado um erro grave na prova de química,(*e) para o
was detected a error serious in.the exam of chemistry and to the
qual ainda não foi apresentada nenhuma explicação.
which yet not was provided no explanation
'A serious error was detected in the chemistry exam, for which no explanation has been provided yet.'

B. Cross-linguistic evidence

Interestingly, ARCs in English may occasionally exhibit a coordinator before the
relative pronoun, as shown in (703)–(706); in these examples, the ARCs are introduced by the coordinator *and* (see (703)–(705)) or *but* (see (706)).

(703) and the new capitol is here, of course, too, built five years before she was
born, **and** which she has always associated with learning Latin. (*COCA*)

(704) "I'm inept—how do you like that word?—at everything but my work and
getting to and from it," was how he liked to phrase it whenever she asked him
to do a chore, **and** which she said was his alibi for doing nothing around the
house. (*COCA*)

(705) Well, Pickering gave me an earful, not directed at me, **and** which I much
enjoyed. (*COCA*)

(706) Eventually I found one willing to sell me a camel at what would have been an
exorbitant price under ordinary circumstances, **but** which I was all too
willing to pay. (*COCA*)

On the basis of English data, it is possible to conclude that the coordinator may show
up: (1) if the nominal antecedent is already modified (see example (706), in which the
antecedent *price* is modified by *exorbitant*);[51] and (2) when no such a modifier is
present (see (704), which involves an ARC with a non-nominal antecedent).

---

[51] Beatrice Santorini (p.c.) reports to me that earlier stages of English behave in a similar fashion.
Consider, for instance, the sequences in (i)–(iii), from Early Modern English (1500–1700); in these
examples, the ARC is preceded by a coordinator (and the antecedent is modified by one or more
adjectives).

(i) and hopes the Pope will not any longer delay gratifying him in so reasonable a request, **and** which
his Majesty desires so earnestly from his Holinesse (17th/18th c., *PPCEME*)

(ii) but the greater power and working of wine may be spied more plainly in colde and withered bodies,
and wherein is lesse naturall heat, as in olde men, and in such as are amended of their sicknesse
(16th c., *PPCEME*)

(iii) That had been too wild and extravagant a supposition, **and** which it is likely in those days had never
entered into any mans mind. (17th c., *PPCEME*)

C. Earlier stages of Portuguese

Earlier stages of Portuguese pattern with English in the possibility of having *o qual*-ARCs preceded by a coordinator; see (707)–(709).

(707)   custumarõ dauer   e   ouuerom no   dicto   Monsteiro
used.3PL   DE.PREP.have.INF and had.3PL   in.the mentioned monastery
bõa   raçom e   mãtijmẽto de pam   aluo boroa.   carne e   vĩho
good ration and provisions of bread white corn.bread meat and wine
e   o   qual   mãtijmẽto os   Priores [...] auiã e   som theudos
and the which provisions the priors   had and are   compelled
de   dar   ao   dicto   conuẽto
DE.PREP give.INF to.the mentioned convent
'they had in the aforementioned monastery good ration and provisions of white bread, corn bread, meat, and wine; and which provisions the priors had and were compelled to give to the aforementioned convent' (14th c., Martins 2001: 215)

(708)   me   outorgo   por biẽ pagada deste   dicto   herdamẽto &
me.CL declare.1SG as   well paid   of.this mentioned land   and
cousas que aqui en esta carta som en ella escriptos &   cõteudos.
things that here in this letter are in it   written   and contained
Et   o   qual   herdamẽto &   cousas sobredictas hã   jazença
and the which land   and things aforesaid   have ±location
no   logar que chama   de Curraes
in.the place that call.3SG of C.
'I declare that I was paid for the aforementioned land and things referred to in this letter. And which land and things aforesaid are located in a place called Curraes...' (13th c., *DCMP*)

(709)   E   nos [...] outorgamos sse formos   contra este prazo   en
and we   declare   if   go.FUT.SBJV.3PL against this ±document in
todo ou en parte que peytemos   aos   sobreditos
all   or in part   that pay.SBJV.1PL to.the aforementioned.persons
cen   mr uelhos de pẽa.   E   a   qual   pẽa   pagada ou nõ,
one.hundred m. old   of penalty and the which penalty paid   or not
este prazo   e   as   cousas que neel sson cõtehudas fiquen   en
this ±document and the things that in.it are   contained stay.SBJV in
ssa firmydõe.
its firmness
'And we declare that, if we go against this document, we must pay to the aforementioned persons one hundred *maravedis* [currency] as penalty. Nevertheless, this document and the things contained in it should be valid independently of the payment of this penalty.' (14th c., *DCMP*)

TABLE 4.5 **Properties of *o qual*-appositive relatives: Different stages of Portuguese**

	CEP	Earlier stages of Portuguese
Internal head	−	+
Generalized extraposition	−	+
Generalized pied-piping	−	+
Clausal antecedent	−	+
Split antecedents	−	+
Coordination of the wh-pronoun with another DP	−	+
Non-declarative illocutionary force	−	+
Coordinator preceding the wh-pronoun	−	+

4.4.9 *Summary*

I have shown that *o qual*-ARCs in CEP behave differently from *o qual*-ARCs in earlier stages of Portuguese with respect to a number of syntactic properties. The contrasting properties analyzed thus far are summarized in Table 4.5. Here a minus indicates that *o qual*-ARCs may display the relevant properties and a plus indicates that they may not.

Additionally, I have demonstrated that Italian *il quale*-ARCs and English ARCs pattern with *o qual*-ARCs in earlier stages of Portuguese with respect to the same syntactic properties.

4.5 Deriving the contrasting properties

The main claim of this section is that the contrasting properties of *o qual*-ARCs can be derived from a dual approach to the syntax of ARCs (see §4.2). Concretely, I submit that both the specifying coordination analysis (De Vries 2006b) and the raising analysis (Kayne 1994; Bianchi 1999) may derive ARCs (see §§1.3.2.5B and 1.3.2.5C respectively). However, the two structures may not be instantiated in all languages nor in all stages of the same language.

In §§4.5.1–8 I provide an explanation for the contrasting properties of *o qual*-ARCs in CEP and in earlier stages of Portuguese, which is summarized in (710).

(710) Dual approach to syntax of *o qual*-ARCs in Portuguese[52]

    a. In earlier stages of Portuguese, *o qual*-ARCs are derived from the specifying coordination structure (and possibly by the raising structure).

---

[52] Note that the formulation in (710) leaves open the possibility of having ARCs derived from raising both in earlier stages of Portuguese and in CEP (see §4.6.1).

b. In CEP, *o qual*-ARCs do not involve specifying coordination, being derived from head raising.

I postpone the discussion of cross-linguistic contrasts until §4.6.

4.5.1 *Internal head*

O qual-ARCs in CEP differ from *o qual*-ARCs in earlier stages of Portuguese in that they disallow an additional internal head (see §4.4.1). Such a contrast can be easily explained under the dual approach to the syntax of ARCs displayed in (710).

Why cannot *o qual*-ARCs in CEP take an additional internal head? According to the raising analysis of relative clauses, the head NP originates as the complement of the relative determiner D_{rel}, as represented in (711). Thus, there is simply no room for an additional internal head because the only NP position available is already filled with the visible head.

(711) $[_{DP}$ D $[_{CP}$ NP$_i$ $[_{DP_{rel}}$ *o qual* t$_i]_k$ C $[_{IP}...t_k...]]]$

Why can *o qual*-ARCs in earlier stages of Portuguese take an additional internal head? Under the specifying coordination account, there are two NP positions in the appositive construction: the external antecedent in the first conjunct and the NP position within the second conjunct, as shown in (712). Because the antecedent is base-generated in the first conjunct, the NP in the second conjunct may be spelled out as an additional internal head.

(712) $[_{CoP}$ $[_{DP}$ *antecedent*$]$ Co $[_{DP}$ D $[_{CP}$ $[_{DP_{rel}}$ *o qual* $[_{NP}$ *internal head*$]]_k$ C $[_{IP}...t_k...]]]]$

Furthermore, the structure in (712) also explains why there may not be categorial, phonological, and semantic identity between the internal head and the antecedent. The eventual non-categorial identity between the antecedent (which may be non-nominal) and the internal head (which must be nominal) can be explained by the structure in (712): regardless of the category of the constituent at which the second conjunct is attached, the internal head is always nominal because it is the complement of D_{rel}. Moreover, nothing forces phonological or semantic identity between both elements because there is no movement chain between the antecedent and the internal head.

4.5.2 *Extraposition*

As already mentioned in §4.4.2, *o qual*-ARC extraposition is possible in all periods of the history of Portuguese. However, the restrictions on extraposition are less constrained in earlier stages of Portuguese than in CEP. I submit that this contrast can be explained by the hypothesis in (713).

(713) Dual approach to *o qual*-ARC extraposition in Portuguese

    a. In earlier stages of Portuguese: (1) *o qual*-ARCs are derived from speci-fying coordination; and (2) extraposition of *o qual*-ARCs is generated by specifying coordination plus ellipsis (involving attachment at different levels of projection).

    b. In CEP: (1) *o qual*-ARCs are derived from head raising; and (2) extra-posed *o qual*-ARCs do not involve specifying coordination plus ellipsis (being instead derived from stranding).

From (713), it becomes clear that there is a strict correlation between the syntax of ARCs and the syntax of ARC-extraposition. In earlier stages of Portuguese, *o qual*-ARCs already involve specifying coordination (see (714)). Thus, extraposition requires two distinct coordination-style structures (see (715)): a specifying coordination struc-ture to derive ARCs (CoP_2) and an additional specifying coordination plus ellipsis structure to derive extraposition (CoP_1), as proposed by De Vries (2002: 279).

(714) $[_{CoP}$ DP Co $[_{DP}$ D $[_{CP}$ [*o qual* (*internal head*)$]_k$ C $[_{IP}\ldots t_k\ldots]]]]$

(715) $[_{CoP1}$ $[_{XP1}\ldots$ *antecedent* YP] $[$Co $[_{XP2}$ $[_{CoP2}$ $[_{DP1}$ ~~*antecedent*~~$]$
            Co $[_{DP2}$ D $[_{CP}$ *o qual* (*internal head*)$]_k$ C $[_{IP}\ldots t_k\ldots]$ ~~YP~~$]]]]]$

In turn, *o qual*-ARCs in CEP are derived from head raising plus covert IP movement (see Kayne 1994; Bianchi 1999), as in (716) (repeated from (77a)). The same basic structure is involved in extraposed *o qual*-ARCs: the antecedent is base-generated inside the ARC and undergoes leftward movement, stranding the ARC in situ, as schematically represented in (717).

(716) $[_{DP}$ D $[_{CP}$ $[_{DP_{rel}}$ NP$_j$ $[D_{rel}$ t$_j$ $]_i]$ C $[_{IP}\ldots t_i]]]$ (*pre-LF*)

(717)

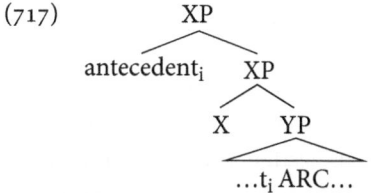

Although the restrictions on *o qual*-ARC extraposition deserve more detailed study (parallel to that developed for RRC-extraposition in Ch. 3), I will show that the dual approach outlined in (713) can derive the contrasting properties of *o qual* ARC-extraposition (see §4.4.2), which I will consider in turn.[53]

---

[53] I will only provide a brief explanation of the restrictions on *o qual*-ARC extraposition. For more technical details, see Ch. 3 (§§3.4.2 and 3.5.2).

A. The definiteness effect

Under the raising analysis, strong noun phrases are not constituents (excluding the ARC) and consequently cannot undergo leftward movement, stranding the *o qual*-ARC in its base position.

Under the specifying coordination analysis, however, strong noun phrases are detached from the relative clause and base-generated in the first conjunct of the coordinate structure. There is simply no movement chain between the antecedent and the position of the gap inside the relative CP; thus, no restriction on movement applies. This is illustrated in the simplified structure given in (718), where the extraposed *o qual*-ARC takes a strong noun phrase as antecedent (*o dicto herdamento* 'the aforementioned land').

(718) [$_{IP}$ ficou [$_{CoP1}$ [$_{VP}$ [$_{DP}$ o   dicto   herdamento] [$_{PP}$ ao   dicto
        went   the mentioned land   to.the mentioned
        Moesteyro de   suso   nomeado]] [Co
        monastery DE.PREP above mentioned
        [$_{VP}$ [$_{CoP2}$ [$_{DP}$ o̶ d̶i̶c̶t̶o̶   h̶e̶r̶d̶a̶m̶e̶n̶t̶o̶] [Co [$_{DP}$ D [$_{CP}$ [$_{DP}$ o   qual
                      the mentioned land   the which
        herdamento   est...]]]]] [$_{PP}$ a̶o̶   d̶i̶c̶t̶o̶   M̶o̶e̶s̶t̶e̶y̶r̶o̶ d̶e̶
        land   is   to.the mentioned   monastery DE.PREP
        s̶u̶s̶o̶   n̶o̶m̶e̶a̶d̶o̶]]]]]
        above   mentioned

B. Pre-verbal positions

Given the possibility of attaching the relative clause at different levels of projection, the specifying coordination analysis plus ellipsis predicts that an extraposed *o qual*-ARC can take any constituent as antecedent. This would be derived thus: when the antecedent is a subject in a pre-verbal position, the second conjunct would be attached at the IP-level projection; when the antecedent is a topic, the second conjunct would be attached at the Topic-level projection (assuming a split CP system). However, the actuality is not so simple because in the historical data considered thus far, extraposed *o qual*-ARCs can take pre-verbal subjects, but not topics, as antecedents.

B1. Pre-verbal subjects

The analysis of *o qual*-ARCs extraposition from a pre-verbal subject is schematically represented in (719).

(719) [$_{\text{CoP}}$ [$_{\text{IP}}$ toda a   outra cidade era devassa] [Co
                  all   the other city   was opened
          [$_{\text{IP}}$ [$_{\text{CoP}}$ [$_{\text{DP}}$toda a   outra   cidade] [Co [$_{\text{DP}}$ na   quall moravam muitas
                      all   the other   city   in.the which lived   many
          gentes]]] era   devassa]]]
          people was opened

Note, however, that according to the Interpretative Principle in (720) (adapted from (426)), extraposition from pre-verbal subjects should not be allowed because a constituent in [Spec, IP] can be semantically interpreted as topic or non-topic.

(720) Interpretative Principle
        The antecedent of an extraposed *o qual*-ARC must occur in a position non-ambiguously interpreted as non-topic (in Kuroda's 2005 sense).

In line with the proposal put forward for Chapter 3, I tentatively submit that CEP and earlier stages of Portuguese may resort to different strategies to resolve the ambiguity expressed by the Interpretative Principle. Although in CEP the ambiguity associated with [Spec, IP] is resolved syntactically and prosodically (through subject inversion), in earlier stages of Portuguese it may be resolved by prosody alone. In this case, a constituent in [Spec, IP] may be unambiguously interpreted as non-topic if it is prosodically marked by pitch accent. Further research is necessary in this domain to warrant the validity of this hypothesis.

B2. Restriction on extraposition from other pre-verbal positions

In the corpus of historical Portuguese inspected thus far, *o qual*-ARC extraposition can take place from preposed foci (see §4.4.2.3B2). In this case, the coordinate structure involves coordination of a dedicated functional projection (say, Focus) of the left periphery. Such a configuration satisfies the Interpretative Principle presented in (720) because the position occupied by the preposed constituent is non-ambiguously interpreted as non-topic.

   In turn, extraposed *o qual*-ARCs with a topic as antecedent are not present in the corpus under consideration. Such a restriction follows from the Interpretative Principle in (720): under a split-CP system, a constituent in [Spec, TopicP] is non-ambiguously interpreted as topic.

C. Prepositional phrases

Under the raising analysis, prepositional phrases are not constituents (excluding the ARC) and consequently cannot undergo leftward movement stranding the *o qual*-ARC in its base position. Under the specifying coordination analysis, such a restriction does not hold because there is no movement chain between the antecedent and the position of the gap inside the relative CP.

D. Extraposition across conjuncts

O qual-ARCs derived from specifying coordination can be attached at different projection levels. Therefore, they can be directly coordinated with the antecedent (see (721a)) or with a multiple coordinate structure including the antecedent in the first conjunct; see (721b), which schematically represents the coordinate structure in (722), repeated from (616).[54]

(721) a. DP Co [$_{DP}$ ARC]
      b. (DP$_1$ Co DP$_2$ Co DP$_3$) Co [$_{DP}$ ARC]

(722) testemunhas que Eram presemtes llopo martjz orjuez e   alluaro
      witnesses that were present L. M. jeweller and A.
      gomcalluez barbeJro e   bento velloso ao   quall llopo marfiz a
      G.   barber   and B.   V.   to.the which L.   M.   the
      dita   catarjna periz rrogou que asynasse   por   sy e
      mentioned C.   P.   asked that sign.SBJV.3SG POR.PREP him and
      por   ella
      POR.PREP her
      'witnesses that were present: Llopo Martjz, a jeweler, Alluaro Gomcalluez, a barber, and Bento Velloso, the which Llopo Martĩz the aforementioned Catarjna Periz asked to sign in her place' (16th c., Martins 2001: 307)

In contrast, *o qual*-ARCs in CEP are derived from head raising, which represents the relative CP as a complement of an external determiner. Under this approach, the configuration in (723) is not allowed because the external determiner and the NP head do not form a constituent excluding the ARC.

(723) *DP$_i$ Co DP Co DP [$_{DP}$ t$_i$ ARC]

E. Extraposition across discourse

In earlier stages of Portuguese, *o qual*-ARCs may refer to an antecedent across the discourse, as in (724), repeated from (622). This configuration has been referred to in

---

[54] As for the referential link between the ARC and its antecedent, see §1.3.2.5B(b)).

the literature by different labels, for instance, *relatif de liaison, connecting relative,* and *relative junction* (see §4.4.2.3).

(724) —Senhor, chegou ally o allmocadẽ, e pareçe-me que diz que lhe he neçessario
de vos fallar llogo amte que amanheça.
'—Sir, the Moorish captain arrived there and it seems to me he is saying
he needs to speak to you promptly, before it dawns.'
O   qual   o   comde mamdou que viesse.
the which the count   ordered   that come.sbjv
'The which (Moorish captain) the count ordered to come.' (15th c., Brocardo
1997: 296)

It is not completely clear whether the clause introduced by *o qual* is syntactically connected. Bianchi (1999: 152) suggests that in these contexts there is simply no relative construction involved. Under that view, *o qual* is used as an anaphoric pronoun or determiner, and the clause is either coordinate to the main clause or parenthetical (see §4.2.3 for further details).

De Vries (2002), commenting on the sentence from German displayed in (725), emphasizes the apparently ambiguous status of the construction. On the one hand, the second sentence in (725) is verb-final, which is the clause structure of subordinate clauses in German. However, its intonation pattern differs from that in ARC constructions, and perhaps may equal the one found in main clauses. Equating these properties, De Vries (2002: 66) concludes, "The relative junction is a special case of a more general pattern whereby, for stylistic reasons, the junction between a main clause and a subordinate clause looks like one between main clauses."

(725) Dieser Wagen ist nicht mehr   verbesserungsfähig. Weshalb
this   car   is not   any.more improvable   for.which.reason
wir ihn unverändert weiterbauen.
we it   unchanged   further.build
'This car cannot be improved any further. Which is why we continue to build
it without changes.' (Lehmann 1984, from De Vries 2002: 66; translation mine)

Cinque (2008: 117–19), in turn, claims that the head and the ARC may be separated across the discourse in *non-integrated* ARCs (see §4.2.3). Assuming Kayne's LCA to hold for Discourse Grammar as well, the author argues that linear precedence in a discourse must also reflect asymmetric c-command. Under this view, a linearly preceding main sentence is placed in the specifier of an (empty) head, which, in turn, takes the main sentence as its complement (726).[55]

---

[55] The structure represented in (726) is instantiated in a sequence such as *John is no longer here. He left at noon.* (Cinque 2008: 118).

(726)

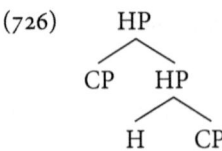

Another hypothesis is that a DP is placed in the specifier of an (empty) head, taking a sentence as its complement (727).[56]

(727)

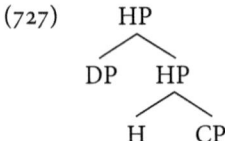

Cinque (2008) takes the configurations in (726) and (727) to underlie the non-integrated ARCs, (726) for the contexts of the *relatif de liaison*, and (727) for the anaphoric relations within a sentence.

In the present study, I propose that the so-called *relatif de liaison* introduces, in fact, an ARC that involves coordination at the discourse level (as opposed to the sentence level). Note that the same is true of regular coordination (see Matos 2003: 576), as in *She said, "Aren't you even curious?" And he looked at her with a strange expression on his face.*

This idea can be implemented by assuming that the discourse unit that contains the antecedent surfaces in the first conjunct of a specifying coordinate structure, while the *o qual*-ARC surfaces in the second conjunct. Under this analysis, a sentence like (724) corresponds to the simplified structure in (728).[57]

(728)

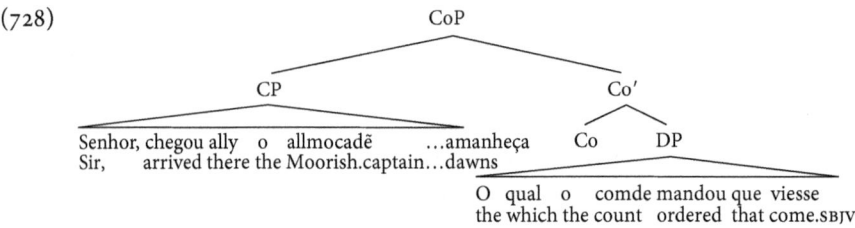

---

[56] Recall from §4.2.3 that this configuration is found in sequences such as *A pink shirt? I will never wear any such thing in my life!* (Cinque 2008: 118).

[57] In the structural representation given in (728), I assume, following Moro (2003), that vocative phrases (such as *Senhor* 'Sir' in (724)) are located in the CP domain. Under Moro's (2003) proposal, vocative phrases are hosted in the specifier of the head projected by a Voc feature governing Force. Hence, the split Comp field is expanded thus:

$C° = ... Voc° > Force° > (Top° > Foc° > Top°) > Fin° ...$

Given that the split CP has no direct bearing on the analysis at hand, in (728) I adopt a non-split representation, labeling the first conjunct simply as CP.

Observe that, given the E-type character of the referential link between the ARC and the antecedent, no adjacency requirement holds between the antecedent and the ARC (see §1.3.2.5B(b)). The abstract pronoun heading the second conjunct is able to pick up the right antecedent in the first conjunct, similarly to how definite anaphoric or demonstrative pronouns refer to a phrase across discourse.

Obviously, the *relatif de liaison* is not available in CEP because the raising analysis cannot derive a sentence like (724): it would involve leftward movement of the antecedent into a different utterance.

4.5.3 Pied-piping

In §4.4.3 I have shown that pied-piping in contemporary *o qual*-ARCs is subject to constraints that appear not to hold in earlier stages of Portuguese. The contrasts are summarized in Table 4.6 (repeated from Table 4.4).

The explanation I provide for these contrasts relies on the assumption that the restrictions on pied-piping found in relative clauses result from restrictions on NP movement.[58]

Let me first consider *o qual*-ARCs in CEP, which are derived from the raising analysis. Recall that one of the basic tenets of the raising analysis is that the head NP is generated inside the relative clause as a complement of D_{rel}. Imagine now that D_{rel} is embedded in a PP, as in (729).

(729) $[_{DP}$ D $[_{CP}$ $[_{PP}$ NP_i $[_{PP}$ P $[_{DP_{rel}}$ DP_{rel} $t_i]]]$ $[C$ $[_{IP}\dots t_j\dots]]]]$

In this case, the wh-movement does not only affect the constituent that bears the wh-feature (D_{rel}) but instead targets a phrase that properly contains the maximal projection of that item (the PP in (729)). But how is this configuration derived?

TABLE 4.6 **Restrictions on pied-piping: Different stages of Portuguese**

	DPs	APs	CPs	AdvPs	PPs	Partitives
CEP	−	−	−	+	+	+
Earlier stages of Portuguese	+	?	+	+	+	+

---

[58] The explanation for the pied-piping found in other structures (e.g. wh-exclamatives, questions) is beyond the scope of this book. Note, however, that the rationale behind my proposal is that the mechanism of *feature percolation* (see Chomsky 1973; Webelhuth 1992; and Grimshaw 2000; among others) applies irrespective of the categories involved. Different restrictions on pied-piping result from the different syntactic environment in which pied-piping takes place.

The standard answer to this question is that there is a mechanism, called *feature percolation*, that spreads the wh-features of the wh-word up to higher phrases. This proposal refers back to Chomsky (1973) and has been revived by many authors, such as Webelhuth (1992) and Grimshaw (2000). In addition to explaining the nature of this mechanism, these studies are concerned with identifying and explaining the restrictions on percolation. Among the questions that arise in this respect are: What prevents wh-feature percolation from occurring freely? Why is it sensitive to the category of the phrases involved?

This line of research does not, however, provide any clue to explain the contrast found in the history of Portuguese: if the same phrasal categories are involved, the same restrictions on percolation should hold in CEP and in earlier stages of Portuguese, which is contrary to the actual situation.

Additional evidence for the idea that feature percolation cannot be the whole story is provided by the fact that pied-piping exhibits construction-specific variation. For instance, pied-piping of DPs and CPs is possible in English ARCs but not in RRCs, as shown in (730)–(731).

(730)   a. Most students are interested in Prof. Rotestern, [the security file on whom] the government won't release.

       b. *Most students are interested in any professor [a security file on whom] the government won't release. (both Emonds 1985: 304)

(731)   a. Egbert, [α to hire whom] would be a real scoop, . . .

       b. *four consultants [to hire whom] would be a real scoop . . . (both Heck 2008: 168)

Such contrasts seem to suggest that the restrictions on pied-piping cannot be simply derived by the restrictions on percolation. Pied-piping appears to be sensitive to the type of relative clause involved; therefore, the syntax of relativization might play an important role in this story.

The hypothesis that I want to put forward here is that percolation exists (or some equivalent of it, as is the case of *feature movement* proposed by De Vries 2006a) and that it applies irrespective of the categories/distance involved. Restrictions on pied-piping are, then, derived not from the restrictions on percolation but rather from the syntactic environment in which pied-piping occurs.

With these ideas in mind, let me show how the raising analysis can explain the restrictions on pied-piping found in CEP. As already mentioned in §1.3.2.4B, the raising analysis involves two basic movement steps: movement of the operator phrase DP_{rel} to the CP domain and subsequent movement of the head NP to the left of D_{rel}. The latter movement usually targets [Spec, DP_{rel}]. However, when DP_{rel} is embedded in another constituent, the head NP targets the highest specifier position within the pied-piped constituent.

The hypothesis I would like to suggest is that the movement of the head within the pied-piped constituent is subject to the Lexical Projection (LP) Condition in (732).

(732) The LP-Intervention Condition on pied-piped constituents[59]
Within pied-piped constituents, NP movement to the highest specifier position cannot cross LPs.

This is illustrated in (733). In (733a), NP movement is allowed because the head does not cross any LP on its path to the highest specifier position; in contrast, in (733b), NP movement is blocked by an intervening LP.

(733) a. Intervening Functional Projection (FP)   b. Intervening LP

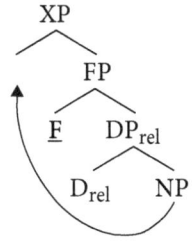   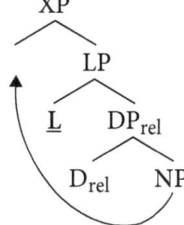

NP movement: *OK*   NP movement: *BLOCKED*
(no intervening LP)   (intervening LP)

Under the standard assumption that N, A, and V are lexical projections, the restrictions found in CEP can be derived from the LP-Intervention Condition in (732). Observe the schematic representation given in (734), where the constituents to be pied-piped are a DP ((734a)), an AP ((734b)), and a CP ((734c)).[60] The examples are from CEP.

---

[59] The idea that the intervention of lexical heads is relevant for constraining pied-piping has already been put forth in the literature by different authors; see Grimshaw (2000), among others. Here, I am inspired by the LP-Intervention Condition proposed by Cable (2007). Although I do not wish to review that proposal here, the basic idea is that wh-words are rendered interpretable through the help of a Q-particle, which heads its own projection—QP—and c-commands the wh-word. Hence, restrictions on pied-piping result from the fact that in some languages, an agreement relationship must be established between a Q-particle and the wh-word. According to Cable, languages showing more limited pied-piping structures are the ones that show Q/Wh-agreement. In technical terms, the Q-interpretable, unvalued instance of Q undergoes agreement with the wh-word, which has a valued instance of Q. The most important constraint that holds in these languages is the LP-Intervention Principle, whereby agreement holds between Q/Wh only if no lexical head intervenes between them.

[60] To keep the representation simple, in (734) I abstract away from movement of the head NP to possible intermediate landing sites.

(734)   a. Pied-piping of DP
        *(O) Pedro, a mulher do qual. . .
        lit. (the) P. the wife of.the which

                                   b. Pied-piping of AP
                                    *(O) João, admirador do qual. . .
                                    lit. (the) J. admirer of.the which

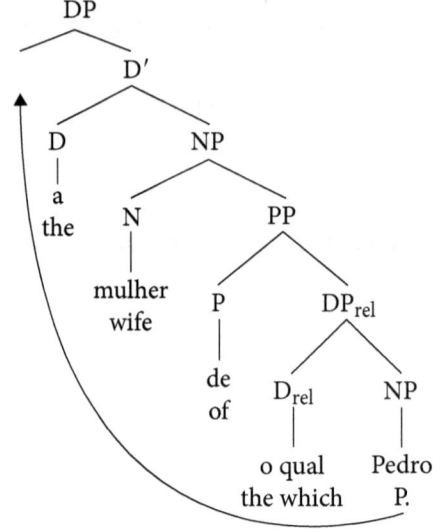

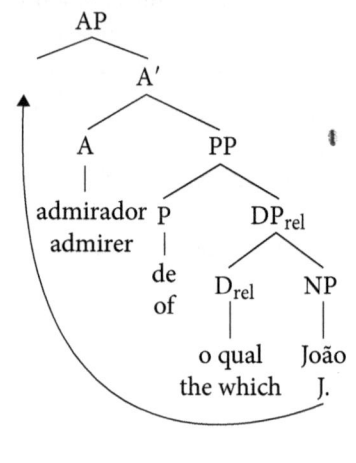

NP movement: *BLOCKED*
(intervening LP: N)

                                    NP movement: *BLOCKED*
                                    (intervening LP: A)

     c. Pied-piping of CP
      *(os) documentos, para analisar os quais. . .
     lit. (the) documents, to analyze the which

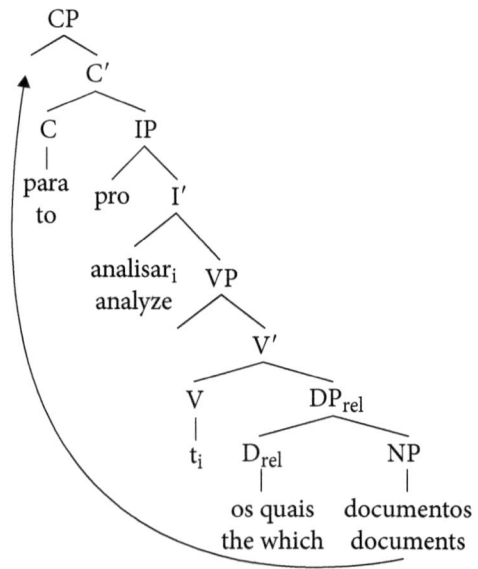

NP movement: *BLOCKED*
(intervening LP: V)

This approach explains the restrictions on pied-piping found in CEP. As shown in (734), pied-piping of DPs, APs, and CPs in CEP is blocked by the LP-Intervention Condition in (732) because the head crosses a lexical projection (N, A, V) on its path to the highest specifier position.

Consider now the pied-piping of PPs and AdvPs (see (735)). The LP-Intervention Condition straightforwardly derives the pied-piping of these phrasal categories: the head NP on its path to the highest specifier position only crosses functional projections. If a PP is involved (see (735a)), the head crosses D_{rel} and P; if an AdvP is involved (735b), the head crosses D_{rel}, P, and Adv.

(735)

a. Pied-piping of PP   b. Pied-piping of AdvP
(este) livro, no qual . . .   (o) pedido . . . relativamente ao qual
lit. (this) book, in.the which   lit. (the) request relatively to.the which

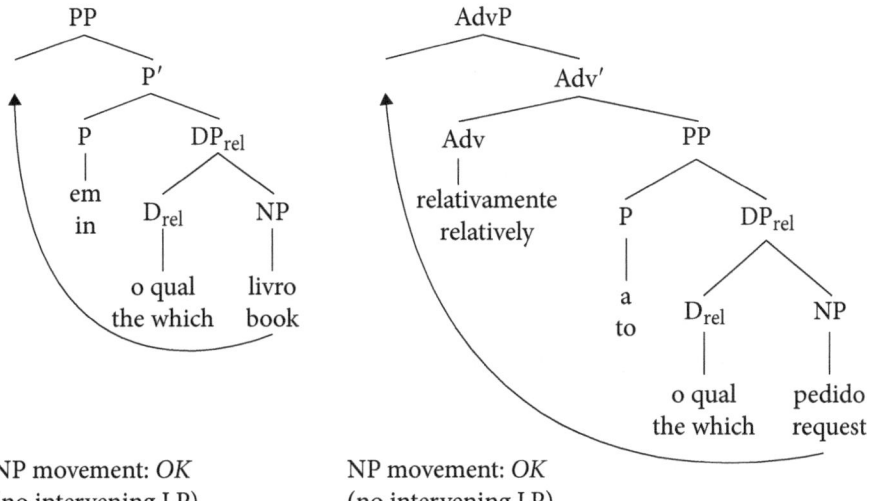

NP movement: *OK*   NP movement: *OK*
(no intervening LP)   (no intervening LP)

Additional evidence for this theory of pied-piping comes from the unexpected pied-piping of partitive constructions found in CEP. Recall from §4.4.3 that, unlike DPs, partitive construction may get pied-piped in *o qual*-ARCs, as shown in (736) (repeated from (628)).

(736)   Este acto terá   levado o   industrial   a   disparar três   tiros,
        this act   have.FUT led   the industrialist to fire.INF   three shots
        [QP dois dos   quais] terão   atingido o   filho no   abdómen.
            two of.the which have.FUT hit   the son   in.the stomach
        'This act might have led the industrialist to fire three shots, two of which
        might have hit his son in the stomach.' (*CRPC*)

Again, this possibility is derived from the approach adopted here: if pied-piping of partitive constructions is involved, the head only crosses functional projections on its way to the highest specifier position. See (737), where the head crosses D_{rel}, P, and Q.[61]

(737)   Pied-piping of partitive constructions
(três) tiros, dois dos quais . . .
lit. (three) shots, two of.the which

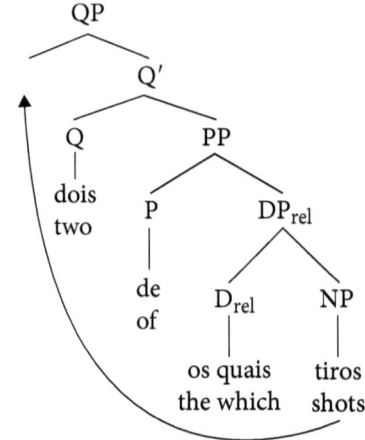

NP movement: *OK*
(no intervening LP)

In sum, the restrictions imposed by the LP-Intervention Condition explain why PPs and AdvPs can get pied-piped in CEP, whereas DPs, APs, and clausal constituents cannot. Note that ultimately, this amounts to saying that the limitations on relative-clause pied-piping follow from a restriction on NP movement.

Consider now the situation in historical Portuguese. Recall from §4.4.3 that pied-piping of DPs, PPs, AdvPs, partitive structures, and clausal constituents occurs in earlier stages of Portuguese. Let me consider how the broader possibilities for pied-piping can be derived by the specifying coordination analysis.

---

[61] In (737), I assume, along with López (2000), that partitive constructions: (1) do not involve an empty nominal head; and (2) involve a syntactic structure in which the quantifier directly selects a PP. One of the most convincing arguments provided by López (2000) in favor of this analysis is that it is not possible to find a counterpart of the null nominal head in partitive constructions (*several (*ones/units) of the students*); by contrast, elided pro-forms can always have an overt counterpart (*several (pictures) made in Canada*). It should be mentioned, however, that the earlier hypotheses proposing a structure of the type: [NP [QP several] [N' ø [PP of the students]]] (see Jackendoff 1977 and Milner 1978, among others) are also compatible with the approach developed here; in this case, it would only be necessary to assume that empty N is not a blocker for NP movement.

Under the raising analysis, the head is base-generated as the complement of D_{rel} and then moves to the highest position within the pied-piped constituent. Recall from the previous discussion that this movement is subject to the LP-Intervention Condition. In the specifying coordination analysis, however, the NP head is null in the second conjunct because the overt antecedent is base-generated in the first conjunct. Proposing a minor change to the basic scheme of specifying coordination presented in §1.3.2.5B(b) (see (45)), I hypothesize that, similarly to the configuration of the ARC with an additional internal head (see (61)), the null NP in the second conjunct stays in the complement position of D_{rel} (see (738)), checking the phi-features of the external D (and DP_{rel}) via Agree. No restriction on pied-piping holds simply because there is no movement of the abstract NP head to the highest specifier position within the pied-piped constituent.

(738)

$[_{CoP}$ DP   Co $[_{DP}$ D $[_{CP}$ $[_{DP}$ D $[_{NP}$N $[_{PP}$ P $[_{DP_{rel}}$ D_{rel} NP]]]]$]_j$ C $[_{IP}..t_j...]]]]$

    o Pedro   Ø   a   mulher   de   o qual Ø

4.5.4 Clausal antecedent

In §4.4.4, I have shown that *o qual*-ARCs in earlier stages of Portuguese, contrary to *o qual*-ARCs in CEP, can take a clausal antecedent. This contrast can be explained straightforwardly by the dual approach to the syntax of *o qual*-ARCs put forward in (710).

Why cannot *o qual*-ARCs in CEP take clausal antecedents? On the raising structure, the NP head originates as the complement of the relative determiner D_{rel}; consequently, it has to be a nominal projection (see (739)).

(739) $[_{DP}$ D $[_{CP}$ $\underline{NP_i}$ $[o\ qual\ t_i]_k$ C $[_{IP}...t_k...]]]$

Why can *o qual*-ARCs in earlier stages of Portuguese take clausal antecedents? On the specifying coordination account, the visible antecedent (i.e. XP in (740)) originates in the first conjunct. Hence, the second conjunct containing the ARC may be attached at different levels (including AP, VP, IP, CP, PP) simply because coordination at any structural level is independently allowed.[62]

(740) $[_{CoP}$ $\underline{XP}$ Co $[_{DP}$ $[_D$ D $[_{CP}$ $[_{DP_{rel}}o\ qual$ NP]$_j$ C $[_{IP}...t_j...]]]]]$

---

[62] Notice that if XP = CP, the coordination is syntactically unbalanced. However, De Vries (2006b) argues that this is permitted if the abstract D element that heads the second conjunct (possibly associated with the head) refers to CP, such that the two conjuncts are functionally equivalent (see §1.3.2.5B). According to De Vries, this is possible because a pronoun, in principle, can refer to any syntactic category.

4.5.5 Split antecedents

In §4.4.5, I have noted that *o qual*-ARCs in earlier stages of Portuguese can take split antecedents, in contrast to the situation found in CEP. Under the dual approach advocated in this chapter (see (710)), the question that arises is how the raising analysis can block split antecedents and how the specifying coordination analysis can account for them.

On the raising analysis, the head of the relative clause is considered to originate inside the relative clause. Hence, when split antecedents are involved, two different hypotheses can be formulated. The first one supposes that the antecedents are generated inside the relative clause as a conjoined noun phrase and are subsequently split and moved to different positions, as in (741).[63]

(741) $[_{CoP} [_{CP} [A man]_k$ entered the room] and $[_{CP} [a woman]_j$ went out $[_{DP} D [_{CP}$ $[_{DP_{rel}}$ who $[_{CoP} t_k [_{Co} Co t_j]]]_i C [_{IP} t_i$ were quite similar]]]]]

This hypothesis would explain the plural agreement found in the relative pronoun and the verb (in those languages that can morphologically manifest it). However, the movement of the two conjuncts in (741) violates the Coordinate Structure Constraint and, more precisely, the Conjunct Constraint (see Grosu 1973), which bars the movement of whole conjuncts of coordinate structures (see §3.6.1.2, n. 53). It is noteworthy that across-the-board raising cannot rescue this violation either because (1) it applies only to movement of constituents contained within a conjunct (as opposed to the conjunct itself); and (2) it involves extraction of the same element from all the conjuncts (and not extraction of two different constituents).

Another hypothesis states (in line with Suñer 2001) that two identical relative clauses modify each noun phrase, with the subsequent deletion of the first one, as in (742).[64]

(742) $[_{CoP} [_{CP} [_{DP} D [_{CP} [a man]_i [_{DP_{rel}}$ who $t_i]_k C [_{IP} t_k$ was/were quite similar]]] entered the room] and $[_{CP} [a woman]_i$ went out $[_{DP} D [_{CP} t_i [_{DP_{rel}}$ who $t_i]_k$ $C [_{IP} t_k$ were quite similar]]]]]]

However, this analysis fails to explain the plural forms found in the relative clause (see Andrews 1975, among others). Consider first the plural agreement of the verb. In a relative clause taking split antecedents, the verb in the relative clause is plural

---

[63] Note that the hypothetical structure given in (741) involves extraposition, as none of the antecedents are adjacent to the ARC. Following Kayne (1994), in this representation I assume that extraposition is derived by VP-internal stranding and that weak determiners are located not in the external determiner but within the NP (see §3.4.2.1). For ease of exposition, in (741) I abstract away from eventual intermediate landing sites of the conjoined heads.

[64] Again, observe that the structure given in (742) involves extraposition of the relative clause modifying *a woman*. See n. 63 for more details of implementation.

(*who were quite similar*). However, the plural agreement is not derived from the structure given in (742); under this structure, the verb should be singular (*was*) because it agrees with a singular head.

The pluralization of the relative pronoun (and of the adjective) raises a similar problem. This can be seen in languages such as Portuguese, where the plural is morphologically visible in relative pronouns and in adjectives (this is evident in the gloss: *os quais eram bastante parecidos* lit. 'the.PL which.PL were.PL quite similar.PL'). Again, the structure in (742) cannot explain the pluralization of the relative pronoun and of the adjective because these elements are supposed to agree with a singular head.

Given these facts, it is reasonable to conclude that split antecedents stand out as an obstacle to the raising analysis. Interestingly, this obstacle is highly desirable for the dual approach proposed here: it explains that *o qual*-ARCs cannot take split antecedents in CEP because they are derived from the raising analysis.

Regarding *o qual*-ARCs in earlier stages of Portuguese, a different scenario emerges. Under the approach adopted here, the specifying coordination analysis is expected to allow for ARCs with split antecedents. This is indeed the case. It is simply necessary to assume that split antecedents appear in the first conjunct, whereas the ARC occurs in the second conjunct. Observe that, in this case, the second conjunct is attached not to a noun phrase but to a higher level, which is schematically represented in (743).

(743) $[_{CoP} [_{XP}...[ ]_{i}...[ ]_{j}] [_{Co'} Co [_{DP} D_{i+j} [_{CP}...D_{rel}...]]]]$ (XP=IP, CP,...)

Under the structure of specifying coordination in (45), with the minor change introduced in (738), I argue that the abstract D heading the second conjunct behaves as an E-type pronoun requiring co-reference with some objects. For this reason, it can be interpretatively linked to the two parts of the antecedent (see the referential indexes in (743)), similar to how a pronoun can refer to split antecedents across the discourse, as in (744).

(744) *A man$_i$* entered the room and *a woman$_j$* went out. They$_{i+j}$ were quite similar.
(Demirdache 1991: 166)

4.5.6 Coordination of the wh-pronoun with another Determiner Phrase

O qual-ARCs in CEP differ from the ones in earlier stages of Portuguese by not allowing coordination of the wh-pronoun with another DP. In accordance with the dual approach adopted here, the question that arises is how the raising analysis blocks the coordination of the wh-pronoun with another DP and how the specifying coordination analysis accounts for it.

One of the basic tenets of the raising analysis is that the antecedent is generated inside the relative clause as a complement of D_{rel}. As shown in §1.3.2.5C, there are two movement steps: movement of the operator phrase DP_{rel} to the CP domain and subsequent movement of the head NP to the left of D_{rel}. Usually, the head NP targets [Spec, DP_{rel}]. However, when pied-piping is involved, a larger constituent is dragged along with D_{rel} to the CP domain and the head NP moves to the highest position within the pied-piped constituent.

Let me start by showing how the raising analysis bans the coordination of the wh-pronoun with another DP in CEP (see (745), repeated from (683)).

(745)   *O presidente elogiou o   João, o   qual   e   a   sua mulher têm
      the president praised the J.   the which and the his wife   have
      desenvolvido um óptimo trabalho naquela instituição.
      developed   a   great   work   in.that institution
      'The president praised João; he and his wife have been developing great
      work in that institution.'

In this construction, DP_{rel} is conjoined with the DP *a sua mulher* 'his wife'. According to the first movement step mentioned earlier, the whole coordinate structure (CoP) is pied-piped to the CP domain. Then, the head NP undergoes movement to the highest specifier position within the pied-piped constituent, which in this case corresponds to the specifier of CoP, as shown in (746).

(746)   *[$_{CoP}$ João$_i$ [$_{CoP}$ [$_{DP_{rel}}$ o qual t$_i$] e [$_{DP}$ a sua mulher]]]

However, note that this step constitutes a violation of the Coordinate Structure Constraint (see Ross 1967: 98–9), because it has to postulate the viability of movement of one conjunct alone. Crucially, this violation explains, as desired, why ARCs generated by the raising analysis fail to allow the property at hand.

Turning now to the specifying coordination analysis, the relevant contrasting fact is that there is no movement chain between the antecedent and the position of the gap inside the relative CP. Hence, the coordination of a wh-pronoun with another DP would involve the structure in (747).

(747)   [$_{CoP}$ *antecedent* Co [$_{DP}$ D [$_{CP}$ [$_{CoP}$ [$_{DP_{rel}}$ D$_{rel}$ (*internal head*)] Co [$_{DP}$ D NP]]$_k$
      C [$_{IP}$...t$_k$...]]]]]

Because in (747) there is no asymmetric extraction of the antecedent, the Coordinate Structure Constraint is not violated, and the possibility of having a wh-pronoun conjoined with another DP follows. According to this approach, the sentence in (686) above, from a fifteenth-century Portuguese text, has the (simplified) structure in (748).

(748)

[$_{CoP}$ DP   Co [$_{DP}$ D [$_{CP}$ [$_{CoP}$ [$_{DPrel}$ D$_{rel}$ NP]

  Dom Henrrique...   o qual   dom Henrrique e   hum seu tio

  D.   H.   the which D.   H.   and a   his uncle

[$_{Co'}$ Co DP]]$_k$ C [$_{IP}$..t$_k$..]]]]

4.5.7 Illocutionary force

O qual-ARCs in earlier stages of Portuguese and *o qual*-ARCs in CEP behave differently with respect to the system of basic clause types: the former allow different clause types, whereas the latter do not allow any clause types beyond the declarative. In what follows, I will show that this divergent behavior with respect to the basic clause types can be interpreted as reflecting a functional difference between coordinate and subordinate constructions in terms of illocutionary force.

Several formal criteria have traditionally been used in the literature to distinguish coordinate structures from subordinate ones, for example, verb second, the possibility of topicalization/preposing, the occurrence of certain adverbs, scopal independence, and illocutionary force. Regarding illocutionary force, the basic claim is that coordinate constructions have independent illocutionary force, whereas subordinate clauses do not. As Verstraete (2005) puts it,

> The basic idea is that coordinate constructions are characterized by the presence of illocutionary force in both clauses in the construction, either separately or shared, whereas subordinate constructions are characterized by absence of illocutionary force in the subordinate clause. In the case of coordination, the presence of illocutionary force in both clauses reflects the 'equality' and 'independence' that has traditionally been associated with coordinate constructions: the clauses are equal and independent in that each constitutes a speech act just like independent main clauses. In the case of subordination, the absence of illocutionary force in the subordinate clause reflects its status as a discursively presupposed or backgrounded proposition relative to the main clause which does have illocutionary force.
>
> (Verstraete 2005: 613)

Let me consider what predictions these ideas make for the raising/specifying coordination analyses. Under the specifying coordination analysis, the ARC surfaces in the second conjunct of a coordinate structure. Recall that coordinate structures have independent illocutionary force, as illustrated in (749), from Verstraete (2005: 614).[65]

---

[65] Note, however, that not all the coordinate constructions allow differing illocutionary types (see example (i) and (ii), from Ross 1967: 103). To account for these examples, I assume, following Verstraete (2005), that all coordinate constructions have an independent illocutionary force, and that the fact that not all of them allow the same range of illocutionary force types can be explained by the semantics of the interclausal relation.

(i)   *Sally's sick and what did you bring me?

(ii)   *(You) make yourself comfortable and I got sick.

(749)   a. John was imprisoned, but did he really rob the bank?
         b. John was imprisoned, but don't forget that he robbed the bank!

This fact straightforwardly captures the possibility of having *o qual*-ARCs with (non-declarative) illocutionary force in earlier stages of Portuguese: the second conjunct of the specifying coordination (just like the second conjuncts of the traditional types of coordination) have independent illocutionary force, which is expressible in terms of different clause types.

Let me now consider what the raising analysis predicts. Under the raising analysis, the relative clause is a complement of the external determiner; consequently, it is syntactically a subordinate clause. Given that no coordinate structure is involved, ARCs unambiguously pair with the subordinate constructions and, consequently, are characterized by the absence of illocutionary force. This explains why *o qual*-ARCs in CEP do not allow any clause types beyond the declarative.

There is, however, one possible complication that I wish to make explicit. As mentioned in §4.4.7, ARCs in CEP are declarative even if the matrix is interrogative or imperative. This is illustrated in (750)–(751) (repeated from (690)–(691), for ease of exposition).

(750)   Será   que o   João, com o   qual   pudemos sempre contar,
         be.FUT.3SG that the J.   with the which could.1PL always count.INF
         estará disponível desta   vez?
         be.FUT available   DE.PREP.this time
         'Will João, who we have always counted on, be available this time?'

(751)   Telefona   aos   teus pais,   os quais estarão   certamente
         phone.IMP.2SG to.the your parents the which be.FUT.3PL certainly
         disponíveis para te   ajudar!
         available   to   you.CL help.INF
         'Phone your parents, who will certainly be available to help you!'

This might suggest that *o qual*-ARCs in CEP are characterized by the presence of illocutionary force. However, as also mentioned in §4.4.7, ARCs in CEP do not allow any clause type beyond the declarative type found in (750)–(751). This is shown by the unacceptability of (752) and (753) (repeated from (692) and (693)), where the matrix is declarative and the ARC is, respectively, interrogative or imperative.

(752)   *O único que   te   apoiou   foi o   João, ao   qual já
         the only that you.CL supported was the J.   to.the which yet
         agradeceste devidamente por tudo o   que   te   fez?
         thanked.2SG properly   by all   the which you.CL made.3SG
         'The only person who supported you was John; have you yet thanked
         him properly for everything he did for you?'

(753) *Acabou de   chegar o João, ao   qual vai   já
       has.just DE.PREP arrive.INF the J.   to.the which go.IMP.2SG now
       oferecer uma bebida!
       offer.INF a   drink
       'João has just arrived; offer him a drink now!'

The divergent behavior of (750)–(751) and (752)–(753) with respect to the different clause types casts some doubt on the presence of illocutionary force in *o qual*-ARCs in CEP. In fact, and in line with Verstraete (2005), if the *o qual*-ARCs in (750)–(751) were genuinely assertive, the assertive force would be expressible with non-declarative clause types, such as interrogatives and imperatives, which is contrary to fact. Therefore, following Verstraete (2005), I submit that the declarative in (750)–(751) should be regarded not as a marker of assertive illocutionary force but rather as the unmarked option that emerges in contexts of neutralization of the illocutionary force.[66]

In sum, the theoretical apparatus adopted here derives the divergent behavior of *o qual*-ARCs from the coordinate/subordinate dichotomy; *o qual*-ARCs in earlier stages of Portuguese involve a coordinate structure and, consequently, are characterized by the presence of illocutionary force; *o qual*-ARCs in CEP do not involve a coordinate structure and, consequently, are characterized by the absence of illocutionary force.

4.5.8 Coordinator

As mentioned in §4.4.8, *o qual*-ARCs in CEP differ from the ones in earlier stages of Portuguese by not allowing a coordinator preceding the relative clause.

---

[66] This line of reasoning is put forward by Verstraete (2005) to account for the contrast between the coordinate construction in (i) and the subordinate construction in (ii). Note that the *but*-clause in (i) structurally allows different clause types beyond the declarative in (ia), such as the interrogative in (ib) and the imperative in (ic). In contrast, the *after*-clause in (ii) does not allow any clause types beyond the declarative in (iia).

(i)   a. John was imprisoned, but he didn't rob the bank.
      b. John was imprisoned, but did he really rob the bank?
      c. John was imprisoned, but don't forget that he robbed the bank! (all Verstraete 2005: 614)
(ii)   a. John was imprisoned after he robbed the bank.
      b. *John was imprisoned after didn't he rob the bank?
      c. *John was imprisoned after do keep in mind that he robbed the bank! (all Verstraete 2005: 614)

Given these contrasts, Verstraete concludes that the divergent behavior of (i) and (ii) can be interpreted as reflecting a functional difference in terms of illocutionary force: the declarative in (ia) functions as a marker of illocutionary force, whereas the declarative in (iia) should be analyzed in terms of "a typical instance of a switch to the unmarked option of a paradigm in contexts of neutralization, in this case neutralization of illocutionary force (comparable to the switch to the unmarked member of the paradigm in contexts of phonological neutralization, as discussed by Trubetzkoy, 1939: 77–9, 81)." (Verstraete 2005: 614).

This contrast can be easily explained by the dual approach adopted here. The presence of a coordinator in earlier stages of Portuguese is straightforwardly derived by the specifying coordination analysis; it corresponds to the spelling out of the specifying coordination position Co, as shown in (754).

(754) [$_{CoP}$ [$_{DP}$ antecedent]
    e.g. bõa raçom e mãtijmẽto de pam aluo boroa.   carne e   vĩho
       good ration and provisions of bread white corn.bread meat and wine
    Co [$_{DP}$ D [$_{CP}$ [$_{DP_{rel}}$ D$_{rel}$ NP]]$_i$ C [$_{IP}$...t$_i$...]]]
    e   o   qual   mãtijmẽto
    and   the which   provisions

On the other hand, the impossibility of having such an element in CEP is straightforwardly explained by the raising analysis; if the relative CP is the complement of the external determiner, and there is no coordinate structure involved, there is simply no room for a coordinating head in the structure.

4.5.9 Summary

The major goal of §4.5 has been to show that the contrasting properties of *o qual*-ARCs in CEP and in earlier stages of Portuguese can be explained by the dual approach to ARCs. In particular, it was argued that *o qual*-ARCs in earlier stages of Portuguese are derived from specifying coordination, whereas *o qual*-ARCs in CEP do not involve specifying coordination, being derived from head raising.

The comparison between different stages of the same language proved to be precious empirical grounds for testing the syntax of ARCs. By controlling important variables (e.g. ARCs introduced by the same relativizer, attested in different periods of the same language), this study offers challenging evidence for the idea that ARCs do not constitute a uniform syntactic phenomenon.

In §4.6, I will show that the non-uniform approach to ARCs can be independently confirmed by synchronic evidence, within a single language and across languages.

4.6 Some comparative remarks

This section is devoted to some comparative remarks on the syntax of ARCs. In light of the dual approach to ARCs advocated in this chapter, it offers an integrated account of the diachronic and synchronic variation found within the same language and across languages. The diachronic change affecting *o qual*-ARCs is discussed in §4.6.1, whereas the synchronic variation within the same language and across languages is considered in §§4.6.2 and 4.6.3 respectively.

4.6.1 Diachronic path

In this section I investigate the diachronic change that affected the syntax of *o qual*-ARCs. Concretely, I will offer two different hypotheses grounded in the dual approach to the syntax of o *qual*-ARCs advocated in this chapter (see §§4.6.1.1–2). The analysis is developed mainly within the model proposed by Lightfoot (see Lightfoot 1991, 1999, and subsequent work), but it also benefits from insights of the competing grammars hypothesis proposed by Kroch (1989, 1994, 2001) (see §1.3.4).

4.6.1.1 Hypothesis I   The first hypothesis that I would like to formulate is that *o qual*-ARCs were reanalyzed from a specifying coordination structure to a raising structure (see Lightfoot 1979, 1991). Concretely, I hypothesize that *o qual*-ARCs have undergone the diachronic path sketched in Table 4.7.

(a) Step 0

The input of the change is the specifying coordination structure proposed by De Vries (2006b) for ARCs (see (755)). In this configuration, the visible antecedent occurs in the first conjunct of a coordinate structure. The second conjunct includes a full RRC with an empty external D and an empty NP head (see §1.3.2.5).

(755) $[_{\text{CoP}}$ DP   Co $[_{\text{DP}}$ D $[_{\text{CP}}$ $[_{\text{DP}\,\text{rel}}$ D_{rel} $\text{NP}]_k$ C $[_{\text{IP}}$ t_k...$]]]]$

o casal de mudelos ø	ø	o	qual ø	ø	he do Monsteiro de
the hamlet of M.		the	which		is of.the monastery
vilarĩo					
of V.					

TABLE 4.7 **Extraposition of *o qual*-appositive relatives: Diachronic path**

Steps	Description	Result	Date (ca.)
0	*o qual*-ARCs derived from the specifying coordination structure		until 16th c.
1	Loss of extraposition derived from specifying coordination (plus ellipsis)	Decrease in frequency of configurations generated by the specifying coordination structure	after 16th c.
2	Reanalysis of *o qual*-ARCs from the specifying coordination structure to the head raising structure	Decrease in frequency of configurations generated by the specifying coordination structure	
3	Loss of the abstract specifying coordinator	No configurations derived from specifying coordination in CEP	

Note: The shading indicates that the line contains a description of an independent change that took place in the history of Portuguese.

As already noted in §4.5, this approach explains why *o qual*-ARCs in earlier periods of Portuguese can have an additional internal head, allow for generalized extraposition and pied-piping, take clausal and split antecedents, allow for the coordination of the wh-pronoun with another DP, have illocutionary independence, and co-occur with a spelled-out coordinator.

(b) Step 1

After the sixteenth century, extraposition generated by specifying coordination (plus ellipsis) ceases to be available in the diachrony of Portuguese (see §3.6.1). Two main consequences of this change are: (1) extraposition is reanalyzed from specifying coordination (plus ellipsis) to stranding (e.g. extraposition of RRCs and possibly PPs); (2) extraposition of some specific constituents (e.g. conjuncts) ceases to be allowed. As for (1), I posit, somewhat tentatively, that the reanalysis of the former specifying coordination (plus ellipsis) structure might have involved the steps represented in (756) (repeated from (491)).[67] First, the two conjuncts are reanalyzed as XP_2 without the application of deletion (see (756b)). Then the visible antecedent is taken to originate in an RRC-internal position, the extraposition being concomitantly derived from stranding (see (756c)). Technically, stranding involves partial movement: the head noun undergoes leftward movement stranding the RRC in situ.

(756)   a. $[_{CoP} [_{XP_1} [_{DP} \textit{antecedent}]_i \text{ YP } t_i] \text{ Co } [_{XP_2} [_{DP} \textit{antecedent} \text{ RRC}]_i \text{ YP } t_i]] \rightarrow$
         b. $[_{XP} [\textit{antecedent}]_i \text{ YP } [_{DP} t_i \text{ RRC}]]$

Although extraposed *o qual*-ARCs involve a more complex structure with two different coordinate phrases (to derive extraposition and apposition), they are expected to have followed a similar path, contrary to fact.

This can be explained by the emergence of conflicting grammatical options. As shown in (757),[68] the output of the reanalysis (see (757b)) is not compatible with a derivation of extraposition in terms of stranding because the raising of the first conjunct (and the stranding of the second conjunct) would violate the Coordinate Structure Constraint and, more precisely, the Conjunct Constraint (see Grosu 1973), which bars the movement of whole conjuncts of coordinate structures.

(757)   a. $[_{CoP_1} [_{XP_1} [_{DP} \text{ D NP}]_i \text{ YP } t_i] \text{ Co } [_{XP_2} [_{CoP_2} [_{DP_1} \text{ D NP}] \text{ Co } [_{DP_2} \text{ D } [_{CP} \text{ NP}$
             o qual-ARC]]]]$_i$ YP t_i]] $\rightarrow$
         b. $[_{XP} [_{CoP} [_{DP_1} \text{ D NP}] \text{ Co } [_{DP_2} \text{ D } [_{CP} \text{ NP } \textit{o qual}\text{-ARC}]]]_i \text{ YP } t_i]$

---

[67] In Ch. 3 I show that the diachronic path of RRC-extraposition can be framed in terms of the competing grammars hypothesis originally proposed by Kroch (1989, 1994). For more details see §3.7.1.2.

[68] In order to distinguish the abstract categories (which are independently available in the derivation of *o qual*-ARCs under the specifying coordination structure) from the deleted material, I represent the abstract categories in gray (see (757) and (759)). For more details about the coordinate-style account adopted for ARCs, see §1.3.2.5B.

Therefore, if no additional change had taken place, *o qual*-ARCs would no longer display an extraposed variant, just like conjuncts, which have lost the possibility of being extraposed in the diachrony of Portuguese (see Chapter 3, Section 3.7.1.1(e)).

(c) Step 2

With the loss of *o qual*-ARC extraposition, the frequency of contexts expressing positive evidence for the derivation of *o qual*-ARC in terms of the specifying coordination structure gradually decreases. Following Lightfoot (1991, 1999), I suggest that such evidence was found in the cue provided in (758), which involves a strong noun phrase or the object of a preposition as the antecedent of an extraposed *o qual*-ARC. In earlier stages of Portuguese, children knew that the antecedent of *o qual*-ARCs was generated in an external position because no movement chain could be established between the antecedent and a position inside the *o qual*-ARC.[69]

(758)   [*strong noun phrase/embedded noun phrase*] XP [*o qual*-ARC]

When the expression of the cue drops below the learnability threshold, *o qual*-ARCs are reanalyzed from a specifying coordination structure to a raising structure. A tentative representation of this process is given in (759).

(759)   a. $[_{\text{CoP}} \text{DP}_1 \text{ Co } [_{\text{DP2}} \text{D } [_{\text{CP}} \text{NP}_i [_{\text{D}_{\text{rel}}} t_i]_k \text{ C } [_{\text{IP}}...t_k...]]]] \rightarrow$
         b. $[_{\text{DP}} \text{D } [_{\text{CP}} \text{NP}_i [_{\text{D}_{\text{rel}}} t_i]_k \text{ C } [_{\text{IP}}...t_k...]]]$

The starting point is the specifying coordination structure in (759a) (see De Vries 2006b): the first conjunct contains the visible antecedent and the second conjunct involves a raising configuration in which the abstract D selects the relative clause as its complement and the abstract NP head is generated in a position internal to the *o qual*-ARC (see §1.3.2.5).

The change might have involved the reanalysis of the two conjoined DPs (DP$_1$ and DP$_2$) as DP$_2$ (see (759b)). In this configuration, the former abstract elements D and NP are spelled out and the antecedent is generated in a position internal to the *o qual*-ARC. The raising configuration, which was independently available in the second conjunct in (759a), involves two movement steps: movement of the operator phrase DP$_{\text{rel}}$ to the CP domain, and movement of the head NP to the left of D$_{\text{rel}}$.[70]

Moreover, in line with Kayne (1994), I assume that the non-restrictive interpretation of *o qual*-ARCs results from LF-movement of the relative IP to [Spec, DP], as represented in (760).[71]

(760) $[_{\text{DP}} [_{\text{IP}}...t_k...]_j [_{\text{D}'} \text{D } [_{\text{CP}} \text{NP}_i [_{\text{D}_{\text{rel}}} t_i]_k \text{ C } t_j]]]$ *(LF)*

---

[69] A more detailed discussion of the cue is provided in §4.7.1.1(e).
[70] For more details about this derivation see Ch. 1 (§1.3.2.4B).
[71] For more details about the raising analysis of ARCs, see §1.3.2.5C.

Importantly, the fact that *o qual*-ARCs after the sixteenth century are exclusively derived from raising explains why these relatives do not display an additional internal head, generalized extraposition or generalized pied-piping, clausal antecedent, split antecedents, coordination of the wh-pronoun with another DP, independent illocutionary force, and a spelled-out coordinator.

(d) Step 4

Given that the specifying coordination structure ceases to be involved not only in extraposition configurations but also in *o qual*-ARCs, I tentatively suggest that children lost evidence for the use of this structure and might have converged on a new grammar that lacked the abstract specifying coordinator &:. Further research is, however, necessary to confirm the validity of this proposal.[72]

A. Excursus

A potential problem with the diachronic path proposed for *o qual*-ARCs is that it does not explain why learners take extraposition and not utterances expressing other unambiguous cues as evidence for the acquisition of the specifying coordination structure. One possible unambiguous cue for this structure is the sequence *o qual N*, which is found in *o qual*-ARCs with an additional internal head. As already observed in §4.5.1, this configuration can only be generated by the specifying coordination analysis; in the raising structure there is simply no room for an additional internal head because the only NP position available is already occupied by the antecedent of the relative clause (see (761)). Such a position is, however, available in the specifying coordination analysis (see (762)): as the antecedent is base-generated in the first conjunct, the complement of D_{rel} may be spelled out as an additional internal head.

(761) $[_{DP} D [_{CP} \underline{NP}_i [_{DP_{rel}} o\ qual\ t_i]_k\ C\ [_{IP}...t_k...]]]$ (*raising analysis*)

(762) $[_{CoP} [_{DP} antecedent]\ Co\ [_{DP} D\ [_{CP} [_{DP_{rel}} o\ qual\ [_{NP} internal\ head]]_k$
       $C\ [_{IP}...t_k...]]]]$ (*specifying coordination analysis*)

Hence, at this point, the question that arises is why utterances manifesting the cue in (758) were more relevant for learners than utterances exhibiting, for instance, the cue *o qual N*. Under a cue-based model of acquisition, the most likely answer to this question is that it depends on the robustness of the cue, that is, on the frequency of utterances that unambiguously express the different cues (see Lightfoot 1999). However, quantification of the degree to which these two cues are expressed in

---

[72] In fact, there are still some questions that remain to be answered, such as: What structure derives regular appositions in CEP? Assuming that regular appositions might involve an implicit relative clause in the second conjunct, is it possible to generate them by raising? Which typology of specifying coordinators needs to be established in order to account for the changes affecting extraposition and apposition in the diachrony of Portuguese? How is it explained that parenthetical constructions have presumably been available throughout the history of Portuguese?

TABLE 4.8 Frequency of appositive relatives with *o qual* (*N*)

o qual	*o qual N*	Total
207 (42.3%)	282 (57.7%)	489

TABLE 4.9 Frequency of appositive relatives with *o qual* (*N*) broken down by century

	o qual	*o qual N*	Total
13th	30 (39.5%)	46 (60.5%)	76
14th	73 (39.2%)	113 (60.8%)	186
15th	68 (47.6%)	75 (52.4%)	143
16th (first half)	36 (42.9%)	48 (57.1%)	84

earlier texts does not permit the drawing of any firm conclusions. In the corpus edited by Martins (2001), the total number of *o qual*-ARCs is 489 but, as illustrated in Table 4.8, no significant contrast is found in the frequency of relative clauses with and without an internal head.[73]

Moreover, no substantial contrast is found between different periods. The frequency of *o qual N*-ARCs (broken down by century) is displayed in Table 4.9.

Additionally, in the corpus edited by Martins (2001), the total number of *o qual*-ARCs with nominal antecedents is 446. As illustrated in Table 4.10, the cases of extraposed *o qual*-ARCs correspond to 36.5% of the total instances of *o qual*-ARCs.

Again, no significant contrast arises across the thirteenth to sixteenth centuries. The frequency of *o qual*-ARCs (broken down by century) is displayed in Table 4.11.

Although more texts must be inspected to confirm these tendencies, I would like to tentatively suggest that the explanation might rely upon the different types of register in which the different cues are expressed. As mentioned in §4.4.1, the presence of an additional internal head is mainly used as a strategy to avoid ambiguity when the relative and the antecedent are non-adjacent, as a way of conferring more precision on the utterance. Recent studies have shown that there are good reasons for assuming that ambiguity avoidance determines syntactic choices (see Temperley 2003), and that this might happen more frequently in written language than in spoken language (because writing allows more time for such considerations to be brought to bear). If this is so, then the explanation for the non-relevance of the cue *o qual N* may rely upon the low frequency of *o qual*-ARCs with an internal head in the spoken language that a child is exposed to during the process of language acquisition.

---

[73] Only *o qual*-ARCs with a nominal antecedent are considered in these figures.

TABLE 4.10 Frequency of (non-)extraposed appositive relatives with *o qual* (*N*)

extraposed *o qual*-ARCs	non-extraposed *o qual* N	Total
163 (36.5%)	283 (63.5%)	446

TABLE 4.11 Frequency of (non-)extraposed appositive relatives with *o qual* (*N*) (broken down by century)

	extraposed *o qual*	non-extraposed *o qual* N	Total
13th	19 (32.8%)	39 (67.2%)	58
14th	58 (35.4%)	106 (64.6%)	164
15th	44 (32.8%)	90 (67.2%)	134
16th (first half)	39 (48.1%)	42 (51.9%)	81

4.6.1.2 Hypothesis II   The second hypothesis that I would like to raise is an attempt to integrate the theory of competing grammars originally proposed by Kroch (1989, 1994) with the diachronic path outlined in §4.6.1.1. It is not my aim to provide a detailed explanation of the change under this scenario, but rather outline how the change affecting *o qual*-ARCs could globally be understood in the light of this model.

The starting point of the diachronic path would involve two variants in competition to generate *o qual*-ARCs in earlier stages of Portuguese: the specifying coordination structure and the head raising structure. The specifying coordination structure would be used in configurations that cannot be derived from the raising structure, namely *o qual*-ARCs with an additional internal head, generalized extraposition and pied-piping, clausal and split antecedents, coordination of the wh-pronoun with another DP, illocutionary independence, and a spelled-out coordinator. The remaining configurations would be derived from the raising structure. Under this hypothesis, the change affecting *o qual*-ARCs would consist in the loss of *o qual*-ARCs generated by specifying coordination. No reanalysis needs to be postulated because the stranding structure was independently available in the grammar.

4.6.2 Synchronic variation

There are some indications in the literature that seem to support the view that *o qual*-ARCs in CEP are subject to synchronic variation. With regard to the presence of an additional internal head, Brito (1991) considers that an internal head is (marginally) possible in CEP, as in (763).

(763) A   falta de monitores na   Faculdade de Direito de Lisboa não permitiu
       the lack of tutors   in.the Faculty   of Law   of L.   not allowed
       ainda que começassem as aulas   das   subturmas, as quais <u>aulas</u>
       yet that start.sbjv   the lessons of.the subclasses the which lessons
       funcionam em regime de avaliação contínua   de conhecimentos.
       function   in   regime of evaluation continuous of knowledge
       'The lack of tutors in the Faculty of Law of Lisbon did not yet allow the
       lessons of the subclasses to start; the lessons function in a system of continu-
       ous evaluation of knowledge.' (Brito 1991: 133)

The same point is made in Bechara (1961/2001), who provides the example in (764).

(764) Ao   livro ninguém fez   referência, o   qual <u>livro</u> merece a   maior
       to.the book nobody made mention   the which book deserves the best
       consideração, no   meu entender.
       consideration in.the my   opinion
       'Nobody made any mention of the book, which deserves the best consider-
       ation, in my opinion.' (Bechara 1961/2001: 488)

Nevertheless, it is worth reiterating here that I do not share these judgments, and that the same is true of the other native speakers I consulted. To support these introspective judgments, I have also inspected a large written corpus of CEP: *CETEMPúblico* (the first million words). This corpus contains some one million words that are taken from the daily newspaper *Público*. In this corpus, there is no occurrence of *o qual*-ARCs with an additional internal head. Moreover, in order to check if this construction is attested in legal documents with a degree of formality comparable to the notarial documents edited by Martins (2001), I have also inspected the subcorpus Law (*CRPC*, Portuguese language), which includes legal processes and decisions of the supreme court of justice, amounting to a total of 2,927,953 words. The results are straightforward, and corroborate my judgments: no occurrence of *o qual*-ARCs with an internal head is found in the subcorpus.

As far as extraposition is concerned, it is possible to find (in written CEP) extraposed *o qual*-ARCs with strong noun phrases as antecedents in a pre-verbal position, as illustrated in (765). Again, according to my intuitions and those of the speakers I consulted, this sentence is ungrammatical.[74]

---

[74] I did not perform any systematic search of extraposition configurations because it would require the availability of a large corpus of CEP with syntactic annotation. At this moment, only *CORDIAL-SIN* is

(765) Na   região da   Trofa, dos   quatro fogos registados, o   mais difícil
in.the region of.the T.   of.the four   fires registered the most difficult
de   combater <u>ocorreu em S. Mamede do Coronado,</u> o   qual
DE.PREP fight.INF occurred in   S. M.   d. C.   the which
implicou ainda a   ajuda dos   bombeiros da   Maia, Matosinhos
required also   the help of.the firemen   from.the M.   M.
e   Santo Tirso.
and S.   T.
'In the region of Trofa, four fires took place. The most difficult fire to fight
occurred in S. Mamede do Coronado, which also required the help of the
firemen from Maia, Matosinhos, and Santo Tirso.' (*CETEMP*)

Regarding pied-piping, Brito (1991) and Peres and Móia (1995) claim that the
pied-piping of DPs and the pied-piping of clausal constituents are possible in
CEP.[75] To support this claim, the authors provide built examples; (766)–(767)
involve the pied-piping of DPs and (768)–(769) the pied-piping of non-finite
clauses.[76]

(766) O João, [$_{DP}$ a   amiga do   qual] tu   conheces, telefonou agora mesmo.
the J.   the friend of.the which you know   called   now right
'João, the friend of whom you know, called right now.' (Brito 1991: 132)

(767) Foram apresentados vários   filmes   portugueses muito interessantes,
were   presented   various movies Portuguese very   interesting
[$_{DP}$ os realizadores dos   quais] o   Estado deveria apoiar.
the directors   of.the which the state   should support
'Various interesting Portuguese movies were presented, the directors of which
the state should support.' (Peres and Móia 1995: 278)

(768) Foram descobertas novas provas, [$_{CP}$ para analisar   as quais] o
were   found   new   proofs   to   analyze.INF the which the

---

available for CEP, but it contains only one occurrence of the relativizer *o qual* (see (770)). Nevertheless,
given that conflicting judgments seem to arise, it may be worth testing the grammaticality of relative clause
extraposition experimentally, which I leave for future research.

[75] I leave aside here the special case of pied-piping of participial clauses. For more details, see §4.4.3A,
n. 39.
[76] Costa, Fiéis, and Lobo (2012) mention that in CEP there are *o qual*-ARCs with pied-piped adverbial
(non-finite) clauses. Note, however, that the empirical evidence provided for the piped-piping of infinitival
clauses includes examples taken from 19th-century literary texts. Moreover, excluding the context in which
a participial clause behaves as a fixed expression (see n. 39 above), these authors provide one built example
to illustrate the pied-piping of participial clauses. Needless to say, for me and the speakers I consulted these
examples are ungrammatical (with the exception of the pied-piped participial clause used as a fixed
expression).

tribunal precisa de   muito tempo.
court   needs   DE.PREP much time
'New proofs were found, to analyze which the court needs much time.'
(Peres and Móia 1995: 279)

(769) Foram descobertas novas provas, [CP considerando as   quais] o   tribunal
were   found   new   proofs   consider.GER the which the court
mudou de   opinião.
changed DE.PREP opinion
'New proofs were found, considering which the court changed its opinion.'
(Peres and Móia 1995: 279)

Note, however, that for me and the informants I consulted, the examples (766)–(769) are ungrammatical. These introspective judgments are corroborated by corpus evidence: in the subcorpus Law (*CRPC*, Portuguese language) no occurrence of *o qual*-ARCs with these pied-piped constituents is found.

As for *o qual*-ARCs with a clausal antecedent, for me and the informants I consulted the ungrammaticality is sharp (see §4.4.4A). Interestingly, the use of *o qual*-ARCs with a clausal antecedent is found in the *Syntax-oriented Corpus of Portuguese Dialects*; see (770). However, it is completely excluded from the standard variety.

(770) e   era tudo   pregado com cravetes,   o   qual   desta forma
and was everything nailed   with ±metal.slivers the which of.this way
é mais fácil, com menos despesa
is more easy with less   expense
'and everything was nailed with metal slivers, which (way) was easier and less expensive' (*CORDIAL-SIN*)

For split antecedents, Brito (1991) asserts that *o qual*-ARCs in CEP can take split antecedents, as in (771) and (772) (see §4.4.5). However, for me and the informants I consulted, the ungrammaticality of these sentences is sharp.

(771) Como a   Maria_i não se   estava a   dar   muito bem com o
as   the M.   not SE.CL was   A.PREP get.INF very well with the
António_j, os   quais_{i+j} de facto não têm muito em comum, ele resolveu
A.   the.M.PL which.PL in fact not have much in common he decided
aceitar o   emprego em Lisboa.
accept.INF the job   in L.
'Since Maria was not getting along with António, who in fact do not have much in common, he decided to accept the job in Lisbon.' (Brito 1991: 133)

(772) Como a Maria$_i$ veio ao   Porto com o Henrique$_j$, com os   quais$_{i+j}$
       as   the M. came to.the P. with the H.   with the.M.PL which.PL
       eu já   não estava há muito tempo, fui   jantar   com eles.
       I already not was   has much time   went.1SG dine.INF with them
       'As Maria came with Henrique to Porto, with whom I was not for long time,
       I had dinner with them.' (Brito 1991: 133)

The examples provided in (763)–(769) manifest "theoretically inconvenient variation" (in the sense of Lightfoot 1991: 98). As the reader may have already
noticed, in these sentences *o qual*-ARCs display a range of syntactic properties
that are unexpected if *o qual*-ARCs are generated by the raising analysis. As
shown in §4.5, the raising analysis cannot derive *o qual*-ARCs with an additional
internal head or extraposed *o qual*-ARCs with strong noun phrases as antecedents; it also fails to derive generalized pied-piping and *o qual*-ARCs with
clausal or split antecedents.

There is another aspect that is worth mentioning here: the sentences outlined
in this section (maybe with the exception of (770)) have a prestigious flavor,
in the sense that they would never be used in "normal" CEP. This means
that they are somewhat artificial and unnatural, even for people who apparently
accept/produce them.

Note additionally that in CEP there are no attestations for most of the properties listed in §4.4. This situation contrasts sharply to what happens in earlier
stages of Portuguese, where *o qual*-ARCs displaying the relevant properties can be
easily found.

Under this scenario, non-trivial questions arise, namely: What structure is
involved in these *o qual*-ARCs? What is the source of the synchronic variation?
Clearly, more research is needed to answer these questions. For example, it
is important to determine whether the speakers who accept/produce the prestige
o qual-ARCs also accept/produce generalized RRC-extraposition. However, by
capitalizing on the investigation already developed in the domain of language change
and variation, at least two hypotheses can be raised to explain the synchronic
variation.

4.6.2.1 Hypothesis I A possible line of explanation is to assume the competing
grammars hypothesis (or *syntactic diglossia*) put forth by Kroch (1989, 1994, 2001).
This approach rests on the assumption that individuals may synchronically instantiate several grammars in a kind of internalized diglossia. The competing grammars
emerge when individuals are exposed to linguistic data that lead to incompatible
analysis; a case in point is the competition between a vernacular language and a
superposed prestige language. I quote: "it could easily be the case that the forms in
competition in syntactic diglossia represent an opposition between an innovative

vernacular and a conservative literary language. Since the former would have both a psycholinguistic advantage and the advantage of numbers, it should win out over time, even in written texts" (Kroch 2001: 723). Crucially, the competing grammars do not have the same acquisitional status. The vernacular grammar is subject to L1 acquisition, whereas the prestige language is learned a bit later in life for the purpose of reading and writing. In light of this view, it seems plausible to assume that Portuguese children have a grammar that generates *o qual*-ARCs with a raising structure. Later in life, upon exposure to a wider range of language, children may be exposed to *o qual*-ARCs of the type illustrated in (763)–(772), which for them have the status of a prestige construction. Given that this sequence has a structure grammatically incompatible with the one generated by their own grammar, the children may develop a diglossic capacity, becoming able to interpret and eventually use the new construction in their own writing.

Under this scenario, it can be assumed that those individuals who replicate the prestige *o qual*-ARCs resort to a grammar that generates *o qual*-ARCs with an alternative structure (e.g. a specifying coordination structure). This hypothesis predicts that the individuals who were not exposed to prestige *o qual*-ARCs or who were exposed to them without sufficient linguistic evidence to develop diglossic grammars would not produce or accept prestige *o qual*-ARCs. Most of the speakers I consulted belong to this latter group, as do I.

4.6.2.2 Hypothesis II   Another hypothesis is to assume that prestige *o qual*-ARCs are not part of the core Portuguese grammar but rather the result of extra-grammatical rules for producing prestige forms, which may be cataloged among what Sobin (1997) and Lasnik and Sobin (2000) have termed *grammatical viruses*. One of the central ideas of these proposals is that sometimes speakers use forms that are not generated by the grammar they acquired during the process of language acquisition. The motive for going against the initial system is the desire to employ (or the need to interpret) prestigious forms. Thus, forms licensed by grammatical viruses have a prestige status and are not typical of child language, and intuitions about their use are strikingly different from intuitions about the use of other grammatical forms.

For the formal implementation of this idea, Lasnik and Sobin (2000) propose that prestige forms are derived from a set of extra-grammatical rules that apply externally to the central computational system in a post-syntactic component. Thus, these rules may change output only at a very superficial level: they may take into account the linear sequence of elements in a sentence, but they can never involve hierarchic arrangement.[77]

---

[77] Lasnik and Sobin (2000) postulate a *virus theory* to account for the use of the wh-pronoun *whom* in English. It is commonly assumed that this wh-pronoun is parallel to *him* and *them* in manifesting the

A possible solution along these lines could be to assume that the computational system generates the structure underlying prestige *o qual*-ARCs in other syntactic environments (for instance in other relative constructions). Later on, this system can be superficially changed to reproduce prestigious *o qual*-ARCs. In this case, individuals would resort to an extra-grammatical rule, which has the task of expanding the use of *o qual* to other syntactic environments.

Clearly, these speculations require a great deal more work before they can really be considered as established hypotheses. Nevertheless, depending on the results obtained, two possible scenarios can be imagined a priori. If contemporary speakers who accept/produce prestige *o qual*-ARCs come to consistently accept *o qual*-ARCs in all of the possible contexts generated by the specifying coordination analysis, then the competing-grammar hypothesis is more promising. By contrast, if speakers come to accept prestige *o qual*-ARCs only in very specific environments, then the virus theory may be favored. However, for now, these scenarios remain mere speculations.

4.6.3 *Cross-linguistic contrasts*

Throughout this chapter, diachronic evidence is presented that points to the existence of two different types of ARC in the history of Portuguese. Whenever possible, cross-linguistic evidence is also considered, showing that *o qual*-ARCs in earlier stages of Portuguese systematically pattern with ARCs in other languages. In this comparison, particular attention is given to *il quale*-ARCs in contemporary Italian and to ARCs in English. In this section, I tentatively provide an integrated account of the facts of cross-linguistic variation considered in this chapter. In doing so, I show how the findings of this study can be integrated into the typological approach to ARCs put forth by Cinque (2008).

As already mentioned in §4.2, Cinque (1982, 2008) proposes a dual approach to ARCs, according to which there are two different types of structure that can generate ARCs (integrated and non-integrated types). These two structures are not, however,

---

pronominal case. Lasnik and Sobin challenge this traditional treatment and claim that *who* is the basic form of the wh-pronoun, which can check either the nominative or accusative case. The suffix *–m* of *whom* is assumed to be associated with an additional accusative feature and has to be checked independently of the accusative feature associated with the stem *who*. This additional feature is checked by rules that have the status of a grammatical virus. These rules are argued to be the product of extra-grammatical devices and are entirely independent from ordinary case-marking mechanisms. Just to give an idea of what a virus rule might look like, see the rule in the example below, from Lasnik and Sobin (2000: 354), which licenses the occurrence of *whom* as object of a verb or preposition:

If: $[_{V/P}]$ who-   -m
         [ACC] [ACC]

    1   2   3
then: check ACC on 3.

instantiated in all languages. From a cross-linguistic perspective, three different types of languages can be identified:

(773) Type I.   Languages that display the integrated and the non-integrated types (e.g. Italian and French).

Type II.   Languages that display only one construction (e.g., English and Romanian display the non-integrated type; Northern Italian dialects and, possibly, Chinese display the integrated type).

Type III.   Languages that lack ARCs (e.g. Gungbe, Bunun, and Mixtecan).

Assuming this tripartite classification, I would like to suggest that CEP may belong to Type-I or to Type-II languages. The present research has demonstrated that *o qual*-ARCs belong to what Cinque (2008) calls the integrated type but has not confirmed that all ARCs found in CEP are derived the same way. Further research is necessary in this domain to clarify this point. Earlier stages of Portuguese (until the sixteenth century) may belong to Type-I or Type-II languages, depending on the theory of language change adopted. Under the reanalysis hypothesis, earlier stages of Portuguese would be paired with Type-II languages of the non-integrated type (see §4.6.1.1). Under the competing grammars hypothesis, earlier stages of Portuguese would be paired with Type-I languages without further ado because *o qual*-ARCs per se can be derived by the integrated and the non-integrated types (see §4.6.1.2).

Importantly, the investigation presented in this chapter provides an important cue to an alternative typology of ARCs based on the presence/absence of the abstract specifying coordinator &:.

(774) Type I.   Languages that lack the specifying coordinator &: (e.g. CEP).

Type II.   Languages that have the specifying coordinator &: (e.g. English, Dutch).

To elaborate on this proposal it may be crucial, for instance, to conduct a grammaticality judgment experiment on "prestige" *o qual*-ARCs (CEP) and *il quale*-ARCs (Italian) in order to determine if these relatives are derived from grammatical or extra-grammatical rules. In this context, it would be important to test if individuals consistently accept *o qual/il quale*-ARCs with all the properties detailed in §4.4. This is an important move because the corpora inspected do not support the view that these constructions are productively used in CEP.

The dual approach adopted here, combined with Cinque's typological proposal, also provides us with a useful insight to understand the cross-linguistic variation reported throughout this chapter. First, it straightforwardly explains that *o qual*-ARCs in earlier stages of Portuguese exhibit the same syntactic properties as English ARCs and Italian *il quale*-ARCs because all of them are generated by specifying coordination. Second, it explains that *o qual*-ARCs in CEP differ from *il quale*-ARCs in contemporary Italian because *o qual*-ARCs have undergone a syntactic change that apparently did not affect their Italian counterpart.

I believe, however, that the dual approach developed in this chapter, which can be cataloged as a generalized constituency approach, is empirically superior to the approach put forward by Cinque (2008). Whereas, according to the Cinque approach, "integrated" and "non-integrated" *o qual*-ARCs have two completely different derivational stories, under the approach developed here both constructions basically involve one structure: the raising structure. Differences among languages and within the same language result from the possibility of having this raising structure in the second conjunct of a coordinate structure.

From a theoretical point of view, the similarity between the two constructions is highly desirable because it shows that it is still possible to pursue the ideal goal of linguistic theory, according to which variation across languages and within the same language can be reduced to some different parametric choices. According to this view, an interesting line of research may be to assume that in the languages of the world the concept of apposition can be syntactically expressed in two different ways: complementation and/or coordination. Languages will then differ in the ways they instantiate these two options.

Importantly, the findings of this chapter also show that a generalized constituency analysis (although not uniform) can account for the dual behavior of ARCs across languages without resorting to a version of the orphanage approach. This is highly desirable because, as De Vries (2006b) notes, proposals involving radical orphanage (see Fabb 1990, among others) or the attachment at some grammatical level beyond LF (see Safir 1986) cannot be easily accommodated in the standard assumptions about the organization of the grammar. ARCs are interpreted and pronounced; therefore, they must be present at the LF interface and the PF interface. The only way to get at these interfaces is via the overt syntax; if ARCs were to be added at or after the LF interface (i.e. after Spell Out in Chomsky's terms), they would not be pronounced.

4.7 Conclusion

This chapter investigates a case of micro-variation in the syntax of ARCs. It shows that different stages of the same language turn out to be precious empirical grounds for testing the syntax of ARCs. In particular, it is possible to demonstrate that within the same language, when dealing with the same construction introduced by the same relativizer, it is still necessary to adopt a dual approach to ARCs. Given the constrained nature of diachronic variation, such an approach is particularly attractive, because it allows the control of important variables that may incidentally interfere with the results obtained in other studies that involve, for instance, the comparison of languages historically and typologically quite distant from each other.

Specifically, this study focuses on Portuguese ARCs introduced by the relativizer *o qual*. The main claim is that *o qual*-ARCs have undergone a change from one syntactic type to another at some point in the history of Portuguese.

From an empirical point of view, I show that *o qual*-ARCs in CEP differ from *o qual*-ARCs in earlier stages of Portuguese with respect to a number of syntactic properties. The contrasting properties discussed in this chapter are as follows: (1) the possibility of having an additional internal head; (2) restrictions on extraposition; (3) restrictions on pied-piping; (4) the possibility of taking a clausal antecedent; and (5) split antecedents; (6) coordination of the wh-pronoun with another DP; (7) illocutionary force; and (8) the presence of coordinator.

From a theoretical point of view, I show that a single syntactic analysis cannot account for the contrasts found in the history of Portuguese. For this reason, I argue for a dual approach to ARCs, according to which *o qual*-ARCs in CEP use the raising structure, proposed by Kayne (1994) and Bianchi (1999), whereas *o qual*-ARCs in earlier stages of Portuguese use the specifying coordination structure, proposed by De Vries (2006b).

The dual approach adopted here provides us with a useful insight to understand the variation in the syntax of ARCs found within a language and across languages, both in the synchronic and diachronic dimensions. In this respect, I have shown that (1) ARCs may undergo a change from one syntactic type to another in the diachronic dimension; (2) two different syntactic structures for ARCs may coexist synchronically within the same language; and (3) languages may differ synchronically with respect to the syntactic types of ARC they display.

This chapter was not intended to establish the chronology of the change affecting ARCs in earlier stages of Portuguese; instead, it focuses on the identification of the change (not yet properly identified in the literature) and on the exploitation of its empirical and theoretical consequences. One important task for future research is to identify the chronology of the change and investigate whether the proposal put forth for *o qual*-ARCs in earlier stages of Portuguese can be extended to other ARCs.

5

Conclusion

This book sheds light on language variation and change from a generative syntactic perspective, based on a case study of relative clauses in the synchrony and diachrony of Portuguese. Furthermore, it contributes to the theoretical debate on the structural analysis of RRCs, ARCs, and extraposition. Two important findings are (1) that competing theoretical analyses need not be either false or true universally, but could be instrumental in explaining language variation (both diachronically and synchronically); and (2) a comparative analysis of phrasal discontinuity can provide an invaluable window into the syntax of different languages (and different stages of the same language).

The research methodology adopted involves comparative syntax (see Cinque and Kayne, eds., 2005, among others), both in the diachronic and the synchronic dimensions: CEP is systematically compared with earlier stages of Portuguese; moreover, Portuguese is compared with other languages, in particular Latin, English, Dutch, and Italian.

Such methodology provided precious insights into the diachronic contrasts found in Portuguese. Of particular interest is the finding that earlier stages of Portuguese, contrary to CEP, are to a large extent Germanic-like, at least with respect to the linguistic phenomena scrutinized. The comparative approach also proved to be an invaluable way of overcoming the limitations of historical inquiry. In this respect, it was shown that studying the behavior of other contemporary languages might provide the means to overcome the difficulties posed by the limited nature of written sources and the impossibility of manipulating data.

The linguistic facts are analyzed in the light of the Minimalist version of the Principles-and-Parameters framework (see Chomsky 1981; Chomsky 1993, 1995, and subsequent work). The interpretation and explanation of grammatical changes is developed within the model proposed by Lightfoot (1991, 1999, and subsequent work), which associates diachronic change with language acquisition. It also benefits from the insights of the competing grammars hypothesis originally proposed by Kroch (1989, 1994, 2001).

The benefits of using theoretical linguistics in studying diachronic (and synchronic) phenomena are substantial. To single out but a few, theoretical linguistics

Portuguese Relative Clauses in Synchrony and Diachrony. First Edition. Adriana Cardoso.
© Adriana Cardoso 2017. First published in 2017 by Oxford University Press.

provided important tools to organize, describe, and explain the data. It also oriented the inspection of large-scale corpora in an advanced phase of the research: with the predictions made by the theory, it was possible to search corpora for specific and theoretically informed purposes.

It may be the case that some readers have certain reservations about the methodological option of combining rich empirical documentation (from contemporary and old languages) with the insights of theoretical linguistics. As Devine and Stephens (2006) note, those with a primarily philological background may not appreciate the technical details of the discussion and "pure" syntacticians may become impatient with the rich philological documentation. However, note that the subject of this book does not permit choosing between philology and linguistics. Each discipline makes its own contribution and the present research demonstrates, I hope, that our understanding of language can benefit from this association. As Devine and Stephens (2006: 6) put it: "If there are no data, there cannot be any theory. If there is no theory, there can hardly be any understanding."

The present book is organized around three main linguistic phenomena: remnant-internal relativization; RRC-extraposition; and appositive relativization. The selection of these phenomena was determined by these criteria: (1) the contrasting properties of the relevant structures in earlier stages of Portuguese with respect to CEP; (2) their novelty (i.e. constructions/properties not yet reported in the literature), and (3) the theoretical relevance of the facts uncovered.

The study on *remnant-internal relativization* (see Ch. 2) is dedicated to the analysis of RRCs in which the head noun and some modifier/complement related to it appear discontinuously, as in (232) and (233), repeated here as (775), from earlier stages of Portuguese.

(775) a. <u>os livros</u> que eu compus <u>da philosaphia</u>
           the books that I wrote of.the philosophy

       b. <u>os livros</u> que <u>da philosaphia</u> eu compus
           the books that of.the philosophy I wrote

From a theoretical point of view, I show that this phenomenon provides important new evidence for the raising analysis of RRCs. From a diachronic perspective, I hypothesize that the loss of remnant-internal relativization with the modifier/complement in the left periphery of the relative clause (see (775b)) might be due to a restriction on movement that emerges inside the DP, which blocks the extraction of the modifier/complement to the left periphery of the RRCs.

Considering this change in the light of recent findings on the history of Portuguese, the global picture that emerges is that until the sixteenth century, Portuguese had more structural positions available to generate phrasal discontinuity. With the loss of a position dedicated to fronted-unmarked/information focus in the clausal left periphery from the thirteenth to the fourteenth century (see Martins, Pereira, and Pinto forthcoming), the loss of IP-scrambling after the sixteenth century (see Martins 2002), and the loss of modifier/complement fronting within the noun phrase (which blocks further step movements to a position outside the noun phrase), the possibilities of displacement operations decrease and discontinuity configurations start to involve a more restricted range of clausal positions.

This scenario opens the way to new research directions. The phrasal discontinuities that emerge in relative clauses seem to be the tip of an iceberg of noun phrase discontinuities found in earlier stages of Portuguese. Hence, a more global approach to the phenomenon, considering a wider range of configurations exhibiting discontinuity, will contribute to tracing other changes taking place in the diachrony of Portuguese and enhance our knowledge of the interaction between information structure and word order.

The second study presented in the book deals with RRC-extraposition (see Ch. 3). From a descriptive point of view, I show that different languages and different stages of the same language may differ with respect to the three main properties of extraposition: definiteness effect; extraposition from pre-verbal positions; and extraposition from prepositional phrases. The main descriptive findings are: (1) that earlier stages of Portuguese contrast sharply with CEP with respect to RRC-extraposition; and (2) the extraposition of RRCs in earlier stages of Portuguese is, to a large extent, Germanic-like, unlike CEP.

From a theoretical point of view, I show that one and the same structural analysis cannot alone derive the contrasting properties of RRC-extraposition. To account for the variation found in the diachronic and cross-linguistic dimensions, I argue that the extraposition of RRCs might involve two different structures, one of them derived from specifying coordination plus ellipsis (De Vries 2002), the other the result of stranding (Kayne 1994). See (776)–(777).

(776)   [$_{CoP}$ [$_{XP_1}$ antecedent YP] [Co [$_{XP_2}$ [~~antecedent~~ RRC] ~~YP~~]]]   (*specifying coordination*)

(777)   [antecedent$_i$ YP [t$_i$ RRC]]   (*stranding*)

In the diachronic dimension, I establish that RRC-extraposition in earlier stages of Portuguese is generated by specifying coordination plus ellipsis (and possibly by stranding), whereas the extraposition in CEP is derived from VP-internal stranding. Two different scenarios suggest themselves to account for this change. The first hypothesis is that the change affecting RRC-extraposition might have involved the reanalysis of extraposition from a specifying coordination plus ellipsis structure to a stranding structure (see Lightfoot 1991, 1999). The second hypothesis builds on the competing grammars hypothesis originally proposed by Kroch (1989, 1994). The idea is that there were two structures in competition to derive extraposition in earlier stages of Portuguese: the specifying coordination and the stranding structures. The stranding structure was available for: (1) cases in which it led to the same overt results as the specifying coordination plus ellipsis structure; and (2) cases that could not be derived from the specifying coordination structure. Conversely, the specifying coordination plus ellipsis structure might have been used in the cases that could not be derived from stranding. Under this view, the change affecting RRC-extraposition in the diachrony of Portuguese might simply have involved the loss of extraposition derived from specifying coordination plus ellipsis. The reanalysis need not to be postulated because RRCs were already generated by the stranding structure in earlier stages of Portuguese.

The grammars competition hypothesis has at least three important advantages with respect to the reanalysis hypothesis. First, under the reanalysis hypothesis, it is a mystery why movement operations, independently available in the grammar, could not derive extraposition until the sixteenth century. This question receives a straightforward explanation under the competing grammars hypothesis because movement operations could in fact give rise to contexts of extraposition derived from stranding.

Secondly, the competing grammar hypothesis can provide a simpler explanation for the change affecting RRC-extraposition by assuming that it results from the loss of the specifying coordination structure. No reanalysis process need be stipulated because the stranding structure was already available in the grammar.

Finally, the competing grammars hypothesis provides important insights into the articulation between diachronic change and synchronic cross-linguistic variation. Building on the hypothesis that the diachronic change affecting extraposition ultimately gives rise to the loss of the abstract specifying coordinator &:, I suggest that two different types of language can be identified:

(778)   Type I. Languages that lack the specifying coordinator &: (e.g. CEP and possibly Italian, Spanish, and French).
    Type II. Languages that have the specifying coordinator &: (e.g. English and Dutch).

Interestingly, this formulation leaves open the possibility that Type-II languages also make use of the stranding structure to derive extraposition. Hence, similarly to earlier stages of Portuguese, which have different structures in competition to generate extraposition, some contemporary languages generate extraposition by the specifying coordination plus ellipsis structure and the stranding structure. Moreover, similarly to historical Portuguese (after the sixteenth century), which ceases to have the specifying coordinator *&*, some contemporary languages lack this abstract coordinator (cf. Type-I languages).

The third and last study of the book investigates a case of micro-variation in the syntax of ARCs (Ch. 4). It focuses on the dissimilar behavior of ARCs introduced by the complex relative pronoun *o qual* in CEP and earlier stages of Portuguese.

From a descriptive point of view, eight contrasting properties are identified, relative to: (1) additional internal head; (2) extraposition; (3) pied-piping; (4) clausal antecedent; (5) split antecedents; (6) coordination of the wh-pronoun with another DP; (7) illocutionary force; and (8) coordinator.

Sticking to the comparative approach adopted in the book, data from other languages (in particular, English and Italian) were inspected in light of the same set of potentially contrasting properties. A finding of particular interest came out of this comparative scrutiny, namely that *o qual*-ARCs in earlier stages of Portuguese pattern with Italian (*il quale*) and English ARCs, unlike CEP.

In order to account for the grammatical contrasts found in the diachronic dimension, I raise two different hypotheses. First, I propose, in line with Lightfoot (1991, 1999), that *o qual*-ARCs might have been reanalyzed from a specifying coordination plus ellipsis structure to a stranding structure. Secondly, adopting the competing grammars hypothesis proposed by Kroch (1989, 1994), I submit that in earlier stages of Portuguese there could have been two structures in competition to derive *o qual*-ARCs in earlier stages of Portuguese: the specifying coordination and the head raising structures. The specifying coordination structure would be used in configurations that cannot be derived from the raising structure, namely *o qual*-ARCs with an additional internal head, generalized extraposition and pied-piping, clausal and split antecedents, coordination of the wh-pronoun with another DP, illocutionary independence, and a spelled-out coordinator. The remaining configurations could have been derived from the raising structure.

Under this hypothesis, the change affecting *o qual*-ARCs might have consisted in the loss of *o qual*-ARCs generated by specifying coordination. The reanalysis need not be postulated because *o qual*-ARCs derived from stranding would be independently available in the grammar. Moreover, the competing grammars hypothesis provides an important basis for the explanation of cross-linguistic variation. Building on the typological contrast in (778), I suggest that languages that have the specifying coordinator *&* might derive ARCs from specifying coordination or raising; in contrast, languages that lack the specifying coordinator *&* do not derive ARCs from the specifying coordination structure, making use of the raising structure instead.

Of course, it is not a coincidence that extraposition and *o qual*-ARCs cease to be derived from specifying coordination in the same period of the history of Portuguese. The changes investigated in the book (see Table 5.1) can be integrated in a cluster of

TABLE 5.1 Series of changes in the diachrony of Portuguese

Steps	Description	Date (ca.)
0.	Earlier stages of Portuguese: • Two structures in synchronic competition to derive extraposition: the specifying coordination (plus ellipsis) structure and the stranding structure • Two structures in synchronic competition to derive *o qual*-ARCs: the specifying coordination structure and the head raising structure	until 16th c.
1.	Loss of IP-scrambling (and PP-scrambling)	after 16th c.
2.	Loss of extraposition derived from the specifying coordination (plus ellipsis) structure	
3.	Loss of *o qual*-ARCs derived from the specifying coordination	
4.	Loss of the abstract specifying coordinator	

phenomena changing at the same time in the history of Portuguese, which might be taken as the result of a parameter change (see Biberauer and Roberts 2008).[1]

Concretely, I propose that the loss of IP-scrambling investigated by Martins (2002) gives rise to a series of changes whose major superficial effect is the reduction of word order patterns available in Portuguese. In more technical terms: (1) the functional head I loses the option of being associated with an Attract-all-F EPP-feature (Martins 2002); and (2) the specifying coordinator &: ceases to generate extraposition and (3) appositive constructions.[2]

Moreover, there are indications that a change parallel to that found at the clausal level (i.e. the loss of IP-scrambling) might have also affected the DP-level. As I show in Chapter 2, PP-complements/modifiers of the noun cease to target the higher specifier position within the DP; as a result, they cease to undergo other potential movements out of the DP. Importantly, Poletto (2014) investigates a similar syntactic change in the diachrony of Italian.

In this book I have demonstrated that this series of changes had the effect of transforming Portuguese from a "Germanic-like" language, with a wide range of phrasal discontinuities, to a "non-Germanic" type, with more restricted possibilities of phrasal discontinuity. This proposal is quite likely to be supported by other syntactic changes taking place in the history of Portuguese, but I leave this open for future research.

---

[1] Note that in Table 5.1, I adopt the competing grammars hypothesis (§§3.6.1.2 and 4.6.1.2) given its advantages over the reanalysis hypothesis (see the discussion presented earlier in this chapter).

[2] In this research I show that the specifying coordinator &: ceases to be involved in *o qual*-ARCs. The hypothesis that this change might have affected other appositive constructions requires further inquiry, which should include a deeper investigation of the typology of specifying coordinators and of the appositional/parenthetical structures available in the synchrony and diachrony of Portuguese and across languages.

References

Primary sources

Bacelar do Nascimento, Maria Fernanda (2000). Corpus de Référence du Portugais Contemporain, in Mireille Bilger (ed.), *Corpus, Méthodologie et Applications Linguistiques*. Paris: Champion, Presses Universitaires de Perpignan, 25–30. Corpus URL: <http://www.clul.ulisboa.pt/en/10-research/713-crpc-reference-corpus-of-contemporary-portuguese>, accessed Feb. 2016.

Bacelar do Nascimento, Maria Fernanda, José Bettencourt Gonçalves, Rita Veloso, Sandra Antunes, Florbela Barreto, and Raquel Amaro (2005). The Portuguese Corpus, in Emanuela Cresti and Massimo Monegli (eds.), *C-ORAL-ROM Integrated Reference Corpora for Spoken Romance Languages*. Amsterdam: John Benjamins, 163–207.

Brocardo, Maria Teresa (1997). *Crónica do Conde D. Pedro de Meneses—Gomes Eanes de Zurara: Edição e estudo*. Lisbon: Fundação Calouste Gulbenkian, Junta Nacional para a Investigação Científica e Tecnológica.

Brocardo, Maria Teresa (2006). *Livro de linhagens do Conde D. Pedro: edição do fragmento manuscrito da Biblioteca da Ajuda (século XIV)*. Lisbon: Imprensa Nacional—Casa da Moeda.

Camões, José (ed.) (1999). *Gil Vicente: todas as obras* [CD-ROM]. Lisbon: Comissão Nacional para as Comemorações dos Descobrimentos Portugueses.

Castro, Ivo (1984). Livro de José de Arimateia (Estudo e edição do COD. ANTT 643). Doctoral Dissertation, University of Lisbon.

CLUL (ed.) (2014). *P.S. Post Scriptum: A Digital Archive of Ordinary Writing (Early Modern Portugal and Spain)* <http://ps.clul.ul.pt/index.php?action=home>, accessed Feb. 2016.

Coelho, António Borges (1987). *Inquisição de Évora: Dos primórdios a 1668*. Lisbon: Caminho, ii.

Davies, Mark (2008–). *Corpus of Contemporary American English*. <http://corpus.byu.edu/coca/>, accessed Feb. 2016.

Davies, Mark, and Michael Ferreira (2006–). *Corpus do português*. <http://www.corpusdoportugues.org/>, accessed Feb. 2016.

Galves, Charlotte, and Pablo Faria (2010). *Tycho Brahe Parsed Corpus of Historical Portuguese*. <http://www.tycho.iel.unicamp.br/~tycho/corpus/en/index.html>, accessed Feb. 2016.

Kroch, Anthony, Beatrice Santorini, and Lauren Delfs (2004). *The Penn-Helsinki Parsed Corpus of Early Modern English (PPCEME)* [CD-ROM]. Department of Linguistics, University of Pennsylvania.

Kroch, Anthony, Beatrice Santorini, and Ariel Diertani (2010). *The Penn Parsed Corpus of Modern British English (PPCMBE)* [CD-ROM]. Department of Linguistics, University of Pennsylvania.

Macchi, Giuliano (1975). *Crónica de D. Fernando—Fernão Lopes*. Lisbon: Imprensa Nacional—Casa da Moeda.

Maia, Clarinda (1986). *História do Galego Português: Estado linguístico da Galiza e do Noroeste de Portugal desde o século XIII ao século XVI (com referência à situação do Galego Moderno)*. Coimbra: Instituto Nacional de Investigação Científica.

Martins, Ana Maria (2001). *Documentos portugueses do Noroeste e da região de Lisboa*. Lisbon: Imprensa Nacional—Casa da Moeda.

Martins, Ana Maria, Sandra Pereira, and Adriana Cardoso (2013–15). *Parsed José de Arimateia*. CC licensed: *WOChWEL*, Centro de Linguística da Universidade de Lisboa. <http://alfclul.clul.ul.pt/wochwel/oldtexts.html>, accessed Feb. 2016.

Martins, Ana Maria, Sandra Pereira, and Adriana Cardoso (2014–15). *Parsed Demanda do Santo Graal*. CC licensed: *WOChWEL*, Centro de Linguística da Universidade de Lisboa. <http://alfclul.clul.ul.pt/wochwel/oldtexts.html>, accessed Feb. 2016.

Martins, Ana Maria (coord.) (2000–10). *Syntax-oriented Corpus of Portuguese Dialects (CORDIAL-SIN)*. Centro de Linguística da Universidade de Lisboa. <http://www.clul.ulisboa.pt/en/11-resources/314-cordial-sin-corpus-2>, accessed Feb. 2016.

Muhana, Adma (1995). *Os autos do processo de Vieira na Inquisição*. São Paulo: Universidade Estadual Paulista.

Neto, Sílvio Toledo (2012–15). Transcrição/edição da *Demanda do Santo Graal*. MS. University of São Paulo.

Pereira, Isaías da Rosa (1987). *Documentos para a história da Inquisição em Portugal: séc. XVI*. Lisbon: n.p., i.

Piel, Joseph (1948). *Livro dos ofícios de Marco Tullio Ciceram, o qual tornou em linguagem o Ifante D. Pedro, duque de Coimbra: Edicao critica, segundo o MS. de Madrid, prefaciada, anotada e acompanhada de glossario*. Coimbra: Universidade de Coimbra.

Piel, Joseph, and Irene Nunes (1988). *Demanda do Santo Graal*. Lisbon: Imprensa Nacional—Casa da Moeda.

Pimpão, Júlio da Costa (1972/2000). Os Lusíadas *de Luís de Camões*. Lisboa: Ministério dos Negócios Estrangeiros, Instituto Camões (4th edn.).

Rocha, Paulo Alexandre, and Diana Santos (2000). *CETEMPúblico*: Um corpus de grandes dimensões de linguagem jornalística portuguesa, in Maria das Graças Volpe Nunes (ed.), *V Encontro para o Processamento Computacional da língua Portuguesa Escrita e Falada (PROPOR 2000)*. São Paulo: ICMC, USP, 131–40. Corpus URL: <http://www.linguateca.pt/CETEMPublico/> accessed Feb. 2016.

Xavier, Maria Francisca (coord.) (1993–). *Digital Corpus of Medieval Portuguese*. Faculdade de Ciências Sociais e Humanas da Universidade Nova de Lisboa. <http://cipm.fcsh.unl.pt/> accessed Feb. 2016.

Secondary sources

Abney, Steven (1987). The English Noun Phrase in its Sentential Aspect. Doctoral Dissertation, MIT.

Alexandre, Nélia (2000). A estratégia resumptiva em relativas restritivas do Português Europeu. Master's Dissertation, University of Lisbon.

Alexiadou, Artemis (1997). *Adverb Placement: A Case Study in Antisymmetric Syntax*. Amsterdam: John Benjamins.

Alexiadou, Artemis, and Elena Anagnostopoulou (2001). The subject-in-situ generalization and the role of case driving computations, *Linguistic Inquiry* 32(2): 193–231.

Alexiadou, Artemis, Paul Law, André Meinunger, and Chris Wilder (2000). *The Syntax of Relative Clauses*. Amsterdam: John Benjamins.

Ambar, Manuela (1992). *Para uma sintaxe da inversão sujeito-verbo em Português*. Lisbon: Edições Colibri.

Ambar, Manuela (1999). Aspects of the syntax of focus in Portuguese, in Georges Rebuschi and Laurice Tuller (eds.), *The Grammar of Focus*. Amsterdam: John Benjamins, 23–53.

Ambar, Manuela, and Rita Veloso (2001). On the nature of wh-phrases—Word order and wh-in-situ: Evidence from Portuguese, French, Hungarian and Tetum, in Yves D'hulst, Johan Rooryck, and Jan Schroten (eds.), *Romance Languages and Linguistic Theory 1999: Selected Papers from Going Romance 1999*. Amsterdam: John Benjamins, 1–37.

Ambar, Manuela, Hans Obenauer, Iris Pereira, et al. (1998). From wh-questions to wh-exclamatives: The internal structure of wh-phrases and the left periphery. Evidence from Portuguese, French and Hungarian. Posted at Chomsky Celebration's site for his 70th anniversary in December 1998.

Andrews, Avery (1975). Studies in the Syntax of Relative and Comparative Clauses. Doctoral Dissertation, MIT.

Androutsopoulou, Antonia (1997). Reduced relatives in DPs: Evidence from adjective extraction in Modern Greek, *MIT Working Papers in Linguistics* 31: 19–40.

Arnold, Doug (2007). Non-restrictive relatives are not orphans, *Journal of Linguistics* 43(2): 271–309.

Avesani, Cinzia, and Mario Vayra (2003). Broad, narrow, and contrastive focus in Florentine Italian, in María Josep Solé, Daniel Recasens, and Joaquín Romero (eds.), *Proceedings of the XVth International Congress of Phonetic Sciences*. Barcelona: Futurgraphic, ii. 1803–6.

Baker, Mark (2003). *Lexical Categories: Verbs, Nouns and Adjectives*. Cambridge: Cambridge University Press.

Baltin, Mark (1984). Extraposition rules and discontinuous constituents, *Linguistic Inquiry* 15: 157–63.

Baltin, Mark (2006). Extraposition, in Martin Everaert and Henk van Riemsdijk (eds.), *The Blackwell Companion to Syntax*. Malden, Mass.: Blackwell, ii. 237–71.

Barbiers, Sjef (1995). *The Syntax of Interpretation*. The Hague: HAG.

Barbosa, Pilar (1995). Null Subjects. Doctoral Dissertation, MIT.

Barbosa, Pilar (2000). Clitics: A window into the null subject property, in João Costa (ed.), *Portuguese Syntax: New Comparative Studies*. New York: Oxford University Press, 31–93.

Barbosa, Pilar (2009). Two kinds of subject pro, *Studia Linguistica* 63(1): 2–58.

Barbosa, Pilar, Maria Eugênia Duarte, and Mary Kato (2005). Null subjects in European and Brazilian Portuguese, *Journal of Portuguese Linguistics* 4(2): 11–52.

Barreto, Mário (1911/1980). *Novos estudos da língua portuguesa*. Rio de Janeiro: Livraria Francisco Alves. (3rd edn., Rio de Janeiro: Presença Edições).

Bašić, Monika (2004). Nominal Subextractions and the Structure of NPs in Serbian and English. Master's Dissertation, University of Tromsø.

Basilico, David (1996). Head position and internally headed relative clauses, *Language* 72: 498–533.

Bassols de Climent, Mariano (1967). *Sintaxis latina*. Madrid: Consejo Superior de Investigaciones Científicas.

Bastos, Ana Cláudia (2001). Fazer, eu faço! Topicalização de constituintes verbais em português brasileiro. Master's Dissertation, Campinas State University.

Batllori, Montserrat, and Maria Lluïsa Hernanz (2015). Weak focus and polarity: Asymmetries between Spanish and Catalan, in Theresa Biberauer and George Walkden (eds.), *Syntax over Time: Lexical, Morphological and Information-structural Interactions*. Oxford: Oxford University Press, 280–98.

Bechara, Evanildo (1961/2001). *Moderna gramática portuguesa*. Rio de Janeiro: Companhia Editora Nacional. (37th edn., Rio de Janeiro: Editora Lucerna).

Belletti, Adriana (1990). *Generalized Verb Movement: Aspects of Verb Syntax*. Turin: Rosenberg & Sellier.

Bhatt, Rajesh (2002). The raising analysis of relative clauses: Evidence from adjectival modification, *Natural Language Semantics* 10: 43–90.

Bianchi, Valentina (1999). *Consequences of Antisymmetry: Headed Relative Clauses*. Berlin: Mouton de Gruyter.

Bianchi, Valentina (2000). The raising analysis of relative clauses: A reply to Borsley, *Linguistic Inquiry* 31(1): 123–40.

Bianchi, Valentina (2002). Headed relative clauses in generative syntax—part II, *GLOT International* 6(8): 235–47.

Biberauer, Theresa, and Ian Roberts (2008). Cascading parameter changes: Internally driven change in Middle and Early Modern English, in Thórhallur Eythórsson (ed.), *Grammatical Change and Linguistic Theory*. Amsterdam: John Benjamins, 79–133.

Biberauer, Theresa, Anders Holmberg, Ian Roberts, and Michelle Sheehan (2010). *Parametric Syntax: Null Subjects in Minimalist Theory*. Cambridge: Cambridge University Press.

Bobaljik, Jonathan David (2002). A-chains at the PF-interface: Copies and covert movement, *Natural Language & Linguistic Theory* 20(2): 197–267.

Borsley, Robert (1997). Relative clauses and the theory of phrase structure, *Linguistic Inquiry* 28(4): 629–47.

Bošković, Željko (1999). On multiple feature checking: Multiple wh-fronting and multiple head movement, in Samuel Epstein and Norbert Hornstein (eds.), *Working Minimalism*. Cambridge, Mass.: MIT Press, 159–87.

Bošković, Željko (2001). *On the Nature of the Syntax-Phonology Interface: Cliticization and Related Phenomena*. Amsterdam: Elsevier Science.

Bošković, Željko (2002). On multiple wh-fronting, *Linguistic Inquiry* 33(3): 351–83.

Bošković, Željko (2004a). On the clitic switch in Greek imperatives, in Olga Tomić (ed.), *Balkan Syntax and Semantics*. Amsterdam: John Benjamins, 269–91.

Bošković, Željko (2004b). PF merger in stylistic fronting and object shift, in Arthur Stepanov, Gisbert Fanselow, and Ralf Vogel (eds.), *Minimality Effects in Syntax*. Berlin: Mouton de Gruyter, 37–71.

Bošković, Željko (2005). On the locality of left branch extraction and the structure of NP, *Studia Linguistica* 59(1): 1–45.

Bošković, Željko, and Jairo Nunes (2007). The copy theory of movement: A view from PF, in Norbert Corver and Jairo Nunes (eds.), *The Copy Theory of Movement*. Amsterdam: John Benjamins, 13–74.

Bowers, John (1987). Extended X-bar theory, the ECP, and the Left Branch Condition, in Megan Crowhurst (ed.), *Proceedings of the West Coast Conference on Formal Linguistics* 6. Stanford: Stanford Linguistics Association, 47–62.

Brito, Ana Maria (1991). *A sintaxe das orações relativas em português: estrutura, mecanismos interpretativos e condições sobre a distribuição dos morfemas relativos*. Porto: Instituto Nacional de Investigação Científica, Centro de Linguística da Universidade do Porto.

Brito, Ana Maria (1995). As orações relativas restritivas nas variantes culta e oral em quatro línguas românicas, com especial incidência em português, *Lusorama* 27: 70–81.

Brito, Ana Maria (2003). Categorias sintácticas, in Maria Helena Mateus, Ana Maria Brito, Inês Duarte, et al. (eds.), *Gramática da língua portuguesa*. Lisboa: Caminho, 323–432.

Brito, Ana Maria (2004). As relativas não restritivas com antecedente nominal como um caso de aposição, in Inês Duarte and Isabel Leiria (eds.), *Actas do XX Encontro Nacional da Associação Portuguesa de Linguística*. Lisboa: APL, 401–19.

Brito, Ana Maria, and Inês Duarte (2003). Orações relativas e construções aparentadas, in Maria Helena Mateus, Ana Maria Brito, Inês Duarte, et al. (eds.), *Gramática da língua portuguesa*. Lisbon: Caminho, 653–94.

Brito, Ana Maria, Inês Duarte, and Gabriela Matos (2003). Estrutura da frase simples e tipos de frase, in Maria Helena Mateus, Ana Maria Brito, Inês Duarte, et al. (eds.), *Gramática da língua portuguesa*. Lisbon: Caminho, 433–506.

Broekhuis, Hans (2007). Object shift and subject shift, *Journal of Comparative Germanic Linguistics* 10: 109–41.

Browning, Marguerite Ann (1987). Null Operator Constructions. Doctoral Dissertation, MIT.

Brucart, José María (1999). La estructura del sintagma nominal: Las oraciones de relativo, in Ignácio Bosque and Violeta Demonte (eds.), *Gramática descriptiva de la lengua española*. Madrid: Espasa Calpe, 395–522.

Büring, Daniel, and Katharina Hartmann (1997). Doing the right thing—extraposition as a movement rule, *Linguistic Review* 14: 1–42.

Butler, Alastair, and Eric Mathieu (2004). *The Syntax and Semantics of Split Constructions: A Comparative Study*. Basingstoke: Palgrave Macmillan.

Cable, Seth (2007). The Grammar of Q: Q-particles and the nature of wh-fronting, as revealed by the wh-questions of Tlingit. Doctoral Dissertation, MIT.

Cardinaletti, Anna (1987). Aspetti sintattici dell'estraposizione della frase relativa, *Rivista di Grammatica Generativa* 12: 3–59.

Cardoso, Adriana (2008). Relativas com núcleo interno e relativo de ligação na história do português, in Sónia Frota and Ana Lúcia Santos (eds.), *Actas do XXIII Encontro Nacional da Associação Portuguesa de Linguística*. Lisbon: Associação Portuguesa de Linguística, 77–92.

Cardoso, Adriana (2010). Variation and Change in the Syntax of Relative Clauses: New Evidence from Portuguese. Doctoral Dissertation, University of Lisbon.

Cardoso, Adriana (2011). Orações relativas apositivas em português: entre a sincronia e a diacronia, *Estudos de Lingüística Galega* 3: 5–29.

Cardoso, Adriana (2012). Extraposition of restrictive relative clauses in the history of Portuguese, in Charlotte Galves, Sonia Cyrino, Ruth Lopes, et al. (eds.), *Parameter Theory and Linguistic Change*. Oxford: Oxford University Press, 77–96.

Cardoso, Adriana, and Mark de Vries (2010). Internal and external heads in appositive constructions. MS. University of Lisbon, University of Groningen, Version 2, May 2010.

Carlson, Greg (1977). Amount relatives, *Language* 53: 520–42.

Carrilho, Ernestina (2005). Expletive *ele* in European Portuguese Dialects. Doctoral Dissertation, University of Lisbon.

Castro, Ivo (1983). Sobre a data da introdução na Península Ibérica do ciclo arturiano da Post-Vulgata, *Boletim de Filologia* 28: 81–98.

Castro, Ivo (1993). Demanda do Santo Graal, in Giulia Tavani and Giuseppe Lanciani (eds.), *Dicionário da literatura medieval galega e portuguesa*. Lisbon: Caminho.

Cecchetto, Carlo (2005). Reconstruction in relative clauses and the copy theory of traces, in Pierre Pica and Johan Rooryck (eds.), *Linguistic Variation Yearbook* 5. Amsterdam: John Benjamin, 73–103.

Chafe, Wallace (1976). Givenness, contrastiveness, definiteness, subjects, topics, and point of view in subject and topic, in Charles Li (ed.), *Subject and Topic*. New York: Academic Press, 25–55.

Chomsky, Noam (1965). *Aspects of the Theory of Syntax*. Cambridge, Mass.: MIT Press.

Chomsky, Noam (1973). Conditions on transformations, in Stephen Anderson and Paul Kiparsky (eds.), *A Festschrift for Morris Halle*. New York: Holt, Reinhart & Winston, 232–86.

Chomsky, Noam (1977). On wh-movement, in Peter Culicover, Thomas Wasow, and Adrian Akmajian (eds.), *Formal Syntax*. New York: Academic Press, 71–132.

Chomsky, Noam (1981). *Lectures on Government and Binding*. Dordrecht: Foris.

Chomsky, Noam (1993). A minimalist program for linguistic theory, in Kenneth Hale and Samuel Keyser (eds.), *The View from Building 20*. Cambridge, Mass.: MIT Press, 1–52.

Chomsky, Noam (1995). *The Minimalist Program*. Cambridge, Mass.: MIT Press.

Chomsky, Noam (2000). Minimalist inquiries: The framework, in Roger Martin, David Michaelis, and Juan Uriagereka (eds.), *Step by Step: Essays on Minimalist Syntax in Honor of Howard Lasnik*. Cambridge, Mass.: MIT Press, 89–156.

Chomsky, Noam (2001). Derivation by phase, in Michael Kenstowicz (ed.), *Ken Hale: A Life in Language*. Cambridge, Mass.: MIT Press, 1–52.

Cinque, Guglielmo (1982). On the theory of relative clauses and markedness, *Linguistic Review* 1: 247–94.

Cinque, Guglielmo (1990). *Types of A-dependencies*. Cambridge, Mass.: MIT Press.

Cinque, Guglielmo (1994). On the evidence for partial N movement in the Romance DP, in Guglielmo Cinque, Jan Koster, Jean-Yves Pollock, et al. (eds.), *Paths towards Universal Grammar: Studies in Honor of Richard S. Kayne*. Washington DC: Georgetown University Press, 85–110.

Cinque, Guglielmo (1999). *Adverbs and Functional Heads: A Cross-Linguistic Perspective*. Oxford: Oxford University Press.

Cinque, Guglielmo (2003). The prenominal origin of relative clauses. Paper presented at the Workshop on Antisymmetry and Remnant Movement, New York University, 31 October–2 November.

Cinque, Guglielmo (2006). *Restructuring and Functional Heads: The Cartography of Syntactic Structures*. Oxford, New York: Oxford University Press.

Cinque, Guglielmo (2007). A note on linguistic theory and typology, *Linguistic Typology* 11: 93–106.

Cinque, Guglielmo (2008). Two types of nonrestrictive relatives, in Olivier Bonami and Patricia Cabredo Hofherr (eds.), *Empirical Issues in Syntax and Semantics* 7, 99–137. At <http://www.cssp.cnrs.fr/eiss7/eiss7.pdf>, accessed February 2017.

Cinque, Guglielmo (2009). The prenominal origin of relative clauses. Paper presented at a research seminar, University of Hong Kong, 5 May.

Cinque, Guglielmo, and Richard Kayne (eds.) (2005). *The Oxford Handbook of Comparative Syntax*. New York: Oxford University Press.

Citko, Barbara (2001). Deletion under identity in relative clauses, in Minjoo Kim and Uri Strauss (eds.), *Proceedings of the North East Linguistic Society* 31. Amherst, Mass.: GLSA, University of Massachusetts, 131–46.

Colaço, Madalena (2006). Coordenação e movimento sintáctico: os dados do português europeu, *Letras de Hoje* 1(1): 75–97.

Corominas, Joan, and José Pascual (1980). *Diccionario crítico etimológico castellano e hispánico*. Madrid: Gredos.

Corver, Norbert Ferdinand Marie (1990). The Syntax of Left Branch Extractions. Doctoral Dissertation, Tilburg University.

Costa, Ana (2003). Construções de relativização numa partição de Chelas de 1425, MS. University of Lisbon.

Costa, Ana (2004). Aspectos das construções de relativização no português do séc. XV, in Tiago Freitas and Amália Mendes (eds.), *Actas do XIX Encontro da Associação Portuguesa de Linguística*. Lisbon: Associação Portuguesa de Linguística, 409–20.

Costa, João (1996). Adverb positioning and V-movement in English: Some more evidence, *Studia Linguistica* 50(1): 22–34.

Costa, João (1998). *Word Order Variation: A Constraint-Based Approach*. The Hague: Holland Academic Graphics.

Costa, João (2001). Postverbal subjects and agreement in unaccusative contexts in European Portuguese, *Linguistic Review* 18(1): 1–17.

Costa, João (2004a). *Subject Positions and Interfaces: The Case of European Portuguese*. Berlin: Mouton de Gruyter.

Costa, João (2004b). A multifactorial approach to adverb placement: Assumptions, facts, and problems, *Lingua* 114(6): 711–53.

Costa, João, and Inês Duarte (2002). Preverbal subjects in null subject languages are not necessarily dislocated, *Journal of Portuguese Linguistics* 1: 157–75.

Costa, João, Alexandra Fiéis, and Maria Lobo (2012). Pied-piping e movimento em estruturas adverbiais, in Armanda Costa, Cristina Flores, and Nélia Alexandre (eds.), *XXVII Encontro Nacional da Associação Portuguesa de Linguística—textos seleccionados*. Lisbon: Associação Portuguesa de Linguística, 185–95.

Costa, João, and Ana Maria Martins (2009). *Scrambling* de média distância com advérbios locativos no português contemporâneo, in Alexandra Fiéis and Maria Antónia Coutinho (eds.), *Actas do XXIV Encontro Nacional da Associação Portuguesa de Linguística*. Lisboa: Lisbon: Associação Portuguesa de Linguística, 225–37.

Costa, João, and Ana Maria Martins (2011). On focus movement in European Portuguese, *Probus* 23(2): 217–45.

Cresti, Diana (2000). Ellipsis and reconstruction in relative clauses, in Masako Hirotani, Andries Coetzee, Nigel Hall, and Ji-Yung Kim (eds.), *Proceedings of the North East Linguistic Society* 30. Amherst, Mass.: GLSA, University of Massachusetts, 153–62.

Cruschina, Silvio (2011). *Discourse-Related Features and Functional Projections*. Oxford: Oxford University Press.

Cuesta, Pilar Vásquez, and Maria Albertina Luz (1971). *Gramática portuguesa*. Madrid: Gredos (1980, Portuguese translation: *Gramática da língua portuguesa*. Lisbon: Edições 70).

Culicover, Peter, and Michael Rochemont (1990). Extraposition and Logical Form, *Linguistic Inquiry* 21(1): 23–47.

Culicover, Peter, and Susanne Winkler (2008). English focus inversion constructions, *Journal of Linguistics* 44: 625–58.

Culy, Christopher (1990). The Syntax and Semantics of Internally Headed Relative Clauses. Doctoral Dissertation, Stanford University.

Cunha, Celso, and Luis Filipe Lindley Cintra (1984/1997). *Nova gramática do português contemporâneo*. Lisbon: Edições João Sá da Costa (17th edn.).

Danckaert, Lieven (2012). *Latin Embedded Clauses: The Left Periphery*. Amsterdam: John Benjamins.

Del Gobbo, Francesca (2008). On the syntax and semantics of appositive relative clauses, in Nicole Dehé and Yordanka Kavalova (eds.), *Parentheticals*. Amsterdam: John Benjamins, 173–201.

Delorme, Evelyne, and Ray Dougherty (1972). Appositive NP constructions, *Foundations of Language* 8: 2–29.

Demirdache, Hamida (1991). Resumptive Chains in Restrictive Relatives, Appositives, and Dislocation Structures. Doctoral Dissertation, MIT.

Devine, A. M., and Laurence Stephens (1999). *Discontinuous Syntax: Hyperbaton in Greek*. Oxford: Oxford University Press.

Devine, Andrew, and Laurence Stephens (2006). *Latin Word Order: Structured Meaning and Information*. Oxford: Oxford University Press.

Dias, Augusto Epifânio da Silva (1933/1970). *Sintaxe histórica portuguesa*. Lisbon: Clássica Editora (5th edn.).

Diesing, Molly (1992). *Indefinites*. Cambridge, Mass.: MIT Press.

Drozd, Kenneth (2001). Metalinguistic sentence negation in child English, in Jack Hoeksema, Holtze Rullmann, Victor Sanchez-Valencia, and Ton van der Wouden (eds.), *Perspectives on Negation and Polarity Items*. Amsterdam: John Benjamins, 49–78.

Duarte, Inês (1987). A construção de topicalização na gramática do português: regência, ligação e condições sobre o movimento. Doctoral Dissertation, University of Lisbon.

Duarte, Inês (1997). Ordem de palavras: sintaxe e estrutura discursiva, in Ana Maria Brito, Fátima Oliveira, Isabel Pires de Lima, et al. (eds.), *Sentido que a vida faz: estudos para Óscar Lopes*. Porto: Campo das Letras, 581–92.

Duarte, Inês (2003). A família das construções inacusativas, in Maria Helena Mateus, Ana Maria Brito, Inês Duarte et al. (eds.), *Gramática da língua portuguesa*. Lisbon: Caminho, 507–48.

Duarte, Inês, and Fátima Oliveira (2003). Referência nominal, in Maria Helena Mateus, Ana Maria Brito, Inês Duarte, et al. (eds.), *Gramática da língua portuguesa*. Lisbon: Caminho, 205–42.

É. Kiss, Katalin (1998). Identificational focus versus information focus, *Language* 74(2): 245–73.

Emonds, Joseph (1976). *A Transformational Approach to English Syntax: Root, Structure-preserving, and Local Transformations*. New York: Academic Press.

Emonds, Joseph (1979). Appositive relatives have no properties, *Linguistic Inquiry* 10(2): 211–43.

Emonds, Joseph (1985). *A Unified Theory of Syntactic Categories*. Dordrecht: Foris.

Enkvist, Nils Erik (1980). Marked focus: Function and constraints, in Sidney Greenbaum, Geoffrey Leech, and Jan Svartvik (eds.), *Studies in English Linguistics for Randolph Quirk*. London: Longman, 134–52.

Ernout, Alfred, and François Thomas (1972). *Syntaxe Latine*. Paris: Klincksieck.

Ernst, Thomas (2002). *The Syntax of Adjuncts*. Cambridge: Cambridge University Press.

Erteschik-Shir, Nomi (2007). *Information Structure: The Syntax-Discourse Interface.* Oxford: Oxford University Press.

Espinal, M. Teresa (1991). The representation of disjunct constituents, *Language* 67: 726–62.

Evans, Gareth (1980). Pronouns, *Linguistic Inquiry* 11: 337–62.

Fabb, Nigel (1990). The difference between English restrictive and nonrestrictive relative clauses, *Journal of Linguistics* 26(1): 57–78.

Fanselow, Gisbert (1988). Aufspaltung von NPn und das Problem der "freien" Wortstellung, *Linguistische Berichte* 114: 91–113.

Fanselow, Gisbert, and Damir Ćavar (2002). Distributed deletion, in Artemis Alexiadou (ed.), *Theoretical Approaches to Universals.* Amsterdam: John Benjamins, 65–107.

Fanselow, Gisbert, and Caroline Féry (2006). Prosodic and morphosyntactic aspects of discontinuous noun phrases: A crosslinguistic perspective. MS. University of Postdam.

Fiéis, Alexandra, and Maria Lobo (2010). Aspectos da sintaxe das orações gerundivas em Português Medieval e em Português Contemporâneo, in Ana Maria Brito, Fátima Silva, João Veloso, et al. (eds.), *XXV Encontro Nacional da Associação Portuguesa de Linguística—textos seleccionados.* Porto: Associação Portuguesa de Linguística, 419–34.

Fiengo, Robert (1977). On trace theory, *Linguistic Inquiry* 8: 35–61.

Finch, James (2006). *Caesar Completely Parsed.* Mundelein, Ill.: Bolchazy-Carducci.

Fiorentino, Giuliana (1999). *Relativa debole. Sintassi, uso, storia in italiano.* Milan: Franco Angeli.

Fox, Danny (2002). Antecedent-contained deletion and the copy theory of movement, *Linguistic Inquiry* 33(1): 63–96.

Fox, Danny, and Jon Nissenbaum (1999). Extraposition and scope: A case for overt QR, in Sonya Bird, Andrew Carnie, Jason Haugen, and Peter Norquest (eds.), *Proceedings of the 18th West Coast Conference on Formal Linguistics.* Somerville, Mass.: Cascadilla, 132–44.

Franks, Steven, and Ljiljana Progovac (1994). On the displacement of Serbo-Croatian clitics, *Indiana Linguistic Studies* 7: 69–78.

Frota, Sónia (1998). *Prosody and Focus in European Portuguese.* Doctoral Dissertation, University of Lisbon.

Frota, Sónia (2002). Nuclear falls and rises in European Portuguese: A phonological analysis of declarative and question intonation, *Probus* 14: 113–46.

Giorgi, Alessandra, and Giuseppe Longobardi (1991). *The Syntax of Noun Phrases.* Cambridge: Cambridge University Press.

Givón, Talmy (2001). *Syntax: An Introduction.* Amsterdam: John Benjamins.

Grimshaw, Jane (2000). Locality and extended projections, in Peter Coopmans, Martins Everaert, and Jane Grimshaw (eds.), *Lexical Specification and Insertion.* Amsterdam: John Benjamins.

Grosu, Alexander (1973). On the nonunitary nature of the coordinate structure constraint, *Linguistic Inquiry* 4: 88–92.

Grosu, Alexander, and Fred Landman (1998). Strange relatives of the third kind, *Natural Language Semantics* 6: 125–70.

Haider, Hubert (1996). Downright down to the right, in Uli Lutz and Jurgen Pafel (eds.), *On Extraction and Extraposition in German.* Amsterdam: John Benjamins, 245–71.

Haider, Hubert (1997). Extraposition, in Dorothee Beerman, David LeBlanc, and Henk van Riemsdijk (eds.), *Rightward Movement.* Amsterdam: John Benjamins, 115–51.

Hale, Ken (1983). Warlpiri and the grammar of non-configurational languages, *Natural Language & Linguistic Theory* 1: 5–47.

Hale, William, and Carl Buck (1966). *A Latin Grammar*. Tuscaloosa: University of Alabama.

Halitsky, David (1974). Deep structure appositive and complement NPs, *Language* 50: 446–55.

Heck, Fabian (2008). *On Pied-Piping. Wh-movement and Beyond*. Berlin: Mouton de Gruyter.

Heim, Irene (1987). Where does the definiteness restriction apply? Evidence from the definiteness of variables, in Eric Reuland and Alice ter Meulen (eds.), *The Representation of (In)definiteness*. Cambridge, Mass.: MIT Press, 21–42.

Henk, Paula (2010). *Information Structure of Estonian—Compared to Finnish and Hungarian*. Osnabrück: Institute of Cognitive Science.

Heringa, Herman (2007). Appositional constructions: Coordination and predication, in Marlies Kluck and Erik-Jan Smits (eds.), *Proceedings of the Fifth Semantics in The Netherlands Day*. Groningen: University of Groningen, 67–82.

Heringa, Herman (2012). A multidominance approach to appositional constructions, *Lingua* 122(6): 554–81.

Hernanz, María Lluïsa, and José María Brucart (1987). *La sintaxis: principios teóricos. La oración simple*. Barcelona: Crítica.

Holmberg, Anders (2000). Scandinavian stylistic fronting: How any category can become an expletive, *Linguistic Inquiry* 31(3): 445–83.

Holmberg, Anders, and Ian Roberts (2010). Introduction, in Theresa Biberauer, Anders Holmberg, Ian Roberts, et al. (eds.), *Parametric Variation: Null Subjects in Minimalist Theory*. Cambridge: Cambridge University Press, 1–57.

Hoof, Hanneke van (2005). Split topicalization, in Martin Everaet and Henk van Riemsdijk (eds.), *The Blackwell Companion to Syntax*. London: Blackwell.

Hoop, Helen de (1992). *Case Configuration and Noun Phrase Interpretation*. Doctoral Dissertation, University of Groningen.

Horvath, Julia (2007). Separating "focus movement" from focus, in Simin Karimi, Vida Samiian, and Wendy Wilkins (eds.), *Phrasal and Clausal Architecture: Syntactic Derivation and Interpretation: In Honor of Joseph E. Emonds*. Amsterdam: John Benjamins, 108–45.

Hualde, José (2002). Intonation in Romance. Introduction to the special issue, *Probus* 14: 1–7.

Huber, Joseph (1933/1986). *Altportugiesisches Elementarbuch*. Heidelberg: Carl Winters (1986, Portuguese translation: *Gramática do português antigo*. Lisbon: Fundação Calouste Gulbenkian).

Huddleston, Rodney, Geoffrey Pullum, and Peter Peterson (2002). Relative constructions and unbounded dependencies, *The Cambridge Grammar of the English Language*. Cambridge: Cambridge University Press, 1031–96.

Inaba, Jiro (2005). Extraposition and the directionality of movement, in Sylvia Blaho, Luis Vicente, and Erik Schoorlemmer (eds.), *Proceedings of ConSOLE XIII*. Leiden: Leiden University, 157–69.

Inada, Shun'ichiro (2007). Towards a syntax of two types of relative clauses, *Linguistic Research: Working Papers in English Linguistics* 23: 1–41.

Jackendoff, Ray (1977). *X-syntax: A Study of Phrase Structure*. Cambridge, Mass.: MIT Press.

Jackendoff, Ray (1990). On Larson's treatment of the double object construction, *Linguistic Inquiry* 21(3): 427–56.

Jelinek, Eloise (1984). Empty categories, case, and configurationality, *Natural Language & Linguistic Theory* 2: 39–76.

Jespersen, Otto (1949). *A Modern English Grammar on Historical Principles*. London: Allen and Unwin.

Johannessen, Janne (1998). *Coordination*. Oxford: Oxford University Press.

Kariaeva, Natalia (2009). Radical Discontinuity: Syntax at the Interface. Doctoral Dissertation, State University of New Jersey.

Kato, Mary, and Jairo Nunes (2009). A uniform raising analysis for standard and nonstandard relative clauses in Brazilian Portuguese, in Jairo Nunes (ed.), *Minimalist Essays on Brazilian Portuguese Syntax*. Amsterdam: John Benjamins, 93–120.

Kato, Mary, and Eduardo Paiva Raposo (2007). Topicalization in European and Brazilian Portuguese, in José Camacho, Nydia Flores, Liliane Sánches, et al. (eds.), *Romance Linguistics: Selected Papers from the 36th Linguistic Symposium on Romance Languages*. Amsterdam: John Benjamins, 213–26.

Kayne, Richard (1984). *Connectedness and Binary Branching*. Dordrecht: Foris.

Kayne, Richard (1994). *The Antisymmetry of Syntax*. Cambridge, Mass.: MIT Press.

Kiss, Tibor (2003). Phrasal typology and the interaction of topicalization, wh-movement and extraposition, in Jong-Bok Kim and Stephen Wechsler (eds.), *Proceedings of the 9th International Conference on Head-Driven Phrase Structure Grammar*. Stanford: CSLI, 109–28.

Kiss, Tibor (2005). Semantic constraints on relative clause extraposition, *Natural Language & Linguistic Theory* 23(2): 281–334.

Klein, Maarten (1977). Appositionele Constructies in het Nederlands. Doctoral Dissertation, Radboud University Nijmegen.

Koopman, Hilda, and Dominique Sportiche (1991). The position of subjects, *Lingua* 85: 211–58.

Koster, Jan (1987). *Domains and Dynasties. The Radical Autonomy of Syntax*. Dordrecht: Foris.

Koster, Jan (1995). Extraposition as coordination. Paper presented at Max-Planck-Institut and Von Humboldt University, Berlin.

Koster, Jan (2000). Extraposition as parallel construal. MS. University of Groningen.

Krifka, Manfred (2007). Basic notions of information structure, in Caroline Féry, Gisbert Fanselow, and Manfred Krifka (eds.), *Working Papers of the SFB632, Interdisciplinary Studies on Information Structure (ISIS) 6*. Potsdam: University of Potsdam, 13–56.

Kroch, Anthony (1989). Reflexes of grammar in patterns of language change, *Language Variation and Change* 1: 199–244.

Kroch, Anthony (1994). Morphosyntactic variation, in Katharine Beals, Jeannette Denton, Robert Knippen, et al. (eds.), *Proceedings of the Thirtieth Annual Regional Meeting of the Chicago Linguistics Society*. Chicago: Chicago Linguistics Society, 180–201.

Kroch, Anthony (2001). Syntactic change, in Mark Baltin and Chris Collins (eds.), *The Handbook of Contemporary Syntactic Theory*. Malden, Mass.: Blackwell, 699–729.

Kunstmann, Pierre (1991). Création et diffusion du rélatif/interrogatif *lequel* en ancien français. Comparaison avec d'autres langues romanes, in Dieter Kremer (ed.), *Actes du XVIIIe Congrès International de Linguistique Romane*. Tübingen: Max Niemeyer, ii. 660–70.

Kuroda, S.-Y. (1965). Generative Grammatical Studies in the Japanese Language. Doctoral Dissertation, MIT.

Kuroda, S.-Y. (1972). The categorical and the thetic judgment: Evidence from Japanese syntax, *Foundations of Language* 9: 153–85.

Kuroda, S.-Y. (1992). *Japanese Syntax and Semantics: Collected Papers*. Dordrecht: Kluwer.

Kuroda, S.-Y. (2005). Focusing on the matter of topic: A study of *wa* and *ga* in Japanese, *Journal of East Asian Linguistics* 14(1): 1–58.

Laka, Itziar (1990). Negation in Syntax: On the Nature of Functional Categories and Projections. Doctoral Dissertation, MIT.

Lambova, Mariana (2004). On triggers of movement and effects at the interfaces, in Anne Breitbarth and Henk van Riemsdijk (eds.), *Triggers*. Berlin: de Gruyter, 231–58.

Lambrecht, Knud (1994). *Information Structure and Sentence Form: Topic, Focus, and the Mental Representations of Discourse Referents*. Cambridge: Cambridge University Press.

Landau, Idan (2007). EPP extensions, *Linguistic Inquiry* 38(3): 485–523.

Larson, Richard (1988). On the double object construction, *Linguistic Inquiry* 19(3): 335–91.

Larson, Richard (1990). Double objects revisited: Reply to Jackendoff, *Linguistic Inquiry* 21(4): 589–632.

Lasnik, Howard, and Nicholas Sobin (2000). The *who/whom* puzzle: On the preservation of an archaic feature, *Natural Language & Linguistic Theory* 18: 343–71.

Lausberg, Heinrich (1967/1972). *Elemente der Literarischen Rhetorik*. Munich: Max Hueber (Portuguese translation: 1972, *Elementos de retórica literária*, 2nd edn., Lisbon, Fundação Calouste Gulbenkian).

Ledgeway, Adam (forthcoming). From Latin to Romance: On the decline of edge-fronting, in Ana Maria Martins and Adriana Cardoso (eds.), *Word Order Change*. Oxford: Oxford University Press.

Lee, Seong-yong (2007). Sideward movement approach to extraposition from DP in English, *Korean Journal of English Language and Linguistics* 7(1): 27–49.

Lees, Robert (1960). *The Grammar of English Nominalizations*. The Hague: Mouton.

Lees, Robert (1961). The constituent structure of noun phrase, *American Speech* 36: 159–68.

Lehmann, Christian (1984). *Der Relativsatz*. Tübingen: Gunter Narr.

Lightfoot, David (1979). *Principles of Diachronic Syntax*. Cambridge Studies in Linguistics 23. Cambridge: Cambridge University Press.

Lightfoot, David (1991). *How to Set Parameters: Arguments from Language Change*. Cambridge, Mass.: MIT Press.

Lightfoot, David (1999). *The Development of Language: Acquisition, Change, and Evolution*. Oxford: Blackwell.

Lobo, Maria (2003). Aspectos da sintaxe das orações subordinadas adverbiais do português. Doctoral Dissertation, New University of Lisbon.

Loock, Rudy (2007). Appositive relative clauses and their functions in discourse, *Journal of Pragmatics* 39(2): 336–62.

López, Luis (2000). Ellipsis and discourse linking, *Lingua* 110: 183–213.

Lucchesi, Dante (1991). Considerações sobre a análise das relativas do Português Contemporâneo e algumas incursões na história dessas estruturas, in Direcção da Associação Portuguesa de Linguística (ed.), *Actas do VI Encontro da Associação Portuguesa de Linguística*. Porto: Associação Portuguesa de Linguística, 175–93.

Maia, Clarinda (1986). *História do galego-português. Estado linguístico da Galiza e do noroeste de Portugal desde o século XIII ao século XVI (com referência à situação do galego moderno).* Coimbra: Instituto Nacional de Investigação Científica.

Martin, Larry (1972). Appositive and Restrictive Relative Clauses in English. Doctoral Dissertation, University of Texas at Austin.

Martins, Ana Maria (1994). Clíticos na história do português. Doctoral Dissertation, University of Lisbon.

Martins, Ana Maria (1999). Ainda «os mais antigos textos escritos em português»: Documentos de 1175 a 1252, in Isabel Hub Faria (ed.), *Lindley Cintra: Homenagem ao Homem, ao Mestre e ao Cidadão.* Lisbon: Cosmos, Faculdade de Letras da Universidade de Lisboa, 491–534.

Martins, Ana Maria (2002). The loss of IP scrambling in Portuguese: Clause structure, word order variation and change, in David Lightfoot (ed.), *Syntactic Effects of Morphological Change.* Oxford, New York: Oxford University Press, 232–48.

Martins, Ana Maria (2004). A emergência do português escrito na segunda metade do século XII, in Rosario Álvarez and Antón Santamarina (eds.), *(Dis)cursos da escrita: estudos de filoloxía galega ofrecidos en memoria de Fernando R. Tato Plaza.* A Coruña: Fundación Pedro Barrié de la Maza, 491–526.

Martins, Ana Maria (2008). Investigating language change in a comparative setting, in Maria Clotilde Almeida, Bernd Sieberg, and Ana Maria Bernardo (eds.), *Questions on Language Change.* Lisbon: Colibri, Centro de Estudos Alemães e Europeus, 99–116.

Martins, Ana Maria (2011). Scrambling and information structure in Old and Contemporary Portuguese, *Catalan Journal of Linguistics* 10: 133–58.

Martins, Ana Maria (2013). Copiar o português duocentista: a *Demanda* e o *José de Arimateia*, in Álvarez Rosario, Ana Maria Martins, Henrique Monteagudo, et al. (eds.), *Ao Sabor do Texto. Estudos dedicados a Ivo Castro.* Santiago de Compostela: Universidade de Santiago de Compostela/Servizo de Publicacións e Intercambio Científico, 383–402.

Martins, Ana Maria (forthcoming). Constituent order in simple declarative clauses, in Mary Kato, Ana Maria Martins, and Jairo Nunes (eds.), *The Syntax of Portuguese.* Cambridge: Cambridge University Press.

Martins, Ana Maria, Sandra Pereira, and Clara Pinto (forthcoming). The diachronic path of *senão*: From conditional subordination to exceptive coordination, in Barbara Egedi and Veronika Hegedűs (eds.), *Functional Heads Across Time: Syntactic Reanalysis and Change.* Oxford: Oxford University Press.

Mathieu, Eric, and Ioanna Sitaridou (2005). Split wh-constructions in Classical and Modern Greek: A diachronic perspective, in Montserrat Batllori and Francesc Roca (eds.), *Grammaticalization and Parametric Change.* Oxford: Oxford University Press, 236–50.

Matos, Gabriela (1992). Construções de elipse do predicado em português. SV nulo e despojamento. Doctoral Dissertation, University of Lisbon.

Matos, Gabriela (2003). Estruturas de coordenação, in Maria Helena Mateus, Ana Maria Brito, Inês Duarte, et al. (eds.), *Gramática da língua portuguesa.* Lisbon: Caminho, 549–92.

Mattos e Silva, Rosa Virgínia (1989). *Estruturas trecentistas: elementos para uma gramática do português arcaico.* Lisbon: Imprensa Nacional—Casa da Moeda.

Meinunger, André (2000). *Syntactic Aspects of Topic and Comment.* Amsterdam: John Benjamins.

Middleton, Roberta (2000). Aspects of the History of Relative Clauses in Italo-Romance. Doctoral Dissertation, University of Oxford.

Milner, Jean-Claude (1978). *De la syntaxe à l'interprétation*. Paris: Seuil.

Milsark, Gary (1974). Existential Sentences in English. Doctoral Dissertation, MIT.

Moro, Andrea (2003). Notes on vocative case: A case study in clause structure, in Josep Quer, Jan Schroten, Mauro Scorretti, et al. (eds.), *Romance Languages and Linguistic Theory 2001: Selected Papers from Going Romance, Amsterdam, 6–8 December 2001*. Amsterdam, Philadelphia: John Benjamins, 247–61.

Munn, Alan (1993). Topics in the Syntax and Semantics of Coordinate Structures. Doctoral Dissertation, University of Maryland.

Nanni, Debbie, and Justine Stillings (1978). Three remarks on pied piping, *Linguistic Inquiry* 9: 310–18.

Ndayiragije, Juvénal (2000). Strengthening PF, *Linguistic Inquiry* 31(3): 485–512.

Neto, Serafim da Silva (1957/1970). *História da língua portuguesa*. Rio de Janeiro: Presença, MEC (2nd edn.).

Neto, Sílvio Toledo (2001). *Livro de José de Arimatéia (Lisboa, AN/TT, Livraria, Cód. 643): Camadas lingüísticas da tradução ibérica ao traslado quinhentista*. Doctoral Dissertation, University of São Paulo.

Nunes, Jairo (1999). Linearization of chains and phonetic realization of chains links, in Samuel Epstein and Norbert Hornstein (eds.), *Working Minimalism*. Cambridge, Mass.: MIT Press, 217–49.

Nunes, Jairo (2004). *Linearization of Chains and Sideward Movement*. Cambridge, Mass.: MIT Press.

O'Connor, Kathleen (2008). Aspects de la syntaxe et de l'interprétation de l'apposition à antécédent nominal. Doctoral Dissertation, University Charles de Gaulle.

Ott, Denis (2009). Multiple NP-split: A distributed deletion analysis, *Groninger Arbeiten zur Germanistischen Linguistik* 48: 65–80.

Peres, João Andrade, and Telmo Móia (1995). *Áreas críticas da língua portuguesa*. Lisbon: Caminho.

Perzanowski, Dennis (1980). Appositive relatives do have properties, in John T. Jensen (ed.), *Cahiers Linguistiques D'Ottawa: Proceedings of the Tenth Meeting of the North East Linguistic Society*. Ottawa: University of Ottawa, 355–68.

Pesetsky, David (1995). *Zero Syntax*. Cambridge, Mass.: MIT Press.

Philips, Colin (1996). Order and Structure. Doctoral Dissertation, MIT.

Pinkster, Harm (2005). Changing patterns of discontinuity in Latin. Paper presented at Latling—13e Colloque international de Linguistique latine, Facultés Universitaires Saint-Louis, 4–9 April.

Pintzuk, Susan (1991). Phrase Structures in Competition: Variation and Change in Old English Word Order. Doctoral Dissertation, University of Pennsylvania.

Poletto, Cecilia (2014). *Word Order in Old Italian*. Oxford: Oxford University Press.

Pollock, Jean-Yves (1989). Verb movement, universal grammar, and the structure of IP, *Linguistic Inquiry* 20: 365–424.

Pollock, Jean-Yves (1994). Notes on checking theory, pro-drop, free variation and economy. Paper presented at the conference Going Romance VIII, University of Utrecht, 8–10 December.

Posner, Rebecca (1996). *The Romance Languages*. Cambridge: Cambridge University Press.

Potts, Christopher (2007). Conventional implicatures, a distinguished class of meanings, in Gillian Ramchand and Charles Reiss (eds.), *Oxford Handbook of Linguistic Interfaces*. Oxford: Oxford University Press, 475–501.

Predolac, Nikol (2009). Information structure and Serbian bipartite NPs, in Wayles Browne, Adam Cooper, Alison Fisher, et al. (eds.), *Proceedings of Formal Approaches to Slavic Linguistics* 18. Ann Arbor: Michigan Slavic Publications, 435–54.

Quer, Josep (1998). *Mood at the Interface*. Utrecht: LOT.

Quirk, Randolph, Sidney Greenbaum, Geoffrey Leech, and Jan Svartvik (1985). *A Comprehensive Grammar of the English Language*. London: Longman.

Ramat, Anna (2005). Persistence and renewal in the relative pronoun paradigm: The case of Italian, *Folia Linguistica Historica* 26(1): 115–38.

Raposo, Eduardo Paiva (1995). Próclise, ênclise e a posição do verbo em Português Europeu, in João Camilo dos Santos and Frederick G. Williams (eds.), *O amor das letras e das gentes: In Honor of Maria de Lourdes Belchior Pontes*. Santa Barbara: Center for Portuguese Studies, University of California, 455–81.

Rebuschi, Georges (2001). Semi-free relative clauses and the DP-hypothesis: Basque evidence and theoretical consequences, in Alex Grosu (ed.), *Proceedings of the The Israel Association for Theoretical Linguistics* 8, 55–64.

Reinhart, Tanya (1980). On the position of extraposed clauses, *Linguistic Inquiry* 2(3): 621–4.

Reinhart, Tanya (1982). *Pragmatics and Linguistics: An Analysis of Sentence Topics*. Bloomington: Indiana University Linguistics Club.

Reinhart, Tanya (1995). Interface strategies, *OTS Working Papers in Linguistics*. Utrecht: Utrecht Institute of Linguistics.

Remberger, Eva-Maria (2010). Left peripheral interactions in Romance. Paper presented at the Worshop on Focus, Contrast and Givenness in Interaction with Extraction and Deletion, University of Tübingen, 26–7 March.

Riemsdijk, Henk van (1989). Movement and regeneration, in Paola Benincá (ed.), *Dialect Variation and the Theory of Grammar*. Dordrecht: Foris, 105–36.

Rizzi, Luigi (1997). The fine structure of the left periphery, in Liliane Haegeman (ed.), *Elements of Grammar: Handbook in Generative Syntax*. Dordrecht: Kluwer, 281–337.

Rooth, Mats (1985). Association with Focus. Doctoral Dissertation, University of Massachusetts, Amherst.

Rooth, Mats (1992). A theory of focus interpretation, *Natural Language Semantics* 1: 75–116.

Ross, John (1967). Constraints on Variables in Syntax. Doctoral Dissertation, MIT.

Safir, Ken (1986). Relative clauses in a theory of binding and levels, *Linguistic Inquiry* 17: 663–89.

Said Ali, Manuel (1931/1971). *Gramática histórica da língua portuguêsa*. São Paulo: Melhoramentos (7th edn.).

Salzmann, Martin (2006). *Resumptive Prolepsis: A Study in Indirect A-dependencies*. Utrecht: LOT.

Santorini, Beatrice (1992). Variation and change in Yiddish subordinate clause word order, *Natural Language & Linguistic Theory* 10: 595–640.

Sauerland, Uli (1998). The Meaning of Chains. Doctoral Dissertation, MIT.

Sauerland, Uli (2003). Unpronounced heads in relative clauses, in Kerstin Schwabe and Susanne Winkler (eds.). *The Interfaces: Deriving and Interpreting Omitted Structures*, Amsterdam: John Benjamins, 205–26.

Schachter, Paul (1973). Focus and relativization, *Language* 53: 19–49.

Schmitt, Cristina (2000). Some consequences of the complement analysis, in Artemis Alexiadou, Paul Law, André Meinunger, and Chris Wilder (eds.), *The Syntax of Relative Clauses*. Amsterdam: John Benjamins, 309–48.

Schönefeld, Doris (2006). Constructions, in Doris Schönefeld (ed.), *Constructions*, special volume 1, Constructions all over: case studies and theoretical implications, http://elanguage. net/journals/index.php/constructions.

Sekerina, Irina A. (1999). The scrambling complexity hypothesis and processing of split scrambling constructions in Russian, *Journal of Slavic Linguistics* 7: 265–304.

Smith, Carlota (1964). Determiners and relative clauses in a generative grammar of English, *Language* 40: 37–52.

Smits, Rik (1988). *The Relative and Cleft Constructions of the Germanic and Romance Languages*. Dordrecht: Foris.

Sobin, Nicholas (1997). Agreement, default rules, and grammatical viruses, *Linguistic Inquiry* 28: 318–43.

Sòla, Jaume (1992). Agreement and Subjects. Doctoral Dissertation, Autonomous University of Barcelona.

Stassen, Leon (2008). Zero copula for predicate nominals, in Martin Haspelmath, Matthew Dryer, David Gil, and Bernard Comrie (eds.), *The World Atlas of Language Structures Online*. Munich: Max Planck Digital Library, ch. 120.

Stjepanović, Sandra (2007). Free word order and copy theory of movement, in Norbert Corver and Jairo Nunes (eds.), *The Copy Theory of Movement*. Amsterdam: John Benjamins, 219–48.

Stone, Jon R. (2005). *The Routledge Dictionary of Latin Quotations; the Illiterati's Guide to Latin Maxims, Mottoes, Proverbs, and Sayings*. New York: Routledge.

Strunk, Jan (2007). Extraposition mythbusting. Paper presented at the Stanford Syntax Workshop, 13 March.

Suñer, Margarita (2001). The puzzle of restrictive relative clauses with conjoined DP antecedents, in Julia Herschensohn, Enrique Mallén, and Karen Zagona (eds.), *Features and Interfaces in Spanish and French: Essays in Honor of Heles Contreras*. Amsterdam: John Benjamins, 267–78.

Takano, Yuji (1998). Object shift and scrambling, *Natural Language & Linguistic Theory* 16(4): 817–89.

Temperley, David (2003). Ambiguity avoidance in English relative clauses, *Language* 79(3): 464–84.

Tognini-Bonelli, Elena (2001). *Corpus Linguistics at Work*. Amsterdam: John Benjamins.

Truckenbrodt, Hubert (1995). Phonological Phrases: Their Relation to Syntax, Focus, and Prominence. Doctoral Dissertation, MIT.

Truswell, Robert (2011). Relatives with a leftward island in Early Modern English, *Natural Language & Linguistic Theory* 29: 291–332.

Vergnaud, Jean-Roger (1974). French Relative Clauses. Doctoral Dissertation, MIT.

Vergnaud, Jean-Roger (1985). *Dépendences et niveaux de représentation en syntaxe*. Amsterdam: John Benjamins.

Verstraete, Jean-Christophe (2005). Two types of coordination in clause combining, *Lingua* 115(4): 611–26.

Vries, Gertrud de (1992). On Coordination and Ellipsis. Doctoral Dissertation, Catholic University of Brabant.

Vries, Mark de (1999). Extraposition of relative clauses as specifying coordination, in Tina Cambier-Langeveld, Anikó Lipták, Michael Redford, et al. (eds.), *Proceedings of ConSOLE VII*. Leiden: SOLE, 293–309.

Vries, Mark de (2002). *The Syntax of Relativization*. Utrecht: LOT.

Vries, Mark de (2005). Coordination and syntactic hierarchy, *Studia Linguistica* 59: 83–105.

Vries, Mark de (2006a). Possessive relatives and (heavy) pied piping, *Journal of Comparative Germanic Linguistics* 9: 1–52.

Vries, Mark de (2006b). The syntax of appositive relativization. On specifying coordination, false free relatives and promotion, *Linguistic Inquiry* 37: 229–70.

Vries, Mark de (2007). Invisible constituents? Parentheses as B-merged adverbial phrases, in Nicole Dehé and Yordanka Kavalova (eds.), *Parentheticals*. Amsterdam: John Benjamins, 203–34.

Vries, Mark de (2009). Specifying coordination: An investigation into the syntax of dislocation, extraposition and parenthesis, in Cynthia R. Dreyer (ed.), *Language and Linguistics: Emerging Trends*. New York: Nova, 37–98.

Webelhuth, Gert (1992). *Principles and Parameters of Syntactic Saturation*. Oxford: Oxford University Press.

Wilder, Chris (1994). Coordination, ATB and ellipsis, *Groninger Arbeiten zur germanistischen Linguistik* 37: 291–329.

Wilder, Chris (1995). Rightward movement as leftward deletion, in Uli Lutz and Jürgen Pafel (eds.), *Extraction and Extraposition in German*. Amsterdam: John Benjamins, 273–309.

Zhang, Niina Ning (2007). The syntactic derivations of split antecedent relative clause constructions, *Taiwan Journal of Linguistics* 5(1): 19–48.

Zimmermann, Malte (2007). Contrastive focus, in Caroline Féry, Gisbert Fanselow, and Manfred Krifka (eds.), *Working Papers of the SFB632, Interdisciplinary Studies on Information Structure 6*. Potsdam: Universitätsverlag Potsdam, 147–60.

Ziv, Yael, and Peter Cole (1974). Relative extraposition and the scope of definite descriptions in Hebrew and English, in Michael La Galy, Robert Fox, and Anthony Bruck (eds.), *Papers from the Tenth Regional Meeting of the Chicago Linguistic Society, April 19-21*. Chicago: Chicago Linguistic Society, 772–86.

Zubizarreta, Maria Luisa (1998). *Prosody, Focus and Word Order*. Cambridge, Mass.: MIT Press.

Zubizarreta, María Luisa (1999). Las funciones informativas: Tema y foco, in Ignácio Bosque and Violeta Demonte (eds.), *Gramática descriptiva de la lengua española*. Madrid: Espasa Calpe, 4215–44.

Zumpt, Karl (1832). *A Grammar of the Latin Language*. London: B. Fellowes.

Zwart, Jan-Wouter (2011). *The Syntax of Dutch*. Cambridge: Cambridge University Press.

Subject index

Language index

OXFORD STUDIES IN DIACHRONIC AND HISTORICAL LINGUISTICS

GENERAL EDITORS: Adam Ledgeway and Ian Roberts, University of Cambridge

ADVISORY EDITORS: Cynthia Allen, *Australian National University*; Ricardo Bermúdez-Otero, *University of Manchester*; Theresa Biberauer, *University of Cambridge*; Charlotte Galves, *University of Campinas*; Geoff Horrocks, *University of Cambridge*; Paul Kiparsky, *Stanford University*; Anthony Kroch, *University of Pennsylvania*; David Lightfoot, *Georgetown University*; Giuseppe Longobardi, *University of York*; George Walkden, *University of Konstanz*; David Willis, *University of Cambridge*

PUBLISHED